Dumbarton Oaks Studies
XLI

THE *HISTORY* OF
LEO THE DEACON

THE *HISTORY* OF LEO THE DEACON
Byzantine Military Expansion
in the Tenth Century

Introduction, translation, and annotations

by Alice-Mary Talbot and Denis F. Sullivan

with the assistance of George T. Dennis and Stamatina McGrath

Dumbarton Oaks Research Library and Collection
Washington, D.C.

Library of Congress Cataloging-in-Publication Data

Leo, the Deacon, b. ca. 950.
  [History. English]
  The History of Leo the Deacon : Byzantine military expansion in the tenth
century / introduction, translation, and annotations by Alice-Mary Talbot
and Denis F. Sullivan ; with the assistance of George T. Dennis and
Stamatina McGrath.
      p. cm.
  History translated into English from the original Greek; critical matter
in English.
  Includes bibliographical references and index.
  ISBN 0-88402-306-0
  1. Byzantine Empire—History, Military—527–1081. I. Talbot, Alice-Mary
Maffry. II. Sullivan, Denis. III. Title.
  DF543.L46 2005

                                                          2005003088

Contents

Preface and Acknowledgments

The *History* of Leo the Deacon presented here in annotated translation is one of the most important sources for the transitional years of the Macedonian dynasty. It covers the reigns of Nikephoros Phokas and John Tzimiskes, a period in which the future Macedonian emperors, Basil II and Constantine VIII, were in their minority, and the empire was ruled by highly successful military officers who had usurped the imperium.

The appearance of this translation has been long delayed, and a few words of explanation are in order. In 1970–1971, Dr. Nicholas Panagiotakes spent a year as a fellow at Dumbarton Oaks working on a critical edition of the Greek text of Leo. For his doctoral dissertation at the University of Athens he had prepared the prolegomena to this edition, consisting of a biographical essay and a discussion of the manuscripts and previous editions. The dissertation was published in 1965 in the Ἐπετηρὶς τῆς Ἑταιρείας Βυζαντινῶν Σπουδῶν, vol. 34, under the title Λέων ὁ Διάκονος, and also appeared as a separate volume (Athens, 1965). In the fall of 1970 Dr. Panagiotakes invited me to prepare an English translation to accompany his Greek text. When I agreed to do so, he sent me a photocopy of his handwritten new Greek text, complete with critical apparatus and *fontes et paralleles*. I finished a first draft that same academic year, most of which Panagiotakes was able to review before his return to Greece. Subsequently he discovered that de Gruyter, with which he had a contract to publish his text in the Series Berolinensis of the Corpus Fontium Historiae Byzantinae, was unwilling to include an English translation, and he therefore released me to publish the translation on its own. Since my translation was, however, based on Panagiotakes' new edition, with different paragraphing from the Bonn edition of Hase, and with a number of different readings and punctuation, I decided to wait for Panagiotakes' Greek text to appear before publishing my translation. Alas, this never came to pass, since Panagiotakes' interests turned away from Byzantium in the 1970s, and he devoted the rest of his career to research on the post-Byzantine history and literature of his beloved homeland of Crete. After his untimely death in 1997, Prof. Athanasios Markopoulos undertook responsibility for completing the posthumous publication of the Greek text of Leo, and it is my fervent hope that this critical edition will soon see the light of day.

About five years ago, at the urging of some of my colleagues at Dumbarton Oaks and in the Washington area, in particular Professor George Dennis of The Catholic University of America, I decided to make Leo's *History* the focus of our weekly Byzantine Greek reading group at Dumbarton Oaks. Over a period of eighteen months we read the text and took turns making oral translations into English. This exercise gave me the opportunity to review my translation, and to discuss problem passages with colleagues. To speed up preparation of the final publication, four of us agreed to share the work of annotation and writing the introduction. The initial division of labor was as follows: Stamatina McGrath drafted the preliminary version of notes to Books I and III, Denis Sullivan Books II and IV, George Dennis Books VI and VII, and myself Books VIII–X. The annotation of Book V was a joint effort. Thereafter Denis Sullivan meticulously reviewed the entire translation and all the notes, and made so many additions, corrections, and suggestions for improvement throughout that he must be considered a coauthor of the translation and all the notes; he is also the principal author of the Introduction. I undertook the final editorial coordination of our contributions. I should also like to acknowledge the active engagement in this project of Alexander Alexakis, an original member of the team, who had to withdraw during the final phase of preparation, but was an invaluable collaborator in the earlier stages, especially in matters of translation and emendations to the Greek text. Let me add a note of gratitude to the two anonymous readers who carefully reviewed the initial draft of the manuscript and made valuable suggestions for corrections and improvement.

Because of uncertainty about the eventual date of publication of the new Greek edition, I have decided to revert to the Bonn text as the basis for the translation, using Hase's paragraphing. Where, however, I felt that Panagiotakes' edition offered a better reading (based either on a more accurate transcription from the manuscripts, an emendation, or a conjecture), I have adopted it and so indicated in a footnote. In a few cases I have suggested readings different from those of Hase and Panagiotakes.

I should also acknowledge my extraordinary debt to the efforts of Panagiotakes to identify *fontes et paralleles*, a task undertaken well before the advent of the *Thesaurus Linguae Graecae*, which has been so beneficial for Greek philologists. The online version of the *TLG* has enabled our team to identify numerous citations that Panagiotakes did not find, and we have also rejected a number of his *fontes* as being too far removed from the text of Leo. Nonetheless his labors have greatly eased our work, and we stand in awe and admiration of his deep knowledge of Greek literature.

Last but not least, I would like to express our appreciation to Leslie MacCoull, who served as copy editor, and to the staff of the Dumbarton Oaks Publications Office, especially Joel Kalvesmaki, for their care in preparing the manuscript for publication and shepherding it through the press.

Alice-Mary Talbot
Dumbarton Oaks, May 2004

Abbreviations

AB
    Analecta Bollandiana
Agath.
    Agathias, *Historiarum libri quinque*, ed. R. Keydell (Berlin, 1967)
    [references cited by page and line number]
Ahrweiler, *Mer*
    H. Ahrweiler, *Byzance et la mer* (Paris, 1966)
Ahrweiler, *Structures*
    H. Ahrweiler, *Études sur les structures administratives et sociales de Byzance* (London, 1971)
AIPHOS
    Annuaire de l'Institut de Philologie et d'Histoire Orientales et Slaves
Anna Komnene, *Alexiad*
    Anne Comnène, Alexiade, ed. B. Leib and P. Gautier, 3 vols. (Paris, 1937–76)
Beck, *Kirche*
    H. G. Beck, *Kirche und theologische Literatur im byzantinischen Reich* (Munich, 1959)
Belke, *Galatien*
    K. Belke, *Galatien und Lykaonien*, TIB 4 (Vienna, 1984)
Belke and Mersich, *Phrygien und Pisidien*
    K. Belke and N. Mersich, *Phrygien und Pisidien*, TIB 7 (Vienna, 1990)
Berger, *Untersuchungen*
    A. Berger, *Untersuchungen zu den Patria Konstantinupoleos* (Bonn, 1988)
BMGS
    Byzantine and Modern Greek Studies
Brokkaar, "Basil Lacapenus"
    W. G. Brokkaar, "Basil Lacapenus. Byzantium in the 10th Century," in *Studia Byzantina et Neohellenica Neerlandica*, ed. W. F. Bakker et al. (Leiden, 1972), 199–234
BSl
    Byzantinoslavica
Bury, *Adm. System*
    J. B. Bury, *The Imperial Administrative System in the Ninth Century* (London, 1911; repr. New York, n.d.)
ByzF
    Byzantinische Forschungen

Abbreviations

BZ
   Byzantinische Zeitschrift
CAG
   Commentaria in Aristotelem Graeca
Cameron, *Agathias*
   A. Cameron, *Agathias* (Oxford, 1970)
Cameron, *Procopius*
   A. Cameron, *Procopius* (Berkeley, 1985)
Canard, "Expéditions mésopotamiennes"
   M. Canard, "La date des expéditions mésopotamiennes de Jean
   Tzimiscès," *AIPHOS* 10 (1950): 99–108
Canard, *H'amdanides*
   M. Canard, *Histoire de la Dynastie des H'amdanides de Jazîra et de Syrie*
   (Alger, 1951)
CFHB
   Corpus Fontium Historiae Byzantinae
Cheynet, "Les Phocas"
   J.-C. Cheynet, "Les Phocas," in Dagron, *Le traité*, 289–315
Cheynet, *Pouvoir*
   J.-C. Cheynet, *Pouvoir et contestations à Byzance (963–1210)* (Paris, 1990)
Christides, *Crete*
   V. Christides, *The Conquest of Crete by the Arabs (ca. 824), a Turning Point
   in the Struggle between Byzantium and Islam* (Athens, 1984)
CPG
   E. L. Leutsch and F.G. Schneidewin, eds., *Corpus Paroemiographorum
   Graecorum*, 2 vols. (Göttingen, 1839–51; repr. Hildesheim, 1958)
Dagron, *Le traité*
   G. Dagron and H. Mihaescu, *Le traité sur la guérilla (De velitatione) de
   l'empereur Nicéphore Phocas (963–969)* (Paris, 1986)
De cer.
   De cerimoniis aulae byzantinae, ed. J. J. Reiske, 2 vols. (Bonn, 1829–30)
Dennis, "Byz. in Battle"
   G. Dennis, "The Byzantines in Battle," in Τὸ ἐμπόλεμο Βυζάντιο, 9–12 αἰ.
   [*Byzantium at War 9th–12th c.*], ed. K. Tsiknakes (Athens, 1997), 165–78
Dennis, "Helepolis"
   G. Dennis, "Byzantine Heavy Artillery: The Helepolis," *GRBS* 39 (1998):
   99–115
Dennis, *Treatises*
   G. Dennis, *Three Byzantine Military Treatises*, CFHB 25 (Washington, D.C.,
   1985; repr. 2000)
DictSpir
   Dictionnaire de spiritualité

Abbreviations

DOC
>A. R. Bellinger, P. Grierson, and M.F. Hendy, *Catalogue of the Byzantine Coins in the Dumbarton Oaks Collection and in the Whittemore Collection*, 5 vols. (Washington, D.C., 1966–99)

Dölger, *Beiträge*
>F. Dölger, *Beiträge zur Geschichte der byzantinischen Finanzverwaltung, besonders des 10. und 11. Jahrhunderts* (Leipzig,1927; repr. Hildesheim, 1960)

Dölger, "Chronologie"
>F. Dölger, "Die Chronologie des grossen Feldzuges des Kaisers Johannes Tzimiskes gegen die Russen," *BZ* 32 (1932): 275–92

Dölger, *Regesten*
>F. Dölger and P. Wirth, *Regesten der Kaiserurkunden des oströmischen Reiches* (Munich–Berlin, 1924–)

DOP
>*Dumbarton Oaks Papers*

DOSeals
>N. Oikonomides and J. Nesbitt, *Catalogue of Byzantine Seals at Dumbarton Oaks and in the Fogg Museum of Art* (Washington, D.C., 1991–)

E
>Escurial gr. Y–I–4

EEBS
>Ἐπετηρὶς τῆς Ἑταιρείας Βυζαντινῶν Σπουδῶν

EI²
>*The Encyclopedia of Islam*, 2nd ed. (Leiden–London, 1960–)

EO
>*Échos d'Orient*

Garland, *Empresses*
>L. Garland, *Byzantine Empresses: Women and Power in Byzantium, AD 527–1204* (London, 1999)

GCS
>Griechische Christliche Schriftsteller

GRBS
>*Greek, Roman, and Byzantine Studies*

Grégoire, "Amorians and Macedonians"
>H. Grégoire, "The Amorians and Macedonians, 842–1025," in *Cambridge Medieval History*, vol. 4.1 (Cambridge, 1966), 105–92

Gr. Nys. 6
>*Gregorii Nysseni opera*, vol. 6, *In Canticum canticorum*, ed. H. Langenbeck (Leiden, 1960)

Grumel, *Chronologie*
>V. Grumel, *La chronologie* (Paris, 1958)

Guidoboni, *Earthquakes*
>E. Guidoboni, *Catalogue of Ancient Earthquakes in the Mediterranean Area up to the 10th Century* (Rome, 1994)

Abbreviations

Guilland, *Institutions*
R. Guilland, *Recherches sur les institutions byzantines*, 2 vols. (Amsterdam, 1967)

Guilland, *Topographie*
R. Guilland, *Études de topographie de Constantinople byzantine*, 2 vols. in 1 pt. (Amsterdam, 1969)

Haldon, *Recruitment*
J. Haldon, *Recruitment and Conscription in the Byzantine Army c. 550–950: A Study of the Origins of the Stratiotika Ktemata* (Vienna, 1979)

Haldon, *Warfare*
J. Haldon, *Warfare, State and Society in the Byzantine World, 565–1204* (London, 1999)

Haldon and Kennedy, "Arab-Byzantine Frontier"
J. Haldon and H. Kennedy, "The Arab-Byzantine Frontier in the Eighth and Ninth Centuries: Military Organisation and Society in the Borderlands," *ZRVI* 19 (1980): 79–116

Halkin, *Inédits byzantins*
F. Halkin, *Inédits byzantins d'Ochrida, Candie et Moscou* (Brussels, 1963)

Halkin, "Translation"
F. Halkin, "Translation par Nicéphore Phocas de la brique miraculeuse d'Hiérapolis (BHG³ 801n)" in Halkin, *Inédits byzantins*, 253–60

Hanak, "The Infamous Svjatoslav"
W. Hanak, "The Infamous Svjatoslav: Master of Duplicity in War and Peace?" in Miller-Nesbitt, *Peace and War*, 138–51

Hild and Hellenkemper, *Kilikien*
F. Hild and H. Hellenkemper, *Kilikien und Isaurien*, TIB 5 (Vienna, 1990)

Hild and Restle, *Kappadokien*
F. Hild and M. Restle, *Kappadokien: Kappadokia, Charsianon, Sebasteia und Lykandos*, TIB 2 (Vienna, 1981)

Honigmann, *Ostgrenze*
E. Honigmann, *Die Ostgrenze des byzantinischen Reiches von 363 bis 1071* [= A. Vasiliev, *Byzance et les Arabes* 3] (Brussels, 1935)

Hunger, *Lit.*
H. Hunger, *Die hochsprachliche profane Literatur der Byzantiner*, 2 vols. (Munich, 1978)

Hussey, *Orthodox Church*
J. Hussey, *The Orthodox Church in the Byzantine Empire* (Oxford, 1986)

Janin, *CP byz.*
R. Janin, *Constantinople byzantine: Développement urbain et répertoire topographique*, 2nd ed. (Paris, 1964)

Janin, *Églises CP*
R. Janin, *La géographie ecclésiastique de l'empire byzantin*, vol. 1, *Le siège de Constantinople et le patriarcat oecuménique*, pt. 3, *Les églises et les monastères*, 2nd ed. (Paris, 1969)

Abbreviations

Janin, *Grands centres*
  R. Janin, *La géographie ecclésiastique de l'empire byzantin*, vol. 2, *Les églises et les monastères des grands centres byzantins* (Paris, 1975)
Jenkins, *Byzantium*
  R. J. H. Jenkins, *Byzantium: The Imperial Centuries, A.D. 610–1071* (London, 1966)
JÖB
  Jahrbuch der Österreichischen Byzantinistik
Karales, Λέων
  B. Karales, Λέων Διάκονος. Ἱστορία (Athens, 2000)
Kazhdan, "Byzantine Family Names"
  A. Kazhdan, "The Formation of Byzantine Family Names in the Ninth and Tenth Centuries," *BSl* 58 (1997): 90–109
Kazhdan, "Polis"
  A. Kazhdan, "*Polis* and *Kastron* in Theophanes and Some Other Historical Writers," in *ΕΥΨΥΧΙΑ. Mélanges offerts à Hélène Ahrweiler*, 2 vols. (Paris, 1998), 2:345–60
Kolias, *Waffen*
  T. Kolias, *Byzantinische Waffen* (Vienna, 1988)
Korres, *Hygron pyr*
  Th. K. Korres, Ὑγρὸν πῦρ: Ἕνα ὅπλο της βυζαντινῆς ναυτικῆς τακτικῆς, 3rd ed. (Thessalonike, 1995)
Kühn, *Armee*
  H.-J. Kühn, *Die byzantinische Armee im 10. und 11. Jahrhundert* (Vienna, 1991)
Lampe, *PGL*
  G. W. H. Lampe, *A Patristic Greek Lexicon* (Oxford, 1961–68)
Laurent, *Corpus*
  V. Laurent, *Corpus des sceaux de l'empire byzantin*, 2 vols. in 5 pts. (Paris, 1963–81)
Lemerle, *Agr. Hist.*
  P. Lemerle, *The Agrarian History of Byzantium from the Origins to the Twelfth Century* (Galway, 1979)
Leo diac.
  Leonis diaconi Caloënsis Historiae libri decem, ed. C. B. Hase (Bonn, 1828)
Liudprand, *Relatio*
  Relatio de legatione Constantinopolitana, in *Liudprandi Cremonensis opera*, ed. P. Chiesa (Turnhout, 1998), 185–218
Loretto, *Phokas*
  F. Loretto, *Nikephoros Phokas "Der bleiche Tod der Sarazenen" und Johannes Tzimiskes: Die Zeit von 959 bis 976 in der Darstellung des Leon Diakonos* (Graz, 1961)

Abbreviations

LSJ
> H. G. Liddell, R. Scott, and H. S. Jones, *A Greek-English Lexicon* (Oxford, 1968)

Magdalino, *Year 1000*
> *Byzantium in the Year 1000*, ed. P. Magdalino (Leiden, 2003)

Mango, *Brazen House*
> C. Mango, *The Brazen House: A Study of the Vestibule of the Imperial Palace of Constantinople* (Copenhagen, 1959)

Mango, "The Palace of the Boukoleon"
> C. Mango, "The Palace of the Boukoleon," *Cahiers Archéologiques* 45 (1997): 41–50

Markopoulos, "History Writing"
> A. Markopoulos, "Byzantine History Writing at the End of the First Millennium," in Magdalino, *Year 1000*, 183–97

Markopoulos, "Ζητήματα κοινωνικοῦ φύλου"
> A. Markopoulos, "Ζητήματα κοινωνικοῦ φύλου στὸν Λέοντα τὸν Διάκονο," in Ἐνθύμησις Νικολάου Μ. Παναγιωτάκη, ed. S. Kaklamanes, A. Markopoulos, et al. (Herakleion, 2000), 475–93

McCormick, *Eternal Victory*
> M. McCormick, *Eternal Victory: Triumphal Rulership in Late Antiquity, Byzantium and the Early Medieval West* (Cambridge–Paris, 1986)

McGeer, *Warfare*
> E. McGeer, *Sowing the Dragon's Teeth: Byzantine Warfare in the Tenth Century* (Washington, D.C., 1995)

McGrath, "Aristocracy"
> S. F.-P. McGrath, "A Study of the Social Structure of Byzantine Aristocracy as Seen Through Ioannes Skylitzes' *Synopsis Historiarum*," (Ph.D. diss., Catholic University of America, Washington, D.C., 1996)

Miller-Nesbitt, *Peace and War*
> *Peace and War in Byzantium: Essays in Honor of George T. Dennis, S.J.*, ed. T. S. Miller and J. Nesbitt (Washington, D.C., 1995)

Moravcsik, *Byzantinoturcica*
> G. Moravcsik, *Byzantinoturcica*, 2nd ed., 2 vols. (Berlin, 1958)

Morris, "Phokas"
> R. Morris, "The Two Faces of Nikephoros Phokas," *BMGS* 12 (1988): 83–115

Morris, "Succession and Usurpation"
> R. Morris, "Succession and Usurpation: Politics and Rhetoric in the Late Tenth Century," in *New Constantines: The Rhythm of Imperial Renewal in Byzantium, 4th–13th Centuries*, ed. P. Magdalino (Aldershot, 1994), 199–214

Abbreviations

Müller-Wiener, *Bildlexikon*
> W. Müller-Wiener, *Bildlexikon zur Topographie Istanbuls* (Tübingen, 1977)

Nikeph., *Short History*
> C. Mango, ed. and trans., *Nikephoros, Patriarch of Constantinople: Short History* (Washington, D.C., 1990)

Obolensky, "Cherson"
> D. Obolensky, "Cherson and the Conversion of Rus': An Anti-Revisionist View," *BMGS* 13 (1989): 244–56

ODB
> A. Kazhdan et al., eds., *The Oxford Dictionary of Byzantium*, 3 vols. (New York, 1991)

Oikonomides, *Listes*
> N. Oikonomides, *Les listes de préséance byzantines du IXe et Xe siècle* (Paris, 1972)

P
> Parisin. gr. 1712

Panagiotakes, *Leon*
> N. Panagiotakes, *Λέων ὁ Διάκονος* (Athens, 1965)

Panagiotakes, *Theodosios*
> N. Panagiotakes, *Θεοδόσιος ὁ διάκονος καὶ τὸ ποίημα αὐτοῦ ῞Αλωσις τῆς Κρήτης* (Herakleion, 1960)

Papadopoulos, Ἱστορία
> Ch. Papadopoulos, Ἱστορία τῆς Ἐκκλησίας Ἀντιοχείας (Alexandria, 1951)

Parani, *Reconstructing the Reality of Images*
> M. Parani, *Reconstructing the Reality of Images: Byzantine Material Culture and Religious Iconography (11th–15th Centuries)* (Leiden, 2003)

PG
> Patrologiae series completus, series graeca, ed. J.-P. Migne, 161 vols. in 166 pts. (Paris, 1857–66)

PO
> Patrologia Orientalis

Preger, *Scriptores*
> *Scriptores originum Constantinopolitanarum*, ed. T. Preger (Leipzig, 1901–7; repr. New York, 1975)

Prokopios, *Buildings*
> *Procopii Caesariensis opera omnia*, ed. J. Haury, vol. 4 (Leipzig, 1974)

Prokopios, *Gothic Wars*
> *Procopii Caesariensis opera omnia*, ed. J. Haury, vol. 2 (Leipzig, 1963)

Prokopios, *Persian Wars*
> *Procopii Caesariensis opera omnia*, ed. J. Haury, vol. 1 (Leipzig, 1962), 1–304

Prokopios, *Vandalic Wars*
> *Procopii Caesariensis opera omnia*, ed. J. Haury, vol. 1 (Leipzig, 1962), 305–552

Abbreviations

Psellos, *Chronographia*
> Michel Psellos. *Chronographie*, ed. É. Renauld, 2 vols. (Paris, 1926–28)

RE
> *Paulys Real-Encyclopädie der classischen Altertumswissenschaft*

REB
> *Revue des études byzantines*

Ringrose, *The Perfect Servant*
> K. M. Ringrose, *The Perfect Servant: Eunuchs and the Social Construction of Gender in Byzantium* (Chicago, 2003)

Runciman, *Bulgarian Empire*
> S. Runciman, *A History of the First Bulgarian Empire* (London, 1930)

Runciman, *Romanus*
> S. Runciman, *The Emperor Romanus Lecapenus and His Reign: A Study of 10th-Century Byzantium* (Cambridge, 1929; repr., 1988)

Russian Primary Chronicle
> S. H. Cross and O. P. Sherbowitz-Wetzor, *The Russian Primary Chronicle. Laurentian Text* (Cambridge, Mass., 1953)

Schlumberger, *Phocas*
> J. Schlumberger, *Un empereur byzantin au dixième siècle: Nicéphore Phocas* (Paris, 1890)

Schove, *Chronology*
> D. J. Schove and A. Fletcher, *Chronology of Eclipses and Comets AD 1–1000* (Woodbridge, Suffolk, 1987)

Schreiner, "Ausrüstung"
> P. Schreiner, "Zur Ausrüstung des Kriegers in Byzanz, im Kiewer Russland und in Nordeuropa nach bildlichen und literarischen Quellen," in *Les Pays du nord et Byzance*, ed. R. Zeitler (Uppsala, 1981), 215–36

Scott, "Historiography"
> R. Scott, "The Classical Tradition in Byzantine Historiography," in *Byzantium and the Classical Tradition*, ed. M. Mullett and R. Scott (Birmingham, 1981), 61–74

SEER
> *Slavic and East European Review*

Seibt, *Skleroi*
> W. Seibt, *Die Skleroi: Eine prosopographische-sigillographische Studie* (Vienna, 1976)

Sidéris, "'Eunuchs of Light'"
> G. Sidéris, "'Eunuchs of Light': Power, Imperial Ceremonial and Positive Representations of Eunuchs in Byzantium (4th–12th Centuries AD)," in *Eunuchs in Antiquity and Beyond*, ed. S. Tougher (London, 2002), 161–75

Siuziumov et al., *Lev D'iakon*
> M. I. A. Siuziumov et al., trans., *Istoriia: Lev D'iakon* (Moscow, 1988)

Abbreviations

Skyl.

    Ioannis Scylitzae Synopsis historiarum, ed. I. Thurn, CFHB 5 (Berlin–New York, 1973)

Sophocles, *Lexicon*

    E. A. Sophocles, *Greek Lexicon of the Roman and Byzantine Periods* (New York, 1900)

Stephenson, *Balkan Frontier*

    P. Stephenson, *Byzantium's Balkan Frontier* (Cambridge, 2000)

Stokes, "Balkan Campaigns of Svyatoslav"

    A. D. Stokes, "The Background and Chronology of the Balkan Campaigns of Svyatoslav Igorevich," *SEER* 40 (1961–62): 44–57

Sullivan, "The *De obsidione toleranda*"

    D. Sullivan, "A Byzantine Instruction Manual on Siege Defense: The *De obsidione toleranda*," in *Byzantine Authors: Literary Activities and Preoccupations: Texts and Translations Dedicated to the Memory of Nicholas Oikonomides*, ed. J. Nesbitt (Leiden, 2003), 139–266

Sullivan, "Prescriptions"

    D. Sullivan, "Tenth-Century Byzantine Offensive Siege Warfare: Instructional Prescriptions and Historical Practice," in *Τὸ Ἐμπόλεμο Βυζάντιο, 9–12 αἰ.* [*Byzantium at War, 9th–12th c.*], ed. K. Tsiknakes (Athens, 1997), 179–200

Sullivan, *Siegecraft*

    D. Sullivan, ed. and trans., *Siegecraft. Two Tenth-Century Instructional Manuals by "Heron of Byzantium"* (Washington, D.C., 2000)

Talbot, *Holy Women*

    A.-M. Talbot, ed., *Holy Women of Byzantium: Ten Saints' Lives in English Translation* (Washington, D.C., 1996)

TAPA

    Transactions and Proceedings of the American Philological Association

Terras, "Ethnology of Kievan Rus'"

    V. Terras, "Leo Diaconus and the Ethnology of Kievan Rus'," *Slavic Review* 24 (1965): 395–406

Theoph.

    Theophanis Chronographia, ed. C. de Boor (Leipzig, 1883)

Theoph. Cont.

    Theophanes Continuatus, ed. I. Bekker (Bonn, 1838)

TIB

    Tabula Imperii Byzantini, ed. H. Hunger et al. (Vienna, 1976–)

TLG

    Thesaurus Linguae Graecae, online version, produced by the Department of Classics, University of California at Irvine, http://www.tlg.uci.edu/

TM

    Travaux et mémoires

Abbreviations

Trapp, *LBG*

> E. Trapp, ed., *Lexikon zur byzantinischen Gräzität* (Vienna, 1994–)

Treadgold, *Army*

> W. Treadgold, *Byzantium and Its Army* (Stanford, 1995)

Treadgold, *Byz. State*

> W. Treadgold, *A History of the Byzantine State and Society* (Stanford, 1997)

Tsougarakis, *Byz. Crete*

> D. Tsougarakis, *Byzantine Crete. From the 5th Century to the Venetian Conquest* (Athens, 1988)

Vasiliev, *Byz. Arabes*

> A. A. Vasiliev, *Byzance et les Arabes*, 1 (Brussels, 1935), 2.1 (1968), 2.2 (1950)

Yahya of Antioch, *Histoire*

> Yahya of Antioch, *Histoire de Yahya-ibn-Said d'Antioche, continuateur de Saidibn-Bitriq*, ed. and trans. I. Kratchkovsky and A. A. Vasiliev, PO 18 (Paris, 1924): 705–833; 24 (Paris, 1932): 349–520; 47.4 (Turnhout, 1997)

Zepos, *JGR*

> J. and P. Zepos, ed., *Jus graecoromanum*, 8 vols. (Athens, 1931; repr. Aalen, 1962)

ZRVI

> *Zbornik radova Vizantoloshkog Instituta*

Zuckerman, "Chronology"

> C. Zuckerman, "On the Date of the Khazars' Conversion to Judaism and the Chronology of the Kings of the Rus' Oleg and Igor," *REB* 53 (1995): 237–70

Introduction

On the whole the era of the Macedonian dynasty (867–1056) was a
time of territorial expansion and flourishing culture for the Byzantine
empire; nevertheless the continuation of the dynasty was at risk on several occasions in the tenth century when an orderly succession to the
throne proved impossible. Fortunately for the empire, the day was saved
by three generals who assumed the throne, in theory as guardians for
junior emperors until such time as they should achieve their majority.[1]

Problems began already with the second member of the Macedonian
line, Leo VI the Wise (886–912), who had difficulties in producing an
heir to the throne. Only one of his first three wives, who were all short-
lived, bore a son and he soon died. Therefore Leo waited until his new
mistress, Zoe Karbonopsina, gave birth to a healthy boy in 905 before
marrying her. This uncanonical fourth marriage split the church hierar-
chy. The child, the future Constantine VII Porphyrogennetos (945–959),
would grow up to be one of the most famous of Byzantine emperors,
known in particular for his patronage of arts and letters and for his
sponsorship of several important compilations, such as *On the Administration of the Empire* and the *Book of Ceremonies*, which provide invaluable
information on the Byzantine state, foreign policy, diplomacy and court
ceremonial in the tenth century. But he had to wait many years to assume real imperial power, since he was not quite seven years old when
his father, Leo, died in 912, and he was relegated to the sidelines by a
series of regents, including the patriarch Nicholas Mystikos and his
mother, Zoe. Into this power vacuum stepped the admiral Romanos
Lekapenos, who first married his daughter to the young Constantine,
and then had himself crowned emperor in 920. Lekapenos held the
throne until 944, when he was deposed by his sons; the next year
Constantine was finally able to assume independent rule of the empire.

---

[1] This brief summary of military and political affairs follows in general the information
provided by Treadgold, *Byz. State*, Part IV.

Introduction

When Constantine passed away in 959, he was succeeded by his son Romanos II. He died unexpectedly four years later, leaving two very young sons, Basil II and Constantine VIII. At this critical moment the general Nikephoros Phokas, who had just distinguished himself by the reconquest of Crete from the Arabs in 961, saw an opportunity to seize the throne. Phokas, a member of one of the great military aristocratic families, was *domestikos* of the East, that is, commander of the armies of Asia, while his brother held the same position for Europe. Nikephoros easily entered Constantinople, was crowned emperor, and married Romanos's widow, Theophano, thus becoming stepfather to the crown princes.

Nikephoros's reign was marked by continuous offensives against the Arabs, who had proved themselves troublesome neighbors of the empire in the ninth and tenth centuries. Their conquest of Crete in the 820s had provided them with a base for pirate raids throughout the islands and coasts of the Aegean, while Arab dynasties in eastern Anatolia and northern Syria, such as the Hamdanids of Aleppo, encroached on former Byzantine territory in this region and launched frequent raids into central Anatolia. Nikephoros's annual campaigns to the east were a series of successes, achieved both in pitched battles and in sieges of cities; he managed to push the Byzantine frontier steadily further east and south, culminating with the capture of Antioch in 969. He also regained the island of Cyprus from the Arabs in 965.

On the northern frontier in the Balkans, the Byzantines' primary concern was the state of Bulgaria, which had proved to be a major threat to the empire during the reign of Tsar Symeon (893–927), who launched an expedition against Constantinople itself in 913. Under Symeon's son Peter (r. 927–969), Byzantium signed a peace treaty that obligated it to pay tribute. By 966 Nikephoros felt strong enough to cancel tribute payments and to go on the offensive. At first he used diplomacy to persuade the Rus' to invade Bulgaria. The Rus', however, under the leadership of Sviatoslav of Kiev, were more successful than Nikephoros had bargained for; in 969 they captured the Bulgarian capital of Preslav and the tsar, Boris II (969–971), so that the Byzantines now had an even more dangerous enemy to the north.

Despite Nikephoros's successes over the Arabs, he was not universally popular in the capital, and his wife Theophano began to scheme for a way to get rid of him. Contacting Nikephoros's nephew John

Tzimiskes, who had for a while succeeded him as *domestikos* of the East but then had fallen out of favor with the emperor, she arranged for him to return to the capital. There he organized a conspiracy to murder Nikephoros with the help of the empress. On a wintry December night in 969 a band of men gained entrance to the imperial bedchamber and killed Phokas as he slept. Tzimiskes succeeded in persuading the patriarch to crown him emperor, despite this dastardly act, but did not gain permission to marry the beautiful Theophano, now widowed a second time.

Tzimiskes, who was to rule from 969 to 976, immediately turned his attention to Bulgaria where the forces of Sviatoslav held sway. Leading an army of perhaps forty thousand men, the emperor quickly captured Preslav and freed the Bulgarian tsar Boris from captivity. He then moved north to Dristra on the Danube, where he blockaded Sviatoslav by land and water and forced his surrender and retreat toward Kiev. As a result the empire was able to annex part of Bulgaria, moving the Byzantine frontier north to the Danube.

In the east Tzimiskes continued Nikephoros Phokas's offensive, attacking the emirate of Mosul and even invading Fatimid territory in southern Syria, and taking some coastal fortresses. His eventual aim may have been to reach Jerusalem itself and restore it to Christian hands; if so, he was forestalled by death early in 976, just after his return to Constantinople from his campaign of 975.

By now Basil II was eighteen years old and able to embark on a reign of forty-nine years (976–1025), the longest of any Byzantine emperor. Thanks to the military prowess of Phokas and Tzimiskes, he inherited an empire with greatly expanded borders. But almost immediately Basil had to face internal dissension with the dangerous revolts of Bardas Skleros between 976 and 979, and of Bardas Phokas between 987 and 989. Basil was able to overcome Phokas only after enlisting the assistance of Rus' troops from Kiev.

In the meantime, taking advantage of the emperor's distractions by civil war, a new, energetic Bulgarian tsar had appeared, Samuel, who cemented his control over western Bulgaria and took several towns in northern Greece in the 980s. Once Basil had put down the revolt of Bardas Phokas, he was able to focus on Bulgaria, where he waged war against Samuel for almost twenty-five years until achieving total victory in 1018.

3

Introduction

B. THE BYZANTINE MILITARY IN THE TENTH CENTURY

Army and Navy[2]

As is evident from their almost unbroken series of victories in the 960s and 970s, the armies led into battle by Nikephoros Phokas and John Tzimiskes were well equipped and trained. Virtually unchanged from the tradition of Roman times was the emphasis on defense, on caution, on constant drilling, on meticulous preparation for campaign and combat, on remaining in formation, and on adaptability and innovation.

In the course of the tenth century significant changes took place, about which we are well informed by a large and varied corpus of contemporary handbooks.[3] At the same time, historians such as Leo the Deacon and John Skylitzes provide detailed and, as far as we can tell, generally accurate accounts of military operations.[4] By studying the manuals together with the histories, then, one can form a fairly reliable picture of the tenth-century army.[5]

The military forces were still, as had been the case for two hundred years, divided into two major groups: the *themata*, that is, the troops of the themes or military provinces, and the *tagmata*, or standing professional army based around Constantinople. But a number of major developments had occurred. While the number of themes had increased, most of them had been reduced in size. Along the frontiers in particular, smaller themes, called just that, "small themes," or Armenian themes, indicating the ethnicity of their soldiers, were set up, or in very rugged

---

[2] This section (to p. 7) was written by George Dennis.

[3] Examples are the *Tactical Constitutions* (*Taktika*) of Leo VI, written ca. 900 (PG 107:669–1120), which include paraphrases of earlier authors, but also material based on the experience of contemporary commanders, especially regarding combat against the Arabs and naval warfare. His son, Constantine VII, oversaw the encyclopedic collection of available military treatises. Later in the century we have the *Sylloge Tacticorum* (ed. A. Dain, *Sylloge Tacticorum* [Paris, 1938]); treatises on guerilla warfare such as the *De velitatione*, "On Skirmishing" (ed. Dagron, *Le traité*); and, on campaign organization, the *Praecepta* of Nikephoros Phokas and the *Taktika* of Nikephoros Ouranos (the first treatise and chaps. 56–65 of the second ed. McGeer, *Warfare*).

[4] For detailed discussion of the specific insights provided by Leo on military affairs, see "Leo on Byzantine Military Operations," 36–47, below.

[5] Among recent works, see McGeer, *Warfare*; Dennis, "Byz. in Battle"; Kolias, *Waffen*; Kühn, *Armee*; Treadgold, *Army*; J. Haldon, *The Byzantine Wars: Battles and Campaigns of the Byzantine Era* (Stroud–Charleston, 2001).

areas *kleisourai* (territorial units smaller than themes) were established. Most were commanded by a *strategos*, but in border areas, such as Antioch, a *doux* or *katepano* was in charge.

The Byzantine navy was also divided into *tagmata* and *themata*, with crews from certain maritime themes manning their ships while a permanent fleet lay at anchor by Constantinople.[6] Large warships called *dromones*, usually with two banks of oars, were designed for ramming and grappling, while archers stationed on wooden towers fired down upon the enemy. The most destructive weapon in the Byzantine arsenal, the mere mention of which terrified their foes, was the so-called "liquid fire" (also known as "Greek fire").[7] Although its composition was a tightly guarded state secret, it seems to have been made from a petroleum-based substance, put under pressure, ignited, and discharged through bronze tubes, engulfing the enemy fleet in roaring flames. Ships equipped with these flame-throwing devices were called "fireships." There were also smaller, faster ships for scouting and skirmishing, as well as large transports for supplies and horses.

The *tagmata*, and in time of war the *themata* as well, were under the command of the *domestikos* of the Schools (originally the commander of the *tagma* of the *scholae*), two of whom emerged during the tenth century, one of the East and another of the West. Looking at the tagmatic units of this time one is immediately struck by their international character, for they included Armenians, Scandinavians, Rus', Bulgarians, Hungarians, Syrians, Arabs, and others. Some tagmatic units were stationed in border areas and new ones were formed, such as the Immortals by Tzimiskes.

Although not as prestigious or memorable as the mounted warrior, the foot soldier assumed a very important role in the tenth-century army and was indispensable in rough terrain. There were about twice as many infantry as cavalry. Squads of seven to ten foot soldiers were grouped in units of fifty and one hundred to make up a taxiarchy, a force of one thousand men, under the command of a taxiarch. The taxiarchy was supposed to have four hundred heavy infantry with shields and leathern or quilted armor, whose chief weapon was the spear, three hundred

[6] See Ahrweiler, *Mer.*
[7] J. F. Haldon and M. Byrne, "A Possible Solution to the Problem of Greek Fire," *BZ* 70 (1977): 91–99; J. R. Partington, *A History of Greek Fire and Gunpowder* (Cambridge, 1960), 1–41; Korres, *Hygron pyr.* See also below, p. 40.

5

Introduction

archers, two hundred light infantry with javelins and slings, and one hundred *menavlatoi*, a new type of foot soldier, chosen for strength and courage, who formed ahead of the front line holding long, thick spears, ideally fashioned from saplings, to blunt the attack of enemy horse.[8]

The cavalry comprised three branches. The first was the light cavalry, scouts and skirmishers who, in battle, were to go out ahead of the main force to harass the enemy and provoke them into breaking up their formation. Then there was the regular cavalry, both lancers and archers. The main force of the cavalry (and this was an innovation of the tenth century, although it had earlier precedents) was composed of the *kataphraktoi*, covered, together with their horses, in very heavy armor and carrying iron maces and swords.[9]

Although the military manuals had always insisted upon proper drilling and training, the tenth-century armies were noted for constant rigorous and methodical drilling, especially in winter quarters, and for engaging in frighteningly realistic mock battles.

On campaign particular importance was given to the expeditionary camp, which was supposed to be set up each night, even in friendly territory. Detailed instructions for setting up such camps are given in the tenth-century manuals, and the histories show that these procedures were closely followed. The camps, which obviously had to be near a good water supply, were generally square with roadways crossing within. Infantry spears and shields formed a sort of palisade around the camp, often strengthened by a ditch and an earthen rampart. The infantry pitched their tents around the perimeter, within which were the cavalry and baggage train, as well as the commander's quarters. The same order was observed by the army on the march, that is, the infantry on four sides with cavalry and baggage in the middle.

Another noticeable change in the tenth century is the more aggressive nature of Byzantine warfare. Not content only with defending their territory, Byzantine emperors more and more took the offensive into enemy lands. But even though they became more aggressive, they preserved the typically Byzantine characteristics of avoiding or postponing a pitched battle until the circumstances were clearly in their favor. They preferred to employ stratagems and ruses to wear down superior enemy

[8] See E. McGeer, "Menaulion—Menaulatoi," *Diptycha* 4 (1986–87): 53–57, and M. P. Anastasiadis, "On handling the menavlion," *BMGS* 18 (1994): 1–10.
[9] J. F. Haldon, "Some Aspects of Byzantine Military Technology from the Sixth to the Tenth Centuries," *BMGS* 1 (1975): 11–47.

forces, for they knew they could achieve victory as often by surprise and deception as by open confrontation.

When it came to actual battle, two innovations stand out. One was the hollow square formed by the infantry, a formation that was developed in the first half of the century. Twelve taxiarchies, three to a side, formed a defensive square, with the baggage and reserve horses in the middle. Intervals between each taxiarchy allowed weary or defeated cavalry to enter for protection and fresh horsemen to charge out.

The second was the cavalry formation. A third line was added, and the middle unit of the first line was composed of *kataphraktoi* in a blunt, wedge-shaped formation ahead of the two wings of the first line. Wielding heavy maces and swords, the first four ranks of the wedge-like formation charged into the foe; they were followed by lancers with heavy spears, while the archers in the middle kept firing over their heads into the enemy lines.

A trumpet sounded the call to battle, the standard of the cross was raised, and the cavalry left the camp in proper order. The horsemen advanced with a precise measured gait, a trot, and, above all, in formation. They trotted forward deliberately, the *kataphraktoi* and their horses encased in metal, in tight formation and in total silence, although both Phokas and Tzimiskes had a fondness for continuous drum rolls. On several occasions the mere sight of the iron-clad, faceless horsemen advancing in an eerie, unnatural silence completely unnerved the enemy, who broke ranks and fled. Friend and foe alike marveled at the incredible precision of the advancing horsemen in their gleaming armor.

Siege Warfare

The challenge of taking a fortified site could be approached in various ways, including a blockade, which brought the city to capitulation through starvation, surprise attacks, direct assaults on the walls, which might involve the use of ladders, or longer-range attacks, which featured bow and arrow, sling, and artillery bombardment, all combined with the use of battering rams and/or excavating through or undermining the walls.[10] Leo VI's prescriptions in the *Taktika*[11] furnish a representative summary. They include: secure your siege camp with a ditch or walls and careful

---

[10] See Sullivan, "Prescriptions," 179–200.

[11] *Constitutio* XV, PG 107:885–908. It draws heavily on the *Strategikos* of Onasander (1st c.) and the *Strategikon* of Maurice (late 6th to early 7th c.).

guards; see to your own supply lines; guard city gates and walls to prevent surprise attacks; begin with careful reconnaissance of the terrain; cut off supplies of food and water; make a show of your best troops; offer easy terms to encourage surrender; assign men carefully to work in shifts, allowing some of your troops rest while constantly harassing the enemy; encircle the walls with troops carrying ladders, and use rams, siege sheds, and mobile towers at chosen locations; focus on difficult and hence unguarded approaches; use fire-arrows and other incendiaries launched by artillery to set fires within; dig mines under the walls; consult military manuals and employ skilled technicians to prepare the siege machines.

The so-called Heron of Byzantium's *Poliorcetica* and *Geodesia* exemplify such manuals.[12] He describes the construction of siege sheds (including the contemporaneous *laisa*), ladders, mobile towers, and excavating tools, and methods of undermining walls; he also provides geometrical methods for estimating precisely the required sizes of these devices while remaining out of the range of enemy fire. The artillery used was most likely the beam-sling traction or rope-pull trebuchet.[13]

Nikephoros Ouranos recommends initially ravaging the countryside and interdicting supply routes to create lack of provisions; creating a secure siege camp with a ditch, and beyond the ditch placement of anti-personnel devices such as caltrops; offering easy terms of surrender and threats of harsh treatment if the first offer is refused; preparation of siege sheds, notably the *laisa*; use of bows, slings, and artillery to bombard the enemy on the walls; rams to break through the fortifications, with the troops working in three teams to allow rest periods; undermining and propping up the walls, then burning the props to cause the wall to collapse. He specifically cites this last method as most effective.[14]

[12] Sullivan, *Siegecraft*. "Heron," who wrote around the 940s, supplies detailed recommendations on construction of siege machines, paraphrasing and updating particularly the work of Apollodoros of Damascus (2nd c.) and Athenaios Mechanikos (1st c. B.C.).

[13] See W. T. S. Tarver, "The Traction Trebuchet: A Reconstruction of an Early Medieval Siege Engine," *Technology and Culture* 36 (1995): 136–67. See also his figures 1 and 2 for examples of trebuchets in use at the sieges of Mopsuestia and Preslav as depicted in the Madrid Skylitzes, the latter showing use of a trebuchet and ladder in combination.

[14] In chap. 65 of his *Taktika*, ed. McGeer, *Warfare*, 152–63. Ouranos, who wrote ca. 1000, offers the views of a distinguished general who had read earlier manuals, but also had practical field experience.

Introduction

As Eric McGeer has noted, the great emphasis in the manuals on undermining the walls suggests that Byzantine artillery in this period was "not powerful enough to shatter the walls of a fortress," and was used rather to fire at enemy troops on the wall "in unison with archers and slingers to keep up a shower of missiles, which would force the defenders away from the ramparts."[15]

C. Biography of Leo the Deacon[16]

One of the best sources for the history of Byzantine warfare in the second half of the tenth century is Leo the Deacon, who wrote a narrative in ten books of the reigns of Romanos II (959–963), Nikephoros II Phokas (963–969), and John I Tzimiskes (969–976), with digressions into the reign of Basil II (976–1025).

The few facts we know about Leo's life are almost all drawn from occasional self-references in his *History*. Son of a certain Basil, he was born ca. 950 in western Anatolia in the small town of Kaloë, a bishopric dependent on Ephesos, and located southwest of Philadelphia in the Kaystros valley. He came to Constantinople as a youth to pursue his secondary education (ἐγκύκλιος παίδευσις).[17] Although he was destined for a clerical career, the language and citations of his *History* show that he had a traditional classical education. He was well read in ancient authors, with a definite predilection for Homer, whom he quotes frequently, and for proverbs. His Christian upbringing is reflected by occasional biblical allusions, to both Old and New Testaments, and some quotations from the church fathers, but these are surprisingly few for the work of a deacon.[18]

Leo was ordained a deacon sometime after 970,[19] and he became a member of the palace clergy after Basil II's accession to the throne in

---

[15] "Byzantine Siege Warfare in Theory and Practice," in *The Medieval City under Siege*, ed. I. Corfis and M. Wolfe (Woodbridge, 1995), 123–29, specifically 125–26, 128.

[16] Much of the following section is based on the conclusions of Panagiotakes in *Leon*, 1–41. We were unable to consult the very recent analysis of Leo and his work by A. Karpozilos in *Βυζαντινοί ιστορικοί και χρονογράφοι: 8ος–10ος αιώνας* (Athens, 2002), 2:475–525, which did not reach Dumbarton Oaks until this book was in page proofs.

[17] Leo diac. 72.17–18 (Book IV, chap. 11).

[18] For a more detailed assessment of Leo's familiarity with classical and Christian authors, see "Leo's Education and Literary Style," 23–25, below.

[19] This is the conclusion of Panagiotakes (*Leon*, 8–9), since the minimum age for the diaconate was 22.

Introduction

976. Around 980 he delivered an encomium in praise of the emperor.[20]
He was evidently in Constantinople ca. 985, at the time of the downfall
of Basil the Nothos, and participated (perhaps as a member of the imperial retinue) in the disastrous Bulgarian campaign of 986, at which
time he narrowly escaped being captured or killed by the enemy during
the battle of Trajan's Gate.

He certainly lived through the 980s, since Book X of his history
mentions the rebellions of Bardas Skleros and Bardas Phokas in the 980s
(including the battle of Abydos of 989), the Bulgarian campaign of 986,
and the earthquake of 989, which severely damaged Hagia Sophia. He
adds that it took six years for Basil II to complete the repairs to the
church,[21] which would bring us to a terminus post quem of 995 for the
composition of the history.[22] Siuziumov has suggested, however, that
the phrase about the repair of Hagia Sophia be bracketed,[23] which would
leave a terminus post quem of 989. At any rate no event dating after
1000 is mentioned, and the fearful millennial premonitions expressed in
two passages strongly suggest that he wrote the work before the end of
the tenth century. On the other hand, he also indicates that he planned
to continue a more systematic treatment of the reign of Basil later on,
which must lead us to believe that he died shortly after completing the
ten books of the history, unless a later work on Basil was written but has
been lost.

Panagiotakes theorized that he retired from his palace duties to write
his history and composed his work at some distance from the palace.[24]
He also hypothesized that Leo lived well beyond 1000 and became bishop
of Caria.[25] The basis for this supposition is his identification of Leo the
Deacon with a certain Λέων Ἀσιανός or Ἀσινός mentioned in Skylitzes'
prologue as his predecessor as a historian,[26] a personage styled as Leo

[20] I. Sykoutres, "Λέοντος τοῦ Διακόνου ἀνέκδοτον ἐγκώμιον εἰς Βασίλειον τὸν Β'," EEBS
10 (1933): 425–34.

[21] Leo diac. 176.4–6 (Book X, chap. 10).

[22] This date of composition is accepted by C. Holmes, "Political Elites in the Reign of
Basil II," in Magdalino, Year 1000, 38 and n. 8.

[23] Siuziumov et al., Lev D'iakon, 223 n. 73, and M. I. A. Siuziumov, "Ob istochnikakh
Lva D'iakona i Skilitsy," Vizantiikoe obozrenie 2 (1916): 106–66, at 137–39. Karales (Λέων,
12) suggests that Leo left Book X unfinished at his death, and that it was revised by
another author. He argues that Leo wrote the work in 994.

[24] Panagiotakes, Leon, 13–14.

[25] Panagiotakes, Leon, 16–29.

[26] Skyl. 3.28.

10

metropolitan of Caria by Kedrenos. The evidence for this identification is somewhat tenuous, however, especially since there is no suggestion in the *History* as we have it that Leo lived beyond 1000.

D. LEO AS A "HISTORIAN"

Purpose

In his opening chapter Leo argues for the "useful and profitable" aspects of history (ἱστορία): it recounts deeds, provides examples "to emulate . . . and avoid," is one of "the useful things in life" (βιωφελῶν), and saves human events from "the depths of oblivion" (τοῖς τῆς λήθης βυθοῖς).[27] He further notes that in the course of his life many unusual events have occurred: astronomical anomalies, earthquakes, torrential rains, wars, displacement of whole populations, and so on,[28] and adds a brief comment on his birthplace. Charles Benoît Hase first noted that many of these themes are modeled (with accommodation to Leo's own circumstances) on the sixth-century historian Agathias.[29] Again citing Agathias, Leo indicates that he will especially strive for the truth (περὶ πλείστου τὸ ἀληθίζειν ποιουμένοις ὡς μάλιστα), which wise men agree is appropriate to history.[30] He also says that he has thus resolved to recount these events as a "lesson to later generations" (παίδευμα τοῖς ὕστερον), perhaps a play on Thucydides' (1.22.4) "possession forever" (κτῆμα ἐς ἀεί).[31]

In the final sentence of the fifth book Leo comments that he writes "so that deeds useful in life may not pass away into the depths of oblivion" (ὡς ἂν μὴ λήθης βυθοῖς παραρρυῇ ἔργα βιωφελῆ), as he completes the

---

[27] Cf. Psellos, *Chronographia* 6.22.8ff: διὰ ταῦτά με βοηθῆσαι ἠξίουν τῇ φύσει τοῦ πράγματος, καὶ μὴ τὰ μὲν ἄνω που πρὸ ἡμῶν ἀναγραφῆς παρὰ τῶν μεταγενεστέρων ἠξιῶσθαι, τὰ δὲ ἐφ᾽ ἡμῶν πεπραγμένα <u>λήθης καλυφθῆναι βυθοῖς</u>; and Anna Comnena, *Alexiad* 1.1.6ff: ὅ γε λόγος ὁ τῆς ἱστορίας ἔρυμα . . . τὰ ἐν αὐτῷ (i.e., χρόνῳ) γινόμενα πάντα . . . οὐκ ἐᾷ διολισθαίνειν <u>εἰς λήθης βυθούς</u>.

[28] He provides similar lists again at X:6 and 10, noting (X:6) that he witnessed them all. While his model, Agathias, also has a list of calamities, Leo is original in linking his list to "signs of the end of the world" found in the New Testament (Matthew 24; Mark 13).

[29] Leo diac. 397. For Agathias see Agath. and for English translation J. D. Frendo, *Agathias, The Histories* (Berlin, 1975); see also Cameron, *Agathias*, and Karpozilos (see n. 16), 492–501.

[30] For doubts about such claims see Scott, "Historiography," 65.

[31] So W. Fischer, "Beiträge zur historischen Kritik des Leon Diakonos und Michael Psellos," *Mitteilungen des Instituts für Österreichische Geschichtsforschung* 7 (1886): 353–77, esp. 358.

11

reign of Nikephoros Phokas and begins that of John Tzimiskes. While Agathias does mention "oblivion" (λήθη), he does not mention its "depths" (βυθοί). The phrase βυθοῖς λήθης, used twice by Leo to frame his narrative of Phokas, is apparently taken from Gregory of Nazianzus,[32] who proposes annual celebrations of remembrance (ἐγκαίνια) "in order that good things may not in time become extinct and may not pass into the depths of oblivion and be rendered invisible" (ἵνα μὴ ἐξίτηλα τῷ χρόνῳ γένηται τὰ καλά, μηδὲ παραρρυῇ λήθης βυθοῖς ἀμαυρούμενα). Given Leo's repetition at the transitional point in his work, and the reuse of a parallel not from his model Agathias, it is reasonable to assume that he is here clearly stating his own personal objective. His intent is to save from oblivion deeds "to emulate and avoid" as his "lesson to later generations."[33] In similar fashion at IV:9 (68.20–23) he comments that God causes earthquakes whenever he sees humans acting contrary to divine law, "in the hope that, terrified in this way, men may avoid base deeds (φαύλων ἔργων) and strive rather for praiseworthy ones (ἐπαινετῶν)." Notably in his opening paragraph Leo says that the "deeds" history describes are "usually brought about by the passage of time and events and especially by the choice (προαίρεσις) of men engaged in the events." Thus he asserts from the outset the particular role of human choice in historical action and hence the value of presenting deeds to "emulate ... and avoid."

Still more telling perhaps is Leo's added comment at the end of the fifth book (V:9), that he finds it necessary "to bring to an end this account (διήγησις) of him (i.e., Nikephoros Phokas) and his deeds" and report those of John Tzimiskes. He thus explicitly indicates that his organizing principle is centered on individuals as opposed to continuous chronological narrative, an approach also particularly characteristic of Byzantine historiography beginning in the tenth century.[34] In this

[32] *In novam Dominicam* (*Oratio* 44), PG 36:608A. Note that Gregory himself in the first half of the sentence is quoting Herodotus 1.1, on preserving human actions from oblivion through passage of time.

[33] See, on new trends in 10th-c. historiography, Markopoulos, "History Writing," 186: "The main concern of this new compositional approach lies not only in the desire to satisfy curiosity about the past, but also—and principally—to gather precisely those features that were to form the basis, via a complex of moral examples and symbols, of the ideals, way of life, and models worthy of emulation." Leo is indeed explicitly stating this.

[34] See, for example, Scott, "Historiography," 64: "The Byzantine histories, from the tenth century on, are often about an individual or a family, or at any rate the focus is on the

regard Alexander Kazhdan has argued that Leo was attempting "to create the image of the emperor as a noble warrior."[35] Rosemary Morris takes this a step further in suggesting that Nikephoros Phokas's military prowess was the achievement for which he was widely known and admired.[36] More generally Athanasios Markopoulos has suggested that the male ideal of strength, especially in time of war, presented in the image of the exemplary warrior, dominates Leo's work.[37]

Sources

At the end of the first chapter of Book I Leo states that he will commit to writing those events "that I saw with my own eyes . . . and those that I verified from the evidence of eyewitnesses" (ὅσα ὀφθαλμοῖς καὶ αὐτὸς τεθέαμαι . . . τὰ δὲ καὶ πρὸς τῶν ἰδόντων ἠκρίβωσα). This reference to his own autopsy and verifying eyewitnesses perhaps recalls Thucydides' similar statement (οἷς τε αὐτὸς παρῆν καὶ παρὰ τῶν ἄλλων ὅσον δυνατὸν ἀκριβείᾳ περὶ ἑκάστου ἐπεξελθών, 1.22.2), but the extent to which Leo observed these stipulations is not easy to determine. His work basically covers the period 959–976, but with digressions that cover earlier and later events. He writes (IV:7) that he personally saw the emperor Nikephoros Phokas riding through Constantinople (in 966 or 967) while he was himself a student there. He notes (IV:11) that he was a student pursuing his "general education" at the time of an eclipse (22 December 968). He indicates (X:8) that he saw a "shooting star" that preceded the death of Basil the Nothos (post 985) and that (X:8) he attended the emperor Basil II as a deacon in the campaign against the Bulgarians (in 986). Finally in a digression he describes conjoined twins whom

individual or family," with numerous later parallels to what Leo says. See also Markopoulos, "History Writing," 186: "The *History* of Leo the Deacon . . . is composed essentially of the biographies of two Byzantine soldier-emperors." See also "Chronological System," 19–23 below.

[35] A. Kazhdan, "Certain Traits of Imperial Propaganda in the Byzantine Empire from the Eighth to the Fifteenth Centuries," in *Prédication et propagande au Moyen-Age*, ed. G. Makdisi et al. (Paris, 1983), 27 n. 29; see also op. cit. 13–18 and idem, "The Aristocracy and the Imperial Ideal," in *The Byzantine Aristocracy, IX to XIII c.*, ed. M. Angold (Oxford, 1984), 47–48.

[36] Morris, "Phokas," 87.

[37] Markopoulos, "Ζητήματα κοινωνικοῦ φύλου," esp. 481.

he claims to have seen (X:3). These are the only instances in which he specifically cites autopsy.[38]

Given his indication of student status as late as 968 and hence his relative youth, it is clear that much of what he records was in fact based, not on autopsy, but on reports from others. In thirty-seven instances[39] Leo uses λέγεται ("it is said"), and in fifteen cases[40] φασί(v) ("they say"), to present information. These items vary from examples of past bravery used to introduce a participant (10.23, 107.19, 109.21), reports of how someone died (30.12, 46.13, 78.10, 177.4), or reports of prophecies (64.13, 83.2, 85.23, 101.3), to battlefield statistics (111.2, 155.8). In most cases Leo's intent appears to be to distance himself from the accuracy of the information: e.g., 30.12: "The emperor Romanos is said (λέγεται) to have died in the following manner," followed by a description of Romanos's excesses, including deer hunting during Lent, and the alternative views about the cause of his death, 31.2: "Some people say (φασί) that he suffered a fatal convulsion as a result ... but most people suspect (ἡ τῶν πλειόνων ὑπόνοια) that he drank some hemlock poison that came from the women's apartments." In other cases he perhaps seeks to indicate that he has not examined the sources directly or is reporting information derived orally: e.g., 63.2: "It is said (λέγεται) that on several previous occasions the Romans came to grief in ... Mysia, and were completely destroyed." Unfortunately Leo makes no mention of who his sources, whether written or oral, might be. Siuziumov, followed by Kazhdan, theorized that Leo the Deacon (and John Skylitzes) used a now lost source favorable to Nikephoros Phokas,[41] which led Leo to

---

[38] He does also comment at 64.19 on Nikephoros Phokas's new palace wall, "which can be seen today" (τὸ νῦν ὁρώμενον); at 129.3 on the restored church at the Brazen Gate and "the beauty and size that is apparent today" (κάλλος, εἰς ὃ νῦν ὁρᾶται, καὶ μέγεθος); and at 138.21 on Dorystolon and "the beauty and size that is apparent today" (εἰς ὃ νῦν ὁρᾶται κάλλος καὶ μέγεθος).

[39] They are 5.17, 10.23, 23.6, 24.21, 27.12, 30.12, 46.13, 63.2, 64.13, 78.10, 81.17, 83.2, 85.23, 97.6, 101.3, 103.18, 104.18, 107.19, 109.21, 111.2, 120.24, 122.11 and 16, 123.23, 129.21, 134.11, 136.16, 148.20, 149.24, 151.22, 153.22, 155.8, 162.16, 164.1, 166.23, and 177.4 and 8.

[40] They are 5.12, 31.2, 38.23, 70.18, 105.4, 123.18, 130.9, 134.7, 150.23, 152.2, 154.2, 9, 156.11, 164.3, and 166.24.

[41] For a recent discussion with earlier bibliography see I. Liubarskii, "Nikephoros Phokas in Byzantine Historical Writings," BSl 54 (1993): 245–53, esp. 252–53. See also Hunger, Lit., 368–69; Morris, "Phokas," 85–86; and the brief comment of Kazhdan, "Polis," 358: "The character of the common source has not yet been clarified; at any rate it could not be much older than Leo himself who described the events of 959–976."

take a relatively positive view of that emperor, although some anti-Phokas material does also appear. Jean-Claude Cheynet proposed that he may have had firsthand information from the Parsakoutenoi, members of the Phokas family.[42] Gyula Moravcsik[43] suggested that Leo used as a source a participant in Tzimiskes' campaign against the Rus'. It has also been suggested that Leo may have employed "official documents"[44] and an "official panegyric" of John Tzimiskes.[45] Leo indeed gives a presentation of Tzimiskes that has been characterized as "almost hagiographical."[46]

Methods

Leo's *History* has been described as midway between a world chronicle and a humanistic memorial of an emperor.[47] As noted above, his work is basically organized around the reigns of the two emperors, Nikephoros Phokas (Books I–V) and John Tzimiskes (Books VI–X). He also implies (X:10) that he intended to cover at least portions of the reign of Basil II, but presumably died before he could do so. Within these two imperial reigns he generally records by major events. He does, however, irregularly note the arrival of spring, summer, or winter, often with rhetorical embellishment, and generally in relation to the beginning or end of weather favorable for campaigns, thus reflecting the military dominance in the work.

His work includes not only narrative but also summaries or ostensibly verbatim texts of speeches, letters and conversations, as well as digressions. The history contains seven speeches, five of them addresses by a general (sometimes the emperor) to troops and/or officers, one by the patriarch to the senate, and one by the emperor to the bishops and the senate. The letters include purportedly verbatim texts of Joseph Bringas's letter to John Tzimiskes, Nikephoros Phokas's missive to the Arab ruler of Carthage; an exchange between John Tzimiskes and Bardas Phokas when the latter revolted in 970; and another between Bardas Phokas and Bardas Skleros, who was dispatched to suppress the revolt.[48] The

[42] Cheynet, "Les Phocas," 303 n. 43.
[43] Moravcsik, *Byzantinoturcica*, 1:399, noting that Skylitzes may have used the same source.
[44] Hunger, *Lit.*, 369.
[45] Morris, "Succession and Usurpation," 209.
[46] Morris, "Phokas," 114.
[47] Hunger, *Lit.*, 367.
[48] See Morris, "Succession and Usurpation," 213: "letters supposedly exchanged."

"verbatim" conversations vary from seemingly private exchanges between Nikephoros Phokas and the empress Theophano (V:5–6) to a court reception of Bulgarian ambassadors. While Leo may possibly have had written sources for some of this material,[49] this is unlikely to be true of most of his supposedly authentic reports of actual speeches and documents,[50] since speeches were typically occasions for authorial invention in the classical[51] and Byzantine[52] traditions. The degree to which the speeches, letters, and conversations in Leo's work reflect in style and content the individuals involved awaits further investigation.

Typical of classicizing historians, Leo includes a number of digressions, among them the cause of earthquakes (IV:9), the origin of the Mysians (Bulgarians) (VI:8–9), the source of the Istros (Danube) (VIII:1), the customs of the Rus' (IX:6 and 8), but also two religious ones, on the "Holy Tile" (IV:10) and on a miraculous icon (X:5). He employs classical terms for contemporary ones: Mysians for Bulgarians and Scythians for Huns, Tauroscythians for the Rus', triremes for *dromones*, and so on, occasionally explaining his usage with the contemporary term (I:3, II:1, VIII:1). Yet he also directly employs contemporary terms, e.g., the Rus' (IX:9). Leo is fond, too, of commenting on the character and physical appearance of prominent individuals,[53] describing Nikephoros Phokas (I:5, III:8, IV:7, V:2 and 8), Tzimiskes (IV:3, VI:3), and Sviatoslav (IX:11) in considerable detail.

Leo's approach to historical causation seems to reflect a conflict between his classicizing style and his Christianity. In twenty-four instances

---

[49] Did the lost pro-Phokas source apparently used by Leo the Deacon preserve actual texts of speeches and letters of Nikephoros and Leo Phokas? The view expressed by Dennis, *Treatises*, 157 n. 2; Dagron, *Le traité*, 223 n. 16; and Cheynet, "Les Phocas," 303–5, that Leo Phokas's speech to his troops (II:3) reflects tactics advocated in the *De velitatione*, would seem to support this possibility for that specific speech.

[50] *Theoph. Cont.* 478.7–18 records a speech of Nikephoros Phokas to the Byzantine forces on Crete demoralized by the winter and lack of supplies. The style contrasts sharply with his speech recorded by Leo the Deacon at I:6.

[51] See M. H. Hansen, "The Battle Exhortation in Ancient Historiography," *Historia* 42 (1993): 161–80; but for possible verbatim speeches N. G. L. Hammond, "The Speeches in Arrian's *Indica* and *Anabasis*," *Classical Quarterly* 49 (1999): 238–53. See M. Whitby, *The Emperor Maurice and His Historian* (Oxford, 1988) for verbatim transcription of letters in Theophylact Simocatta.

[52] See Cameron, *Procopius*, 148–49.

[53] See Hunger, *Lit.*, 369, who calls it a "Somato-Psychogramm," and Markopoulos, "Ζητήματα κοινωνικοῦ φύλου."

Introduction

Leo uses the classicizing concept τύχη[54] ("fortune,""chance," or the like) to designate a force that controls events. A few examples will give the flavor. At 9.9–12, quoting Prokopios's *Persian Wars* (2.9.1–2), he says: "Men's good fortune, however, does not remain forever unmixed, but is mingled with adversity. Misfortunes follow upon good fortunes" (εὐτυχήμασι). At 10.13 he says, in phrasing reminiscent of Diodorus Siculus as preserved in the *Excerpta Constantiniana*,[55] that Nikephoros Phokas acted "since he still feared the reversals and mutability of fortune"; at 12.8 he comments that Crete had come under Arab control "through the wickedness of fortune" (μοχθηρία τῆς τύχης);[56] at 31.17 (= 10.13) he indicates that "the reversals and mutability of fortune gave the man (Nikephoros Phokas) no rest"; at 41.16 Phokas "reflected on the instability and uncertainty of fortune";[57] at 44.17 Phokas acted so "that fortune would not be angry with him, but would rather smile upon him cheerfully and benignly"; at 48.23, again quoting Prokopios (*Vandalic Wars* 1.21.7), Leo says one could see "fortune priding herself on and exulting in the turn of events, and attributing all human affairs to herself"; at 66.10 "malicious fortune" (βάσκανος τύχη) sent adverse winds against the Byzantine fleet in Sicily; at 146.17 he says of Leo Phokas "fortune devised for him bitter blindness, . . . mocking the man's hopes."

By contrast, Leo also speaks frequently of Providence (πρόνοια), sometimes qualified by the adjective "divine." At 4.20 he says "unless Providence has decided to bring the transport ship of life . . . into the harbor of the end [of the age]"; at 12.12 he has Nikephoros Phokas say of the Arabs of Crete "Providence . . . has brought us here to repay them sevenfold"; at 42.10 Phokas calls on "Providence, which guides everything"; at 83.6 a monk predicts Phokas's death, as revealed to him by Providence; at 105.19 John Tzimiskes says, "since we believe that there is a Providence that guides everything"; at 167.3 a miracle is set in motion "by some divine providence"; and at 173.5 Leo says he was himself saved on the battlefield "by some divine providence." In a related passage (68.10ff) on the cause of an earthquake, Leo notes the pagan (Aristotelian) explanation, which he calls "the foolish babbling of the Greeks,"

---

[54] See generally *ODB* 3:2131.

[55] *Bibliotheca historica* 34/35.28.3.10–11 (ed. K. T. Fischer and F. Vogel, *Diodori bibliotheca historica*, vol. 6 [Stuttgart, 1969]): τὸ τῆς τύχης ἄστατον, τὸ παλίντροπον τῶν ἀνθρωπίνων.

[56] Cf. Prokopios, *Vandalic Wars* 4.6.23: ἡ τύχη μοχθηρά.

[57] Cf. Agathias 15.18, τὸ ἀστάθμητον . . . τῆς τύχης; 42.1 and 63.3, τῇ ἀδήλῳ τύχῃ.

but then says: "I would go along with the holy David[58] and say that it is through the agency of God (ἐπισκοπῇ τοῦ Θεοῦ) that such quakes happen to us."[59]

In two passages Leo seems to attempt to reconcile these conflicting views. At 80.7 he begins, citing Lucian (*Ploion* 26), saying that "human fortunes (τὰ ἀνθρώπινα) . . . are as if suspended from a slender thread, and are wont to turn also in the opposite direction." He continues: "Some people[60] rightly (ἀνεπισφαλῶς) believe that a certain divine wrath . . . attack[s] the most prominent." He continues emphatically stating his own position: "And I will say this: that it is through the unfathomable forethought of the Almighty[61] (ἀμηχάνῳ τοῦ κρείττονος προμηθείᾳ) that mankind's prospering affairs change to the opposite. . . ." Then he notes in explanation that some such prominent men have "insult[ed] Providence itself," seemingly equating "fortune" to the forethought of God. At 90.5f again Leo emphatically comments: "But I say that, if some malicious fortune (βάσκανος . . . τύχη) had not begrudged his [Nikephoros Phokas's] prospering affairs . . . , the Roman empire would have obtained greater glory than ever before." He immediately continues: "But Providence, which abhors harsh and overweening spirits in men, curtails[62]

---

[58] Psalm 103 (104):32.

[59] Leo is in part drawing here on Agathias (Agath. 2.15), who describes an earthquake at Alexandria and mentions the pagan explanation; Agathias's reaction, however, is less polemical than Leo's. After mildly skeptical comments on the pagan theory ("their conclusions do not lack a certain plausibility"), he concludes: "It is sufficient for us to know that all things are controlled by the workings of a divine mind." On the passage in Agathias and the Aristotelian theory see Cameron, *Agathias*, 113–15; the translations of Agathias are those of Frendo.

[60] He is citing here Dionysius of Halicarnassus, *Roman Antiquities* 8.52: ταῦτ᾽ ἐμοὶ φόβου μεστὰ ἦν ἐνθυμουμένῃ τὸν ἀνθρώπινον βίον, ὡς ἐπὶ μικρᾶς αἰωρεῖται ῥοπῆς, καὶ ἐκ πολλῶν ἀκουσμάτων τε καὶ παθημάτων μαθούσῃ, ὅτι τοῖς ἐπισήμοις ἀνδράσι θεία τις ἐναντιοῦται νέμεσις ἢ φθόνος τις ἀνθρώπινος πολεμεῖ.

[61] One may also note that Leo often uses τὸ κρεῖττον and occasionally τὸ θεῖον, as well as ὁ Θεός, to refer to God; while the former terms are found in classical authors, they are also found in Christian ones and need not be seen as classical imitations. See Cameron, *Procopius* 35–36 and n. 16.

[62] Leo here is presumably thinking of the famous passage in Herodotus 7.10, which has Φιλέει γὰρ ὁ θεὸς τὰ ὑπερέχοντα πάντα κολεύειν. He is also again reflecting phrasing found in the *Roman Antiquities* of Dionysius of Halicarnassus (8.25): ὅτι μεταβολὰς ἔχει πάντα τὰ πράγματα καὶ οὐδὲν ἐπὶ τῶν αὐτῶν φιλεῖ διαμένειν, νεμεσᾶταί τε πάντα ὑπὸ θεῶν τὰ ὑπερέχοντα, ὅταν εἰς ἄκρον ἐπιφανείας ἀφίκηται, καὶ τρέπεται πάλιν εἰς τὸ μηδέν. μάλιστα δὲ τοῦτο πάσχει τὰ σκληρὰ καὶ μεγάλαυχα φρονήματα καὶ τοὺς ὅρους ἐκβαίνοντα τῆς ἀνθρωπίνης φύσεως.

and checks them and reduces them to nothing, with its incomprehensible decisions steering the transport ship of life on an expedient course." Thus he seems in these two passages to equate pagan τύχη and Christian πρόνοια, although the match is not a compatible one. Averil Cameron[63] has noted a similar incompatibility in Prokopios, who, she notes, had "a strong sense of the unexpectedness of events, as of the role of the irrational in history . . . and found the classical conception of *Tyche* a useful one . . . [but] was not successful in developing a uniform philosophy of history." Leo, who in two and perhaps three instances cites Prokopios on τύχη, seems to share the same dilemma, perhaps exacerbated by his role as a member of the clergy.

Chronological System

Leo provides four specific dates that include a year reckoned from 5508 B.C. (the *annus mundi*, i.e., creation),[64] although three of these contain errors and the text must be emended. He records that (I:2) Constantine VII died "in the month of November, during the third indiction, in the year 6467";[65] that (III:8) Nikephoros Phokas first entered Constantinople as emperor on 16 August, the sixth indiction, 6470;[66] that (VI:1) Phokas died and John Tzimiskes was hailed as emperor on 11 December, thirteenth indiction, 6478 (= 969); and that (X:11) John Tzimiskes died on 10 January, fourth indiction, 6485.[67] He also notes that Phokas held the imperium for "six years and four months" (V:8) and John Tzimiskes for "six years and thirty days" (X:11).

Otherwise Leo's chronological indications are usually by inconsistent notice of change of seasons, particularly the coming of spring or winter. Book I begins with the reign of Romanos II following his father's death in November 959 and with the expedition to Crete under Nikephoros Phokas. The change to the year in which the expedition

[63] Cameron, *Procopius*, 118.

[64] Since the Byzantine year and indiction (year of the tax cycle) began on 1 September, for any date from September through December one needs to subtract 5509 from the year of creation to obtain the corresponding date AD. See *ODB* 1:342–43.

[65] November 6467 would be 958, while the third indiction conforms to 959 and Constantine is known to have died in the latter year. The erroneous year must be emended to 6468 = 959. See Book I, n. 20.

[66] Again an erroneous *annus mundi* date; it should be 6471 = 963. See Book III, n. 68.

[67] Again an erroneous *annus mundi* date; it should be 6484 = 976. See Book X, n. 117.

actually sailed, 960, is not indicated. At I:9 and II:1 it is noted that Nikephoros Phokas "spent the winter" on Crete, that is 960/61. Book II:1 also indicates that "meanwhile" (ἐν τούτῳ) Sayf ad-Dawla began ravaging Byzantine territory in Asia Minor and (II:4–5) was defeated by Leo Phokas, a battle externally dated to November 960. At II:6, again with "meanwhile" (ἐν τούτῳ), the narrative returns to Phokas on Crete, his winter encampment, and renewal of hostilities "just as spring was . . . emerging" (March 961). The narrative continues with Phokas's success on Crete, triumph in Constantinople, return to campaigning in Asia Minor (in late 961),[68] having great success there, sending his troops home, and beginning to return to Constantinople, when news of the death of Romanos II (15 March 963) was received. The spring of 962 is not indicated.

At III:1 Leo notes that "spring time (963) was at its midpoint" and subsequently (III:8) states that Phokas's entry into Constantinople as emperor took place on 16 August 963.[69] At III:10 he indicates the spring equinox (964), followed by Phokas's initial attack on Tarsos, his capture of Adana and Anazarbos and twenty other fortresses plus Mopsuestia, then (III:11) the coming of the "hardships of winter" (964/65).

Book IV:1 indicates that Phokas spent the winter (of 964/65) in Cappadocia and "as soon as spring shone forth, and the bitter cold of winter changed considerably to the warmth of summer" (965), he gathered his troops for an attack on Tarsos. After Tarsos fell, he returned to the capital and entertained the people with chariot races. In what follows, Leo's chronological sequence omits any indication of change of year and places at least one event significantly out of sequence. IV:5 begins, "Just as he was concerned with these affairs" (i.e., the victory celebrations), and then reports the arrival of a Bulgarian embassy demanding tribute, Phokas's brief expedition to Bulgaria, his dispatch of his representative Kalokyres to bribe the Rus' to attack the Bulgarians, his brother Leo's entrepreneurial activities during a famine, a public riot against Phokas, the launching of an expedition against the Arabs of Sicily, an earthquake at Klaudioupolis (IV:9: "During the same year, when summer was just turning to autumn"), a severe storm in Constantinople (IV:9: "Also during this year, around the middle of summer, just as the sun was entering the sign of Cancer . . . it was Friday"), Phokas's campaign

[68] See Canard, H'amdanides, 805, and Book II, n. 54.
[69] With the emendation of the year noted above in n. 66.

to Antioch, "Palestine," "Edessa," Mempetze, Tripolis, and Arka, an eclipse of the sun (IV:11:"about the time of the winter solstice"), and Phokas's return north to Antioch. The Bulgarian embassy and the brief Bulgarian campaign most likely occurred in 966;[70] the dispatching of Kalokyres in 966 or 967,[71] likewise the famine and public protest against the emperor; but the Sicilian expedition took place in 964 or perhaps 965.[72] The earthquake is presumably that also reported by Skylitzes as occurring in September 967,[73] and the summer storm also occurred in 967.[74] Leo's description of the campaign to Antioch, "Palestine," and elsewhere seems to conflate the campaigns of 966 and 968 into the latter year, while the eclipse is securely dated to 22 December 968.[75] The book ends with Phokas stationing troops near Antioch and returning to the capital, which occurred in early 969. Thus Book IV begins in 965 and ends in early 969, but with only the spring of 965 indicated and misplacement of the Sicilian expedition.

The narrative of Books V–IX, covering in detail events of the years 969–971, proceeds in a relatively smooth temporal sequence with no apparent errors. Book V begins without direct chronological reference, but continues to describe events of the year 969 (although it backtracks a bit to include Kalokyres' embassy to the Rus', probably to be dated to 966 or 967).[76] The first chronological indication (V:5) is the commemoration of the Archangels (8 November), and at V:9 "it was Saturday, the eleventh of December" when the slain Nikephoros Phokas's body lay in the snow. Book VI starts with the extremely precise indication of the beginning of the reign of John Tzimiskes noted above. It covers the period from 11 December 969 into 970 and ends (VI:13) with orders to troops to spend the winter (hence 970–71) awaiting the spring campaign. Book VII, beginning with the word "While" ('Εν ᾧ), relates events (the revolt of Leo Phokas) that are simultaneous with those of Book VI and hence still in 970. At VII:9 Leo notes that John Tzimiskes married in "November, in the second year of his reign," an error since Tzimiskes

[70] See Book IV, n. 39.
[71] See Book IV, n. 44.
[72] See Book IV, n. 63.
[73] See Book IV, n. 70.
[74] See Book IV, nn. 76 and 78.
[75] See Book IV, n. 99.
[76] See Book V, n. 13 and Book IV, n. 44.

Introduction

married in November 970, still in the first year of his reign.[77] The first
words of Book VIII, "As soon as the gloom of winter changed to . . .
springtime," signal early 971, as Tzimiskes began his campaign against
the Rus'. The description of this expedition continues into Book IX,
where Leo records the final Byzantine victory at Dorystolon (IX:8) as
occurring on Friday, 24 July[78] (in 971). The book ends with John returning to Constantinople for the winter (of 971/72).

The chronology of Book X is perhaps even more confused than that
of Book IV. It begins "When summer arrived," presumably that of 972,[79]
and describes a campaign of Tzimiskes against "Upper Syria," mentioning
specifically Amida, Meyyafariqin (Martyropolis), Nisibis, and Ekbatana (an
error for Baghdad), and Tzimiskes' return to Constantinople for a triumph. At X:4 one reads "When spring appeared once again" and Leo
describes Tzimiskes' campaign in "Palestine," mentioning specifically
Mempetze (Hierapolis), Apameia, Damascus, Borzo, Balanaiai, and Beirut.
At X:6 one reads "After he took Balanaiai and Berytus by force, he attacked Tripolis . . . [and other] coastal towns," followed immediately by
mention of a comet that can be securely dated to August–October 975.

It is generally thought that Tzimiskes conducted campaigns in
Mesopotamia and Syria in 972, 974, and 975. Leo seems to describe
only two such campaigns, conflating events of 972 and 974[80] and omitting some seasonal notices. Book X ends with the death of Tzimiskes
and the specific date 10 January 6485 (= 975, but which must be emended
to 6486 = 976). Within Book X Leo presents a lengthy digression (chaps.
7–10) on events from the reign of Basil II, the "four-year" (X:7) revolt
of Bardas Skleros (976–79), dated as "after the death of the emperor
John"; Basil II's disastrous campaign against the Bulgarians (986), dated
(loosely) as "when Bardas Skleros's robber band of conspirators was completely dispersed" (X:8); and the revolt of Bardas Phokas (987–89), dated
as "Before the effects of this disaster [Basil II's defeat in Bulgaria] had
completely passed" (X:9), as well as portents including the appearance
of Halley's comet and an earthquake of the same year, which are externally dated to 989 (X:10).

[77] For the likely source of the error see Book VII, n. 79.
[78] The day must be in error since 24 July 971 was a Monday, not a Friday. For an
explanation see Book IX, n. 43.
[79] Hase, however, says 973 (Leo diac. 488); see Book X, n. 2 for discussion of the date.
[80] See Book X, nn. 1, 2, 9, and 47.

22

Thus the sequence of Leo's narrative, while it contains significant errors, differs in important respects from the approach of chronographers. The four specific dates and two regnal lengths clearly reflect his organizational principle, the reigns of emperors. His indications of change of seasons are primarily related to military campaigns, his primary focus, but are used inconsistently and in some instances are totally absent. His concern is presumably more with persons and deeds, and only peripherally with year of occurrence.

Leo's Education and Literary Style

Leo the Deacon indicates that he studied συλλογὴ λόγων (IV:7) and the ἐγκύκλιος παίδευσις (IV:11) in Constantinople. The latter term, referring to general education at the "secondary" level, would typically include grammar, rhetoric, and philosophy; the former term specifically referring to training in Aristotelian logic.[81] The study of grammar focused on Homer,[82] especially the *Iliad*, and Leo frequently cites this poet, a natural choice given Leo's emphasis on warfare.[83] In his text Leo cites by name among pagan authors Herodotus, Homer, and Arrian, and refers generally to the "Holy Scripture," which he cites a number of times, and specifically by name to David (Psalms) and Ezekiel. His unattributed references indicate that he was well acquainted with Agathias and Prokopios and almost certainly with Thucydides. His comments particularly on "Fortune" (τύχη) draw on quotations from Lucian, Diodorus Siculus, and Dionysius of Halicarnassus, whether directly or in excerpts is uncertain. His apparent references to Aristophanes, Dio Cassius, Euripides, and Sophocles present a similar uncertainty. He makes frequent use of proverbial sayings. Citations of the church fathers are infrequent, but his reference to Jacob of Nisibis (X:1) may reflect a knowledge of Theodoret's *Historia ecclesiastica*, and his digression on a miraculous icon (X:5) may echo Ps.-Athanasios's *Sermo et narratio de imagine Christi Berytensi*. Brief phrases seem to reflect familiarity with the works of Basil the Great (γαστρὶ δουλεύων καὶ τοῖς ὑπὸ γαστέρα),[84] Gregory of

---

[81] On the phrase συλλογὴ λόγων see Book IV, n. 60.

[82] R. Browning, "Homer in Byzantium," *Viator* 6 (1975): 15–33.

[83] Markopoulos has in fact suggested ("Ζητήματα κοινωνικοῦ φύλου," 488) that Leo's emphasis on single combats and sieges may imitate Homer's account of events from the siege of Troy. For another view see below, 43.

[84] See 30.16–17.

Introduction

Nazianzus (μηδὲ παραρρυῇ λήθης βυθοῖς),[85] and Gregory of Nyssa (λύει τὴν τοῦ χειμῶνος κατήφειαν).[86]

Leo attempts an artistic style befitting a classicizing historian, using rhetorical flourishes notably when introducing the coming of spring, e.g., "As soon as the gloom of winter changed to the fair weather of springtime" (VIII:1), instead of simply "at the beginning of spring." Karl Krumbacher, however, characterized Leo's style as "trivial and ponderous," and Leo's attempts at periodic sentence structure as "insufferably monotonous."[87] The harsh verdict is perhaps not completely undeserved. Leo's long sentences are often a series of participles in the nominative followed by the main verb. At I:3 (8.3–7) for example, a literal rendering would give: "Nikephoros the general of the Romans, having deployed his formation in three sections, and having studded it with shields and spears, and having sounded the war trumpet, and having ordered the standard of the cross to be brought forward, advanced directly against the barbarians." The following sentence is similar, but begins with two genitives absolute: "When a terrible battle broke out, and missiles were being carried down like hail, the barbarians were not for long able to withstand the spears of the Romans; but having turned their backs and having dissolved their formation, as quickly as they could run, they went back to their fortification."

Leo's vocabulary often tends to substitute poetic or less used terms for the more common ones, as Krumbacher observed. For brother (ἀδελφός) he also uses αὐτάδελφος, ὁμαίμων, and σύναιμος; for "relatives" (of Nikephoros Phokas) he employs οἱ ἐξ αἵματος προσήκοντες (37.21), οἱ ἀγχιστεῖς (43.11), and οἱ ἐξ αἵματος … ἀνήκοντες (96.1). The imperial palace is the βασιλεία ἑστία (31.19, 64.15), τὸ ἀνάκτορον (32.14, 64.18), or τὰ βασίλεια (33.14). In describing Joseph Bringas's position as parakoimomenos he uses τοῦ τῶν βασιλείων κατάρχοντος (33.2–3), ὁ τῆς βασιλικῆς κατάρχων, αὐλῆς (39.1), and τὸν τῶν τυραννείων κατάρχοντα (45.1–2). In referring to Constantinople he employs πόλις, ἄστυ, and βασιλεύουσα.[88] He also has a stylistic compulsion for doublets in

---

[85] See 92.6, and the remarks above, 11–12.

[86] See 51.6, 69.21, 111.13, and 128.1.

[87] K. Krumbacher, *Geschichte der byzantinischen Litteratur von Justinian bis zum Ende des oströmischen Reiches (527–1453)*, 2nd ed. (Munich, 1897), 267–68.

[88] On these see Kazhdan, "Polis," 358–59.

adjectives and verbs, often quite close in meaning, e.g., I:1 "useful and profitable" (ἐπωφελές . . . καὶ λυσιτελές) and "strive after and emulate" (ἀσπάζεσθαι καὶ ζηλοῦν). He employs rare terms, e.g., χαλκοτυπία (9.1), σκυτοτρώκτης (62.5), μουζακίτζης (92.4), and πανσίδηρος (140.11, 151.3–4); provides etymologies, e.g., "troglodytes" ("they dwell in caves," τρώγλαις . . . ὑποδύεσθαι) (35.6–7); and employs figures of speech, e.g., paronomasia, βλυστάνουσα . . . ἀναβλαστάνουσα (162.24–163.1), and homoioteleuton, ἀφέξοιντο . . . ἀνθέξοιντο (68.23). Leo's similes tend to be brief and banal. Twelve are introduced by δίκην, and include "slaughtered like sheep," "missiles fell like hail," and "howling like wild animals"; those with ὡς and ὥσπερ are similar. His rhetorical flourishes are generally brief, but at IV:5 (62.13–20) in describing the terrain of Bulgaria he employs eleven adjectives (with repetition), seven of them with the suffix -ώδης:[89] "densely wooded," "full of cliffs," "full of caverns and cliffs," "densely wooded and overgrown with bushes," "a marshy and swampy area," "damp," "heavily forested," and "surrounded on every side by impassable mountains." He is perhaps carried away here by his opening citation of Homer (ποιητικῶς εἰπεῖν), *Iliad* 16.111: "in every way evil was heaped upon evil."[90]

At the same time Leo is capable of lively description, such as his narrative of the undermining of the fortification walls of Chandax (II:7) and his memorable account of the murder of Nikephoros Phokas (V:6–9). He gives vivid portraits of some of the protagonists of his history, such as John Tzimiskes (VI:3) and Sviatoslav (IX:11). He enlivens his narrative with vignettes: the woman who exposed herself to the Byzantine troops during the siege of Chandax (II:6), the woman who threw a flowerpot at the *patrikios* Marianos (III:7), and the tale of the conjoined twins from Cappadocia (X:3). He includes picturesque details such as Tzimiskes playing a polo-like sport that involved hitting with a stick a leather ball off a glass cup while riding on horseback (VI:3), and the sleeping arrangements of Nikephoros Phokas, on a leopard skin and scarlet felt cloth spread out on the floor before icons (V:5–6).

---

[89] See Hunger, *Lit.*, 369.

[90] He may also be influenced here by Prokopios's description of the land of the Tzani (*Gothic Wars* 4.1.9), which has ὄρη . . . ἄβατα καὶ ὅλως κρημνώδη . . . χαράδραι ἀνέκβατοι καὶ λόφοι ὑλώδεις καὶ σήραγγες ἀδιέξοδοι.

Introduction

Leo the Deacon as an Ordained Cleric

Leo the Deacon is somewhat unusual among Byzantine narrative historians in being an ordained clergyman at the time he was writing his
work[91] and in placing a heavy emphasis on warfare. His personal experience
of battle[92] in Bulgaria under Basil II (X:8) and his presumed audience,
the Byzantine social establishment and provincial military elite with their
interest in warfare,[93] perhaps explain the martial focus. His clerical position
may be detected in a number of other themes in the work.

Leo presents numerous Christian elements without any attempt to
disguise them with classicizing phraseology,[94] as he does with
contemporary military terminology. Patriarchs, particularly Polyeuktos,
play a significant role in events, and their ascetic qualities are praised at
some length: for example, Polyeuktos (32–33 and 101), Basil I
Skamandrenos (102 and 163–164), Antony III Stoudites (164–165), and
the patriarchs of Antioch, Christopher and Theodore of Koloneia (100–
101). Leo supports their actions when in opposition to imperial policies,[95]
and ecclesiastical issues are given prominence, such as the question of the
legitimacy of Nikephoros Phokas's marriage to Theophano (50) and
the conditions for John Tzimiskes' crowning by the patriarch, including
the nullification of Phokas's unlawful assumption of ecclesiastical
authority (98–99), the appointment process for patriarchs (100–101 and
101–102), and the deposition of a patriarch (163–164). Nikephoros Phokas's
religiosity is frequently referred to: he offers prayers of thanksgiving
after victory in Crete (23) and after the return of captives (77), visits

---

[91] George Pachymeres is one of the few other examples of a deacon writing narrative
history. His work on the reigns of Michael VIII and Andronikos II places a special
emphasis on the ecclesiastical controversies that divided the empire of that time (see
ODB 3:1550). George of Pisidia, also a deacon, wrote historical epics, and various monks,
e.g., Theophanes, wrote chronicles. Leo's contemporary, Theodosios the Deacon, wrote
an account of the reconquest of Crete in 961 in verse.

[92] On the role of the clergy in battle see G. Dennis, "Religious Services in the Byzantine
Army," in *ΕΥΛΟΓΗΜΑ: Studies in Honor of Robert Taft, S.J.*, ed. E. Carr et al. (Rome,
1993), 107–17.

[93] See below, 43, "Single Combats."

[94] On this affectation in 6th-c. historians see Cameron, *Procopius*, 115–16 and Cameron,
Agathias, 75–88. However, compare the remarks above on fortune and Providence
(16–19).

[95] On this see Morris, "Phokas," 86.

churches (44 and 70), honors and is influenced by monks (49), sleeps on the floor in preparation for taking the sacraments (83), studies Scripture and prays before icons (86), and is known for his concentration during the singing of hymns (89). John Tzimiskes is pictured as concerned to appoint a new patriarch for Antioch (100–101), visits three churches (restoring one of them) prior to his expedition against the Rus', celebrates "the Holy Resurrection of the Savior" while on campaign (138), has an icon of the Theotokos precede him in a chariot in triumph (158), and on his deathbed confesses his sins to a bishop (178).

Leo frequently dates events by a Christian feast day, often with a brief comment on the nature of the commemoration (the Ascension [64], the Feast of the Archangels [83], the Sunday of Orthodoxy [102], Holy Thursday [134], and the Feast of St. Demetrios [175]); and, as noted above, he includes digressions on the Holy Tile of Edessa (70–71) and a miraculous icon (166–167). He presents vignettes, some quite tangential to the main narrative, of people suffering punishment for insolence (25), disobedience to a superior officer (10) and to a father (161), and for plundering churches (148); notably, three of these incidents conclude with the same phrase, "paid the price" (ἀπηνέγκατο τὰ ἐπίχειρα [13.3, 148.19, and 161.14–15]). He also suggests as one possible reason for the death of Romanos II his "unseasonable" (i.e., during Lent, which Leo comments was devised "for the purification of souls and their guidance toward virtue") deer-hunting expedition (30). Leo finds the sources of the Danube (129) and the Euphrates (160) in the rivers mentioned in Genesis, and comments (72) that a contemporary eclipse was surpassed only by that which occurred at the crucifixion of Christ (69), and that after a contemporary flood Providence placed a rainbow in the sky (69). In speaking of Nisibis (162) he recalls its famous fourth-century bishop "the great Jacob," who defeated the Persians with a miraculous army of gnats and mosquitoes. He notes the discovery at Mempetze of relics, the sandals of Christ and the hair of John the Baptist, and their subsequent dedication in churches in Constantinople (166.1ff). Finally he begins (4.16) by noting that some think that "the Second Coming of the Savior God is near, at the very gates," citing Matthew 24:33. Curiously, however, he omits any mention of Nikephoros Phokas's close spiritual bonds with Athanasios of Mt. Athos, the latter's foundation of the Great Lavra with financial support from Phokas, and the rechristianizing of Crete following Phokas's victory.

The Historian in the History[96]

Roger Scott has suggested that another feature characteristic of post-seventh-century Byzantine historians is the intrusion of the author's personality into the subject, in contrast to the more detached approach of his/her classical or classicizing predecessors. He comments: "A number of Byzantine historians chose their subject just because it did concern them personally, and their object in writing was to ensure that their viewpoint was represented."[97]

Iakov Liubarskii has examined how the personality of the author reveals itself in Byzantine literature, suggesting (with caution) four evaluative criteria: "1) immediate self-presentation of the author, who becomes one of the acting persons of composition or at least a witness commenting on the action. . . ; 2) direct commenting on the events and persons, as a rule deviating from the objectivity of the narrative; 3) emotional evaluation of events and persons by using emotionally colored epithets and adverbs (without deviating from the objectivity of the narrative); 4) references of different kind to the sources of the author's knowledge. These references . . . demonstrate the author's interest in the trustfullness [sic] of the narrative."[98] Liubarskii does not consider Leo the Deacon in detail, but does comment that the four criteria can be applied positively to Leo, while noting that he was an eyewitness rather than an immediate participant.

As noted above, in his introductory chapter Leo mentions his birthplace, Kaloë, which he describes as "a very beautiful village," near the source of the river Kaystros, which offers "a most pleasant vista to the beholder" and empties into the sea near Ephesos, "that famous and celebrated city." He comments (IV:7) that when he saw the emperor Nikephoros Phokas in person he was "astonished at the imperturbable spirit of the man, how fearlessly he maintained the nobility of his spirit under difficult circumstances" as he was being assailed with insults by the angry populace. He describes in detail (IV:11) the eclipse of

---

[96] The title is taken from R. Macrides, "The Historian in the History" in Φιλέλλην, *Studies in Honour of Robert Browning*, ed. C. N. Constantides et al. (Venice, 1996), 205–24, who examines the works of Michael Psellos, Anna Comnena, and George Akropolites for this phenomenon.

[97] Scott, "Historiography," 63–64.

[98] "Writers' Intrusion in Early Byzantine Literature," *XVIIIe Congrès international des études byzantines, Rapports pléniers* (Moscow, 1991), 433–56, esp. 435.

Introduction

22 December 968:"One could see the disk of the sun dark and unlighted, and a dim and faint gleam, like a delicate headband, illuminating the edge of the disk all the way around," and says "At that time I myself was living in Byzantium, pursuing my general education." At Book X:3 he describes with admiration the dignity and good dispositions of conjoined twins whom he says he often saw in Asia; at X:6 a comet that appeared from August to October 975, foretelling, he says, various calamities all of which he witnessed; and (X:8) his service as a deacon to the emperor Basil at Tralitza, where he barely escaped death at enemy hands. Thus while Leo is not a major actor in the events he reports, he describes with emotion and partiality those he witnessed.

In directly commenting on events he indicates what action a person "should" have taken, but did not (or the opposite): Pastilas and his men "should (δέον) have observed the warnings of their general, as was fitting" (9.16–17); Romanos II invited questionable persons into the palace, "as he ought not" (ὡς οὐκ ὤφελεν [6.10]); Manuel in Sicily "should (δέον αὐτῷ) have guarded the cities he had captured" (66.19); Leo Phokas "should (δέον αὐτῷ) have scattered [gold] in the streets to win the favor of the citizens" (95.7–9); the scribe Niketas disobeyed his father's orders (161.9), "as he should not have" (ὡς οὐκ ὤφελεν). In commenting on the willingness of the troops to cut off enemy heads and bring them in for a reward, Leo says, "the soldiers, especially (μάλιστα) the corps of Armenians, received this command gladly" (14.20–21); in noting that Leo Phokas fought with divine aid, Leo adds "I believe" (οἶμαι); and after describing Nikephoros Phokas's construction of a wall to ensure the security of the palace in which he was subsequently murdered, Leo adds "as he thought" (ὡς ὑπετόπαζεν [64.20–21]). Commenting on Nikephoros Phokas's attempt to have authority in the ecclesiastical sphere, he remarks, "which was a violation" (ὅπερ ἔκσπονδον ἦν [98.24]); in observing the lack of typical turmoil following Tzimiskes' usurpation of power, he adds "I know not how" (οὐκ οἶδ᾽ ὅπως [98.7]). He also offers quite explicit opinions with the comment "But I say this" (ἐγὼ δὲ τοῦτό φημι [80.15]), and expresses his personal amazement (ἔμοιγε οὖν ἔπεισι θαυμάζειν) at "how men in olden times were moved by some inspiration to give to places names that were fitting and appropriate to the course of subsequent events" (122.13–15).

When describing individuals, Leo's evaluative comments are ubiquitous and often clichéd, usually in the form of a short judgment on their character and ability, though sometimes longer. Nikephoros Phokas is "an active and energetic man, good at warfare and irresistibly strong" (7.13–14), his brother Leo "a courageous and vigorous man, of exceptionally good judgment" (18.14–15); John Tzimiskes is "extremely daring and more reckless than anyone else" (59.10–11), Marianos "extremely quick to anger and hot-headed" (37.3), Manuel (Phokas) "a hot-headed and self-willed man, likely to yield to thoughtless impulse" (66.4–5). In some instances Leo adds to such comments the phrase, "of anyone we know" (ὧν ἴσμεν). He inevitably comments negatively about eunuchs: Constantine Gongyles, who led the failed expedition to Crete in 949, is "a eunuch of the bedchamber, an effeminate fellow from Paphlagonia" (7.4–5); he has John Tzimiskes in a speech (40.3) call Joseph Bringas "a wretched eunuch from the wastes of Paphlagonia" and earlier in the chapter "an effeminate fellow, whose very sex is doubtful, an artificial woman. . . ." In describing eunuchs who are successful Leo comments "although he happened to be a eunuch" (εἰ καὶ τομίας ἐτύγχανε [66.1, 94.6–7]) or "although a eunuch" (καίτοι τομίαν ὄντα [107.20]). Markopoulos notes that not only eunuchs but also women are marginalized in Leo's narrative.[99]

Leo's discussion of the purpose of his work (I,1) also provides a major indicator of his personal presence. While noting that his intent is to leave a "lesson to later generations" (παίδευμα τοῖς ὕστερον), he has just stated that some believe the Second Coming is at hand and thus adds to his intent the Pauline caveat "unless Providence has decided to . . . cause *the form of the world to pass away*." His lists of various calamities (I:1, X:6 and 9) and references to comets and meteors as omens of disaster, as well as mentions of an eclipse, earthquakes and a flood, suggest his gloomy outlook. Whether these references may be connected with the approach of the year 1000 remains an open question. While the Byzantines reckoned time, not from the Incarnation, but from the beginning of the world, dated to 5508 B.C., there are indications in some tenth-century texts of increasing eschatological tension.[100]

Two formal aspects of his presentation also break the objective narration of events and reveal his personality. First of all, while for the most part using classicizing terms for contemporary ones, he occasionally breaks this affectation and mentions the contemporary term: triremes are

---

[99] "Ζητήματα κοινωνικοῦ φύλου," 490–92. On the ambiguities see Ringrose, *The Perfect Servant*, 37–41, 135–38; and Sidéris, "'Eunuchs of Light'," 161–75.

[100] See Book I, n. 8 for further discussion and bibliography; also Magdalino, *Year 1000*.

Introduction

dromones, the Tauroscythians are the Rus', and so on. He also does the reverse, adding an etymology: the "difficult and narrow paths leading to Mysia" are given their contemporary technical name, "which they call *kleisourai* because they are so closed in" (130.16–17). A second characteristic is his frequent and pedantic references to the "sequence of the narrative" (εἰρμὸς λόγου). Sections are introduced with such comments as "I will relate briefly" (ἐρῶ ἐπιτροχάδην [6.16]), or "as (my) narrative will now relate" (ὅπερ ὁ λόγος αὐτίκα δηλώσει [12.2]), and a digression concludes with "for the narrative should now return again . . . after digressing from its sequence" (δεῖ γὰρ τὸν λόγον τοῦ εἰρμοῦ ἐκτραπέντα . . . τοῦτον αὖθις ἐπαναγαγεῖν [72.18–19]), or "But enough about this" (ἀλλὰ περὶ τούτων μὲν ἅλις [165.16]).

Leo as a Historical Source

Leo the Deacon is one of a number of extant sources for the reigns of Romanos II, Nikephoros II Phokas, John I Tzimiskes, and Basil II. Other relevant material includes John Skylitzes,[101] Michael Psellos's *Historia Syntomos*,[102] John Zonaras,[103] Liudprand of Cremona,[104] the Christian Arab Yahya of Antioch,[105] vitae and *typika* particularly of Athanasios of Athos[106] as well as other hagiographical texts, the Armenian Matthew of

[101] *Ioannes Scylitzes: Synopsis historiarum*, ed. I. Thurn (Berlin–New York, 1973) and J. Wortley, "John Skylitzes: A Synopsis of Histories (811–1057 A.D.): A Provisional Translation" (typescript, University of Manitoba, 2000). We have been unable to consult the recently published annotated French translation of Skylitzes, *Jean Skylitzès. Empereurs de Constantinople* (Paris, 2003), trans. B. Flusin with notes by J.-C. Cheynet.

[102] *Michaelis Pselli Historia syntomos*, ed. W. J. Aerts (Berlin–New York, 1990), with English translation.

[103] *Ioannis Zonarae Epitomae historiarum*, ed. M. Pinder and M. Büttner-Wobst, 3 vols. (Bonn, 1841–97).

[104] *Antapodosis; Homelia paschalis; Historia Ottonis; Relatio de legatione Constantinopolitana*, in *Liudprandi Cremonensis Opera*, ed. P. Chiesa (Turnhout, 1998) and Liudprand of Cremona, *Relatio de Legatione Constantinopolitana*, ed. and trans. with intro. and comm. by B. Scott (London, 1993).

[105] *Historie de Yahya-ibn-Said d'Antioche, continuateur de Said-ibn-Bitriq*, ed. and trans. I. Kratchkovsky and A. A. Vasiliev, PO 18 (Paris, 1924): 705–833; 23 (Paris, 1932): 349–520; 47.4 (Turnhout, 1997).

[106] *Vitae duae antiquae Sancti Athanasii Athonitae*, ed. J. Noret (Turnhout, 1982), and *Byzantine Monastic Foundation Documents: A Complete Translation of the Surviving Founders' Typika and Testaments*, ed. J. Thomas and A. C. Hero, 5 vols. (Washington, D.C., 2000), 1:205–80, nos. 11–14, trans. G. Dennis.

31

Introduction

Edessa,[107] various legal documents[108] and poetry,[109] as well as letters, short chronicles, seals, and coinage. As noted above, Leo himself apparently used now lost sources, one quite favorable to the Phokas family, others favorable to John Tzimiskes. As a result, there are significant internal inconsistencies in his work, notably the positive treatment both of Nikephoros Phokas and of Tzimiskes, who had planned and participated in the murder of his predecessor.[110] There are conflicts as well with the other sources. R. Morris has shown that this results in large part from propaganda as well as actual war on the part of the Phokas family and from the efforts of Tzimiskes' imperial propagandists to whitewash his guilt in the murder of Phokas, "their partial success . . . reflected in the chronicles."[111] Leo also omitted reporting or lacked the knowledge to report numerous items found in the other sources, e.g., Phokas's close relation to Athanasios of Athos and generous patronage in the foundation of the Lavra; his controversial legislation restricting the growth of many monastic and church properties; his devaluation of the currency; the eviction of the Arabs from Cyprus in 965; Phokas's request, denied by the synod, to have soldiers killed in battle declared martyrs; relations with Otto the Great; the report (actually a propagandistic rumor) that the empress Theophano aided Tzimiskes because Phokas intended to emasculate her sons by Romanos II so that his nephews might succeed to the imperium, or, by contrast, that Theophano herself intended to poison them and they were spirited away to safety by Tzimiskes; the marriage of Tzimiskes' niece Theophano to Otto II, and so on. Thus, in seeking to establish historical fact one should use Leo's work with caution and juxtaposed to other sources, with their own biases and shortcomings.

[107] *Chronique de Matthieu d'Edesse*, trans. E. Dulaurier (Paris, 1858).
[108] See E. McGeer, *The Land Legislation of the Macedonian Emperors* (Toronto, 2000).
[109] See *Theodosii Diaconi, De Creta capta*, ed. H. Criscuolo (Leipzig, 1979); John Geometres in PG 106:812–1002 and M. Lauxtermann, "John Geometres—Poet and Soldier," *Byzantion* 68 (1998): 356–80, esp. 367–68 with n. 48; also McGeer, *Warfare*, 223 and 250.
[110] See Morris, "Succession and Usurpation," 208: "the (to us) schizophrenic pages of Leo the Deacon." For extensive analysis of the background to Nikephoros Phokas's murder and subsequent attempts to sanctify him at the Great Lavra, see E. Patlagean, "Le basileus assassiné et la sainteté impériale," in *Media in Francia . . . Recueil de mélanges offert à Karl Ferdinand Werner* (Paris, 1989), 345–61.
[111] Morris, "Succession and Usurpation," 212.

32

A comparison of Leo the Deacon's and Skylitzes' treatments of the reign of Romanos II provides an instructive view of the different approaches of these two most comprehensive sources. Leo (Books I and II) notes that he will begin after the death of Constantine VII (9 November 959), and introduces Romanos II as just coming to manhood, a good person but given to youthful indulgences. He cites Romanos's decision to destroy the Arabs of Crete and avenge the failed expedition of 949. Romanos appoints as commander of the expedition Nikephoros Phokas, who is characterized in highly positive terms by Leo and then dominates the remainder of the first book. Phokas arrives at Crete, uses ramps to disembark fully armed cavalry, and successfully drives the Arab defenders back into the fortifications of Chandax. He then pitches camp and anchors his ships in a safe harbor. Phokas sends his subordinate Pastilas on a reconnaissance mission, but he and his men disobey orders (the New Testament admonition "be sober and vigilant") and are slaughtered by the Arabs. Phokas carefully examines the fortifications of Chandax and builds a stockade to prevent Arab attacks by land, giving a speech to the troops on again "keeping sober and vigilant" and on seeking out Arab ambushes. Phokas himself then leads a group of picked men out by night and successfully destroys an Arab force of forty thousand. After an unsuccessful assault on the walls of Chandax, Phokas decides to let famine weaken the enemy, strengthens his camp with a palisade and ditch, and spends the winter drilling his troops and having siege machines built.

Leo's second book begins with the decision of the emir of Aleppo, Hamdan (Sayf ad-Dawla), to attack and pillage Roman territory in Asia Minor. Romanos dispatches Nikephoros Phokas's brother Leo Phokas, already a successful commander against the Magyars, to oppose Hamdan. Since Leo's force is smaller than that of Hamdan, he decides to use guerrilla tactics, makes a speech to his troops, and ambushes Hamdan in a defile, slaughtering the Arab force, although Hamdan himself escapes. Leo Phokas returns to the capital, is welcomed by Romanos, and celebrates a triumph. Meanwhile in Crete, at the coming of spring (961) Nikephoros Phokas again attacks Chandax, bringing to bear artillery, a ram, and sappers, eventually breaching the wall and taking the city. He is then described as building a fortification (Temenos), pacifying and re-settling the entire island, and returning to the capital to be welcomed by Romanos and celebrate a triumph. Romanos then dispatches Nikephoros Phokas to Asia Minor, where he is said to capture sixty Arab fortresses.

As he begins his return, he learns of the sudden death of Romanos (963), which Leo the Deacon says was due to his questionable companions and an untimely (i.e., Lenten) deer-hunting expedition that exhausted the emperor, or ("as some say") to poisoning. Leo then describes the decision of the patriarch Polyeuktos and the senate to confer the imperium on Romanos's infant sons Basil and Constantine and their mother Theophano; Nikephoros's intent to seize the imperium himself, but to delay until he has regathered his army; the role of the *parakoimomenos* Joseph Bringas in opposing Phokas; Phokas's conversation with the patriarch Polyeuktos; and finally the patriarch's speech to the senate, which results in Nikephoros Phokas's reappointment as commander in Asia Minor, to the great displeasure of Joseph Bringas.

Skylitzes' treatment of the same period,[112] written in the second half of the eleventh century, several decades later, is part of a history that encompasses a much larger span of time (811–1057) and is consequently much briefer. He does, however, present interesting contrasts. He begins by noting Romanos's appointment of officials who were loyal to him, the crowning of his son Basil as co-emperor, and the birth of his second son Constantine. He records that Romanos was devoted to personal pleasure and unsavory associates, entrusting public affairs to Joseph Bringas. He indicates that Romanos gave the already militarily successful Nikephoros Phokas an army and fleet to attack Crete. Phokas on landing initially defeated the Arabs, built a strong palisade with a surrounding ditch, moored his fleet in a safe harbor, and besieged "the cities of the island," capturing cities and strongholds. On 7 March he captured Chandax and took prisoner the emir Kouroupas. He was going to remain to reestablish order in Crete, but owing to a rumor that the conqueror of Crete would become emperor was recalled by Romanos. Skylitzes indicates that there was concern that Hamdan might come to the aid of Crete; therefore Romanos dispatched Leo Phokas, who won a great victory over Hamdan at a place called Adrassos, killing and taking prisoner numberless Arabs, although Hamdan himself escaped. Leo was welcomed by Romanos on his return to the capital and celebrated a triumph.

Skylitzes reports a plot to overthrow Romanos led by the magister Basil Peteinos, a plot betrayed by one of the conspirators with the result

---

[112] Skyl. 248.92–255.65.

that Joseph Bringas had most of the conspirators arrested, tortured, exiled and tonsured, although they were soon recalled by Romanos. The leader Basil, however, died on Prokonnesos. The emperor's brother-in-law Saronites, seeing what happened to the plotters and fearful that his prominence might result in his suffering the same fate, gave his money to his children and the poor and became a monk at the monastery of Elegmoi. Skylitzes records the appearance of a certain Philoraios who put on exceptional equestrian exhibits in the Hippodrome; the end of a cattle-disease (*krabra*) that had begun in the reign of Romanos I; and Romanos's decision, at the urging of his wife, to expel his mother and sisters from the palace. His mother successfully pleaded to be allowed to stay, but the sisters were tonsured and their mother, in grief at their fate, soon died.

Skylitzes reports that on his return from Crete Nikephoros Phokas was not allowed to enter the capital city, but was sent to Asia Minor to repel the resurgent Hamdan, which he did, occupying Berrhoia (Aleppo) with the exception of its citadel. He then reports the death of Romanos, "some say due to debauchery, some to poison," and in summing up his character says that Romanos was "courteous, gentle, and intelligent, capable of governing, but subverted by his intimates who sought to maintain their own positions." He records that Romanos was succeeded by his sons and their mother Theophano, who invited Nikephoros Phokas to come to the capital (despite Joseph Bringas's opposition) and celebrate a triumph with the spoils of Crete and Berrhoia. Skylitzes reports that Phokas then deceived Bringas, by showing him the hair shirt he was wearing, into thinking that he (Phokas) intended to become a monk.

Perhaps the most obvious difference here is that of focus. Leo the Deacon is primarily concerned with the Phokas brothers and their military exploits; Romanos and his reign are presented largely as the source of the appointment of the two brothers to take action in Crete and Asia Minor. Leo's narrative of military events provides numerous details. While Skylitzes devotes a section to the military campaigns, his narrative is broader and concerns many other aspects of Romanos's reign that are not mentioned by Leo. A related aspect is Leo's emphasis on the attack on Chandax and the detail he devotes to the siege of that single city. Skylitzes, on the other hand, mentions attacks on many cities and strongholds on Crete and only briefly mentions the capture of Chandax, but does add the names of prominent captured Arabs, Kouroupas and Anemas. A third aspect concerns factual contradictions. Skylitzes, for example,

Introduction

says Phokas set up a camp with ditch and palisade on Crete after landing and initially driving the Arabs back into the city. Leo describes the initial landing and victory, a camp, the disastrous reconnaissance mission of Pastilas, the success of Phokas's night mission, and an unsuccessful attack on the walls of Chandax, all taking place before the establishing of a camp specifically said to have a palisade and ditch, linked to the need to stay through the winter.[113] Likewise, Leo says Nikephoros Phokas was welcomed into the capital by Romanos after his victory in Crete and celebrated a triumph, whereas Skylitzes says he was denied access to the city and was immediately sent to Asia Minor. A fourth issue reflects the differing styles of the authors. Leo attributes three speeches to participants in his narrative, one each by the Phokas brothers to their troops and one by the patriarch Polyeuktos to the Senate, whereas Skylitzes has no speeches. Notably, both authors reflect the view that Romanos was for the most part a good ruler who owing to his youth was led astray to a life of dissipation by questionable companions.[114]

Leo on Byzantine Military Operations

Warfare constitutes a major portion of Leo the Deacon's *History* (see the section "The Byzantine Military," above, 4–9). The following attempts to summarize what he says about the Byzantine military, particularly those instances where he seems to provide unique information. It should again be noted that Leo generally uses archaic and literary vocabulary for military units, equipment, ships, and so on, and is not always consistent in its application. His terminology bears little relation to what is found in contemporary military manuals,[115] making identification of contemporary realities questionable in some instances. Nevertheless, his descriptions often otherwise reflect what the manuals recommend.

---

[113] Neither author comments on the bitter winter, on which see *Theoph. Cont.* 478.1ff.

[114] For comparative comments on Leo's and Skylitzes' treatments of the reign of Basil II see C. Holmes, "Basil II (976–1025)," De Imperatoribus Romanis, http://www.roman-emperors.org/basilii.htm. See also S. McGrath, "The Battles of Dorostolon (971): Rhetoric and Reality," in Miller-Nesbitt, *Peace and War*, 152–64. The article compares the descriptions of the battles by Leo and Skylitzes.

[115] For example, the *Praecepta militaria* of Nikephoros Phokas and the *Taktika* of Nikephoros Ouranos (in McGeer, *Warfare*).

Command Structure and Tactical Organization

Leo (7.12) notes that when Nikephoros Phokas was sent to capture Crete in 960 he held the well-known title "*domestikos* of the Schools,"[116] in effect (after the emperor) the commander-in-chief of the army; when elsewhere referring to this position prior to 960, he uses the same term. Subsequently Leo notes that Nikephoros's brother, Leo Phokas, was appointed "*domestikos* of the West" (18.12–13) while Nikephoros was still in Crete,[117] and that Nikephoros on becoming emperor appointed John Tzimiskes "*domestikos* of the East" (44.9–10). Leo the Deacon in these designations reflects a major change in command structure, known also from other sources,[118] in which the supreme command in the time of Romanos II was divided (although the commander of the East apparently held a somewhat superior position) to facilitate military operations on the two fronts.

Leo also records the title *stratopedarches* (81.19),[119] newly employed by Nikephoros Phokas in appointing as commander his family retainer Peter, a eunuch who for that reason could not be appointed as *domestikos*.[120] He further notes the title "supreme commander" (*stratelates*)[121] when John Tzimiskes appoints Bardas Skleros (117.9–11) to command the military expedition against the rebellion of Bardas Phokas. Leo mentions the "*droungarios* of the fleet,"[122] noting (IX:4) that the holder of this office was entrusted with responsibility for Constantinople by John Tzimiskes during the latter's absence from the city and in that capacity foiled the attempted rebellion of Leo Phokas. He also refers to taxiarchs (*taxiarchai*), a title used in the later tenth-century for commanders of units of a thousand men,[123] and to captains (*lochagoi*).

---

[116] See *ODB* 1:647–48.

[117] After the death of Romanos, Nikephoros Phokas was appointed by the Senate "commander-in-chief" (αὐτοκράτωρ στρατηγός) "of Asia," apparently an alternative phrase for "*domestikos* of the East." See Guilland, *Institutions*, 1:383.

[118] For bibliography see Book I, n. 38 and Book II, n. 11.

[119] See *ODB* 3:1966–67.

[120] See Oikonomides, *Listes* 334, Cheynet, "Les Phocas," 306.

[121] See *ODB* 3:1965.

[122] See *ODB* 1:663–64 and below, Book VI, chap. 2, with n. 19.

[123] The term appears in the *Praecepta militaria* of Nikephoros Phokas, signaling a recent restructuring of the unit and command structure of the infantry. See McGeer, *Warfare*, 203; Haldon, *Warfare*, 115; Oikonomides, *Listes*, 335–36; Treadgold, *Army*, 113; and 5–6, above.

Leo (VIII:4) records John Tzimiskes' formation of the new regiment *(tagma)* of the "Immortals" (107.12),[124] describing them as "sheathed in armor" (132.18), noting that they charged the Rus' at Dorystolon holding "their spears before them" (133.23–134.1), and describes what is apparently the same *tagma* as "armed horsemen adorned with gold" (156.17–18) and as "the imperial bodyguards" (149.4–5).

Leo's terms for the army as a whole and its tactical units are archaic. McGeer[125] has plausibly suggested that at IV:11 (74.17–20), Leo's reference to a five-hundred-man cavalry "phalanx" and thousand-man "cohort" may be respectively equated to the tenth-century *parataxis* and *taxiarchia* of those known sizes. Leo also mentions service units carrying siege machinery, selected craftsmen who constructed siege machines on site, and bilingual spies sent into Rus' camps and abodes to gain information.

Training

Leo makes numerous references to training and drilling of troops. Most of these are general statements on the constant emphasis on such drilling (an emphasis also well documented in other sources),[126] which produced the discipline and order for which the army was known. In three instances he provides specific information on the type of training involved. Nikephoros Phokas is said to have used daily drills consisting of "whirl[ing] about while armed" (ἐνόπλιος περιδίνησις), "blow[ing] the trumpets often and beat[ing] the drums and sound[ing] the cymbals," "vault[ing] onto a horse," "hit[ting] the mark with the bow," and "hurl[ing] a javelin with utmost accuracy" (36.5–8). He is said to employ daily drills for his servants and household retainers consisting of "draw[ing] the bow unerringly," "pull[ing] the arrow to the chest," "aim[ing] precisely at the target," "brandish[ing] and twirl[ing] spears," "wield[ing] swords accurately," and "vault[ing] nimbly onto horses" (III:9). He also describes a mock combat in the Hippodrome with drawn swords, which terrified the civilian population (IV:6). In a related comment Leo has Nikephoros Phokas tell troops departing for winter to repair their arms, sharpen their swords, and care for their horses (54.1–2). One might also note in this connection Leo's list of the finely-honed martial skills of John Tzimiskes: throwing the javelin, drawing and shooting the bow

124 See *ODB* 1:22, s.v. "Athanatoi."
125 *Warfare*, 203 n. 14.
126 See McGeer, *Warfare*, 217–21.

Introduction

(with exceptional accuracy), and leaping over three horses and landing on a fourth (VI:3). Two items here are of particular interest. The maneuver called "whirling about while armed" is also mentioned when John Tzimiskes is said to drill his select troops on a daily basis.[127] The technique is found in Leo's frequent source Agathias (40.6), but is also referred to in Michael Attaliates and Skylitzes Continuatus.[128] It is apparently a reference to the so-called "Pyrrhic" or "dance in arms"[129] and, given the later references, was perhaps still practiced in the middle Byzantine period. The reference to "pulling the arrow to the chest" may reflect the re-emergence of the three-finger Mediterranean release.[130]

Equipment

For weapons Leo mentions swords,[131] spears or lances,[132] javelins,[133] slings, the bow and arrow, the mace,[134] and artillery. In describing lances Leo adds in an aside that "the Romans use … very long ones (ἐπιμήκεις) in battle";[135] McGeer notes that this corresponds with the evidence of the treatises.[136] Leo's terms for artillery are always generic,[137] e.g., "stone-throwing machines," but almost certainly referring to traction trebuchets.[138]

[127] 127.17–18: τὴν ἐνόπλιον κατὰ θάτεραν δίνησιν.

[128] E.Th.Tsolakes, Ἡ συνέχεια τῆς Χρονογραφίας τοῦ Ἰωάννου Σκυλίτζη (Thessalonike, 1968), 112.10–11: πολεμικῇ ὀρχήσει καὶ περιδινήσει ἀγχιστρόφῳ; and M. Attaleiates, Michaelis Attaliotae historia, ed. W. Brunet de Presle and I. Bekker (Bonn, 1853), 158.9: τὴν Πυρριχεῖον ὄρχησιν.

[129] E.Wheeler, "Hoplomachia and Greek Dances in Arms," GRBS 23 (1982): 232 suggests regarding the ancient training: "Probably the most that can be concluded from our knowledge of the Pyrrhic is that this dance might have increased physical fitness, agility, and dexterity in handling the shield."

[130] Haldon, Warfare, 215.

[131] He generally uses the terms ξίφος and μάχαιρα, employing ἀκινάκης twice and φάσγανον once.

[132] For spear he chiefly employs δόρυ, also δοράτιον, ἄκων, and ἔγχος; κοντός has been translated "lance."

[133] For "javelin" Leo uses ἀκόντιον. Kolias (Waffen, 186) comments that distinctions between terms for spear and javelin are not always precise, citing Leo the Deacon 15.20 δοράτων ἀκοντιζομένων ("spears were thrown").

[134] The mace (κορύνη) is mentioned at 125.12 and 145.2.

[135] See 143.21–22; cf. 132.16–17: δόρυ …μήκιστον of John Tzimiskes' personal weapon.

[136] McGeer, Warfare, 206 and n. 21. See also Kolias, Waffen, 205.

[137] E.g., πετροβόλα ὄργανα, ἀφετήριαι μηχαναί, ἑλεπόλεις.

[138] See Dennis, "Helepolis," 102–3, and above, p. 8.

For defensive armor Leo records helmets,[139] shields,[140] and the breast-plate.[141] He also refers to the "iron-clad" horsemen, the term (πανσίδηρος)[142] occurring for the first time in Leo's text and designating the heavily armored cavalrymen on heavily armored horses, the *kataphraktoi*, "the most significant development in the Byzantine army in the tenth century."[143] He uses the presumably Homeric term μίτρα (47.2), apparently in the (contested) sense of a "waistguard," and also ζωστήρ of a "waistguard" or "belt" worn by a Scythian (110.20).[144] At 89.6 he describes an otherwise unattested instrument called an ἀκούφιον, a kind of pick used to kill Nikephoros Phokas.

The Navy

Leo uses the term "trireme" for the largest Byzantine warship, specifically identifying it with the contemporary term *dromon*[145] at 7.17–18. In a number of instances these ships are described as "fire-bearing," i.e., capable of projecting the incendiary often called "Greek fire" and referred to by Leo in two instances as "Median fire" (144.7, 156.2–3). Notably in two instances (65.19, 126.23) Leo indicates that these "fire-bearing triremes" must be ballasted, a piece of information we have not found elsewhere. Presumably such ships had to be securely stabilized in order to perform this specific function. He also mentions troop transports, which in one instance are said to be unloaded by using ramps, devices that startled the Cretan Arab enemy (7.20–21). At 65.20 Leo mentions "merchantmen" as used to transport troops and equipment, and at 129.12 "cargo vessels." In the emperor John Tzimiskes' review of the navy in the Golden Horn Leo includes, in addition to "triremes," "galleys and patrol boats,"[146] while at 144.22 he refers to "grain transports" supplying the Byzantines at Dorystolon.

---

[139] He employs κρανός, κόρυς, and κυνῆ. Kolias, *Waffen*, 75 n. 2 observes that this last term for a "leather helmet" seldom appears in the Byzantine period and is in both instances used by Leo as a synonym for κόρυς.

[140] Leo primarily uses ἀσπίς and θυρεόν, in three instances σάκος, and once πέλτη.

[141] θώραξ. He specifically describes Scythians (Rus') as wearing chainmail breastplates (ἀλυσιδωτὸς θώραξ, 108.6, 144.5, and 153.2).

[142] 59.4–5, 78.21, 140.11, and 151.3–4.

[143] McGeer, *Warfare*, 214.

[144] On this uncertain usage see Book III, n. 60 and Book VI, n. 116.

[145] See *ODB* 1:662.

[146] See Book VIII, n. 14.

Introduction

Encampment

Leo most frequently uses the term χάραξ (literally, "palisade") for a military encampment. While the term can refer to a "palisaded camp," at I:9 (16.18–19) Leo says that Nikephoros Phokas returned to his previously established χάραξ and "fortified it strongly all around with a stockade and a ditch";[147] thus it seems that the term does not necessarily imply a palisade.[148] It can, however, refer specifically to the palisade itself, as at IX:1 (142.1–2), where John Tzimiskes is said to fortify his camp (στρατόπεδον) with a secure palisade.[149] Leo gives a full description of the camp at IX:1. He relates the excavation of a trench all around, with piling up of the dirt on the inside of the trench, planting of spears in the dirt, and placement of contiguous shields leaning against the spears, commenting that "it was customary for the Romans to set up their camp in this way in enemy territory." McGeer has shown the essential accuracy of this description, comparing it to similar descriptions in military manuals.[150]

Battles

Ambushes. Leo describes instances of Byzantine commanders employing guerrilla methods when they were facing great numerical superiority of the enemy. At II:2 Leo Phokas's tactics in defeating the "Huns" (i.e., Magyars) are described as "unexpected" and "stealthy." He observed the enemy without being seen, attacked at night, and by "sudden attack" slaughtered vast numbers. He used similar tactics in his defeat of Sayf ad-Dawla. Again faced with superior enemy numbers, he decided to occupy strategic positions on the precipices, lie in ambush, and guard escape routes. Addressing his troops (II:3–4), he advocated "cautious planning," "cunning," "reasoned delay," "unexpected attacks," and "to lie in ambush in these steep places, waiting for them to arrive and pass through." When the enemy forces were caught in narrow and rough terrain, trumpets sounded the battle charge and the fresh Byzantine forces slaughtered the enemy, who had been wearied by their march. Dennis, Dagron,

---

[147] Κυκλόθεν ἑρκίῳ καὶ ταφρείᾳ ἱκανῶς ὀχυρώσας. See Book I, n. 47.

[148] See also IV:3 (58.12).

[149] Ἐρυμνῷ χάρακι. The term is also employed of a palisade used to surround a city under siege at 51.13, 58.12, 106.22, and 173.21.

[150] McGeer, *Warfare*, 350–54.

41

and Cheynet have noted[151] that Leo the Deacon has Leo Phokas use the same directives as are found in the *De velitatione (On Skirmishing)*, a text compiled from notes written by Nikephoros Phokas.[152] Ambush techniques (avoidance of confrontation with superior numbers, feigned retreat, and the like) are also employed by Bardas Skleros against the forces of the Rus' prince Sviatoslav (VI:11–12).

Pitched Battles. Leo also presents a number of examples of direct confrontations between Byzantines and both Arab and Rus' forces. On first landing his army "fully armed and mounted" on Crete (I:3), Nikephoros Phokas attacked the Arab forces. He drew up his army in three sections,[153] studded it thickly with shields and spears, had the trumpets sound the charge, and launched a frontal assault preceded by the standard of the cross. Unable to withstand the Roman spears, the Arabs retreated. At Tarsos (IV:3) Nikephoros Phokas deployed the "iron-clad horsemen" in the front line, other cavalry on either wing, and archers and slingers in the rear with orders to shoot at the enemy from behind. At the sound of the trumpets the army advanced "with incredible precision" and the "thrusts of spears" and the "missiles . . . from behind" turned the enemy to flight. At Preslav (VIII:4) John Tzimiskes deployed his forces in "deep formations," ordering the trumpets to sound, cymbals to clash, and drums to roll.[154] At a critical point the emperor commanded his special cavalry forces, the "Immortals," to charge the left wing of the Scythians. They did so with "spears before them," and the enemy, unable to withstand the spears, turned to flight. At Dorystolon (VIII:9–10) John Tzimiskes deployed the "Romans" in the center, the "iron-clad horsemen" on both wings, and again archers and slingers in the rear ordered to maintain steady fire. For some time the battle was evenly balanced until "the emperor threw the cavalry against them in force" with trumpets sounding the call to battle, causing the enemy to retreat.[155]

---

[151] Dennis, *Treatises*, 157 n. 2; Dagron, *Le traité*, 223 n. 16; and Cheynet, "Les Phocas," 303–5. See also Book II, n. 20.

[152] See *ODB* 1:615.

[153] On this tripartite line see also II:2 and VI:12, and Haldon, *Warfare*, 205.

[154] On this combination of trumpets, drums, and cymbals, apparently unique to Leo the Deacon, see also III:1, and N. Maliaras, "Die Musikinstrumente im byzantinischen Heer vom 6. bis zum 12. Jahrhundert," *JÖB* 51 (2001): 94–95.

[155] On the general correspondence between Leo's descriptions and the tactics advocated in the *Praecepta militaria* of Nikephoros Phokas, see McGeer, *Warfare*, 313–16.

Single Combats. Leo records a number of examples of individuals showing courage, heroism, and honor in battle and in one-on-one combat. At VI:11 Peter the *stratopedarches* is described as accepting the challenge of a Scythian commander to single combat; "filled with inconceivable valor and spirit," Peter charged the man and drove a spear right through his opponent's chainmail breastplate and out the back.[156] At VI:12 a Scythian "who boasted of his courage" rode out from his unit and attacked Bardas Skleros. The Scyth delivered only a glancing blow, and Bardas's younger brother Constantine, who "had an enormous body, with irresistible and invincible strength," killed first the Scythian's horse, then the Scythian himself. At VI:13 Bardas Skleros himself killed a Scythian, driving his sword through the enemy's helmet and breastplate and cutting him in two. At VII:8 the defeated rebel Bardas Phokas, in retreat and chased by a "bold and arrogant" pursuer, "spouting threats," urged the pursuer to withdraw out of pity for his (Bardas's) fate and in knowledge of fortune's reversals. When the pursuer did not relent, Bardas crushed his helmet and skull with a mace. At VIII:6 in the siege of Preslav the young Theodosios Mesonyktes was the first to climb a siege ladder set up against the wall, decapitated the Scythian trying to defend the battlement, and then mounted the wall and killed others. "The Romans cheered loudly at the novel deed." At IX:2 Theodore Lalakon is said to have killed great numbers of the enemy with an iron mace, which he wielded with such force as to crush helmet and skull simultaneously. At IX:6 Anemas, one of the imperial bodyguard, upon seeing Ikmor, the second in command of the Rus', killing many Byzantines, charged him with drawn sword and decapitated him. At IX:8, however, when Anemas attacked Sviatoslav in the same manner, he only knocked him from his horse, and Anemas was himself killed.

John Haldon has characterized such descriptions as "reflecting the values and interest in warfare characteristic of the provincial military elite," and "the realities of warfare of the period," but also "a new attitude toward the representation of warfare in the literature of the period, generated by the demands of the Byzantine social establishment as well as the preferred self-image of the soldiers themselves."[157] Eric McGeer has noted the importance of soldiers in the "private service of military magnates, who themselves were coming to form a distinctly military aristocracy during the tenth century."[158]

---

[156] The same feat is attributed to Nikephoros Phokas at I:5.

[157] Haldon, *Warfare*, 244. For another view see above, 23 and n. 83.

[158] McGeer, *Warfare*, 219.

Introduction

Assaults on Fortified Positions and Sieges. Leo mentions the taking of many sites "by surprise," "at first assault," and "by assault"; he describes in some detail the sieges of Chandax (Books I–II), Mopsuestia (Book III), Tarsos (Book IV), Antioch (Books IV–V), and Preslav (Book VIII).

At Chandax, after two initial victories against Arab forces outside the city, Nikephoros Phokas attacked the walls. Leo's brief description (I:8) indicates only that the trumpet was sounded, spears were thrown in all directions, and stone-throwing machines hurled rocks against the battlements. Arrows, axes, and stones came down from the wall in response. Phokas decided to withdraw, and deliver the city to famine, until he could "prepare siege engines and other machines suitably devised for storming walls" (I:9). During the winter he had "siege engines constructed by selected craftsmen."

The following spring Phokas attacked again (II:6–7). He organized his army in "deep formation," trumpets sounded and drums rolled, and the squadron in the van was strengthened with the forces being put into an "oblong formation." Artillery engines began to hurl stones, a battering ram was employed, and sappers undermined the wall, propping it up with wooden uprights that were eventually burned, causing two towers and the intervening wall to collapse.[159] The Romans entered through the breach, despite Arab resistance.

The description of the siege of Mopsuestia is briefer (III:10–11). Phokas surrounded the city and bombarded it from all sides with siege engines. After making a reconnaissance, he ordered sappers to dig a tunnel, beginning some distance away to conceal the activity from the besieged. Eventually two towers and the intervening wall were undermined and propped up by wooden uprights; then the uprights were burned causing the wall to collapse. The city fell.

Nikephoros Phokas initially encircled Tarsos and invested the city (III:10), but was unable to take it. Frustrated at his inability to do so "at first assault," he ordered the fields around Tarsos to be clear-cut to prevent ambushes, but realizing the city could not be taken "by assault," decided to employ starvation. The Tarsians eventually capitulated (IV:1, 3). In a brief but interesting comment (71.19–20), Phokas is said by way of contrast to have attacked the fortress of Arka, surrounding it with three palisades and demolishing its towers with siege machines (ἐλεπόλεσι).

---

[159] Hase, Leo diac. 419, noted that the description is modeled on Agathias's description of the siege of Cumae (Agath. 21.15–22.20).

44

Phokas initially besieged Antioch briefly and terrified its inhabitants with a show of strength (IV:10). He then decided to use a strategy of attrition, stationing troops nearby in a newly-fortified position to carry out daily raids and plunder the city's provisions (IV:11). Subsequently, however, the *stratopedarches* Peter and Michael Bourtzes observed where the wall might be scaled, had ladders constructed of the required height, and secretly entered by night, killing the guards and gaining control of the city (V:4).

As John Tzimiskes marched toward Preslav (VIII:4), the support personnel were in the rear transporting the siege machines. Hoping to take the city "at first assault" (VIII:5), Tzimiskes organized his troops into an unbroken close formation, had the trumpets sound the charge, and attacked the wall. The resistance from the battlements consisted of javelins, missiles, and stones. The Romans responded with bows, stone-throwing devices, slings, and javelins, to keep the enemy from leaning over the battlements. The emperor then ordered ladders set up and personally encouraged the troops. As noted above, Theodosios Mesonyktes climbed a ladder, mounted the wall, and killed numerous defenders. Many other Romans followed up the ladders and the Scythians retreated. Other Romans then broke through the gates.

In his description of Basil II's attack on Tralitza, Leo notes that "the siege machines and the other contrivances accomplished nothing, because of the inexperience of the men who brought them up against the walls, and they [the machines] were set on fire by the enemy" (171.17–19).

While, as noted above, the literary influence of Agathias can be seen on Leo's description of the siege of Chandax (and, given the similarities, also on that of Mopsuestia), much here is similar to the prescriptions of the military manuals. In Chapter 65 ("On siege warfare") of his *Taktika* Nikephoros Ouranos recommends burning crops and interdiction of supplies to create starvation, and attacking the walls with the entire army, using arrows, slings, and stone-throwing devices, while employing battering rams to break the wall, tunneling to the wall, excavating under and propping its foundations, then burning the props to cause the wall's collapse. He specifically recommends the undermining operation as the most effective. One point perhaps worthy of note is Leo's reference to the demolition of the towers of Arka with "siege machines" (ἑλεπόλεις). Which specific machines are meant is not clear, but if the reference is to artillery—it would be odd to apply *helepolis* to a sapping operation—the result is unusual, since traction trebuchets have generally been viewed as antipersonnel weapons,[160] used to drive the enemy from the battlements. Leo's statement may be exaggeration.

The Army and Society

Leo provides a few interesting comments on the place of the army in Byzantine society and its effects upon it. At a number of points he describes troops being sent home following a campaign and subsequently regathering.[161] At III:1, for example, Nikephoros Phokas sets up his headquarters in Cappadocia and awaits the arrival of his troops, while at the very end of Book III he sends his troops home for the winter. Leo reflects here the mustering and dismissal of provincial armies who served on a seasonal basis.[162] At II:8 Leo says that Phokas settled Crete after its conquest with "bands of Armenians, Romans, and other rabble," reflecting the policy of providing plots of land to soldiers in return for the obligation of military service.[163] At various points we learn that a portion of the war booty was distributed to the troops, an important aspect of their income. In a related vein at IV:6 he notes that Phokas "mercilessly introduced taxes that had never before been conceived of, saying that he needed a lot of money for the army, and he oppressed his subjects with these [taxes]," a source of great public anger against the emperor.

At III:4 it is the army of the East that acclaimed Phokas as emperor and marched on Constantinople with him to effect that choice. Within the city (III:7) the opposition to Phokas used other troops, the "Macedonian unit," to resist. The civilian population successfully fought them, however, and their commander Marianos was killed when a flowerpot thrown from a rooftop struck him on the head. In addition, Basil the Nothos armed three thousand of his "householders" and attacked the houses of those opposing Phokas; subsequently he brought triremes from the dockyards over to Phokas on the Asiatic shore. We also read about civilians terrified by a military mock combat in the Hippodrome and the ensuing deaths in the rush to escape (IV:6), while during the imperial procession to Pege a fight took place between civilians and "Armenians," i.e., Phokas's troops in the city, resulting in civilian deaths (IV:7).

---

[160] See Leo's references to stone-throwing machines harming men or driving them from the battlements at II:7, VIII:5, and IX:5. See also above, 9 and n. 15.

[161] See II:9 and 11, III:1 and 11.

[162] See Haldon, *Warfare*, 182, 338 n. 128.

[163] See Book II, n. 49.

Leo also provides a number of comments on Byzantine attitudes toward war. At II:7 Nikephoros Phokas stopped his men from killing the Cretans who threw down their arms, "saying it was a sign of inhumanity to cut down and slay like an enemy men who had given themselves up in surrender." Indeed the captured son of the emir of Crete, Anemas, subsequently appeared in the narrative fighting prominently against the Rus' as a member of the Byzantine imperial bodyguard (IX:6–8). At IV:6, rather than risk his troops in a war against the Bulgarians, Phokas sent an ambassador with a huge sum of money to bribe the Rus' to attack the Bulgarians. At IX:11 Tzimiskes is said to accept reconciliation with the Rus' "for he very much preferred peace to warfare, since he was aware that the former preserves the people, whereas the latter, on the contrary, destroys them." Notable also is the Christian element in battles and resulting conquests. The standard of the cross regularly precedes the army, and the recovery of lost military crosses and their subsequent dedication in Hagia Sophia is prominently related.[164] Commanders indicate that their tactics, "with the help of God," "with the help of Providence," and "with the help of the Almighty" will lead to conquest. The recovery of holy relics is the result of a number of conquests—the *keramion* at Edessa, the sandals of Christ and the hair of John the Baptist at Mempetze, and so on—and an icon of the Theotokos was carried at the head of John Tzimiskes' triumphal procession into the capital after his defeat of the Rus' in Bulgaria (IX:12).

Leo on Tenth-Century Constantinople

Leo provides numerous references to Constantinople, which he generally calls "Byzantium," but also the "imperial city" (βασιλεύουσα); he refers to it as both a πόλις and an ἄστυ. He emphasizes its strong fortifications as when Nikephoros Phokas describes it (43.2–4) as "surrounded by the sea and well-walled, and enclosed on all sides by strong towers," and notes that Nikephoros Phokas built "a wall from one side of the palace, which sloped toward the sea, and brought it to the sea on the other side, and constructed a lofty and secure wall, which can be seen today, and protected the imperial palace, as he thought" (64.17–21). He describes Nikephoros Phokas, in preparation for a possible Russian attack, positioning artillery on the walls and securing the entrance to (presumably) the Golden

---

[164] See Haldon, *Warfare*, 22.

Horn[165] with an iron chain between two towers, called Kentenarion and Kastellion (V:2). He comments that the earthquake of 989 "demolished to the ground the fortifications of Byzantium" (175.24–176.1).[166] Leo notes that Leo Phokas "slipped out [of the city] through pipes under the wall" (45.23–24); mentions the acropolis and nearby gate beneath the sanctuary of St. Phokas,[167] through which the rebel Leo Phokas entered the city (146.12–13); and also refers to the dockyards where the firebearing triremes were harbored (47.6).

A number of churches are mentioned, often in connection with imperial ceremonies and processions, and as sites of prayers before leaving on military campaigns or of prayers of thanksgiving upon return. The building most often mentioned is Hagia Sophia, which Leo refers to as "the holy and great church of the Wisdom of God," "the celebrated and holy church," "the celebrated church of God,"[168] and "the Great Church." It is the scene of asylum-seeking, once by Bardas Phokas, twice by Leo Phokas, and apparently once by Joseph Bringas where it is simply called "the church." Nikephoros Phokas goes to Hagia Sophia to meet with the patriarch Polyeuktos, is crowned emperor there, and deposits there the gold cross-standards recovered from Tarsos. John Tzimiskes is crowned in the church, on the ambo where Leo says the patriarch customarily crowned a new emperor. Tzimiskes also prays in Hagia Sophia before beginning his campaign against the Rus' and there ends his triumphal procession following his successful expedition. Finally Leo describes how the earthquake of 989 "brought down and knocked to the ground the half dome of the upper part of the Great Church, together with the west apse," adding that these were rebuilt by the emperor Basil II in six years (X:10).

The other churches mentioned by Leo are "the very beautiful church ... built in honor of the Virgin" at Pege (64.23) outside the walls, in connection with the traditional imperial procession celebrating the feast of the Ascension; "the church of the Mother of God, which is in the imperial palace" (71.12–13) (i.e., the church of the Virgin of the Pharos), where Nikephoros Phokas dedicated the *keramion* from Edessa and

---

[165] See the related note (Book V, n. 22), where the possibility that the chain blocked the Bosporos is considered.

[166] This must be an exaggeration.

[167] Leo is sole source for this gate. See Book IX, n. 20.

[168] See Book III, n. 69.

Tzimiskes dedicated the sandals of Christ; the church of Christ the Savior at the Brazen Gate, which Tzimiskes visited prior to his campaign against the Rus' and which he rebuilt from "a narrow chapel... in a more splendid and sacred fashion" (128.5–129.1), where he dedicated the hair of John the Baptist, and where he had his tomb constructed and was buried; the church of the Holy Apostles (91.11–13), where Nikephoros Phokas's body was taken and secretly buried in one of the adjacent mausolea (Leo uses the classical term ἡρῷον) where Constantine the Great was also buried; and the church "of the Mother of God at Blachernai" (129.7–8), to which John also made a prayerful procession prior to the campaign against the Rus'. Leo also mentions one monastery within the city, that "of the Abramitai, which they call Acheiropoietos" (47.9–10), where Nikephoros Phokas made his initial headquarters on coming to the city as emperor.

On occasion Leo gives an intimate glimpse into palace life, as when he describes Theophano's conversation with the emperor in his bedchamber and her solicitude for the Bulgarian princesses sent to Constantinople to marry the young princes Basil and Constantine. He mentions the palace terrace above the Boukoleon harbor (Leo notes [87.8–9] that it is so called from the stone statue of a lion seizing a bull located there), from which John Tzimiskes and his fellow conspirators were hauled up in a basket and subsequently entered the imperial bedchamber to murder Phokas, and the iron gates (90.21–22) that Phokas's bodyguards tried to break through to rescue him. He notes that after the murder of Phokas John Tzimiskes went "to the splendid hall of the imperial palace (they call the structure the Chrysotriklinos) ... [and] sat on the imperial throne" (90.13–16). Leo also on three occasions mentions the "women's apartments" of the palace.

Leo is a prime source for triumphal processions in tenth-century Constantinople. He says that Nikephoros Phokas first entered Constantinople as emperor through the Golden Gate (48.3). The Hippodrome (Leo calls it τὸ θέατρον) is frequently mentioned. Leo Phokas celebrates a triumph there, "astounding the spectators with the quantity of slaves and plunder" (24.3); Nikephoros Phokas does the same, "before all the assembled people who marvelled at the magnitude and splendor of the booty" (28.11–15); he also organized chariot races and ordered his soldiers to engage in the mock combat there, which caused a panic resulting in many spectators being trampled and suffocated; Tzimiskes, following his wedding, entertained the people there. In describing Tzimiskes' triumph

over the Rus' (IX:12) Leo notes that "the middle of the city . . . was
everywhere decorated with purple cloths and, like a bridal chamber, was
thickly bedecked with laurel branches and with fabric interwoven with
gold." He briefly describes a subsequent triumphal procession of
Tzimiskes, after victory over the Arabs, as going through the "marketplace" (ἀγορά) (163.6), i.e., the main street or Mese.

Leo also provides rare glimpses of private life in Constantinople. He
notes that Bardas Phokas had his home "on the south side of the town,
next to the steep part of the street that leads to the sea, where the harbor
of Sophia spreads out" and that his body was laid out there prior to
burial (83.22–84.1); that John Tzimiskes met in his home with fellow
conspirators to plot the murder of Nikephoros Phokas (85.19–22); and
that Leo Phokas hid in a private home in the quarter of Sphorakion
awaiting his fellow conspirators (146.20–21). Leo also refers to angry
women throwing rocks from the rooftops at the emperor riding in procession (65.3–5), and a similar incident in which a woman threw a flowerpot from a rooftop, killing the general Marianos as he led the
Macedonian troops through the streets in an effort to prevent Nikephoros
Phokas from entering the city (46.13–17).

E. Manuscript Tradition of the History[169]

The *History* of Leo is preserved in a single primary manuscript, Parisin.
gr. 1712 (P), fols. 272r–322r, dating most probably to the twelfth century,[170] and in a sixteenth century apograph, Escurial gr. Y–I–4 (E), fols.
83v–121v. In the Paris manuscript Leo's *History* is flanked by the work
of the so-called pseudo-Symeon[171] (fols. 18v–272r) and the *Chronographia*
of Michael Psellos (fols. 322r–422r). Since Symeon's chronicle includes
the years 813–961, the *History* of Leo covers the period 959–976, and the
Chronographia of Psellos goes from 976 to 1078, the scribe (or the patron)
evidently considered the three works as a continuous historical work by

---

[169] The sections on manuscript tradition and on previous editions and translations for
the most part summarize the extensive analysis and findings of Panagiotakes in *Leon*,
42–129.

[170] For a detailed description of this manuscript, see K. Snipes, "Notes on Parisinus
Graecus 1712," *JÖB* 41 (1991): 141–61. Note that B. Crostini dates the manuscript to
the 13th c. ("The Emperor Basil II's Cultural Life," *Byzantion* 66 [1996]: 55–80, at 57 n.
15), as does D. DelCorno in his introduction to S. Impellizzeri, ed., *Michele Psello. Imperatori
di Bisanzio (Cronografia)* (Milan, 1984), 1:xxxiii n. 4.

[171] See *ODB* 3:1983.

three authors. The close links among the three works are emphasized by the way in which the scribe does not even start a new page at the beginning of the works of Leo and Psellos.

The seventeenth-century Dominican friar Franciscus Combefis was the first to begin the preparation of an edition of Leo, but his work was interrupted by his death in 1679. Part of his edition was published posthumously in Paris in 1685, included in a volume entitled *Historiae byzantinae scriptores post Theophanem*. He also prepared a Latin translation of the first seven books, but this never appeared in print. It was not until 1819 that the noted German philologist C. B. Hase published the first complete edition in Paris, with the title *Leonis diaconi Caloënsis Historia scriptoresque alii ad res Byzantinas pertinentes*. This was a deluxe edition in the tradition of the seventeenth-century folio volumes of Byzantine historians produced by the royal Louvre Press in Paris, and included beautiful engravings. Hase's edition was accompanied by a Latin translation that has won praise for its style and accuracy,[172] and by substantial philological and historical notes. This limited edition was reprinted in Bonn in 1828 as volume 11 of the Corpus Scriptorum Historiae Byzantinae, and reproduced once more (with a few tacit corrections) in volume 117 of Migne's *Patrologia Graeca* (Paris, 1864).

The Combefis and Hase editions were based solely on the Paris manuscript. In the 1960s Nicholas Panagiotakes prepared a new critical edition, based on the Escurial manuscript as well, which has not yet been published (see Preface); it is hoped that this edition will soon see the light of day in the series Berolinensis of the Corpus Fontium Historiae Byzantinae, thanks to the efforts of Athanasios Markopoulos.[173]

---

[172] See Panagiotakes, *Leon*, 121.

[173] In 1937 Lester Houck prepared a new edition of the *History* as a Ph.D. dissertation at the University of Michigan. We have not been able to consult this dissertation, entitled "The History of Leo the Deacon, An Edition." By coincidence Dr. Houck was the first junior fellow appointed to Dumbarton Oaks, during its inaugural year 1940–41. His announced topic was the edition of Leo the Deacon, but he never brought the work to press.

G. Translations

Combefis and Hase both produced Latin translations, as we have seen. Less well known is the Russian translation of D. Popov, *Istoriia Lva D'iakona Kaloiskago* (St. Petersburg, 1820), which appeared only a year after the deluxe Paris edition. Almost a hundred and fifty years passed before Leo's history was translated into a modern Western European language, Franz Loretto's German version of 1961, *Nikephoros Phokas "Der bleiche Tod der Sarazenen" und Johannes Tzimiskes. Die Zeit von 959 bis 976 in der Darstellung des Leon Diakonos*, in the Graz series Byzantinische Geschichtsschreiber. In 1988 a new Russian translation by M. M. Kopylenko with commentary by M. I. A. Siuziumov and S. A. Ivanov appeared.[174] A modern Greek translation by Vrasidas Karales has been recently published.[175] Finally, it should be noted that after our English translation went to press, Dr. Leslie MacCoull kindly informed us of an undated English translation by Harry Turtledove that never appeared in print.

---

[174] *Lev D'iakon. Istoriia* (Moscow, 1988). We have profited primarily from the notes to this translation.

[175] B. Karales, Λέων Διάκονος. Ἱστορία (Athens, 2000).

Note To The Reader

In the English translation words or phrases in italics are direct quotations. Citations from the Septuagint usually follow the translation of L. C. L. Brenton, *The Septuagint with Apocrypha* (London, 1851; repr. Peabody, Mass., 1992); citations from the New Testament follow the Revised Standard Version.

In an attempt to retain some of the classicizing flavor of the text, we have kept archaizing terms such as Istros for Danube, Tauroscythians for the Rus', and triremes for warships. We have also maintained the Greek spelling of Rus' names such as Sphendosthlavos (Sviatoslav). We have, however, rendered *theatron* as Hippodrome.

As much as possible we have endeavored to give a consistent translation of Greek terms, even though Leo himself is inconsistent in his use of them. As an example, he refers to Constantinople, Preslav, and Antioch as both *polis* (city) and *astu* (town).

The footnotes do not attempt to provide comprehensive bibliography. Many of the citations, to the *ODB* for example, will lead the reader to additional scholarship on a given topic.

The *History* of Leo the Deacon

From the death of the emperor Constantine, to the
death of the emperor John, called Tzimiskes[1]

Book I

[annis 959–961]

AMONG THE GOOD THINGS THAT ARE OF BENEFIT IN LIFE, *history* is not one of the least, but one of the most important, since it is by nature something useful and profitable.[2] For it recounts manifold deeds of all kinds, such as are usually brought about by the passage of time and events, [p. 4] and especially by the choice of men engaged in the events; it also *ordains for men*[3] to strive after and emulate some deeds, while rejecting and avoiding others, so that they may not inadvertently neglect that which is useful and beneficial, and attach themselves to that which is abominable and harmful. Therefore history is agreed to be as profitable as the other useful things in life, inasmuch as it brings mortal affairs back to life or gives them youthful vigor, and does not allow them to be swept away and concealed in *the depths of oblivion*.[4] Many extraordinary and unusual events have occurred in novel fashion *in the course of my lifetime*:[5] fearsome sights have appeared in the sky, unbelievable earthquakes have occurred,[6] thunderbolts have struck and torrential rains have

[1] I.e., from November 959 to January 976. This title must have been composed by an editor or scribe, rather than by the author, since parts of Book X (chaps. 7–10) describe events from the early years of the reign of Basil II (976–1025) and Leo states that he planned to write in greater detail about the late 10th c.; see Leo diac. 176.12–13. This plan was evidently frustrated by Leo's death.

[2] See Agath. 4.4–7.

[3] The phrase ἱστορία ... τοῖς ἀνθρώποις νομοθετεῖ (Leo diac. 3.2, 4.2–3) may be borrowed from Gregory of Nyssa, *De vita Mosis* 2.146.8 ed. J. Daniélou, *Grégoire de Nysse. La vie de Moïse*, 3rd ed. (Paris, 1968).

[4] See Gregory of Nazianzus, *Or.* 44.1 (PG 36:608). See Leo, Book V, chap. 9, p. 92.6, and n. 88, for a similar expression; and the Introduction, 11–12, for discussion.

[5] See Agath. 5.5, whose subsequent list of calamities Leo has altered in what follows to fit the situation in the 10th c.

[6] Earthquakes were reported in Constantinople in 948, 986, and 989: see Grumel, *Chronologie*, 479–80.

Book I

poured down, wars have broken out and armies have overrun many parts of the inhabited world, cities and whole regions have moved elsewhere,[7] so that many people believe that life is now undergoing a transformation, and that the expected Second Coming of the Savior and God is *near, at the very gates*.[8] For these reasons I have resolved not to pass over *in silence* events that are full of horror and *worthy of amazement*,[9] but to recount them openly, so that they may be a lesson to later generations,

---

[7] Lists of notable events and natural disasters, such as the one constructed here by Leo, are nearly a topos of classical and Byzantine historiography. See n. 5 above on Agathias, and M. Whitby, "Greek Historical Writing after Procopius: Variety and Vitality," in *The Byzantine and Early Islamic Near East*, ed. A. Cameron and L. I. Conrad (Princeton, N.J., 1992), 1:31.

[8] See Matt. 24:33, Mark 13:29. Earlier in the same chapters, e.g., Matt. 24:3–7, 29, Christ in his sermon on the Mount of Olives lists the signs of the end of the world (συντέλεια τοῦ αἰῶνος): "And ye shall hear of wars and rumors of wars . . . For nation shall rise against nation, and kingdom against kingdom: and there shall be famines, and pestilences, and earthquakes, in divers places . . . the sun shall be darkened, and the moon shall not give her light, and the stars shall fall from heaven." While Leo's model, Agathias, has a list of calamities, Leo is original in some items and in linking his list to this New Testament passage, which he also reflects in subsequent mentions of an eclipse, earthquakes, famines, and falling stars, and in similar lists in Book X, chaps. 6 and 9.

On the concept of the Second Coming of Christ, see *ODB* 3:1591, s.v. "Parousia." Studies regarding Byzantine views about the end of the world and the Second Coming of Christ show that in Byzantium there was little focus specifically on the year 1000. Although some authors, such as Theophanes, employed among other methods of calculating time the years from the incarnation (AD) to place events in history, Dionysius's era was not widely used in Byzantium until after the fall of Constantinople in 1453. Paul Magdalino has recently, however, presented evidence for "a build-up of eschatological tension in the tenth century": see "The History of the Future and its Uses: Prophecy, Policy and Propaganda," in *The Making of Byzantine History: Studies Dedicated to Donald M. Nicol*, ed. R. Beaton and C. Roueché (Aldershot, 1993), 3–34, esp. 24–25; and idem, *Year 1000*. Recently Ihor Ševčenko has published an unedited computus that provides evidence that some Byzantines did expect the end of the world 1000 years after the birth of Christ: see "Unpublished Texts on the End of the World about the Year 1000 AD," in *Mélanges Gilbert Dagron*, TM 14 (Paris, 2002), 561–78, esp. 572 and n. 23, where he discusses and translates this passage in Leo.

Leo's allusion to the Second Coming being close at hand may have been influenced by the writings of Niketas David Paphlagon, who had calculated that the end of the world would take place in 1028. See C. Mango, *Byzantium: The Empire of New Rome* (London, 1980), 211; A. Vasiliev, "Medieval Ideas of the End of the World: West and East," *Byzantion* 16 (1942–43): 487–89; and L. G. Westerink, "Nicetas the Paphlagonian on the End of the World," in Μελετήματα στὴ μνήμη Βασιλείου Λαούρδα (Thessalonike, 1975), 177–95.

[9] See Agath. 5.14 and 5.12.

unless Providence has decided to bring the transport ship of life in the very near future into the harbor *of the end* [of the age],[10] and cause *the form of the world to pass away*.[11] My wish is that, since I have undertaken such [p. 5] an insuperable task, I may not fall short of my intent, but may *succeed* in proportion to *the magnitude* of events,[12] and recount them as they should be told. Therefore I will set forth the history in detail, to the best of my ability.

I, the one who composed these words, am Leo, son of Basil. My birthplace was Kaloë,[13] a very beautiful village in Asia, located on the slopes of Mt. Tmolos, near the sources of the river Kaystros, which, after flowing past the Kelbianon region and offering a most pleasant vista to the beholder, empties out into the gulf of Ephesos, that famous and celebrated city, and forms an estuary. But I must move on to an account of public affairs, *viewing it of special importance to strive for the truth*,[14] as is more appropriate to history than to other [genres]. For wise men of letters say that *forcefulness* is appropriate *in rhetoric, imaginative invention in poetry*, and *truth* in history.[15] Therefore I have decided to omit the events of the reign of Leo's son, Constantine, who was named Porphyrogennetos[16] (it is said that, when he was born and when he died, a comet appeared in the sky, foretelling his birth and death),[17] for they have been adequately

---

[10] See Matt. 13:39, 24:3, etc.

[11] See 1 Cor. 7:31.

[12] See Agath. 6.7–8.

[13] Kaloë, modern Kiraz (Panagiotakes, *Leon*, 3), was a bishopric in Asia Minor on the slopes of Mt. Tmolos by the banks of the Kaystros river in the Kelbianon (also Kilbianon) region, approximately 55 km NE of Ephesus; for map location, see Map 1 and *Tübinger Atlas des Vorderen Orients*, B VI 8 (Kleinasien—Das Byzantinische Reich) and B VI 12 (Kleinasien—Kirchliche Organisation des Byzantinischen Reiches).

[14] See Agath. 7.12–13.

[15] See Prokopios, *Persian Wars* 1.1.4.

[16] On Constantine VII Porphyrogennetos (945–59), son of Leo VI, see *ODB* 1:502–3. Porphyrogennetos means "born in the purple." On his insistence on the title "as a matter of survival," given his illegitimacy and the usurpation of Romanos I and his sons, see I. Ševčenko, "Re-Reading Constantine Porphyrogenitus," in *Byzantine Diplomacy*, ed. J. Shepard and S. Franklin (Aldershot, 1992), 175.

[17] These comets are mentioned in a number of extant sources, e.g., *Theoph. Cont.* 370.9–11 and 463.10–14, who noted the coincidence that a comet appeared in both 905 and 959, the years of Constantine's birth and death, and in the so-called pseudo-Symeon 756.8–10. On the comets, see Schove, *Chronology*, 297 and Grumel, *Chronologie*, 472.

described by others.[18] But I will now set down in writing subsequent events, both those that I saw with my own eyes (if indeed *eyes are more trustworthy than ears*, as Herodotus said),[19] and those that I verified from the evidence of eyewitnesses.

2. Just after the aforesaid emperor Constantine departed this life and went to his rest in the next world, in the month of November, during the third indiction, in [p. 6] the year 6467,[20] the imperial[21] rule passed into the hands of his son Romanos,[22] who was nearing the end of his adolescence and becoming a full-grown man.[23] On the whole he was a good man, of pleasing countenance and speech, distinguished in appearance, and filled with every sort of noble virtue, benign and fair to all his subjects, but he was also distracted by youthful indulgences and amusements, and introduced into the palace, as he ought not to have done, people who encouraged him in this behavior. Now this emperor Romanos decided to eradicate, with the support of the Almighty, the tyranny of the Arabs of Crete,[24] who were arrogant and had murderous

---

[18] Siuziumov et al., *Lev D'iakon*, 167, suggest a possible reference to Symeon the Logothete or Theophanes Continuatus, also noting that Leo may be simply imitating his model Agathias (9.13–16), who states that he is beginning where Prokopios left off. Loretto, *Phokas*, 163, suggests that the reference is to Theophanes Continuatus. In a yet unpublished portion of his *History of Byzantine Literature*, A. Kazhdan wrote: "Who these 'others' are we can only guess: neither the Chronicle of Symeon Logothete that stopped at 948 nor the last section of the Continuatio of Theophanes (the chronicle by Theodore Daphnopates?) that dealt with the reign of Romanos II are plausible candidates. Some texts now lost were available to Leo, but this sentence could be an empty phrase created to justify the point of departure chosen by the historian."

[19] Cf. Herodotus 1.8.10–11. Interest in the works of this 5th-c. B.C. Greek historian was rekindled in 10th-c. Byzantium: see *ODB* 2:922.

[20] Constantine died on 9 November 959. Leo, who only rarely expresses dates in terms of the so-called Byzantine era (see Introduction, 19 above), is one year off here, since November 6467 = 958, but Constantine VII is known to have died in 959. For the rules for converting Byzantine era dates to AD dates, see *ODB* 1:342–43. The indiction is a 15-year tax cycle; 959/60 does in fact correspond to the third indiction.

[21] Reading with Panagiotakes τὴν αὐτοκρατορίας . . . ἀρχὴν rather than the tacit correction to αὐτοκρατορίαν by Hase.

[22] On Romanos II (959–63), son of Constantine VII Porphyrogennetos, see *ODB* 3:1806–7.

[23] Romanos was born in 939, and was thus 20 years old when he ascended the throne.

[24] The island of Crete (*ODB* 1:545–46) was captured by Arab forces ca. 824 (Christides, *Crete*, 85–88). The term "Arab Cretans" clearly refers to the Muslim population of Crete. Elsewhere in his text Leo uses the term "Cretans" or "*barbaroi*" to identify the Arabs of Crete.

intentions against the Romans.[25] For they exulted immeasurably over the recent disaster[26] suffered by the Romans, and were plundering the shores of the Roman empire on a large scale. I will relate briefly how this misfortune befell the Romans. The emperor Constantine, unable to bear the insolence of the Cretans [p. 7] and their sneak attacks, assembled a worthy army, fitted out a good number of fire-bearing triremes,[27] and sent them against Crete, in the hope of capturing the island at the first assault. But on account of the cowardice and lack of experience of the commander,[28] who was a eunuch[29] of the *bedchamber*, an *effeminate fellow*[30] from Paphlagonia,[31] named Constantine and surnamed Gongyles,[32]

---

[25] The inhabitants of the Byzantine Empire referred to themselves as "Romans" throughout their history. Hieronymus Wolf (1516–80) introduced the term "Byzantium" for the Eastern Roman Empire: see *ODB* 1:344.

[26] Reference to the failed Byzantine expedition against the Cretan Arabs in 949, described below.

[27] Leo uses the classical term "trireme" for a fast warship (usually called a *dromon* in Byzantine Greek, as in Leo diac. 7.18) with two banks of rowers and two or three masts and equipped with Greek fire; see Ahrweiler, *Mer*, 409–18. On the composition of this flammable liquid, see J. F. Haldon and M. Byrne, "A Possible Solution to the Problem of Greek Fire," *BZ* 70 (1977): 91–99.

[28] The Greek term is *strategos*, commander of an army and in some cases military governor of a theme: see Ahrweiler, *Structures*, no. VIII, 1–52, and *ODB* 3:1964.

[29] On the various posts held by eunuchs in the imperial palace see Guilland, *Institutions*, 1:165–380; for *thalamepolos*, 269. The role of eunuchs in Byzantine society is examined in Ringrose, *The Perfect Servant* (here esp. 136) and S. Tougher, "In or Out? Origins of Court Eunuchs"; M. Mullett, "Theophylact of Ochrid's *In Defence of Eunuchs*"; and N. Gaul, "Eunuchs in the Late Byzantine Empire, c. 1250–1400," all in *Eunuchs in Antiquity and Beyond*, ed. S. Tougher (London, 2002), 143–59, 177–98, and 199–219; as well as Sidéris, "'Eunuchs of Light.'"

[30] See Agath. 19.16–17.

[31] Cf. the similar phrase ("a wretched eunuch from the wastes of Paphlagonia") used of Joseph Bringas at 40.3. Paphlagonia was a region of northern Asia Minor situated between Galatia and the Black Sea: see *ODB* 3:1579. For Byzantine attitudes towards Paphlagonians, see P. Magdalino, "Paphlagonians in Byzantine High Society," in *Byzantine Asia Minor (6th–12th cent.)* (Athens, 1998), 141–50, esp. 144–45.

[32] Constantine was elevated to power along with his brother Anastasios by the empress Zoe ca. 914: see Ringrose, *The Perfect Servant*, 136, 188–91 and S. Tougher, "In or Out? Origins of Court Eunuchs," in *Eunuchs in Antiquity and Beyond*, ed. S. Tougher (London, 2002), 149. He was in the service of Constantine VII in 949 as servant of the bedchamber when he was appointed general to head the expedition against Crete: see Skyl. 245.40–246.52 and Guilland, *Institutions*, 2:185–86. For the inventory of men and supplies for this campaign, see J. F. Haldon, "Theory and Practice in Tenth-Century Military Administration: Chapters

even though he was the proud bearer of the very distinguished dignity of *patrikios*,[33] the entire above-mentioned army, with the exception of a few men, was cut to pieces by the barbarians[34] and utterly destroyed.

3. The emperor Romanos was eager to make good this defeat, and appointed as commander-in-chief[35] of the expedition against the Cretans Nikephoros Phokas,[36] distinguished among *magistroi*[37] and commander of the troops of the East (the Romans give to this position the title *domestikos* of the Schools),[38] an active and energetic man, good at warfare and irresistibly strong.[39] Accordingly Nikephoros, upon the order of the emperor, mustered the army of Asia and embarked them on ships, and after a swift voyage he also brought up a large number of fire-bearing triremes (the Romans call these *dromones*)[40] to anchor at Crete. When it seemed to be an opportune moment for disembarkation, he

---

II, 44 and 45 of the *Book of Ceremonies*," *TM* 13 (2000): 201–352 (Greek text, English translation, and commentary).

On the naming convention used here, personal name (ὄνομα) and surname or sobriquet (ἐπίκλησις), see Kazhdan, "Byzantine Family Names."

[33] A high dignity without administrative responsibilities; see Guilland, *Institutions* 2:132–69, and *ODB* 3:1600.

[34] Here the term *barbaroi* is used for the Cretan Arabs, but a combination of Byzantine snobbery and patriotism assigned the term to anyone with a different culture: see *ODB* 1:252–53.

[35] For the military title *autokrator strategos*, see Guilland, *Institutions*, 1:382–84, and *ODB* 3:1964, s.v. "strategos."

[36] The future emperor Nikephoros II Phokas (963–69) embarked for Crete in 960.

[37] On *magistros*, a high-ranking dignity without administrative responsibilities, see R. Guilland, "Études sur l'histoire administrative de l'Empire byzantin: L'ordre (τάξις) des Maîtres (τῶν μαγίστρων)," *EEBS* 39–40 (1972–73): 14–28, and *ODB* 2:1267.

[38] Reforms during the reign of Romanos II (959–63) divided the unified high command of the army by the *domestikos ton scholon* into two positions, the *domestikos ton scholon* of the East and of the West. It is unclear whether the change had already been made at the time of Nikephoros's expedition to Crete. Leo's explanation of the military titles lacks precision. See Guilland, *Institutions*, 1:405–68 and Ahrweiler, *Structures*, VIII, 55–58, as well as Book II, n. 11.

[39] The phrase ἀγαθόν τε τὰ πολεμικά (and its close parallel, ἀγαθὸν τὰ πολέμια, at 34.4 and 37.13–14 [here used of Tzimiskes] is no doubt borrowed from Prokopios's histories of the Justinianic wars (*Gothic Wars, Persian Wars, Vandalic Wars*), where ἀγαθ(ὸς) τὰ πολέμια occurs in 32 instances; the phrase is at least as old as Herodotus (7.238 and 9.122). The phrase τὴν ἰσχὺν ἀνυπόστατον may derive from Josephus, *De bello judaico* 1.135.4.

[40] See n. 27, above.

displayed in deed the experience that he had in military affairs. For he had brought ramps with him on the transport ships, which he set up on the beach, and thus transferred the army, fully armed and mounted, from the sea on to dry land.[41] The barbarians were astonished at this strange and novel [p. 8] sight, but stayed assembled in place and maintained their close formation[42] unbroken, to await the Roman assault against them.[43]

The Roman commander Nikephoros drew up the army in three sections,[44] studded it thickly with shields and spears, and, after ordering the trumpets to sound the charge[45] and the standard of the cross to precede them,[46] launched a frontal assault against the barbarians. A terrible

[41] On the landing ramps, see the 10th-c. *De obsidione toleranda*, ed. H. van den Berg (Leiden, 1947), 72.1, with annotated trans. in Sullivan, "The *De Obsidione Toleranda*," 203 and n. 154; J. H. Pryor, "The Transportation of Horses by Sea During the Era of the Crusades: Eighth Century to 1295 A.D.," *The Mariner's Mirror* 68 (1982): 9–27, 103–25, at 10 and 18; V. Christides, "Naval History and Naval Technology in Medieval Times: The Need for Interdisciplinary Studies," *Byzantion* 58 (1988): 309–32, esp. 319–20.

For further discussion of Phokas's landing on Crete, which probably took place at Almyros, west of Chandax, see Panagiotakes, *Theodosios*, 55–56, and Tsougarakis, *Byz. Crete*, 64ff. and 177–78.

[42] On the term here, συνασπισμός, literally "shields together," see for a technical definition Aelian's *Tactica* 11.4 and in the 10th c. the *Sylloge Tacticorum* (ed. A. Dain [Paris, 1938]) 43.6, and Sullivan, *Siegecraft*, scholion 124–25. Leo uses it normally of formations of the Byzantine army, but also of the Arabs of Tarsos and of the Rus'. It occurs as well in Anna Komnene and in Michael Psellos's *Chronographia*.

[43] Other sources (Theophanes Continuatus and Theodosios the Deacon) report, however, that the landing was unopposed; see Christides, *Crete*, 177.

[44] Similar tripartite battle formations are found in Leo diac. 19.9 and 109.11, and also in Anna Komnene, *Alexiad* 7.1.2, ed. Leib, 2:88.12. For the division of military units into two or three sections see also Dennis, "Byz. in Battle," 172. Nikephoros Ouranos, *Taktika*, 65.101, 113 (ed. McGeer, *Warfare*, 158.101, 160.113), recommends dividing the army into three units during a siege to allow work in relays.

Haldon, *Warfare*, 205, writes that "the basic formation for Byzantine armies from the later 6th c. onwards was, according to the military handbooks, a tripartite line—left, center, and right."

[45] From parallel passages in Leo (e.g., 22.18, 133.6), it is clear that the term ἐνυάλιον referred to the trumpet signal for battle. See N. Maliaras, "Die Musikinstrumente im byzantinischen Heer vom 6. bis zum 12. Jahrhundert," *JÖB* 51 (2001): 73–104, at 84.

[46] Battle standards in the shape of a cross (*labarum*) were placed in front of the army as both apotropaic devices and signaling mechanisms for the troops: see M. Green and J. Ferguson, "Constantine, Sun-Symbols and the Labarum," *Durham University Journal* 80 (1987): 9–17; R. Grosse, "Die Fahnen in der römisch-byzantinischen Armee des 4.–10. Jahrhunderts," *BZ* 24 (1923/4): 359–72; and G. T. Dennis, "Byzantine Battle Flags," *ByzF* 8 (1982): 51–9.

Book I

battle broke out, and the arrows poured down like hail. The barbarians could not long endure the Roman spear thrusts, but turned their backs, broke ranks, and ran back as fast as they could to their fortress. The Romans pursued them, and wrought unspeakable slaughter. In this way the first attack and battle turned out favorably for the Romans. When, as I have said, the barbarians had shut themselves up in their own fortifications, the general summoned his troops, and pitched camp[47] in front of the town of the Cretans.[48] He ordered the triremes and other cargo ships to anchor all together in a safe harbor and control the sea, and, if they should see any barbarian transport ship sailing out, they were to pursue it and incinerate it with liquid fire.

When he had carefully made these plans, and seen them carried out, he entrusted a cohort of picked men to the general Nikephoros, surnamed Pastilas,[49] who was brave and had taken part in many wars; he had been captured many times by the Agarenes,[50] and had escaped from them an equal number of times, and [p. 9] he carried on his face and chest numerous scars of sword wounds[51] inflicted in battle. At that time he was military commander of the Thrakesian theme. He took command of the cohort, and was sent out to raid and reconnoiter the island.

[47] The Greek term here rendered "camp" is χάραξ, which may refer to a palisade and/or entrenchment around an encampment (as at 58.12, 71.18, 106.22, 142.1, and 143.8), or more commonly to the encampment itself. Leo uses the term in reference to this same encampment below at 13.17, 13.19, and 16.18. In the last passage he says Phokas returned to the χάραξ and "fortified it strongly all around with a palisade (ἑρκίον) and a ditch (ταφρεία)." Thus the nature of the initial χάραξ is unclear, but apparently in Leo's version of events Phokas hoped to take Chandax by storm, and only after failing to do so constructed a long-term fortified siege camp. This is supported by Theodosios the Deacon, De expugnatione Cretae, 1.143–73, ed. C. B. Hase (Bonn, 1828), 269–70, who indicates that only after three days and a survey of the situation did Phokas build a fortified camp. For discussions of Phokas's landing and initial encampment, see Christides, Crete, 177; McGeer, Warfare, 353; Panagiotakes, Theodosios, 54–55; and Tsougarakis, Byz. Crete, 66–67. For recommendations on siege camps in the military manuals and other examples, see Sullivan, "Prescriptions," 184–85.

[48] I.e., Chandax. Regarding the city and its walls, see Christides, Crete, 91–111.

[49] As Leo notes below, Pastilas was a strategos of the Thrakesian theme, located in western Asia Minor: see ODB 3:2080.

[50] The Byzantines commonly gave the Arabs the name of (H)agarenes, or children of Hagar the maidservant of Abraham (Gen. 16:15).

[51] χαλκοτυπία, a rare word, in the 10th c. attested only here and in the Suda; see Suidae Lexicon, ed. A. Adler (Leipzig, 1935), 783.

Book I

Nikephoros Phokas gave him many instructions: *to be vigilant and sober;*[52] never to turn to indolence and luxury, lest the enemy inflict upon them irreparable damage; and that after raiding the area and conducting themselves bravely they should quickly return to camp.

4. *Men's good fortune,* however, does not remain forever *unmixed, but is mingled with adversity. Misfortunes* follow upon *good fortunes, and sorrows upon pleasures, and do not allow one to enjoy in a pure manner the prosperity bestowed upon him.*[53] This is indeed what then befell the Romans. For when they advanced into the countryside, and found every sort of delicacy (for the land is fertile, and generally bears heavy crops of all varieties of seasonable produce and juicy fruits, and *is abundant in cattle and sheep*),[54] they should have observed the warnings of their general, as was fitting, but, disregarding them and dismissing them from their mind, they indulged in indolence and luxury. The barbarians, lurking in very advantageous positions in dense mountain thickets, saw the Romans' lack of discipline and precautions. So they emerged from the thickets and clefts, drew up their ranks into a disciplined unit and compact formation, and attacked them. Although the Romans, in their intoxicated condition, were somewhat tipsy and unsteady on their feet, still they moved to meet the barbarians and [p. 10] resisted strongly. But just as the general Pastilas was fighting stoutly and cutting down the barbarian ranks, the horse that he was riding was struck in the chest by arrows and small spears, collapsed to the ground, and died. Pastilas, however, quickly leapt from the horse, and was able to ward off his attackers with his sword for some time, killing many of the barbarians. But after *he lost a lot of blood and was stricken by many arrows,*[55] he fainted and collapsed on the battlefield. When he fell, the Romans turned to flight, and were slaughtered by the barbarians like cattle, so that only a very few men from the aforementioned cohort returned safe to camp.

When Nikephoros Phokas learned of this disaster, he greatly criticized the fallen men for their folly and negligence. And since he still

[52] See 1 Thess. 5:6, 1 Pet. 5:8. Phokas uses the same biblical phrase below at 42.17 (see Book III, n. 32 below) and a close paraphrase (νήφειν καὶ προσέχειν) at 13.4.
[53] Prokopios, *Persian Wars* 2.9.1–2.
[54] Homer, *Odyssey* 15.406.
[55] See Dionysius of Halicarnassus, *Roman Antiquities* 2.42.5. The word order seems curious, but exactly the same phrase is used by Leo at 155.7.

feared *the reversals and mutability of fortune*,[56] he decided not to delay any longer and waste time, thus giving the barbarians an opportunity to set up traps and ambushes and organize their ranks for close combat, but that the Romans should continue fighting with all their might, and with every sort of stratagem.

5. While he was analyzing the situation and trying to reach a decision—for he was *shrewd and energetic*,[57] the most clever of any man we know at grasping the best solution and carrying it out, had a temperate disposition, and was not tempted by pleasures; at the same time he was skillful at making the proper use of opportunities and events, and unequaled in strength and vigor. For it is said that once, when a champion of the most valiant barbarians attacked him, Nikephoros aimed his spear at his chest [p. 11] and thrust it with both hands, and the force was so great that the spear went right through him, piercing both sides of his breastplate—the idea occurred to him of making a circuit of the town and reconnoitering carefully, so that he might attack wherever it was vulnerable.[58]

Therefore he made a circuit and saw that the town was by nature very difficult to attack and assault. For on one side it had the sea as a sure defense, and on the other side it was set on a nearly flat and level rock, on which the walls[59] were laid, and its construction was something new and unusual. For it was built of earth, and goat and pig hair, mixed together and compressed thoroughly;[60] and it was wide enough so that two wagons could easily make a circuit on top of the ramparts and pass each other, and it was quite high, and in addition two extremely wide and deep moats were dug around it.[61] When he (Nikephoros) realized

---

[56] See Diodorus Siculus, *Bibliotheca Historica* 34/35.28.3.10–11, ed. K. T. Fischer and F. Vogel, *Diodori bibliotheca historica*, vol. 6 (Stuttgart, 1969).

[57] The phrase ἀγχίνους καὶ δραστήριος, used also of Hamdan at 17.8 and of Basil the Nothos at 94.7, is borrowed from Prokopios, *Persian Wars* 1.6.19.5.

[58] For recommendations in the military manuals and examples of such reconnaissance of a city prior to beginning a siege, see Sullivan, "Prescriptions," 186. For another translation of much of the last part of this paragraph, see McGeer, *Warfare*, 327.

[59] The term γεῖσα literally means "cornice," but Leo applies it to the entire fortification walls; see also Leo diac. 26.1 and 129.2.

[60] For similar use of goat hair in protective coatings for siege sheds, see Sullivan, *Siegecraft*, "Parangelmata," chap. 15.5–6.

[61] N. Platon, "Πάλιν περὶ τῶν Βυζαντινῶν τειχῶν τοῦ Χάνδακος," *Κρητικὰ Χρονικά* 4 (1950): 359, indicates that the excavated portion of the Arab wall was barely 2.5 m, but

the strength of the wall, as has been described, and that it was virtually impregnable, he countered with the following stratagem. Beginning to build from the sea's edge to the south as far as the beach on the other side, he fortified this expanse of dry land with a stockade, and confined the town of the Cretans to the sea, so that the barbarians could not easily advance on dry land whenever they wanted, and it would be his decision whether or not to fight, whenever the moment seemed right. [p. 12] After Nikephoros had thus seen to the quick completion of this wall, he pressed on to another victory, as my narrative will now relate. He summoned his officers to the command tent, and spoke as follows in quite a loud voice:

6. "I think that none of you is unaware of the *cruelty and ferocity*[62] of the descendants of the maidservant,[63] and the raids and enslavement that they have murderously perpetrated against Romans (and this when they were living on an island that was subordinate to [the Romans], although it had come to the Agarenes through the wickedness of fortune). Isn't it true that almost all of our coastline is uninhabited as a result of their rapine? Aren't most of the islands deserted because of their raids?[64] Therefore Providence has by no means tolerated that these *liars, these most evil beasts, these lazy gluttons*[65] feed forever off the Christian people, but, with the help of the Almighty, it has brought us here to *repay them sevenfold*[66] the evil fortunes they have mercilessly brought upon us. Proof of my words is our recent victory. For when we had just landed, and had not even yet completely recovered from seasickness, with the assistance of the Almighty we put to the sword large numbers of the barbarians as soon as we arrived on the island; and we easily confined the survivors within the town. And so, my fellow soldiers, I beg you not to turn to

---

notes (*Κρητικὰ Χρονικά* 6 [1952]: 459) that precise estimation is not possible without further excavation. If Leo is exaggerating, he may have been influenced by Diodorus Siculus (*Bibliotheca historica* 2.7.4, ed. F. Vogel, 3rd ed. [Stuttgart, 1964]) on Semiramis's walls of Babylon: τὸ δὲ πλάτος πλέον ἢ δυσὶν ἅρμασιν ἱππάσιμον. Leo refers to the walls of Babylon below at 56.9–11.

[62] See Plutarch, *Pericles* 10.8.1.

[63] On the (H)agarenes, see n. 50 above.

[64] For the desertion of Aegean islands such as Aegina, see Talbot, *Holy Women*, 166 and n. 25. On the raids of Cretan Arabs, see V. Christides, "The Raids of the Moslems of Crete in the Aegean Sea: Piracy and Conquest," *Byzantion* 51 (1981): 76–111.

[65] Titus 1:12.

[66] See Sir. 32:11 (ed. Brenton) and 35:10 (ed. Rahlfs).

Book I

indolence and luxury; for our recent disaster should serve as a lesson for us. For if the men who were sent out with Nikephoros Pastilas to reconnoiter the area [p. 13] had heeded my warnings, and had not *turned*[67] *to luxury*[68] and other pleasures, they would not have been so utterly destroyed. But now, since they disregarded my warnings, they have paid the price for their folly. Therefore you should beware of the fate of your comrades, keep sober and remain attentive, and with all speed and strength search out and track down the barbarous wild beasts who are lying in ambush here, draw them out of their dens and lairs and destroy them. Let us not waste[69] our time in idleness and drunkenness, but acting like Romans we will demonstrate the vigorous and brave spirit of our noble people in [military] contests."

7. These were the general's words, and indeed the troops regained courage and applauded, drew their swords from their scabbards, and were inspired to follow and obey him wherever he wished. But he bade them quiet down and rest for the time being, until he should order them to go into action, whenever it was necessary. Presently, in the dead of night, accompanied by a selected group of young and vigorous soldiers, he slipped quietly out of the camp, so that the barbarians would not notice their departure and devise some disaster for the army that was left behind. After he left the camp, and traversed some distance in the countryside, he learned from some captives that a barbarian army, numbering about forty thousand, was assembled on a hill, in order to attack the Romans unexpectedly in force, [p. 14] drive them from the island, and deliver their own men from the blockade of the town. After the general listened to these men, he allowed the army of picked men which was following him to rest all day. Then late in the evening he set off, taking with him native-born men[70] as guides to the region. And since the moonlight was shining (since it was the time of the full moon), *he strained every effort to hurry on, without letting up the pace;*[71] and then he surrounded the

---

[67] Reading ἀπέκλιναν for ἀπέκλεισαν with Hase and Panagiotakes.

[68] See Diodorus Siculus, *Bibliotheca historica* 11.87.4.6–7.

[69] Reading προησώμεθα for προϊστάμεθα with Panagiotakes. The allusion is to Rom. 13:13.

[70] These ἰθαγενεῖς ἄνδρες were most likely Christian inhabitants of Crete who collaborated with the Byzantine forces. Elsewhere (17.3), Leo uses the terms "native-born barbarians" (ἰθαγενεῖς βάρβαροι) to identify the Cretan Muslim Arabs. See below, Book II, n. 2.

[71] Reading ἀνιείς with Hase (see apparatus), and following Philo Judaeus, *De Abrahamo* 233.1–2 and *De vita Mosis* 1.168.6, which Leo seems to quote here.

66

hill where the barbarians were sleeping soundly. Then, after ordering the trumpets to sound and the drums to roll, he advanced toward the hill. The barbarians, who were unarmed and unprepared when they heard the clangor of weapons, were dumbfounded at the unexpected attack, and turned to flight. They were unable, however, to escape, since the entire base of the hill was held by the Roman contingent. And so in a short time the entire host of forty thousand barbarians from youth upwards was easily killed, victims of the Romans' swords.

And now the general prepared yet another triumph on top of this new triumph. He ordered his men to cut off the heads of the fallen host, and to put them in leather satchels to carry them back to camp, and he promised to give a reward in silver[72] to every man who carried a head. The army, especially the corps of Armenians,[73] received this command gladly, and cut off the barbarian heads and put them in satchels. Then the general returned to camp by night.

8. The next day, as soon as the sun rose above the horizon [p. 15] and began to climb toward the vault of heaven, Nikephoros ordered his men to impale some of the barbarian heads on spears and set them up in a row next to the wall that he had built, and to hurl the others at the town with stone-throwing machines.[74] When the Cretans saw the line of spears and the heads impaled on them, and the heads that were hurled at the town and crushed against its battlements, and when they clearly recognized them as the heads of fellow countrymen and relatives, straightaway they were seized with horror and mental confusion, and were paralyzed at the piteous and unexpected sight. Then the *lamentations* of men and the *wailing*[75] of women were heard, and the town took on

---

[72] An interesting indication of payment to the soldiers in *miliaresia* (1 *miliaresion* = 1/12 gold solidus). Since virtually no coinage at all is attributed to the short reign of Romanos II, payment was probably made in issues of Constantine VII, on which see *DOC* 3.2:554–58.

[73] For the Armenians in the Byzantine army, see E. McGeer, "The Legal Decree of Nikephoros II Phokas concerning the Armenian *stratiotai*," in Miller-Nesbitt, *Peace and War*, 123–37, esp. 132–35; McGeer, *Warfare*, 199–200; also A. P. Kazhdan, "The Armenians in the Byzantine Ruling Class Predominantly in the Ninth through Twelfth Centuries," in *Medieval Armenian Culture*, ed. T. J. Samuelian and M. E. Stone (Chico, Calif., 1984), 439–51; and M. Bartusis, *The Late Byzantine Army: Arms and Society, 1204–1453* (Philadelphia, 1992), 196–97 and n. 6. See also below, Book IV, n. 54.

[74] Πετρόβολα ὄργανα, generic term for missile-firing weapons: see Dennis, "Helepolis," 107–8.

[75] See Homer, *Iliad* 22.409.

the appearance of one that had been conquered, with everyone lamenting and bewailing his loved ones. But even so the town would not yet yield to the Romans and surrender; but confident in the strength of their town, they summoned up their courage and waited fully armed for the Roman assault, so that if anyone attacked they might defend themselves.

Then the general, after giving the signal for battle with a trumpet, and ordering his men to face any danger most vigorously, led the army towards the fortifications. And when the battle broke out, one could see *violent deeds* full of *daring*,[76] as spears were thrown in all directions, arrows fell like *snowflakes* in *winter*,[77] and the rocks hurled incessantly by the stone-throwing machines crashed against the battlements. As for the barbarians, they resisted stoutly under the pressure of necessity, defending themselves and shooting arrows from the wall, [p. 16] hurling axes from above, and dropping enormous stones;[78] they overlooked no means of defense in the battle, and retaliated for everything they suffered. For, the obvious danger and their despair of survival inspired them to fight beyond their strength, and desperately to withstand the enemy.

9. When Nikephoros, the Roman general, saw that the town wall was really strong, and that it was very difficult to attack and impregnable (for it could not be captured by assault, since it was raised to such a great height, and was encircled by two moats dug to comparable depth), and when he saw the reckless despair of the barbarians and their extraordinary resistance, he decided not to fight from below against men who were eager to die and desperate, nor to attempt the impossible. He decided he should not let missiles be cast down on them from above and let the Roman army be destroyed to no good purpose, but rather that he should deliver the town into the hands of famine, until he should have a chance properly to prepare siege engines[79] and other machines suitably devised for storming walls. Therefore he postponed the attack, and after recalling the troops with a trumpet, he departed for camp. And he fortified it strongly all round with a stockade and a ditch, and trained the army, and gave the troops a great deal of experience through daily exer-

---

[76] See Josephus, *De bello judaico* 3.152.2.

[77] See Homer, *Iliad* 12.278–79.

[78] For stones dropped from walls, see Sullivan, *Siegecraft*, 161 nn. 8–9.

[79] The term *helepolis* in classical usage referred to mobile towers, but among the Byzantines to various siege devices including battering rams (see Leo diac. 25.13), and in particular stone-throwing machines, most likely trebuchets: see Dennis, "Helepolis."

cises. He also had siege engines constructed by selected craftsmen,[80] and had the soldiers practise attacking and skirmishing whenever practicable, and spent the winter[81] there before the town with all his army.

[80] On the construction of siege engines in 10th-c. Byzantium see Sullivan, *Siegecraft.*
[81] The winter of 960/61.

Book II

[*annis 960–963*]

AFTER NIKEPHOROS, THE ROMAN COMMANDER, had transported Roman forces to the island of Crete, as I have already related,[1] and in close combat put to the sword some of the native-born barbarians,[2] he easily and quickly shut the remainder up in the town, and spent the winter there,[3] training the army daily in warfare. Meanwhile, Hamdan,[4] the ruler of the Agarenes who lived near Cilicia,[5] a *shrewd and energetic* man,[6] [p. 18] who from the time of his youth unquestionably surpassed all his countrymen in his experience of warfare, learned that the Roman troops had set forth on a naval expedition against the Cretans. He decided that this was an opportunity for him to raid all the Roman territory in the east with impunity,[7] to plunder it without bloodshed, amass enormous wealth, and gain eternal glory. So, after

---

[1] In Book I. We have followed Panagiotakes' punctuation, with the comma after rather than before ἤδη.

[2] The use of the term ἰθαγενεῖς for the relatively recent (ca. 824) Arab invaders of Crete is surprising and may be intended to convey their entrenched position. However, there had been certainly enough time for Muslim descendants of the original invaders to be born on the island. Elsewhere Leo uses ἰθαγενής of Christian descendants of Greek natives of Crete prior to the Arab conquest (14.4), and below (56.15) of native inhabitants of Tarsos. See Book I, n. 70.

[3] The winter of 960/61.

[4] Ali ibn Hamdan (916–67), better known as Sayf ad-Dawla ("Sword of the Dynasty"), emir of the Hamdanid dynasty of Aleppo and "between 947 and 967... the Byzantines' archenemy in the east" (McGeer, *Warfare*, 226): see Canard, *H'amdanides*, 595–664 and 741–828, and *ODB* 3:1848.

[5] Sayf ad-Dawla was based in Syrian Berrhoia (modern Aleppo; see *ODB* 1:283), but with strongholds in Cilicia in southeastern Asia Minor, namely Adana, Mopsuestia, and Tarsos; see McGeer, *Warfare*, 228 and for Cilicia *ODB* 1:462.

[6] Leo uses the same characterization (ἀγχίνους καὶ δραστήριος) above (10.18–19) of Nikephoros Phokas and of Basil the Nothos (94.7). The combination occurs also in Prokopios (*Persian Wars* 1.6.19) of the Persian Kabades.

[7] For the extent of Byzantine territory and contested areas in Asia Minor in the 960s, see the map in McGeer, *Warfare*, 227, and Haldon and Kennedy, "Arab-Byzantine Frontier," 97.

assembling an army of vigorous and youthful Arabs and Agarenes,[8] he set out against Roman territory, burning and looting everything on his way. When the emperor Romanos heard about his invasion and violent attack, right in the open, he sent against Hamdan Leo Phokas,[9] Nikephoros's brother and commander of the troops of Europe[10] (the Romans call this position *domestikos* of the West).[11] He [Leo] was a courageous and vigorous man, of exceptionally good judgment, and the cleverest[12] of anyone we know at devising the proper course of action[13] at times of crisis. Some divine force, I believe, used to fight alongside him in battles, overcoming all adversaries and making them surrender.

2. For although many wars broke out during the time of his command, he was never defeated by an opponent, but always emerged victorious. Thus when a Scythian army (they call the people Huns)[14] crossed

[8] McGeer (*Warfare*, 68) cites this passage as an example of the use of "Arabs" ("Αραβες) specifically for Bedouins, and (*Warfare*, 238–42) describes the role of these light nomadic horsemen in the Hamdanid armies as revealed in the Byzantine sources. While Leo diac. (6.11, 42.22 and 103.4) and other Byzantine authors do also use "Αραβες generally of Arabs, not Bedouins specifically, the suggestion in this context is plausible.

[9] On Leo Phokas (born ca. 915–20, died after 970) see *ODB* 3:1667–68 and Cheynet, "Les Phocas," 301–6. Various aspects of his later career are depicted by Leo the Deacon in subsequent books, where he is referred to as Leo the *kouropalates* or simply the *kouropalates*. On the granting of that title to him see below, Book III, chap. 8.

[10] The term here (κατάλογοι) is a classical expression as old as Thucydides (6.43, 7.16), literally the "muster rolls," lists of officers and men of the regular army, but used also of the army in general. See Dölger, *Beiträge*, 21; Haldon, *Recruitment*, 44, 46, 50, 60, 63–64; M. Bartusis, *The Late Byzantine Army* (Philadelphia, 1992), 237–38; and D. F. Sullivan, *The Life of Saint Nikon* (Brookline, Mass., 1987), chap. 65.1–3 and note, p. 301. For the specifically Byzantine term, τὸ ἀδνούμιον, see *ODB* 1:21.

[11] From the time of Romanos II (959–63) the office of *domestikos* of the Schools (see Book I, n. 38), in effect the commander-in-chief of the army, was divided into two, *domestikoi* of the East and West: see *DOSeals* 1:1. Cheynet, "Les Phocas," 302, dates the change to spring 960 with the promotion of Leo to this post, since his brother was occupied in preparation for the expedition against Crete. See also Bury, *Adm. System*, 51; Guilland, *Institutions*, 1:405–68; and Oikonomides, *Listes*, 329.

[12] Reading ἐπηβολώτατον with Panagiotakes; see next note.

[13] Cf. this characterization (τὸ ξυνοῖσον . . . ἐπιφράσασθαι . . . ἐπηβολώτατον) with the similar one used above of his brother Nikephoros (10.19–20: ἐννοῆσαί τε τὸ ξυνοῖσον . . . ἐπηβολώτατος).

[14] The terms "Scyths" and "Huns" are used by Byzantine authors of various nomadic peoples (see *ODB* 3:1857–58 and 2:957–58), in this instance of the Magyars. For the identification see Moravcsik, *Byzantinoturcica*, 1:399.

the Istros[15] at that time, the commander Leo, unable [p. 19] to fight them in a pitched battle because [the enemy] enjoyed vastly superior numbers of troops, whereas he was leading a small and ill-prepared band of soldiers, decided not to expose himself and his men to certain danger, but rather to attack the Scythians unexpectedly,[16] accomplish a brave and courageous feat, and acquire glorious fame for himself. Therefore he passed stealthily through the thickets, and, while keeping out of sight, observed the encampment of the Huns, and carefully spied out their numbers. Then in the dead of night he divided his army into three sections and attacked the Scythians; and by his sudden attack he wrought so much slaughter in a short time that only a few of the untold multitudes escaped.[17] It was this commander Leo whom the emperor Romanos transferred to Asia,[18] in the hope that somehow he might be able to check the invasions of the barbarians and repel their reckless and daring attacks.

After the general left Europe and arrived in Asia, he began to hear about Hamdan's insolence and lack of mercy, and to see churches and villages that had been burned, the ruins of fortresses, and the land that was deserted because of the violent abduction of its inhabitants. And he decided not to expose the army to certain danger, nor to face the barbarian host in the open. For they had won many victories, and were exultant over their unexpected good fortune; moreover, they were composed of divisions with thousands of men who were thoroughly equipped, [p. 20] while he was leading a small and weak army, which was terrified at the successes of the Agarenes and their daily victories. Leo decided instead to occupy the most strategic positions on the precipices, to lie there in ambush and guard the escape routes, and then confront the

---

[15] I.e., the Danube.

[16] On Leo Phokas's guerrilla tactics here and in his defeat of Sayf ad-Dawla below and their apparent influence on recommendations for similar tactics in the *De velitatione* (a treatise compiled from notes written by Nikephoros II Phokas), see Dennis, *Treatises*, 139–40, and Cheynet, "Les Phocas," 305.

[17] According to Cheynet, "Les Phocas," 302, Leo Phokas won this victory over the Magyars in 960. The same victory is apparently also recorded in the vita of Athanasios of Athos: see *Vitae duae antiquae Sancti Athanasii Athonitae*, ed. J. Noret (Turnhout, 1982), *Vita A*, chap. 55.3–5, and *Vita B*, chap. 20.3–5. The battle has been variously dated 958/59 (L. Petit), 960 (Cheynet, as above), and 961 (G. Moravcsik). For discussion and earlier bibliography, see M. Gregoriou-Ioannidou, "Οι Ούγγροι και οι επιδρομές τους στον δυτικό-ευρωπαϊκό και στον βυζαντινό χώρο (τέλη 9ου-10ος αι.)," *Byzantina* 20 (1999): 65–135, at 128 n. 298.

[18] I.e., Asia Minor or Anatolia, the westernmost extension of Asia: see *ODB* 1:205–7.

barbarians at the most dangerous and perilous sections of the path,[19] fighting vigorously, whenever they [the enemy] should pass through.

3. After the general Leo thought this over and decided on this course of action, it occurred to him that he should inspire the army with words and encourage them with exhortations, whenever it should be necessary to advance on the barbarians, so as to make them fight more courageously in the battle. So, after standing up before the host and pausing a moment, he began the following speech of exhortation:[20]

"My fellow soldiers, the lord and emperor of us all, in the knowledge that your corps in its entirety was the best, experienced in warfare and practised in tactical skills, transferred you to Asia, which has now been exhausted and brought to its knees by the attacks and ravages of Hamdan, and he entrusted me with the command. Therefore I exhort and advise you, not so that you may face the enemy bravely (*for I believe that there is no need of words to inspire to courageous deeds you men,*[21] who from your childhood have practiced bravery and daring), but so that you may face the enemy after planning the best course of action. *For wars* are usually *won* not so much by a pitched battle, as by cautious *planning*[22] and victories won with cunning at the opportune moment. [p. 21] You know clearly the deployment of the enemy, that they are spread out through the plains here, and are numerous, indeed countless in number. I myself would say that your army was brave and vigorous in strength and in spirit, but no one would argue that it has sufficient numbers and divisions. Therefore, inasmuch as we are Romans, we must prepare and plan properly, so as to find a good solution to a difficult problem, and choose an expedient rather than a dangerous course of action. So let us not rush headlong into certain disaster with a reckless assault and hazardous endeavors. For an unbridled *act of daring* usually thrusts one into danger, whereas a reasoned *delay* can *save*[23] the lives of those who make use of it.

---

[19] Cheynet ("Les Phocas," 304 n. 47) suggests that Leo the Deacon's choice of the terminology ἀταρπιτός here recalls the ἀτραποί in *De velitatione* 3 (ed. Dennis, *Treatises*, 154.35)

[20] *De velitatione* 23 (ed. Dennis, *Treatises*, 230.29ff) advocates and provides a brief example of such a speech of exhortation by a general about to lead an army into combat.

[21] See Prokopios, *Persian Wars* 2.16.6.

[22] See Prokopios, *Persian Wars* 2.16.7.

[23] See Prokopios, *Persian Wars* 2.19.10.

4. "Therefore, men, I urge you not to endanger yourselves by unrestrained attacks against the barbarians in level areas, but to lie in ambush in these steep places, waiting for them to arrive and pass through; then attack them vigorously and fight bravely. For I think that in this way (let me say, with the help of God) we will overcome the enemy, and will recover all the plunder that was taken from our fellow countrymen. *For the enemy can* usually *be defeated by unexpected*[24] attacks, and their insolent and arrogant attitude is likely to be shattered by sudden assaults. Therefore, upon my signal with the trumpets, go forth to meet the enemy, maintaining your innate valor and the courage that is your companion in battle."

When the general finished delivering the above exhortation, the army raised the war cry [p. 22] and applauded, and was ready to follow him anywhere he should lead, as one who would give them excellent advice. Therefore he set ambushes at intervals on the road,[25] which had sheer mountain ridges above, for the most part precipitous and full of caves, while the foot of the mountain was filled with ravines and thick with trees and all kinds of brushwood. After laying the ambuscade in this way, the general settled down to await the approach of the barbarians. Meanwhile Hamdan, confident in and priding himself on the multitude of his followers and his formations, and elated and bragging at the quantity of plunder and the number of captives carried off, was rushing this way and that, riding on a mare extraordinary for her size and speed. Now he was at the rear of the army, now he led the way, brandishing his spear,[26] tossing it to the winds, and then retrieving it with a flourish.

When he had traversed the section of the road that was passable by horses, and reached difficult terrain, the barbarians had to crowd to-

---

[24] See Prokopios, *Vandalic Wars* 1.15.25.

[25] The location is given by *Theoph. Cont.* (479.21) as τόπος Ἀνδρασσός and by Skylitzes (Skyl. 250.53) as ἔν τινι χωρίῳ Ἀδρασσῷ. Hase (Leo diac. 418) transcribes a portion of the anonymous chronicle in Vat. gr. 163 (fol. 60v), which gives the location as the *kleisoura* Κύλινδρος. For the chronicle see now A. Markopoulos, "Le témoignage du Vaticanus gr. 163 pour la période entre 945–963," *Symmeikta* 3 (1979): 83–119. Hild and Restle (*Kappadokien*, 218–19, s.v. "Kylindros") describe the site as "on the Cappadocian-Cilician border, precise position unknown." For a tentative identification (Balabolu), with earlier bibliography, see E. Alföldi-Rosenbaum, *The Necropolis of Adrassus (Balabolu) in Rough Cilicia (Isauria)* (Vienna, 1980), 13–15.

[26] Leo is here apparently describing a known trait of Hamdan; cf. the description of Hamdan by a commentator on Mutanabbi: "Mutanabbi était à l'avant-garde. S'étant retourné, il vit Saif ad-Daula qui sortait des rangs et faisait tournoyer sa lance" (Vasiliev, *Byz. Arabes*, 2.2:307).

gether in the very narrow and rough places, breaking their formations, and had to cross the steep section each one as best he could. Then the general ordered the trumpets to sound the battle charge to make his troops spring up from ambush, and attacked the barbarians.[27]

5. Everyone had his right hand on his sword, and they drew them and slaughtered on all sides their opponents, who were wearied by their march, whereas the attacking Romans were fresh. And Hamdan himself might almost have been taken captive by the Romans, [p. 23] but, being very shrewd and clever at finding a solution to difficulties, he ordered that the silver and gold that he was carrying with him be scattered in heaps on the path.[28] By thus diverting the attack of the Romans, who busied themselves picking up the gold, he narrowly escaped this danger with a few of his bodyguards. It is said that so many of the barbarian host were killed by the Romans in this battle that piles of human bones can still be seen to this day in many places there.[29]

With such victories and stratagems the general prevailed over the numerous host of barbarians and destroyed them, breaking the insolent arrogance of Hamdan and reducing him to ignoble and unmanly cowardice and flight. Then he assembled his men and gathered together the booty, some of it barbarian, some Roman property that had been collected by the barbarians as plunder, and distributed most of it to the army; and after supplying the [Roman] captives with provisions, he sent them off to return to their usual abodes. Then he secured with fetters the Agarenes who had been captured in the battle, had songs of victory chanted, offered up prayers of gratitude to Providence, and prepared to return to the seat of imperial power, to celebrate a triumph at Byzantium. The army applauded the general, admiring him, as was fitting, and

---

[27] The battle took place on 8 November 960: see Cheynet, "Les Phocas," 302. The *De velitatione* (ed. Dennis, *Treatises*, 157 and n. 2) refers to this victory of Phokas; for the similarities between his tactics and those recommended in the *De velitatione*, see Dennis, *Treatises*, 139–40, and Cheynet, "Les Phocas," 304–5.

[28] The use of such a diversion is recommended and reported elsewhere (e.g., Polyaenus, *Strategemata* 3.7.1, and Skyl. 188.6–7), and is not necessarily a literary invention here. For concern in military manuals with Byzantine soldiers plundering rather than pursuing the enemy, and with specific reference to this passage, see McGeer, *Warfare*, 321–23. See also Canard, *H'amdanides*, 802 n. 186.

[29] See Book VII, chap. 7 for a similar pile, in that case, of Roman bones after the battle of Anchialos. Anna Komnene (*Alexiad* 10.6.4, ed. Leib, 2:211–12) describes a "mountain" of bones remaining from a slaughter of the Crusaders by the Turks in Anatolia.

Book II

declaring him to be a man superior to any other that generation had produced; they also praised him for his good fortune, since they saw that in warfare everything went in a favorable manner for him. [p. 24] Upon his arrival at Byzantium, after making his entrance with enormous amounts of booty and myriads of Agarene prisoners, he was received generously by the emperor Romanos. He then celebrated his triumph at the Hippodrome,[30] astounding the spectators with the quantity of slaves and plunder, and received from the emperor rewards and honors commensurate with his labors. In this way the general Leo saved Asia, by prevailing over Hamdan, and reducing him to a *wandering fugitive*.[31]

6. Meanwhile, after Nikephoros Phokas, the brother of the aforesaid Leo, arrived at Crete (for I should recapitulate and continue with my narrative in sequence), he spent the winter there, keeping his army in military training, and had siege machines[32] constructed. When everything had proceeded according to his plans, just as spring was softly emerging from the winter season,[33] he equipped his army with weapons and organized it into a deep formation.[34] Then, after making the trumpets sound and the drums beat, he advanced against the town. While the general was strengthening the squadron in the van, and organizing the troops into an oblong formation,[35] a rather bold and shameless prostitute, acting in a provocative and wanton manner, leaned over the battlements and made certain spells and incantations (for the Cretans are said

[30] On triumphs in the Hippodrome see *ODB* 3:2121–22, and for brief comments on that of Leo Phokas here specifically, see McCormick, *Eternal Victory*, 166–67.

[31] Apparently a rhetorical exaggeration on the part of Leo the Deacon, who may have borrowed a phrase from Aeschylus, *Agamemnon* 1282–83. Skylitzes (Skyl. 252.22–23) notes that Sayf ad-Dawla returned to his own land, where he later prepared for new hostilities against the Byzantines. While significantly weakened by this defeat, he remained a problem, although a decreasing one, until his death in 967.

[32] On siege machines (*helepoleis*), see Book I, n. 79.

[33] March 961.

[34] Asklepiodotos (2.5) comments that "everything behind the front (μέτωπον) of the phalanx is called its depth (βάθος)"; see also Aelian, *Tactica* 7.1. See also Prokopios, *Gothic Wars* 4.35.19: Γότθοι ... μετωπηδὸν εἰς βαθεῖαν φάλαγγα ἔστησαν ἅπαντες. For 10th-c. recommendations on deep infantry formations, 7 deep as contrasted with the 16, 12, or 10 of the Macedonian phalanx, see McGeer, *Warfare*, 182.

[35] Aelian, *Tactica* 37:8, defines the oblong formation (πλαίσιον) as "when the heavy infantry are drawn up on all sides of the formation in the shape of an oblong." For examples see the Περὶ στρατηγίας (ed. Dennis, *Treatises*), 94.7; 96.42, 48; 100.55; 106.23, and Psellos, *Chronographia*, 2.182.11.

to be addicted to divination, ribaldry, and wrongful beliefs, which they learned of old from the Manichaeans and from Muhammad).[36] [p. 25] That bold woman indicated not only in this way her shamelessness and licentiousness, but she also pulled up her tunic more than was proper, exposing her naked body, and cursed and mocked the general.[37] Then one of the skilled archers drew his bowstring, hit the licentious woman, and made her fall to the ground from the tower; she was instantly crushed and breathed out her wretched soul, suffering this piteous fate as retribution for her insolence. Now the battle broke out fiercely, and the Cretans resisted for some time, fighting bravely from the walls, and wounding many of the Romans.

7. When the general realized this, he had the artillery engines[38] quickly moved up, and gave the order to hurl stones at the barbarians. He also had the siege engine[39] brought near the walls (this is the device the Romans call a battering ram, because the piece of iron that is joined to the beam and batters the town walls is shaped like a ram's head). When the stone-throwing machines began to hurl heavy rocks incessantly, the barbarians were easily checked. And after the ram was dashed against the walls and was battering them mightily, a number of men crept into the

---

[36] Leo here apparently reflects the Byzantine legend that Mani was a Saracen (see *Socratis Scholastici Ecclesiastica Historia*, ed. R. Hussey, 2 vols. [Oxford, 1853], 1:124–29 [= Book I, chap. 22], and *Acta Archelai* [PG 10:1427C]) or settled among them (see *ODB* 2:1285). On Manichaeanism see *ODB* 2:1285–86; on the Byzantine view of Muhammad, see *ODB* 2:1422.

[37] Loretto (*Phokas*, 167 n. 24.3) cites on the actions of this woman F. Altheim, *Die Krise der Alten Welt* (Berlin, 1943), 1:141, for the Arab custom of having women on the battlefield to exhort and shame the men, often with sexual comments, into fighting bravely. For similar examples, see J. Glubb, *The Great Arab Conquests* (London, 1963), 71–72, and W. Kaegi, *Byzantium and the Early Islamic Conquests* (Cambridge, 1992), 127. Here, however, Leo the Deacon depicts the woman as insulting the Byzantines rather than exhorting the Arabs. A very similar episode is recounted by John Kinnamos when describing the Byzantine siege of Zeugmion in 1165: *Ioannes Cinnamus, Epitome rerum ab Ioanne et Manuele Comnenis gestarum*, ed. A. Meineke (Bonn, 1838), 246.2–10. I. Liubarskii, who cites this passage from Kinnamos but is not aware of its similarity with the passage in Leo the Deacon, suggests on other grounds that Kinnamos was familiar with Leo's *History*: see I. Liubarskii, "John Kinnamos as a Writer," in *Polypleuros Nous. Miscellanea für Peter Schreiner zu seinem 60. Geburtstag*, ed. C. Scholz and G. Makris (Leipzig, 2000), 164, 169 n. 20.

[38] The terminology (ἀφετήριοι … μηχαναί) is general, but most likely refers to trebuchets: see Dennis, "Helepolis."

[39] Here *helepolis* is used of a battering ram; see Book I, n. 79, and Dennis, "Helepolis," 103.

moat, carrying *stone cutting tools*. They began to dig there, *quietly chipping away* and cutting through the rock at the point where the foundation of the wall was set. Since by chance the rock was partly sandy[40] here, it yielded and gave way quite easily. Meanwhile, the ram continued to batter the wall, and gradually broke through the structure, even though it was carefully [p. 26] packed together and hard to break. When the men assigned to this task rendered the walls hollowed out and hanging [perilously], as was likely where they were digging, they propped them up *with wooden uprights*; then, after *heaping dry kindling material* and setting it *on fire*, they emerged from the underground passage. As *the flame* was kindled and *the supports were burned to ashes*, two *towers* together with the intervening section of wall *suddenly broke off, sank down, slipped slightly*, and collapsed to the ground.[41]

The Cretans were astonished at the novel spectacle, and stopped fighting for a while, stupefied by this extraordinary event. But then, after reflecting on the danger of captivity and enslavement, they assembled in an unbroken formation, and stood ready to intercept bravely the Roman army, which was entering through the breach in the walls, and, since their lives were at risk, they fought like demons. After many of them were killed, and they could no longer withstand such an irresistible onslaught (for the troops pressed heavily upon them from behind, and the shoving was overwhelming), they turned to flight, withdrawing through the narrow streets, as the Romans pursued and slaughtered them mercilessly. The survivors, and those whom the warfare had not succeeded in mowing down, threw down their arms and turned to supplication. When the general observed this, he spurred his horse to quicken its pace, and entered the city. He restrained[42] the soldiers' onslaught, persuading them not to kill the [p. 27] men who had thrown down their

[40] Reading ψαμμώδης as in P, rather than the ψαμμῶδες of Hase.

[41] As noted in part by Hase (Leo diac. 419), the siege description is partially modeled on Agath. 21–22 (Book I, chap. 10) with some exact verbal repetition, including the stone cutting tools and the quiet chipping at the stone, the flammable material, the burning props, and the collapse of the two towers. Yet Leo also makes necessary adaptations to the different situation at Chandax. The basic prop-and-burn technique is the one found in Byzantine as well as classical military manuals and historians (for examples, see Sullivan, *Siegecraft*, 186–87). Leo also describes Nikephoros Phokas using the same prop-and-burn technique below in his siege of Mopsuestia (Book III, chap. 11).

[42] Reading ἀνεχαίτιζε (as in E and the Hase apparatus) for ἀνετείχιζε; cf. 103.8–9 and 137.10, where Leo uses the phrase ὁρμὴν ἀνεχαίτισε.

Book II

arms, nor to attack cruelly and inhumanely men without armor or weapons, saying it was a sign of inhumanity to cut down and slay like an enemy men who had given themselves up in surrender.[43] With these words the general was able to restrain with difficulty the murderous impulses of the army.

8. After the city was taken by force,[44] the general separated off the first spoils,[45] placed in bondage the pick of the prisoners, and set them aside, saving them especially for the triumph he was going to lead; then he handed over everything else to the soldiers as plunder. So they went through the houses and were rewarded with abundant and valuable booty. For it is said that [the] city of the Cretans contained great and inexhaustible wealth, since it had been very prosperous for a long time, had enjoyed good and kindly fortune, and had not suffered any of the abominations, such as disasters, that the vicissitudes of time usually bring about. By making use especially of the expeditions of pirates and corsairs, it had plundered the shores of both lands,[46] and had stored away untold wealth as a result of such pursuits. So in this way the town was taken and captured by Roman forces. When everything inside had been brought out, Nikephoros ordered his men to raze the circuit wall to the ground; and when it had been demolished in many places,[47] he led his forces out

[43] Panagiotakes (*Theodosios*, 82), basing his views on comments in Theodosios, *De expugnatione Cretae* (5.92–93, 98–103; Bonn ed. pp. 304–5), expresses scepticism about Nikephoros's act of mercy here, although noting a comment in Nuwairi similar to that of Leo the Deacon. Christides (*Crete*, 182), who cites a description in *De ceremoniis* (695) of leniency to Muslim prisoners of war, argues against Panagiotakes' skepticism. Sparing the subjugated is also recommended for practical reasons by Leo VI (*Taktika* 15.37–41 [PG 107:896–97]), following and elaborating on Onasander (see Sullivan, "Prescriptions," 192–93). Thus Leo the Deacon appears trustworthy here.

[44] Chandax fell on 7 March 961.

[45] The legal texts (e.g., *Ecloga*, trans. E. H. Freshfield, *A Manual of Roman Law. The Ecloga* [Cambridge, 1926], 18:1) and the *Sylloge Tacticorum*, ed. A. Dain (Paris, 1938), chap. 50, indicate that one-sixth of the booty was reserved for the imperial treasury, the rest given to the soldiers (see *ODB* 1:309); Leo VI, *Taktika* 20.192 (PG 107:1065), gives one-fifth. The treasury's share is referred to here (also in Leo diac. 82.21 and 158.22) with the classical term πρωτόλεια. On the importance of booty in a soldier's income, see McGeer, *Warfare*, 321 and n. 76.

[46] On Arab-controlled Crete as a center of large-scale piracy, see *ODB* 3:1679–80. "Both lands" may refer to Europe and Asia.

[47] The walls were not entirely demolished, and the site soon attracted new inhabitants: see N. Platon, "Νέα στοιχεῖα διὰ τὴν μελέτην τῶν Βυζαντινῶν τειχῶν τοῦ Χάνδακος," *Κρητικὰ Χρονικά* 6 (1952): 439–59, and Panagiotakes, *Theodosios*, 59.

again into the countryside. After he had plundered this area and taken captives, and had subdued every foe without bloodshed, he went to a lofty and steep hill, [p. 28] which was not very far away from the ruined town, and ordered all the soldiers to build a wall. For the place seemed safe, and good for a defensive position, since it was cut off by cliffs and steep ravines on both sides, and gave forth perpetual springs from the summit, and was watered with their streams.

After the defense works were made very secure and strong, he settled a sufficient army there, and named the town Temenos.[48] Then he pacified the entire island, settling it with bands of Armenians, Romans, and other rabble;[49] and he left behind fire-bearing triremes to defend the island, while he himself took the booty and captives and sailed back to

[48] Christides (*Crete*, 179) notes that Temenos was preserved until the 17th c. (he reprints [his Fig. 61] a 17th-c. drawing, "Castel Temene," by M. Boschini). Tsougarakis (*Byz. Crete*, 72) suggests that, while perhaps Chandax was intended to replace Chandax, Temenos remained no more than a military camp, since Chandax was soon revived. The name Temenos survives today as one of the administrative districts of the nome of Herakleion.

[49] The phrasing here ('Αρμενίων τε καὶ 'Ρωμαίων καὶ συγκλύδων ἀνδρῶν φατρίας ἐνοικισάμενος) presumably reflects in part the settlement policies for areas conquered by the Byzantines evidenced more widely in Cilicia and northern Syria: use of ethnic groups, particularly Armenians, who, as *stratiotai*, received plots of land in return for the obligation of military service. The term φατρία (here rendered "band") in Homeric usage meant a "tribe" or "clan," and, given Leo's frequent use of Homer, is apparently used here to reflect such ethnic groups.

For the presence of "Romans," see M. Georgopoulou, "The Meaning of the Architecture and the Urban Layout of Venetian Candia" (Ph.D. diss., UCLA, 1992), 489–90 n. 39, who transcribes an interesting portion of the 16th-c. commentary in the Venetian archives of Antonio Calergi, who states that Phokas ordered that Chandax be populated with Armenians and certain aristocratic families from Constantinople. Calergi in the same passage notes that he traces his lineage to Phokas.

The final "bands" are called σύγκλυδες ἄνδρες, a term that in classical authors (e.g., Thucydides 7.5.4; Plato, *Republic* 569a) has the sense of "rabble." Leo may be using it in this pejorative sense, although it may be less strong; see Tsougarakis (*Byz. Crete*, 73), who renders the concluding phrase "soldiers of diverse other races" and (238) "groups of peoples of various races."

On the settlement policy see N. Oikonomides, "L'organisation de la frontière orientale de Byzance aux Xe–XIe siècles et le *Taktikon* de l'Escorial," in *Actes du XIVe congrès international des études byzantines* (Bucharest, 1974), 1:285–302, repr. in *Documents et études sur les institutions de Byzance (VIIe–XVe s.)* (London, 1976), no. XXIV, here 295–97; G. Dagron, "Minorités ethniques et religieuses dans l'Orient byzantin à la fin du Xe et au XIe siècle: l'immigration syrienne," *TM* 6 (1976): 177–216; and E. McGeer, "The Legal Decree of Nikephoros Phokas Concerning Armenian *Stratiotai*," in Miller-Nesbitt, *Peace and War*, 123–37, here 124–25 and n. 6.

Byzantium. After a magnificent reception by the emperor Romanos, he celebrated a triumph at the Hippodrome,[50] before all the assembled people, who marveled at the magnitude and splendor of the booty. For a vast amount of gold and silver was to be seen, as well as barbarian coins of refined gold,[51] garments shot with gold, purple carpets, and all sorts of treasures, crafted with the greatest skill, sparkling with gold and precious stones. There were also full sets of armor, helmets, swords, and breast-plates, all gilded, and countless spears, shields, and *back-bent bows*[52] (if some-one happened by there, he would think that the entire wealth of the barbarian land had been collected at that time in the Hippodrome). The quantity was so great that it resembled an abundantly flowing river. [p. 29] After it came the enslaved barbarians, assembled in a numerous throng.

9. After Nikephoros celebrated this triumph and received the admira-tion of all the people, the emperor Romanos presented him with generous gifts, and entrusted him with the command of Asia. So he took on again the rank of *domestikos*;[53] and, after crossing the Bosporos, assembling his troops, and organizing them into an irresistible and invincible army, he marched through the land of the Agarenes.[54] At the news of Nikephoros's invasion, they decided it was not possible to stay where they were, to set ambushes, and fight in a pitched battle; but they decided to retreat to their fortresses, and to repel the assaults from their defense works, fighting as best they could with missiles from a distance. For they were absolutely terrified of meeting such a mighty and strong-minded man in close

---

[50] Skylitzes (Skyl. 252.19–21) states that Phokas was not allowed to enter the city in 961. As a contemporary, Leo's version is more trustworthy; see McCormick, *Eternal Victory*, 167 n. 141. McCormick also notes that in his division of the spoils earlier (Leo diac. 27.6–10) Phokas was preparing for this triumph.

[51] See G. C. Miles, *The Coinage of the Arab Emirs of Crete* (New York, 1970), and idem, "Byzantium and the Arabs: Relations in Crete and the Aegean Area," *DOP* 18 (1964): 1–32, esp. figs. 3–10, for examples and discussion. In the latter article (p. 17) he also comments on the general absence of surviving examples of the other treasures mentioned here as displayed in the triumph, while noting and presenting (fig. 11) two pairs of earrings from a 10th-c. hoard of coins and jewelry in Crete. Cf. the items from Syria in Tzimiskes' triumph below, in Book X, chap. 2.

[52] Homer, *Iliad* 8.266, 10.459, etc. On these bows, see Kolias, *Waffen*, 214 and n. 4.

[53] I.e., *domestikos* of the East. On this position, see n. 11 above, and Book I, n. 38.

[54] Here Leo presents a concise and general summary of Nikephoros's successful campaigns of late 961 to early 963 against the Hamdanids in Cilicia and Syria; surprisingly he makes no mention of the Byzantine entry into Aleppo in December 962; see Canard, *H'amdanides*, 805–17.

Book II

combat. So Nikephoros devastated the surrounding regions like a thunderbolt, ravaging the fields and enslaving whole towns with thousands of inhabitants. When he had destroyed everything in his path with fire and the sword, he attacked the fortresses, most of which he captured at the first assault. As for those that had strong defenses because of their walls and the multitude of inhabitants, he brought up his siege machines against them, and waged a relentless war,[55] urging his men to fight fiercely. Each one readily obeyed his commands. For it was not only with words that he encouraged and persuaded them to be of good courage but also by his [very] deeds, [p. 30] since he always used to fight in an extraordinary fashion in the van of the army, ready to meet any danger that came his way, and to ward it off valiantly.[56] Thus in a very short time he captured and destroyed more than sixty Agarene fortresses, carried off an enormous amount of booty, and crowned himself with a victory more glorious than that of any other man. Then he recalled his forces from there and sent them to their own homes, after they had amassed untold wealth. He himself hurried off to the emperor, to receive the reward for his labors.

10. But just as the general was in the middle of his return journey, a report reached him announcing the death of the emperor Romanos.[57] Stunned at the unexpected news, he halted his journey, and remained where he was. The emperor Romanos is said to have died in the following manner. When he ascended the throne, he revealed himself as a reasonable and temperate man and a benefactor of his subjects, but then certain depraved persons, who were *slaves to their stomachs and to their sexual appetites*, insinuated themselves into his favor and corrupted him; they destroyed the young man's noble character by exposing him to luxury and licentious pleasures, and whetting his appetite for unusual passions.[58]

[55] The Greek here, ἀκήρυκτον . . . πόλεμον, literally "a war without a herald," or "an unheralded war," is as old as Herodotus. It could have two meanings, "unannounced by a herald," that is, "sudden," or "truceless," that is, "relentless." In classical usage heralds were inviolable and so could be safely sent to begin peace negotiations; hence the term often means "a fight to the finish." See also Leo diac. 76.9.

[56] The military manuals recommend that the commander not put himself at risk, since his death could cause the army to panic: see Dennis, "Byz. in Battle," 165–78, esp. 174–75, and McGeer, *Warfare*, 308 and n. 55.

[57] Romanos II died on 15 March 963.

[58] Leo gives a briefer but similar characterization of Romanos II above in Book I, chap. 2. For the expression "slaves to their stomachs, etc.," see Basil, *Homily 9 in Hexaemeron* 2.40, ed. S. Giet, *Basile de Césarée. Homélies sur l'hexaéméron*, 2nd ed. (Paris, 1968), 488.1. (The allusion is also to Phil. 3:19.)

Thus, during the season of Lenten fasting, which God-inspired men devised for the purification of souls and their guidance towards virtue, these pestilent fellows took Romanos and went off to hunt deer, riding through difficult mountain terrain. When they returned, they brought back the emperor [p. 31] in a grievous condition, breathing his last. Some people say that he suffered a fatal convulsion[59] as a result of his unseasonable excursion on horseback; but most people suspect that he drank some hemlock poison that came from the women's apartments.[60] Whatever the cause of his death, Romanos departed this world in the prime of life, after ruling the empire for three years and five months.[61] After his death, Polyeuktos, who was serving as patriarch,[62] and the senate[63] entrusted imperial rule to his sons, Basil and Constantine (who were still infants, in the care of nurses),[64] and to their mother Theophano.[65] Although born of an obscure family, she surpassed all the women of that time in beauty and in the grace of her body, and had married the emperor Romanos.

---

[59] Lit., "a convulsion in his vital parts."

[60] The alternative causes of death offered here by Leo are also found in Skyl. 253.33–35, although Skylitzes gives no hint that the poison may have come from the women's quarters. Schlumberger (*Phocas*, 252–54) notes that most contemporary sources agree that Romanos succumbed to the physical consequences of his excesses and concludes that the empress Theophano was in this case probably not culpable. Jenkins (*Byzantium*, 270, 276) argues even more strongly that there is no evidence to support such a charge against Theophano and that Romanos's death put her in an "exceedingly awkward position." See also Garland, *Empresses*, 126–35.

[61] 9 November 959–15 March 963.

[62] Polyeuktos, patriarch from 956 to 970, and a eunuch, with the support of the senate, required Nikephoros to take solemn vows to preserve the rights of the minor sons of Romanos II. The patriarch subsequently opposed Phokas consistently: see *ODB* 3:1696; also Ringrose, *The Perfect Servant*, 62, 86, 118, 241 n. 39; and Sidéris, "'Eunuchs of Light'," 165.

[63] By the 10th c. the senate of Constantinople was a largely ceremonial institution, but, as in this case, it could advise on the appointment of a regent: see *ODB* 3:1868–69.

[64] The future Basil II was five years old in 963, and his brother Constantine (VIII) was two or three.

[65] On Theophano (born after 940, died after 976), who subsequently married Nikephoros Phokas and then plotted his assassination, see below, Book V; *ODB* 3:2064–65; and Garland, *Empresses*, 126–35.

Book II

When Nikephoros learned of the change in the supreme rule (for again I return to the sequence of the account),[66] he was extremely agitated, distressed first by one thought, then by another. For the untrustworthiness of events and *the reversals and mutability of fortune*[67] gave the man no rest, especially since he was suspicious of the power of Joseph, a eunuch of great influence at the imperial palace (for he was the proud bearer of the title of *parakoimomenos*), who was ill-disposed toward Nikephoros.[68]

11. He therefore resolved to rebel immediately; but since it so happened that he did not have sufficient forces at his disposal (for at his command the soldiers had returned to their native [lands]), he was afraid of becoming involved in such a struggle for the time being. And so he decided [p. 32] to postpone the rebellion, and to return to Byzantium, and celebrate a triumph; and if the regents[69] should entrust him with the army (for he knew that as long as he was alive, no one else would be better able to resist the barbarian attack), he would take the troops and fight for the supreme power with due deliberation and without running any risk. After thinking it over and deciding on this course of action, he went to Byzantium, received a great welcome from the people and the senate, and displayed at the triumph all the booty he had brought back.[70] Then he deposited the wealth of the barbarians in the public treasury,[71] and rested at home.

Joseph was afraid that Nikephoros would rebel against the state while he was in Byzantium, particularly since he had the great affection of the

[66] Leo the Deacon frequently expresses a pedantic concern with maintaining the sequence of his narrative (see Leo diac. 70.3–4, 72.18–19, 148.1, 176.12–13). For analysis see G. Wartenberg, "Das Geschichtswerk des Leon Diakonos," *BZ* 6 (1897): 106–11; also above, Introduction, 19–23.

[67] See Book I, n. 56.

[68] On Joseph Bringas (died after 965), who administered the empire under Romanos II and bitterly opposed Nikephoros Phokas, see *ODB* 1:325–26; Ringrose, *The Perfect Servant*, 36, 37, 41, 62, 130. His plot against Phokas is described below in Book III. On the office of *parakoimomenos* (lit. "sleeping at the side [of the emperor]"), the imperial chamberlain, see *ODB* 3:1584, and Guilland, *Institutions*, 1:202–15.

[69] Theophano was nominally regent for her two young sons, but actual power was in the hands of Joseph Bringas and the patriarch Polyeuktos.

[70] On this triumph of April 963, see McCormick, *Eternal Victory*, 168.

[71] For other references to the imperial treasury, see Leo diac. 53.18, 77.15, and 97.22. On the treasury see *ODB* 1:610, s.v. "Demosios," where it is noted: "It remains disputable whether the distinction between *demosios* and the private imperial (*basilikos*) treasury . . . reflects reality."

84

army and the admiration of the people, on account of his victories and heroic deeds in the wars. So he summoned Nikephoros to the palace, in the hope that he might catch him defenseless, blind him, and send him into exile. But the general, who was truly a man of action and quick to guess at a man's evil nature, was aware of Joseph's villainy and wickedness, and went to the Great Church.[72] There he talked with the hierarch Polyeuktos, a man extremely well versed in both divine and human philosophy; from his youth he had chosen a monastic life of poverty, and possessed a superhuman confidence,[73] which was not instilled in him by nature alone, since he was a eunuch and had attained a great age, but also by his renunciation of worldly goods, his blameless existence, [p. 33] and his frugal and simple way of life. When Nikephoros began to talk with this Polyeuktos, he said: "What fine rewards I receive for all my toil and labor from the man who is in charge of the imperial palace! For in the belief that he can elude the Great *Eye* of God, *which nothing escapes*,[74] he did not hesitate to plot my death, although with the help of the Almighty I have expanded the Roman frontiers, and have never harmed the public interest, but rather have made a greater contribution than any man alive today, by ravaging so much Agarene territory with fire and the sword, and razing so many cities from their foundations. I would have thought that a member of the senate would be a reasonable and moderate man, and would not bear great animosity against a person, especially for no reason."

12. Upon hearing these words the zeal of the patriarch was aroused, and he went to the palace, accompanied by Nikephoros. He summoned the senate, and said: "It is unfair that men who have not spared themselves for the sake of Roman prosperity, who have endured great trials and dangers, and have shown themselves as kind and considerate toward their fellow citizens, should be treated with contempt and dishonor, but rather they should be glorified and rewarded. If then you will heed me as I advise you on a better course of action, I will tell you my opinion

---

[72] Hagia Sophia.

[73] On *parrhesia*, the freedom, conferred by a righteous life, to confront authority, see *ODB* 3:1591. On Polyeuktos see above, n. 62.

[74] For comparable expressions, see Leo diac. 102.4–5 (Book VI, chap. 7) and 116.9 (Book VII, chap. 3). A parallel is found in Makarios of Egypt, *Prayers* (PG 34:448A): ἐνώπιον τῶν ἀλαθήτων σου ὀφθαλμῶν. The concept has classical roots; see Hesiod, *Works and Days* 267: "the all-seeing eye of Zeus."

Book II

forthwith. Since we are Romans, and regulate our lives according to divine commands, we should maintain the young children of the emperor Romanos in ancestral honor, rendering them the respect [p. 34] that we gave to their forebears, inasmuch as they were proclaimed emperors by us and all the people. Since, however, the barbarian nations have not ceased to ravage Roman territory, and, since this man here"— pointing to Nikephoros—"is shrewd and good at warfare, and has won a great number of victories, as you yourselves will agree, and you idolize him above all other men, I advise you, after binding him with oaths that he will not plan anything undesirable against the state and the senate, to proclaim him as commander-in-chief,[75] and entrust him with the troops of Asia,[76] so that he may ward off and check the barbarian attack. For the emperor Romanos, while he was still alive, granted him this honor, and, on his deathbed, he stipulated in his testament that the man should not be removed from this command, as long as he remained of good will."

After the patriarch expressed this opinion, the senate approved it with a vote; even the *parakoimomenos* Joseph concurred, albeit unwillingly, compelled by the pressure of the senate. So they bound Nikephoros with the most frightful oaths that, as long as the young children and emperors lived, he should never plot any wrongdoing against their rule. They in turn swore not to remove any of the officials without his approval, or promote anyone to a higher rank, but to administer public affairs by common consent with the help of his advice. Then, after proclaiming him commander-in-chief of Asia, they adjourned the meeting, and, upon their departure from the palace, each returned to his home.

[75] Literally αὐτοκράτωρ στρατηγός; see above, Book I, n. 35.

[76] I.e., appoint him *domestikos* of the East; see above, n. 11, and the phrase αὐτοκράτορα στρατηγὸν τῆς Ἀσίας at the very end of this chapter. On this, see Guilland, *Institutions*, 1:383.

Book III
[annis 963–965]

WHEN SPRINGTIME WAS AT ITS MIDPOINT, and the sun was slowly moving toward the northern pole, driving its chariot in the sign of the Bull,[1] Nikephoros left Byzantium and crossed over to the opposite shore of Asia. Upon arrival in Cappadocia (whose people were formerly called troglodytes,[2] because they dwelt in caves,[3] hollows, and labyrinths, as if in dens and holes), he established his quarters there, [p. 36] and sent off dispatches in every direction, mobilizing his army and summoning them to him in full force.[4] While *the troops* were assembling, *he trained* the men he had with him *in military exercises, sharpened their mettle and strengthened them with daily drills.* He taught them how *to whirl about when armed*, urging them to blow *the trumpets often*[5] and beat the drums and sound the cymbals; he also taught them how to vault onto a horse,[6] hit the mark with a bow, and hurl a javelin with utmost accuracy; indeed he omitted no skill devised for warfare.[7]

Thus the general drilled the army, while awaiting the arrival of the remaining troops (for he had decided to take the field against Hamdan and the Tarsians[8] with as much strength as possible). Meanwhile the

---

[1] I.e., 20 April–20 May 963.

[2] On Cappadocia in central Asia Minor see *ODB* 1:378–79. The 10th-c. Arab geographer Ibn Hauqal makes reference to the same Cappadocian cave dwellings and their inhabitants, whom he also describes as "troglodytes" in his work *Configuration de la terre (Kitab surat al-ard)*, trans. J. H. Kramers and G. Wiet (Beyrouth–Paris, 1964), 1:194–95. See also Haldon and Kennedy, "Arab-Byzantine Frontier," 96–97.

[3] The Greek here is τρώγλαις ... ὑποδύεσθαι, hence the etymology.

[4] For the obligation of military service, see Haldon, *Recruitment*, 41–65.

[5] See Agath. 40.2–6.

[6] The Greek here, ἐφ᾽ ἵππων τε ὑπεράλλεσθαι, is ambiguous, since the ἐπὶ implies that they vaulted *onto* horses, the ὑπερ- that they vaulted *over* them. Cf. similar phrases at Leo diac. 51.3 and 97.7–8; in this last case jumping *onto* a horse is clearly meant. This is also the interpretation in the translations of Hase and Karales. See n. 82 below.

[7] On the training of Phokas's troops, see McGeer, *Warfare*, 197–98, 217–22.

[8] Preparations for the campaign described here took place in 963. Nikephoros's intentions were to attack the emirs of Aleppo (Ali ibn Hamdan: see Book II, chap. 1, 17.7) and Tarsos (a city in Cilicia: *ODB* 3:2013). For a study of the Byzantine-Hamdanid wars, see Canard, *H'amdanides*, 805–17; for a study of the tactical warfare in this campaign see McGeer, *Warfare*, 225–48.

parakoimomenos Joseph, aware of Nikephoros's diligence and intelligence, and, moreover, of his valiant and noble courage, and suspicious that he might scheme a revolt once his army was gathered around him, trembled in his heart and blamed himself for his lack of resolution, how when he had caught this *bloodthirsty warrior*[9] alive, as in a net, he had not killed him, but had let him protect himself with so many armed troops. He was so consumed with anxiety that he was unable to rest, and deemed *life not worth living*.[10] While considering the situation, and turning over many plans in his head as to how he could deprive the general of such a position of strength, there occurred to him a stratagem whereby he thought he could strip him of his power, which was *pressing* like an *axe against his neck*.[11] [p. 37]

2. Thus he summoned Marianos, a man honored with the dignity of *patrikios*, who had already been commander of the Italian army,[12] a man who was extremely quick to anger and hot-headed. After talking to him in some dark corner, he told him his secret: "If you follow my advice and assume the command of the East, I will soon declare you emperor, and raise you to the imperial throne." "Hush," replied Marianos, "stop provoking and inciting a monkey to fight with a fully armed giant, who is feared not only by neighboring tribes of peoples, but also by all those on which the sun shines as it rises and sets. But if you want me to give you an opinion, since you are at a loss and worried, I will tell you forthwith. You know that John, whom they call Tzimiskes,[13] is ambitious, extremely aggressive, and good in warfare; and the soldierly ranks honor

---

[9] Ps. 5:6, 25(26): 9, 54(55): 23, et alibi.

[10] See Aristophanes, *Plutus* 969 et alibi.

[11] For a parallel to this expression, see Leo diac. 80.4; Herodian, *Ab excessu divi Marci*, ed. K. Stavenhaven (Leipzig, 1922), 8.6.8.8; and Constantine Porphyrogenitus, *De insidiis*, ed. C. de Boor, *Excerpta historica iussu imp. Constantini Porphyrogeniti confecta* (Berlin, 1905), 3:107.18.

[12] Marianos Argyros, κατεπάνω τῶν δύσεων (= Domestikos of the Schools of the West). On his career, see V. von Falkenhausen, *Untersuchungen über die byzantinische Herrschaft in Süditalien vom 9. bis 11. Jahrhundert* (Wiesbaden, 1967), 81; J. Gay, *L'Italie méridionale et l'empire byzantin* (Paris, 1904), 216–18; and Guilland, *Institutions*, 2:179–80. On the family, see J.-F. Vannier, *Familles byzantines: les Argyroi (IXe–XIIe siècles)* (Paris, 1975), 30–32. See also below, 96 n. 49.

[13] John Tzimiskes, who was to become emperor from 969–76 (see *ODB* 2:1045), the nephew of Nikephoros Phokas, was a member of the Kourkouas family; his father, whose first name is unknown, was married to Nikephoros's sister. On his sobriquet Tzimiskes see Book V, n. 87.

him and consider him second only to the commander. Thus, if you agree, entrust the troops to him instead; since the man is extraordinarily venturesome and very daring, I think he will accept the undertaking, the host will follow wherever he leads, and your wishes will be carried out. Don't think that you can overthrow this immovable and unshakeable tower in any other way."

Joseph accepted this suggestion, immediately deprived Nikephoros's blood relatives and other associates of their military rank, and sent them into exile. Then he affixed seals to a letter and sent it to the above-mentioned John, who was a *patrikios* [p. 38] and military commander of the Anatolic theme, a robust and vigorous man, possessed of almost irresistible and insuperable strength. The content of the letter was as follows: "Since I am suspicious of Phokas's ill will and malice, and want to put an end to the wicked thoughts that he nourishes in his heart, I have decided to reveal this secret to your Excellency, in the hope that with your cooperation we might be able to check his irresistible assault. For he intends to rebel as soon as possible and usurp the imperial rule. In order to check his unwarranted[14] attack, however, I am removing him immediately from responsibility for the army, and entrusting it to your distinguished self. Shortly afterward I will elevate you to the very summit of empire. But you must put the bellicose[15] and insolent Phokas in chains and quickly send him to me."

3. After John had received this letter, opened it, and read its contents (as I have already said, the letter promised him the command of the East, and then the supreme power and authority, if he could separate Nikephoros from his army and deprive him of his host), he left the area where he had been staying, and hastened to the general. Proceeding to the general's tent, he sat down beside him (for John was Nikephoros's nephew on his mother's side), and said, "You, my good man, have been sleeping a very deep sleep, deeper even than the sleep of Endymion,[16] as they say, [p. 39] while the good Joseph, the man in charge of the imperial court, is plotting your death with murderous frenzy. As far as he is con-

---

[14] The Greek reads ἔκσπονδον; see Leo diac. 43.9 and 14, where Phokas mentions the broken agreements.

[15] Or perhaps emend ὑπέρμαχον to ὑπέραυχον with Panagiotakes and translate "boastful"; see Philo Judaeus, *De congressu eruditionis gratia* 42.1, ed. P. Wendland, *Philonis Alexandrini opera quae supersunt* (Berlin, 1898), 3:80: ἀλαζὼν καὶ ὑπέραυχος.

[16] *CPG* 1:75, 238; 2:25, 111.

cerned, the invincible commander of the Romans is as good as dead, and his blood has been shed. [To think of] your labors and battles and prowess, while this [dastardly deed] is planned by an effeminate fellow, whose very sex is doubtful, an *artificial woman*[17] who knows nothing except what goes on in the women's quarters! So rouse yourself, my good friend, if you agree; and let us make use of our wits, so that we may not die in slavery. Let us rather act gallantly and courageously, so that Joseph, and anyone else who thinks like him, may realize that they are not contending with delicate and sheltered women, but with men possessed of invincible strength, who are feared and admired by barbarians."

With these words he drew the letter out from the folds of his garment, and handed it to the general. As he perused it and grasped its *deadly*[18] and grievous message, he faltered for a moment, feeling faint (for at the time he happened to be slightly ill), but soon recovered and said, "Tell me, my brave friend, what should we think about this?" He replied, "Are you still saying that we should think about what we must do? My good man, won't you wake up now before it is too late, won't you shake this drowsiness from your eyes? When we are caught in unavoidable peril, you ask me what we should do? I say we must run every risk to obtain the supreme power, after providing ourselves with so many weapons and so great an army, [p. 40] bursting with brave spirits and abounding in physical strength. For I think it is wrong, nay intolerable, for Roman generals to be led and *to be dragged* by the nose, hither and thither, *like slaves*,[19] by a wretched eunuch from the wastes of Paphlagonia,[20] who has insinuated himself into political power. So follow me as quickly as possible, unless you want to be captured alive and suffer the ultimate fate."

4. When John exhorted him in this manner, Nikephoros was aroused to action; after arming himself, he hastened to Caesarea[21] with John and all the soldiers. Then he set up a camp to receive the army [that was arriving]. Within a few days all the troops of Asia gathered round him. As day was dawning, and the rays of the sun were spreading over the

---

[17] See G. Zanetto, *Theophylacti Simocattae epistulae* (Leipzig, 1985), ep. 43.2. See Ringrose, *The Perfect Servant*, 36, 37, 41.

[18] Homer, *Iliad* 6.169.

[19] See Aristotle, *Nicomachean Ethics* 7.2.1, and Plato, *Protagoras* 352b.

[20] On the connection of Paphlagonia with eunuchs, see Book I, n. 31.

[21] Metropolis of Cappadocia and important military base in central Asia Minor in the 10th and 11th centuries; see *ODB* 1:363–64, and Hild and Restle, *Kappadokien*, 193–96.

earth (it was the beginning of July),[22] the men who had been invested with army commands and the general John bared their swords and surrounded the commander's tent (this order was given to the generals and captains by John, who considered it a disgrace for a lowborn eunuch, together with infants still under the care of nurses,[23] to lord it over *bloodthirsty warriors*[24] however he wished); and they proclaimed Nikephoros emperor of the Romans and mighty king, wishing him a long reign. At first he refused such office, as he was wary of the supreme position that attracts envy, and he put forward as an excuse the death of his wife[25] and his son, Bardas.[26] Bardas had been in the prime of life, with his chin just beginning to glisten with a fiery bright beard, when, while at sport [p. 41] not many years before, he was wounded in the eyelid with a lance[27] by his own cousin, a young man named Pleuses.[28] In his terror at the injury he had caused, Pleuses let the lance slip from his hand; when the butt end hit the ground, the rebound was so great that the point went right through Bardas's head,[29] and he instantly fell from his horse without a sound.

[22] July 963.

[23] See Book II, n. 64 regarding Basil II and Constantine VIII.

[24] Ps. 5:6, 25 (26): 9, 54 (55): 23, et alibi.

[25] See Schlumberger, *Phocas*, 282. Cheynet ("Les Phocas," 301) suggests that this first wife belonged to the Pleustes family, of Pontic origin. On the variant spelling, see n. 28 below.

[26] The accidental death of Nikephoros's son Bardas is described both by Leo and Skylitzes (Skyl. 260.74–78), although the latter refers to the episode as the reason for Nikephoros's ascetic diet prior to becoming emperor.

[27] The Greek term is κοντός, translated as Stoßspeer (i.e., a thrusting weapon or lance used by cavalrymen) by Kolias (*Waffen*, 187, 191, 203, 209). In two subsequent passages (Leo diac. 107.23, 143.20) the weapon is described as "long" (ἐπιμήκης); see Josephus, *De bello judaico* 3.96. The interpretation of the weapon as a lance is borne out by the information that after the accident Pleuses still retained the weapon in his hand, so clearly he had not thrown it. Skylitzes on the same incident (260.77) has μετὰ δόρατος.

[28] Panagiotakes has identified this individual as a member of the noble family of Pleustai, suggesting that scribal error may account for the different spelling in Leo's text. See N. Panagiotakes, "Ἡ Βυζαντινὴ οἰκογένεια τῶν Πλευστῶν: Συμβολὴ στὰ γενεαλογικὰ τῶν Φωκάδων," *Dodone* 1 (1972): 243–64.

We have translated αὐτανεψιός as "cousin," but it apparently sometimes means "nephew"; see Book IV, n. 65. Leo the Deacon is the only 10th-c. author in *TLG* to use the term.

[29] This translation roughly concurs with those provided by Loretto (*Phokas*, 44) and Siuziumov et al. (*Lev D'iakon*, 25–26). Karales, *Λέων*, 163, mistranslates the phrase τοῦ σαυρωτῆρος . . . ἀντέρεισιν as ὁ χαλκὸς τρύπησε μὲ σφοδρότητα τὸ δέρμα καὶ κλόνισε τὸν καβαλάρη. We have translated ἐνερεισθέντος as "hit," although literally it should mean "be implanted, be fixed."

Book III

Offering this excuse, Nikephoros refused the imperial rule, and permitted John Tzimiskes to assume this honor and claim the scepter instead. But no one in the army, or even John himself, would stand for these words, but all together they acclaimed him, declaring him the august emperor of the Romans. So he accepted the imperial rule, and put on the scarlet boots, which are the most prominent emblem of the emperor,[30] with little thought for the most frightful oaths that he had sworn before the patriarch Polyeuktos and the senate.[31] For when he reflected on the instability and uncertainty of fortune, and the implacable hostility of Joseph, he hastened to anticipate the man's villainy, by setting his own affairs in good order and securing his position as best he could. Therefore he placed previous events second to his own safety, ascribing little importance to his oaths. After receiving [the] imperial power in this way, Nikephoros emerged from his tent, girt with a short sword and supporting himself with a spear, and, taking his stand under the open sky on a conspicuous and lofty height, he spoke as follows: [p. 42]

5. "My fellow soldiers, the fact that I did not assume this imperial regalia through any desire for rebellion against the state, but was driven to it by the compulsion of you, the army, you yourselves bear witness who forced me to accept such a responsibility and concern for the empire, even though I was unwilling and tried to avoid it. I want all of you to know that it was rather as a result of my goodwill toward you and for my own safety that I have given myself to this struggle. I call as a witness Providence, which guides everything, that I am ready to lay down my very life for your sakes; nothing unpleasant would divert me from this purpose. Since then you could not bear that the unwarranted madness of the eunuch and his rabid and irate insolence should achieve its goal, but you have shaken him off as a harsh overseer, and have chosen me as your ruler, I will show you clearly indeed that I both knew how to be ruled and now know well how to rule securely with the help of God. Thus, since I have goodwill towards you, like a loving father, I advise all of you, as sons who love their fathers, not to turn to indolence and luxury, but *to be vigilant*

---

[30] For the emperor's exclusive right to wear this footgear, see Prokopios, *Buildings* 3.1.23. See also Parani, *Reconstructing the Reality of Images*, 30–31, and N. Gioles, "Byzantine Imperial Insignia," in *Byzantium: An Imperial Empire* (Athens, 2002), 68. We have translated the term πέδιλα, which can also mean "sandals," as "boots," since Nikephoros is on military campaign.

[31] See Book II, n. 62.

and sober,[32] and ready to meet in a well-prepared manner[33] whatever may occur. For I anticipate that the affair will not be resolved without bloodshed, for, just as the imperial power ascends to an unattainable height, to such an extent envy and battle increase in their struggle for it.

"Thus your struggle is not against Cretans, nor against Scythians and Arabs, whom we have slain through your prowess, but against the [p. 43] capital of the Romans,[34] to which goods[35] flow from all directions, and which it is impossible to capture at the first assault like any ordinary fortress. For it is surrounded by the sea, and well-walled, and enclosed on all sides by strong towers, and teeming with a vigorous people, and exceeds the rest of the world by far in gold and wealth and dedicatory offerings. Thus you must adopt the brave stance that you used in battle to overwhelm all opposition, and advance against the enemy with the greatest possible strength. For I am convinced that in this struggle you will have as your helper even the Almighty. For it is not we who have broken the agreements and oaths, but the hostility of Joseph, who for no good reason has sent my relatives into exile and, although I have not wronged him,[36] he has cruelly and mercilessly devised death against me. For usually[37] those who break agreements are not those who first resort to arms, but those who plot against their countrymen after coming to agreement. Taking into account my fame, which has led you to win countless victories, and stirring up your innate valor more than ever before, follow me without hesitation, wherever Providence may lead us, and I will start off."

---

[32] See 1 Thess. 5:6 and 1 Pet. 5:8, a phrase used earlier (Leo diac. 9.5) by Phokas as an admonition to his troops, and perhaps his personal mantra, since it coincides closely with what Leo says of his character (e.g., 78.16–17).

[33] Reading εὐτρεπισμένως with Hase and Panagiotakes instead of εὐπρεπισμένως.

[34] I.e., Constantinople.

[35] The Hase ed. reads ἄκρατα, meaning "pure, unmixed, perfect." Previous translators (Hase, Loretto, Karales) have all rendered it as a synonym for ἀγαθά, "good things," and perhaps an emendation is needed. Cf. Themistius, Εἰς τὸν αὐτοκράτορα Κωνστάντιον, *Themistii orationes quae supersunt*, ed. G. Downey and H. Schenkl (Leipzig, 1965), 1:86.18: ὅτι ἔρχεται εἰς αὐτὴν [Κωνσταντινουπόλιν] ἅπαντα ἁπανταχόθεν τὰ ἀγαθά. Cf. also *Synaxarium ecclesiae Constantinopolitanae. Propylaeum ad AASS Novembris*, ed. H. Delehaye (Brussels, 1902), 899.21–23: Ἐπεὶ δὲ πρὸς τὴν βασιλεύουσαν τῶν πόλεων τὰ πανταχόθεν συνερρύη κάλλιστα, introducing the decision to bring the mandylion of Edessa to the city.

[36] Reading τοῦτον ἠδικηκότι with Panagiotakes.

[37] Reading εἰώθασιν.

6. When Nikephoros related this to the army, he encouraged the spirits of all, and instilled ineffable ardor into their souls, so that no military resistance [p. 44] could be a match for such momentum. For the troops loved him extraordinarily, and everyone exulted in his glorious achievements. For he had been nurtured on warfare since his youth, and was seen to be fearsome in exploits both in battle-line formation and in combat, and was not only invincible in might and very skilful but also mentally prepared and unrivalled in every sort of valor.[38] Therefore [he went] straight to the church of Caesarea,[39] and then returned to the camp; after honoring John with the dignity of *magistros*, he proclaimed him *domestikos* of the East,[40] and despatched orders and commands throughout the Roman empire; and after appointing generals he sent them to the Euxine [region],[41] and all the seacoast and Abydos,[42] bidding them depart with utmost speed. As it seems, he may have made these arrangements before the report of his proclamation [as emperor] should spread, so as to secure the straits and sea routes. For he thought that thus matters would proceed as he planned, and that Fortune would not be angry with him, but would rather smile upon him cheerfully and benignly, if he were quickly to capture the most strategic positions.

After Nikephoros did these things and compressed the units into an unbreakable close formation, and bolstered their strength with secure armaments, he left Caesarea and headed for the imperial city. He wrote

---

[38] For another English translation of these lines, see McGeer, *Warfare*, 327.

[39] The reading of the text here is uncertain. P has εἰς τὸν τῶν Καισαρέων ἐκκλησίας νεὼν; Hase emends to εἰς τὴν τῶν Καισαρέων ἐκκλησίαν νέων (i.e., participle from νέω, to go?); Panagiotakes suggests εἰς τὸν τῆς Καισαρέων ἐκκλησίας νεὼν, and postulates a lacuna thereafter. Leo uses νεώς for "church building" elsewhere (at 19.17, 64.24, and 129.5), whereas he reserves ἐκκλησία for "the Church" as an institution; therefore Panagiotakes' reading is probably to be preferred.

[40] See Book I, n. 38.

[41] I.e., the Black Sea; see *ODB* 1:293–94. Oikonomides (*Listes*, 358, n. 393), citing this passage of Leo, comments that apart from this text, which seems to have a technical significance, the term Εὔξεινος Πόντος is used to designate many regions of the Black Sea. One might speculate that the reference might include Hieron (see *ODB* 2:930–31), the fortress and customs station for ship traffic going between the Bosporos and the Black Sea. This, with Abydos mentioned next, would allow control of all shipping to Constantinople through the Dardanelles and the Bosporos.

[42] Modern Çanakkale, city on the Asiatic shore of the Hellespont, and customs post that controlled goods shipped to and from Constantinople. See *ODB* 1:8–9.

a letter and entrusted it to Philotheos, bishop of Euchaita,[43] and [p. 45] sent it to Polyeuktos, who held in his hands the helm of the church, and to Joseph, who was in authority over the palace,[44] and to the senate. The contents of the letter were, in brief, something like this: that they should accept him as emperor, and he would protect the sons of lord Romanos until they reached maturity, and would oversee their physical training; and moreover he would greatly benefit the state, and expand the sway of Roman rule through his military exploits. If they did not wish this, they would subsequently regret their stupidity, when matters should be determined by the sword and bloodshed. And that there is no opportunity for justification for those who have chosen the worse course over the better.

7. Joseph received this letter like the proverbial *Scythian saying*,[45] and, pierced through the heart as if by a stake or a spur, he cast the bishop into fetters and sent him to prison. And taking as his associates Marianos[46] and Paschalios[47] and the Tornikioi,[48] who were *patrikioi* and appeared hot-headed, he entrusted them with a Macedonian unit,[49] and offered a strong resistance, blockading Nikephoros from access to Byzantium.

[43] Euchaita (modern Avkat) was a city and metropolis of Pontos, in the Armeniakon theme, located west of Amaseia: see *ODB* 2:737.

Philotheos probably became metropolitan in the 950s: see J. Darrouzès, *Epistoliers byzantins du Xe siècle* (Paris, 1960), 274. The same bishop was used by Nikephoros as a messenger in 969: see Leo diac. 79.16.

[44] Here as elsewhere (116.6, 162.14), Leo uses the term τυραννεία for a palace controlled by the opposition or a foreign enemy.

[45] The "Scythian saying" was "you shall repent it"; see *CPG* 2:216–17 and Herodotus 4.127.

[46] See n. 12 above.

[47] According to Skylitzes, the *patrikios* Paschalios was involved in an attempt on the life of Romanos II in 962. The rebellion was revealed and Paschalios and his associates were scourged, tonsured as monks and exiled, but were later granted amnesty by Romanos and allowed to return to Constantinople (Skyl. 250–51).

[48] Most probably Nicholas and Leo Tornikioi, who were mentioned by Skylitzes as having supported Constantine VII in occupying the imperial throne in 945 (Skyl. 236.83). On the family see *ODB* 3:2096–97, and D. Polemis, *The Doukai: A Contribution to Byzantine Prosopography* (London, 1968), 184–85.

[49] The Macedonian *tagmata* made up the majority of the troops under the command of Marianos (on whom see above, Book III, n. 12); see O. Kresten, "Sprachliche und inhaltliche Beobachtungen zu Kapitel I 96 des sogenannten 'Zeremonienbuches'," *BZ* 93 (2000): 485, who concludes that they made up a regimental bodyguard in the capital.

Book III

Meanwhile, as affairs were thus hanging in the balance, Nikephoros's brother Leo, whose victorious battles my narrative has already described in passing,[50] seizing the opportunity (for he happened to be staying in Byzantium), donned the garb of a common workman and slipped out through pipes under the wall,[51] and embarked on a small boat and sailed over to Nikephoros, [p. 46] who had arrived somewhere in the vicinity of the palace at Hieria,[52] and was deploying his army. Then Bardas, their father, who was a *magistros* and had reached extreme old age, suspecting danger from Joseph, was gripped with fear and sought asylum at the Great Church.[53] He was a man nurtured since youth on battles and warfare, and for some time had held the distinguished office of *domestikos* of the Schools. Marianos and Paschalios, moving the Macedonian cohort[54] through the streets, swaggering with empty boasts and tossing their heads, constantly devised new schemes, so that the people became enraged and resorted to force, and resisted them in close combat, and forced them into open flight like delicate youths with no experience of battle. It is said that then a woman picked up in her hands a ceramic pot[55] full of earth, like those suitable for plants, and hurled it from the roof at Marianos, and struck him on the forehead. And the blow proved fatal, so that it broke his skull and splattered his brain, and he died the next day.

---

[50] On these victories, see Book II, chaps. 1–5.

[51] Most likely drainage pipes as in Prokopios's *Gothic Wars*, 1.9.11–21, or water conduits as in Kinnamos, Book 6, chap. 8, ed. A. Meineke, *Epitome* (Bonn, 1836), 275.9–10. Justinian II and his colleagues entered Constantinople through a waterpipe in 705; see Theoph. 1:374.21. Another possible translation is "tunnel": see Sullivan, "The *De obsidione toleranda*," 161 and n. 55, and 185.

[52] The palace of Hieria was built by Justinian on the Asiatic side of the Bosporos: see Janin, *CP byz*. 148–50, 498–99.

[53] See Skyl. 257.24–258.54. Bardas Phokas (879–969) served as *domestikos ton scholon* (945–55): see Cheynet, "Les Phocas," 297–99. The Great Church is the church of Hagia Sophia; see *ODB* 2:892. This is the first of three cases of seeking asylum described by Leo; the other cases involved Joseph Bringas (Book III, chap. 7) and the *kouropalates* Leo Phokas (Book IX, chap. 4). On the law of seeking asylum in churches, see *ODB* 1:217. The article of R. Macrides, "Killing, Asylum and the Law in Byzantium," *Speculum* 63 (1988): 509–38, focuses on asylum for murderers and does not discuss these cases.

[54] See n. 49, above.

[55] In the version of *Theoph. Cont.* 438.13–14, the woman threw a tile instead of a flowerpot; on similar examples of urban violence in antiquity, see W. D. Barry, "Roof Tiles and Urban Violence in the Ancient World," *GRBS* 37 (1996): 55–74.

As a result Basil [the Nothos][56] took courage; he was a eunuch who had held the office of *parakoimomenos*[57] during the reign of the emperor Constantine,[58] and was an illegitimate son of the emperor Romanos the Elder by a Scythian woman[59] and, since [p. 47] he was of mixed race, was energetic and most resourceful in carrying out every idea that occurred to him. At that time, since he was ill-disposed and very hostile to Joseph, he armed his household, who were more than 3000 [in number], with breastplates and waistguards,[60] helmets and shields, javelins and swords, and attacked the houses of Joseph and his accomplices together with the mob. And after subjecting the houses to plunder and looting and destruction, he set off for the dockyards,[61] and prepared to bring the fire-bearing triremes from there over to Nikephoros, with the approval of the people and the senate. Nikephoros at once embarked upon [one of] them, and soon arrived at the monastery of the Abramitai, which they call Acheiropoietos.[62] And from there he dispatched men to seize the palace. When Joseph saw them approaching, he was terrified and seized with ungovernable fear (for his bodyguards had already gone over to Nikephoros), and he left the palace and ran to the church. And one could see a man who shortly before was *arrogant* and with eyebrows raised above his forehead, turned into a *piteous suppliant*[63] who cowered at the slightest

---

[56] On Basil the Nothos, see Brokkaar, "Basil Lacapenus," and Ringrose, *The Perfect Servant,* 38, 39–40, 62, 92, 129–31, 136–38, 203. See also below, Book III, chap. 8, for his title *proedros*, Book VI, chap. 1 for *proedros* again and his support of John Tzimiskes' usurpation, Book VIII, chap. 4 for his command of the siege train in Tzimiskes' campaign against the Rus', Book X, chap. 8 on a star presaging his death, and Book X, chap. 11 on his "predatory" acquisition of estates in Cilicia and Cappadocia and plot to kill Tzimiskes.

[57] On the *parakoimomenos* (guardian of the imperial bedchamber), the highest office granted to eunuchs, see Book II, n. 68.

[58] On Constantine VII (945–59), see Book I, n. 16.

[59] The archaism "Scythian" applied to different peoples at different times, including Avars, Khazars, Bulgars, Hungarians, Pechenegs, and Rus', to name a few; see *ODB* 3:1857–58. On Basil's mother, see Brokkaar, "Basil Lacapenus," 199–200 and n. 3.

[60] Μίτρα, a word unattested in the 10th c. except in the Suda. Leo seems to be following Homeric usage (e.g., *Iliad* 4.137, 187, 216, etc.), but the Homeric meaning is unclear. It was apparently a piece of armor that covered the abdomen and thighs; see G. S. Kirk, *The Iliad: A Commentary* (Cambridge, 1985), 1:344–45. For another later example see S. P. Lambros, *Neos Hellenomnemon* 5 (1908): 18.2–3.

[61] Most probably the dockyards of Neorion, on which see Janin, *CP byz.*, 235–36.

[62] On the monastery *ton Abramiton* near the Golden Gate, see Janin, *Églises CP*, 4–6.

[63] See Gregory of Nazianzus, *Or.* 43.57 (PG 36:569). The same phraseology is used at 147.16 for the *kouropalates* Leo Phokas, who sought asylum at the Great Church.

sound, and demonstrated by his example that *nothing in human life is firm*[64] or immovable, but subject to reverses and transitory, and tossed and moved like dice this way and that. His seeking refuge in the church[65] was a deliverance for Nikephoros's father Bardas, and a cause of his safe return to his son.

8. Since matters were turning out as Nikephoros wished, he stripped off and threw away his own tunic, and fastened on the imperial and royal robe, [p. 48] and made himself more regal. He mounted on a proud white horse, adorned with imperial ornaments and purple cloths,[66] and entered through the Golden Gate,[67] applauded and honored by all the people and officials. It was the sixteenth of August, of the sixth indiction, in the year 6470,[68] when these things occurred. Then, when he went to the celebrated church of God[69] and received worthy honors from the clergy, he was crowned at the age of fifty-one with the imperial diadem by Polyeuktos, who was guiding the patriarchate.

His appearance was as follows: his complexion tended to be swarthy rather than fair, and his hair was thick and dark. His eyes were black, concentrated in thought, beneath bushy brows. His nose was neither narrow nor wide, ending in a slight hook. His beard was of moderate size, sprouting sparse gray hairs on his cheeks. He was stooped[70] in stature and

---

[64] See Dio Cassius 65.1.2.1, ed. U. P. Boissevain, *Cassii Dionis Cocceiani historiarum Romanarum quae supersunt*, vol. 3 (Berlin, 1901).

[65] The church is probably Hagia Sophia; on seeking asylum see n. 53 above.

[66] On horse trappings, see *ODB* 1:411–12.

[67] Gate located at the south end of the land walls in Constantinople: see *ODB* 2:858–59 and Janin, *CP byz.*, 269–72. It was historically the entrance site for a triumph or, as here, an imperial *adventus*. See C. Mango, "The Triumphal Way of Constantinople and the Golden Gate," *DOP* 54 (2000): 173–88.

[68] Leo seems to have mistakenly written August 6470 (= 962) instead of 6471 (= 963); 6471, the correct date, does indeed coincide with the sixth indiction; see Grumel, *Chronologie*, 253. McCormick, *Eternal Victory*, 169 (see also 162) suggests that Phokas chose the specific day, the feast of the Virgin's victory over the Arab besiegers of Constantinople in 718, to exploit "his image as a winner protected by the Virgin." One might add that it is also the anniversary of the entrance nineteen years earlier of the mandylion, the "palladium" of the city taken from Edessa in 944, through the Golden Gate and in procession to Hagia Sophia and then to the palace. Both feasts are included in the *Synaxarium Constantinopolitanum* for August 16.

[69] Most probably Hagia Sophia, as reported by Skylitzes (259.62–63) and where the emperor was traditionally crowned; see below, Book VI, chap. 4. Elsewhere Leo refers to Hagia Sophia as τὸν περίπυστον τῆς τοῦ Θεοῦ σοφίας . . . σηκὸν (95.18) and τὸν θεῖον καὶ περίπυστον νεὼν τῆς τοῦ Θεοῦ σοφίας (129.4–5). See above, Introduction, 48.

[70] Trapp, *LBG*, s.v., translates ἀγκυλαῖος as "gekrümmt, krumm," "crooked, bent."

Book III

sturdy, with extremely broad chest and shoulders, indeed like the legendary Hercules in courage and strength.[71] And he surpassed all the men of his generation in wisdom and good sense and in expressing the right and prudent course of action.

Thus after he had been crowned with the imperial crown, he went to the palace, escorted by the populace[72] and officials, and after making his entrance he sat upon the imperial throne. Thus *it was possible to see fortune priding herself on* and exulting in the turn of events, and [p. 49] attributing all human affairs to herself, and to see that *nothing* ephemeral *was the personal property*[73] of any man. When he embarked upon imperial rule and grasped the helm of empire in a sure and firm manner, he promoted his father Bardas to the honor of caesar.[74] And he appointed John, with the sobriquet of Tzimiskes, who had assisted him at the beginning of the rebellion, as *magistros* and *domestikos* of the East. He appointed his brother Leo as *kouropalates*[75] and *magistros*, and Basil, who had overpowered Joseph, as I have described, he promoted to the dignity of *proedros*.[76]

9. Nikephoros himself claimed that he wished to maintain his customary moderate lifestyle unaltered, avoiding cohabitation with a wife, and refraining from eating meat. But those who pursued the monastic life and really guided his lifestyle (for he held monks in exceedingly great honor) did not permit the man to continue in the manner he preferred, but urged him to get married and not to avoid the eating of meat as something abominable. For they were afraid that he might incline toward luxuries and revelry, as was likely, and be seduced into perverted pleasures, which an independent and self-governing person is

[71] For a less flattering description, see Liudprand, *Relatio* 3; Eng. trans. F. A. Wright, *The Works of Liudprand of Cremona* (London, 1930), 236–37.

[72] The Greek term here (πλήθους) is ambiguous. Above at 48.4, Leo describes Phokas's entrance through the Golden Gate being applauded by "the people (δῆμος) and officials," whereas here he writes παρὰ τοῦ πλήθους καὶ τῶν ἐν τέλει. Πλῆθος can mean "populace, mob" (LSJ, s.v. I.2b), but elsewhere Leo uses it for the "army" or "host." Loretto translates the word as "die Menge" ("crowd, throng"), Karales as πλῆθος λαοῦ, and Hase as "populus."

[73] See Prokopios, *Vandalic Wars*, 1.21.7.

[74] On this dignity see Guilland, *Institutions*, 2:25–43, and *ODB* 1:363.

[75] On Leo Phokas, see Book II, n. 9; on the title *kouropalates* see *ODB* 2:1157 and Oikonomides, *Listes*, 293.

[76] On this high-ranking civilian dignity (although the title was also bestowed upon ecclesiastics), see *ODB* 3:1727; C. Diehl, "De la signification du titre de 'proèdre' à Byzance," in *Mélanges offerts à M. Gustave Schlumberger* (Paris, 1924), 1:105–17; and Guilland, *Institutions*, 1:182, 200, 266, 303.

99

likely to engage in, once he obtains power. Therefore he yielded to the entreaties of the monks, and renounced his usual and customary lifestyle. And he took in marriage the wife of Romanos,[77] who was distinguished in beauty, and was indeed a Laconian woman;[78] and he altered his dietary regime from an abstemious diet to more luxurious meat-eating. [p. 50] It was whispered about that the marriage was not lawful, but was somewhat irregular, since Nikephoros was the baptismal sponsor of the children of the emperor Romanos and of Theophano.[79] The rumor spread with incredible speed to the ears of the hierarch Polyeuktos, and he tried with all his might to bar the ruler from the holy precincts. For since the man was filled with divine zeal, and unsurpassed in all kinds of knowledge and virtue, he was not abashed to rebuke even emperors. The emperor, on the one hand, endeavored to appease the patriarch, and at the same time defended himself, saying that not he but his father Bardas was the baptismal sponsor of the children of the augusta Theophano, and thus he besought the patriarch and cleverly persuaded him to agree to accommodate his marriage with the augusta Theophano. Since matters were going in the right direction for him, he amassed an untold amount of imperial regalia, and set aside vast stretches of fertile land abounding in all sorts of juicy fruits and a multitude of grain crops, and gave them to Theophano, his consort and empress. And spending the winter[80] in Constantinople, he did not cease to entertain his officials with horse races and all sorts of spectacles, and with the customary imperial largesse. As for the servants and household retainers in attendance upon him, he gave them military training, especially through intensive daily drills, to draw the bow unerringly, and to pull the arrow to the chest,[81] and to aim precisely [p. 51] at the target, and to brandish and twirl spears easily this way and that, and to wield swords in the air accurately,

---

[77] On Theophano, see Book II, n. 65.

[78] I.e., Helen of Sparta. Leo describes the beauty of Theophano as similar to that of Helen of Troy.

[79] In Byzantium spiritual relationships, such as serving as a godparent, were considered an impediment to marriage up to the 7th degree: see *ODB*, s.vv. "godparent" (2:858) and "marriage impediments" (2:1306), and R. Macrides, "The Byzantine Godfather," *BMGS* 12 (1987): 139–62.

[80] The winter of 963/64.

[81] Haldon (*Warfare*, 215) suggests that this phrase may indicate the re-emergence of the three-finger Mediterranean release.

and to vault nimbly onto horses,[82] so that at the time of battle they should not appear inferior to their enemies, especially since they ought to bear the brunt of the danger and maintain their ranks in formation.

10. When the spring equinox changed *the gloom of winter*[83] into calm and cheery weather,[84] Nikephoros gave orders for a campaign against the Agarenes,[85] and departed from Byzantium. After making an encampment in Cappadocia and mustering a battleworthy army, he marched toward Tarsos, which at that time exulted in and proudly boasted of the prowess of its men and their multitude and expertise in military tactics, and openly engaged in many surprise raids. When he neared this city, he constructed a strong camp and invested [the city] all around, and settled down to maintain a blockade. The Agarenes within, who were surfeited with an abundance of provisions, were confident in the strength of their fortifications; for the structure of the circuit walls soared to an extraordinary height, in a double circuit, and the city was encircled by a moat of very great depth, fashioned of hewn white stones, and terminating in battlements. And the wall had cutting through its middle the Kydnos River, which had a strong current from its very sources, and flowed cold and clear, providing great security for Tarsos, and within the town it was crossed by three bridges. [p. 52] And when *war pressed upon*[86] them, they would release the river into the moat and in one hour it would be filled to overflowing. Thus taking confidence in these defenses the barbarians mocked the emperor and fearlessly insulted him, and making sallies and attacks killed many Romans.

After the emperor Nikephoros spent considerable time there, since he realized that he was attempting the impossible, he departed from there and, changing his course, attacked the nearby inhabited fortresses, and took Adana and Anazarbos and more than twenty other fortresses at

---

[82] Ἵππων κούφως ὑπεράλλεσθαι; perhaps ἐφ' should be added before ἵππων to parallel Leo diac. 36.7 (see n. 6 above). Hase, Karales, and McGeer (*Warfare*, 221) all interpret the phrase to mean jumping onto a horse. See also Leo diac. 97.7–8.

[83] See Gregory of Nyssa, *Commentarius in Canticum canticorum*, Or. 5 (*Gr. Nys.* 6:155.16). The same (or very similar) phrase is used by Leo at 111.13 and 128.1.

[84] Spring of 964.

[85] On the term "(H)agarenes" see Book I, n. 50. Regarding the campaigns of 964–65, see Canard, *H'amdanides*, 818–23.

[86] See Homer, *Iliad* 7.343.

the first assault.[87] Then he attacked Mopsuestia[88] and surrounded it, and vigorously besieged it, bombarding it on all sides with artillery engines. The inhabitants resisted bravely, shooting burning arrows and hurling heavy stones against the Romans, warding them off from the towers with all their might.

11. The emperor, who was energetic and clever at finding a way in impossible circumstances, walked around and figured out which part of the towers was vulnerable, and in the middle of the night brought men up and ordered them to dig quietly, starting from the banks of the Pyramos River, which flowed by there, so that the barbarians should not realize [what they were doing], and their endeavor come to naught. So they dug and carried away the dirt and dumped it into the stream of the river. When the work was accomplished, two of the towers together with the portion of wall that linked them [p. 53] had been completely undermined and in their suspended state were propped up with timbers, to prevent their collapse. As soon as the rays of the sun dawned on the earth, the Agarenes, white-robed as usual,[89] leaned over the towers, and stretched their bows, and prepared their other devices, and abused the emperor with insults. He ordered fire to be set to the subterranean supports of the towers, and he himself, completely armed, went forth to marshal the troops. The supports burned quickly, and the part of the wall that was hollowed out underneath and suspended came crashing down to the ground,[90] pulling down with it the Agarenes who were standing upon it, most of whom were instantly crushed to death. The rest were taken captive by the Romans and lamented the fortune that had overtaken them. Since the demolition of the wall provided access to anyone at will, the emperor entered Mopsuestia with all his troops and enslaved it, and sent the surviving barbarians into slavery.[91]

---

[87] Hild and Hellenkemper, *Kilikien*, s.vv. Adana, 154–56 (which fell to the Byzantines at the end of 964), and Anazarbos, 178–85.

[88] Hild and Hellenkemper, *Kilikien*, 351–59. Mopsuestia, held by the Arabs since the early 8th c., was a base for Arab raids into Anatolia.

[89] On the white clothes required of Arab prisoners of war at the imperial court, see L. Simeonova, "In the Depths of Tenth-Century Byzantine Ceremonial: The Treatment of Arab Prisoners of War at Imperial Banquets," *BMGS* 22 (1998): 75–104, at 83, 87, 91, 95. However, these are defenders still in their city.

[90] For an earlier example of this siege tactic, see Book II, chap. 7.

[91] According to Skylitzes (Skyl. 268–69) and two Arab historians, Yaqut and al-Miskawayh, Mopsuestia fell in the summer of 965, while Leo the Deacon places its fall in 964; see S. Apostolopoulou, "Ἡ Ἅλωση τῆς Μοψουεστίας (±965) καὶ τῆς Ταρσοῦ (965) ἀπὸ

Book III

After he himself took the best of the booty and assigned it to the imperial treasury, and recalled the army from its sack of the town, when the sun passed through Sagittarius[92] and was moving into Capricorn,[93] and the hardships of winter were upon them, he departed from there and returned to Roman territory. When he reached Cappadocia, he handed out donatives to the host, as was fitting, and ordered them to return home, but to remember to come back to him at the beginning of spring, [p. 54] with all their arms repaired, their swords sharpened, and having taken special care of their horses. Thus the host returned home, while he spent the winter there with the remaining troops, and made ready for war.

βυζαντινὲς καὶ ἀραβικὲς πηγές," *Graeco-Arabica* 1 (1982): 157–67. Yahya of Antioch, *Histoire*, 796, also places the fall of Mopsuestia in 965, as do most modern historians, e.g., Treadgold (*Byz. State*, 501), *ODB* (s.v., "Mopsuestia," 2:1408), and Hild and Hellenkemper (*Kilikien*, 354).

[92] 22 November–21 December 964.

[93] 22 December 964–19 January 965. See Agath. 166.20–26 for the description of the onset of winter.

Book IV

[annis 965–969]

THUS THE EMPEROR NIKEPHOROS CAPTURED MOPSUESTIA and reduced the neighboring fortresses by force in the manner I have
related. Then he spent the winter in Cappadocia,[1] vexed and
worried and disheartened because he had not captured Tarsos at the first
assault, but had been driven away from it, like a *blunt dart*[2] falling on
something harder, and had accomplished nothing mighty or courageous.
He considered the matter a disgrace, a downright insult and an ineradi-
cable reproach; for when he, Nikephoros Phokas, [p. 56] had previously
been a general and was later proclaimed *domestikos* of the Schools, he
had destroyed untold numbers[3] of cities, plundered them, and reduced
them to ashes. He had enslaved prosperous regions, and routed and subdued warlike peoples in pitched battle, nor had they been able to withstand at all his power and invincible force of weapons; but now that he
had assumed leadership of the Romans through his courage and wits,
and was leading an army numbering four hundred thousand,[4] he was
driven back, having done nothing but shadow-fight. Furthermore, he
had been driven off, not from Babylon, which Semiramis fortified with
seven circuit walls,[5] nor from Old Rome, which was built by the might

---

[1] The winter of 964/65; for Leo's dating of the capture of Mopsuestia in 964, see Book
III, n. 91.

[2] Homer, *Iliad* 11.390; *CPG* 2:494.

[3] Lit. "myriads," a term best not taken at face value. Leo above (Book II, chap. 9) says he
captured "more than sixty" Agarene fortresses, while Skylitzes (271.65–66) says he took
"more than one hundred cities and fortresses."

[4] Schlumberger (*Phocas*, 480) comments that the figure 400,000, while also found in
some Arab historians, is an exaggeration perhaps indicative of the effort made here by
Nikephoros and its effect on Arab observers. Treadgold (*Byz. State*, 948 n. 3) comments
that this would be twice the number of soldiers the empire had at this time. He too
suggests significant exaggeration or a possible scribal error of "forty" for "four" myriads
(i.e., 40,000). As the figure is later repeated, exaggeration seems more likely. G. Dagron
("Minorités ethniques et religieuses dans l'Orient byzantin à la fin du Xe et au XIe
siècle: l'immigration syrienne," *TM* 6 [1976]: 180 n. 10) comments: "le chiffre de 400,000
hommes . . . est évidemment fantaisiste. . . ." See also Treadgold, *Army*, 75–80.

[5] For Semiramis (the historical Sammu-ramat of Assyria, 9th c. B.C.), see *Oxford Classical
Dictionary*, 3rd ed. (Oxford, 1996), 1383. The legendary story of her construction of

of the Romans, nor from the walls of Judaea, whose solid height[6] seemed to be a tall tale, devoid of truth, to those who had only heard about it with their ears and not seen it,[7] but he had been repelled from Tarsos, a city of modest size,[8] on a plain suitable for cavalry, with a combined population of immigrants and natives. As he brooded on this, trying to reach a decision, he was annoyed and uncontrollably angry that, when their neighbors had been killed, and those who had escaped the point of the sword had exchanged freedom for servitude, the Tarsians alone had gone scot-free, and were laughing loudly at his bravery, making fun of his military experience. Therefore he drilled his men rigorously in battle skills, while he waited for the right time of year. As soon as spring shone forth,[9] and the bitter cold of winter changed considerably to the warmth of summer, [p. 57] the troops started to assemble round the emperor following his orders. He arrayed the army, which was composed of over four hundred thousand men, in compact fashion, and, after raising the standard,[10] set off toward Tarsos.

2. In the course of this march, one of the lightly armed soldiers, who was exhausted by the rough terrain (for it so happened that the army was marching through a very deep defile, which was hemmed in by cliffs and caves), took off the shield he was carrying on his shoulder, and dropped it on the path. The emperor saw this with his own eyes as he passed by, and ordered one of his attendants to pick up the shield. When he arrived at their halting place, he asked to which captain was assigned the man who threw away his shield and tossed away his own arms, when there was no danger of battle. The guilty party did not escape detection, but was quickly seized. The emperor gave him a grim and baleful look,

---

Babylon is told in detail by Diodorus Siculus, 2.7–10, drawing on and preserving Ktesias's account (see F. Jacoby, *Die Fragmente der griechischen Historiker*, IIIC [Leiden, 1958], 428ff). Leo's reference to seven walls here is an exaggeration.

[6] Hase (Leo diac. 436) notes that the phrase τὸ ναστὸν ὕψος is a recurring formula for the walls of Jerusalem, citing Josephus, *De bello judaico* 5.157, 166, etc.

[7] Cf. Leo diac. 5.20, ὀφθαλμοὶ ὤτων πιστότεροι, a modified quotation from Herodotus, 1.8.10.

[8] Tenth-c. accounts, however, speak of Tarsos's impressive fortifications and thoroughly military character: see McGeer, *Warfare*, 231–32, and the bibliography cited there.

[9] This must be the spring of 965.

[10] The standard of the cross: see Leo diac. 8.6 (σταυρικὸν . . . τρόπαιον) and 128.2 and 138.22 (σταυρικὸν σημεῖον), the last a reference to the vision of Constantine I the Great. See also Leo diac. 61.2–3.

and said, "Tell me, you scoundrel, if there were an unexpected attack, what defense would you use to ward off the enemy, since you threw away your shield on the path?" The man remained speechless, paralyzed with terror. The emperor ordered the captain to flog the soldier, who was bent on his own destruction, to cut off his nose and parade him through the camp.[11] But, whether seized with pity for the man, or softened by bribes, [the captain] let the man go unharmed. The next day the emperor saw him passing by, and summoned the captain, and said, "O, stubborn and [p. 58] bold man, how dare you not carry out my order? Or do you think that you have greater concern for this army than I do? I ordered that the man who tossed away his arms receive such a punishment as a lesson for the others, so that none of them might do the same thing in imitation of his carelessness and laziness, and be caught at the time of battle without their arms, and fall easy prey to the enemy." Then he flogged the captain severely, and cutting off his nose, he instilled fear in all the army, so they would no longer be careless about their own equipment.

3. Upon arrival in the vicinity of Tarsos, he pitched camp there and surrounded it with a palisade; he then ordered his men to clear-cut and mow down thoroughly the fields and meadows, which were filled with flowers and all sorts of trees, so that he could launch an attack in the open, and it would be impossible for any of the barbarians to set up an ambush in thickly grown areas, and attack the Roman army from a concealed spot. Thus one could see the area losing its inherent beauty; for it was all fertile and abounding in pasture, and thickly grown with all kinds of trees, which produced every sort of succulent fruit. The Tarsians, exulting in their previous victories over the Romans,[12] again were shown to be rash and arrogant,[13] and could not bear to restrain their anger, but went out from the town, assembled[14] in a powerful close formation for a

---

[11] The *Ekloga* (Appendix 1:17, trans. E. H. Freshfield, *A Manual of Roman Law: The Ecloga* [Cambridge, 1926] 124) indicates that the penalty for a ῥίψασπις ("a man who threw away his shield") in battle was death. The penalty here was lighter, apparently since the act took place while on the march. On ῥινοτομεῖν ("cutting off/slitting the nose") see *ODB* 2:1428, s.v. "Mutilation," and for discretion in type of punishment, *ODB* 3:1622, s.v. "Penalties." On this incident, see McGeer, *Warfare*, 335, 338.

[12] Skyl. 144.48ff and 270.40–43 and *Theoph. Cont.* 286.15–288.9 report that a late 9th-c. *domestikos* of the Schools, Stypeiotes, appointed by Basil I, had subjected his army to complete destruction at Tarsos owing to his poor planning. See also below, n. 26.

[13] There is a play on words: Ταρσεῖς and θρασεῖς.

[14] Reading παρεκρατοῦντο as in E instead of παρεκροτοῦντο as emended by Hase.

pitched battle, [p. 59] revealing themselves as daring and overweeningly confident before they engaged in the battle. The emperor himself led out from the camp the bravest and most robust soldiers, and arranged the divisions on the battlefield, deploying the ironclad horsemen[15] in the van, and ordering the archers and slingers to shoot at the enemy from behind. He himself took his position on the right wing, bringing with him a vast[16] squadron of cavalrymen, while John who had the sobriquet Tzimiskes,[17] and was honored with the rank of *doux*,[18] fought on the left.[19] He was a man of unbridled courage, extremely daring and more reckless than anyone else; although his body was shorter than average, like the fabled *warrior Tydeus*,[20] there was still a certain heroic strength

[15] On the heavily armed cavalry (*kataphraktoi*), the core of Nikephoros Phokas's army, see *ODB* 2:1114 and McGeer, *Warfare*, 214–17. According to the *TLG*, Leo is the first author to use the term πανσίδηροι. On the use of heavy cavalry as an indication of the "renewal of interest in methods of waging warfare, and the re-emergence of the Byzantine armed forces from comparative isolation," see J. Haldon, "Byzantine Military Technology from the Sixth to the Tenth Centuries," *BMGS* 1 (1975): 11–47, esp. 44 and n. 142.

[16] This rendering by McGeer (*Warfare*, 315) seems preferable to the literal figure of 10,000. While that many regular cavalry would be possible, the specific number would not be in accord with technical recommendations in the *Praecepta*: see Treadgold, *Army*, 113 and n. 78.

[17] For "sobriquet," read ἐπώνυμον with Panagiotakes rather than the ἐπώνυμα of the Hase ed.; note the rhyming of εὐώνυμον and ἐπώνυμον. On the naming convention here, personal name and sobriquet, see Kazhdan, "Byzantine Family Names," 108 (his reference in line 18 to 93.3–5 should be corrected to 92.3–5). For discussion of the meaning of Tzimiskes (translated by DuCange as "adolescentulus" or "youth"), see Book V, n. 87.

[18] The title δοὺξ—given Leo the Deacon's report earlier (Book III, chap. 8) that Nikephoros Phokas appointed Tzimiskes *domestikos* of the East and given the absence of any geographical limitation here on *doux* (see Book VI, n. 26: Bardas Phokas "*doux* . . . of Chaldia")—is apparently used for *domestikos*; see Oikonomides, *Listes*, 344. The relatively few references in the sources to Tzimiskes during the period 965–68 and the unknown date of his dismissal from his military command by Nikephoros Phokas (see Book V, n. 53) leave much of this portion of his career obscure. For Tzimiskes' various titles, though omitting this use of *doux*, see R. Guilland, "Les Logothètes," *REB* 29 (1971): 55.

It should be noted that Leo the Deacon's description of the fall of Tarsos differs significantly from other accounts; see Canard, *H'amdanides*, 820–23 with nn. 228–30.

[19] For close correspondence between the battle tactics described here and recommendations in the *Praecepta* attributed to Nikephoros Phokas, see McGeer, *Warfare*, 315.

[20] In classical legend one of the Seven against Thebes, a fierce warrior characterized by Homer (*Iliad* 5.801) as Τυδεύς τοι μικρὸς μὲν ἔην δέμας, ἀλλὰ μαχητής, hence aptly chosen to exemplify Tzimiskes, characterized as diminutive by Leo.

and force in his diminutive frame. When the emperor ordered the trumpets to sound the charge, one could see the Roman divisions move into action with incredible precision,[21] as the entire plain sparkled with the gleam of their armor. The Tarsians could not withstand such an onslaught; forced back by the thrusts of spears and by the missiles of the [archers] shooting from behind, they immediately turned to flight, and ingloriously shut themselves up in the town, after losing most of their men in this assault. They were overwhelmed by a terrible cowardice, when they saw such an experienced multitude advancing [against them]. Therefore they assigned positions on the circuit wall of the town, fortifying it with artillery engines, and remained patiently inside, awaiting the enemy's attack. [p. 60]

4. Since the emperor Nikephoros realized that the city was extremely difficult to attack and capture, and that it could not be taken by force, he decided not to take any chances by fighting in an ill-advised manner, but to deliver the city into the grip of famine, which through cruel necessity would make it surrender, even against its will. After making this plan, he encircled the town with diligent guards. The Tarsians kept hurling javelins at the Romans from the towers, as long as the famine had not yet grown serious and completely overwhelmed them. But when it began pitilessly to consume them, and their bodies were weakened by the lack[22] of food, then one could see the dreadful suffering and severe depression that overwhelmed the city; the men were cadaverous, no different from *ghostly shadows*.[23] *Starvation* is a *most piteous* and devastating *fate*; it wastes away the body's *mass*, quenches its *warmth* with cold, makes the skin stretch over *the bones like a spiderweb*,[24] and summons death to prevail slowly.

Since they were not able to fight both invincible suffering from starvation and so great an army, they came to terms with the emperor and surrendered, on condition that anyone who wished could proceed unimpeded to the interior of Syria. After making this concession and agreement with them, he ordered them to leave the city quickly, taking

---

[21] The Greek term κόσμος here indicates the product of the intensive drilling and training to which Nikephoros Phokas subjected his army.

[22] Reading ἀπορίᾳ with Panagiotakes instead of ἀπορία of Hase.

[23] See Plato, *Republic* 532c2.

[24] Some of the vocabulary and phrasing of this passage is reminiscent of Basil of Caesarea, Ὁμιλία ῥηθεῖσα ἐν λιμῷ καὶ αὐχμῷ, PG 31:321.

Book IV

only themselves and necessary[25] clothing. [p. 61] When he captured the city in this way, he distributed to the army some of the booty, which amounted to countless wealth, taking himself the cross-standards made of gold and precious stones that the Tarsians had seized in various battles, when they defeated the Roman forces;[26] after securing the city with a sufficient army, he returned to the imperial city. After arriving there, being magnificently received by the populace,[27] he deposited the captured crosses in the celebrated and holy church,[28] and entertained the people with chariot races[29] and other sights. For the Byzantines are fonder of spectacles[30] than any other people.

5. Just as he was concerned with these affairs, Mysian ambassadors came to him to say that their ruler[31] demanded the customary tribute,[32] and for that reason now sent them to the emperor. He was seized with unaccustomed anger (for he was of strong character, and was not easily

---

[25] Reading τὸν ἀναγκαῖον for τῶν ἀναγκαίων as suggested by Hase and accepted by Panagiotakes.

[26] On the standards carried into battle, see n. 10 above. Skyl. 270.39–43 states that crosses were captured when a *domestikos* of the Schools appointed (ca. 882) by Basil I was defeated at Tarsos; see n. 12 above. On the nature of the crosses, see G. Dennis, "Byzantine Battle Flags," *ByzF* 8 (1982): 51–59, esp. 57. He notes that the text does not indicate whether these were large processional crosses or crosses attached to regular flags. His third option, however, crosses simply depicted on regular flags, seems at variance with Leo's description of ornamentation with actual gold and gemstones.

[27] In October 965.

[28] Hagia Sophia; see McCormick, *Eternal Victory*, 169–70 and Skyl. 270.43–44.

[29] On chariot races in 10th-c. Constantinople, "a traditional and indispensable prop of the monarchy . . . to celebrate important political events," see *ODB* 1:412.

[30] For examples of the sorts of entertainment that the Byzantines enjoyed, see *ODB*, s.vv. "Entertainment" (1:702) and "Sports" (3:1939–40).

[31] Peter, tsar of Bulgaria (927–69).

[32] This payment to the Bulgarians had been arranged by Romanos I, apparently in connection with the marriage of his granddaughter, Maria Lekapena, to the Bulgarian tsar Peter (8 October 927). Runciman (*Romanus*, 99) suggests that the payment was to enable the princess to live at the Bulgarian court as befitted her station, and may have been due only during her lifetime, and that the Bulgarian demand here was illegitimate. Jenkins (*Byzantium* 280) suggests that Nikephoros made a serious error in not honoring the status quo and leaving Bulgaria as a buffer between Byzantium and the Magyars and Rus'. For a recent review of Phokas's Bulgarian policy, with specific discussion of Leo the Deacon's presentation of it here, see Stephenson, *Balkan Frontier*, 48–51. According to Stokes ("Balkan Campaigns of Svyatoslav," 57), this embassy occurred sometime between October 965 and the middle of 966. Stephenson (*Balkan Frontier*, 48) dates it "probably" to 966.

consumed with rage), swelled up inordinately, and, speaking in a louder voice than usual,[33] replied: "It would be a dreadful fate now to befall the Romans, who destroy their every foe with armed force, if they would have to pay tribute like captives to the particularly wretched and abominable Scythian people!"[34] Turning to his father Bardas (who happened to be sitting beside him, having been proclaimed caesar),[35] he asked him in perplexity what was the reason for the exaction of tribute that the Mysians [p. 62] were demanding from the Romans: "Did you unawares beget me as a slave? Shall I, the revered emperor of the Romans, be reduced to paying tribute to a most wretched and abominable people?" Therefore he ordered that the ambassadors be immediately slapped in the face, and said, "Go tell your leather-gnawing[36] ruler who is clad in a leather jerkin[37] that the most mighty and great emperor of the Romans is coming immediately to your land, to pay you the tribute in full, so that you may learn, O you who are thrice a slave through your ancestry,[38] to proclaim the rulers of the Romans as your masters, and not to demand tribute of them as if they were slaves."

With these words he dismissed them to return to their own country, while he assembled a sufficient army and set forth against the Mysians.[39]

---

[33] Reading ἢ ἧπερ εἴθιστο with Panagiotakes for ἤπερ εἴθιστο.

[34] "Scythians" is used here of Bulgarians, above (Book II, chap. 2) of Magyars. See Book III, n. 59, and ODB 3:1857–58, for generic application of the term to various nomadic peoples.

[35] On Bardas Phokas, see Book III, n. 53. For the title of caesar see ODB 1:363 and Oikonomides, Listes, 293.

[36] The Greek here, σκυτοτρώκης, is a hapax (according to the TLG), apparently devised by Leo the Deacon (or Nikephoros Phokas himself) for the situation; for a similar insult, see A.-J. Festugière, Vie de Théodore de Sykéôn, 1 (Brussels, 1970), chap. 35.5: σιδηροφάγε.

[37] The leather jerkin (διφθέρα) was the dress of boors in classical comedy; in Aristophanes, Clouds 70–72, it is contrasted as the attire of a goatherd with the ξύστις, a long robe of fine material worn by great men as a symbol of their status.

[38] The phrase τρίδουλος ... ἐκ προγόνων occurs in Eustathios of Thessalonike (Eustathii Archiepiscopi Thessalonicensis Commentarii ad Homeri Iliadem pertinentes, ed. M. van der Valk [Leiden, 1976], 2:623.7) to explain τρίδουλος in Sophocles, Oedipus Rex 1063, suggesting the origin of the insult: a slave born of a slave born of a slave. On the emperor's insulting behavior toward the Bulgarian envoys, see L. Simeonova, "The Short Fuse. Examples of Diplomatic Abuse in Byzantine and Bulgarian History," ByzF 23 (1996): 55–73, at 60–62.

[39] The date of this brief campaign against the Bulgarian frontier has been the subject of considerable debate. Treadgold (Byz. State, 502), following Stokes ("Balkan Campaigns of Svyatoslav," 57), places the expedition in 966, as does Stephenson (Balkan Frontier, 48).

He took by assault all the fortresses that bordered on Roman territory; but then he surveyed the region, and saw that it was densely wooded and full of cliffs (for, to use the language of the poet, in the land of the Mysians *in every way evil was heaped upon evil*;[40] an area full of caverns and cliffs followed upon a region that was densely wooded and overgrown with bushes, and then immediately after that would be a marshy and swampy area; for the region located near the Haimos and Rhodope [mountains],[41] which is watered with great rivers, is extremely damp, heavily forested, and surrounded on every side by impassable mountains). When the emperor Nikephoros observed this, he did not think he should lead the Roman force [p. 63] through dangerous regions with its ranks broken, as if he were providing sheep to be slaughtered by the Mysians; for it is said that on several previous occasions the Romans came to grief in the rough terrain of Mysia, and were completely destroyed.[42]

6. He decided therefore not to run any risks in impassable and dangerous territory. So he took the army and returned to Byzantium;[43] and after honoring with the rank of *patrikios* a particularly impulsive and hot-headed man named Kalokyres,[44] he sent him to the Tauroscythians (who are usually called Russians in the popular language)[45] to distribute

---

[40] Homer, *Iliad* 16.111.

[41] Reading Αἷμον with Panagiotakes instead of Αἷμον of Hase ed. On this range see *ODB* 1:248–49, s.v. "Balkans," with accompanying map; on the Rhodope, see *ODB* 3:1793. See also Anna Komnene, *Alexiad* 14.8.6 (ed. Leib, 3:180) for a description of the Haimos mountains as being a long range parallel to the Rhodope mountains.

[42] Among the most memorable of these defeats would be the losses suffered by Nikephoros II's uncle Leo Phokas at the hands of Symeon on 20 August 917 near Anchialos (described by Leo the Deacon below in Book VII, chap. 7), and later that year or early in 918 at Katasyrtai; see Runciman, *Romanus*, 54–56.

[43] For another English translation of the preceding passage describing the dangers of a Bulgarian campaign, see McGeer, *Warfare*, 328.

[44] Skyl. 277.28–29 adds that he was the son of the chief magistrate of Cherson (on which see *ODB* 1:418–19). Runciman, *Bulgarian Empire*, 200, notes that Kalokyres was thus "admirably fitted to deal with the savage neighboring tribes, knowing their languages and habits as well." According to Stokes ("Balkan Campaigns of Svyatoslav," 57) this embassy took place in 966, while Stephenson places Kalokyres' mission "probably in 967" (*Balkan Frontier*, 48). On Kalokyres' embassy to the Rus' and his attempt to use it to make himself emperor see below, Book V, chaps. 1–3 and Book VIII, chap. 5.

[45] On the Rus' of Kiev see *ODB* 3:1818–20, and on the term "Tauroscythians" for them see *ODB* 3:1857–58, s.v. "Scythians." On the emperor's use of the Rus' here as mercenaries against the Bulgarians, an incident on which Leo the Deacon is less precise than Skylitzes, see *ODB* 3:1979, s.v. "Svjatoslav."

to them the gold that he entrusted to him, a sum of 15 *kentenaria*,[46] and lead them to Mysian territory to conquer it. So Kalokyres hastened to the Tauroscythians, while Nikephoros ascended into the Hippodrome, and sat watching the chariot races he organized. He also gave orders to his soldiers to descend into the stadium, divide into opposing units, draw their swords, and attack each other in sport, to train in this way for battle. But the inhabitants of Byzantium, who knew nothing of military exercises, were panic-stricken at the flash of the swords, and, frightened by the assault of the soldiers in close quarters and by the clattering [of their arms], in their terror at the novel spectacle they turned to flight and ran to their homes. Quite a few deaths resulted from the shoving and the chaotic rush, as many were trampled underfoot and miserably suffocated. This tragic event was a beginning of hatred [p. 64] for the emperor in Byzantium.[47]

Hard on the heels of this came the outrageous conduct of his brother, Leo the *kouropalates*,[48] who abandoned his manly and soldierly life, exchanging it for that of a city-dwelling and greedy entrepreneur, and was unable to resist making money and unjust gains, and heartlessly brought about famine and a scarcity of provisions; for he bought grain at a low price and sold it at a high one. A rumor ran through the town, spread by the citizens, to the effect that the two brothers were making private profits off the sufferings of the masses, *stuffing* the goods of the people *into their bulging wallets*.[49] For the emperor mercilessly introduced taxes that had never before been conceived of, saying that he needed a lot of

---

[46] A *kentenarion* was a unit of weight (100 lbs.) often applied to gold coins; see *ODB* 2:1121. Runciman (*Bulgarian Empire*, 200–201) notes that 1500 pounds of gold was "a sum of money enormous even in those days of wholesale bribery of nations."

[47] See Skyl. 273.37–275.87, who also provides a more detailed list of the causes of the popular hatred of Nikephoros II. For contrasting analysis of the accuracy of and motives for the charges against the emperor, see Jenkins, *Byzantium*, 280–82, and Morris, "Phokas," 87–88, 97ff.

[48] On Leo Phokas, see above, Book II, n. 9. On the title *kouropalates* granted to him by his brother, the emperor, see Book III, n. 75.

[49] A proverbial expression; see *CPG* 2:201, cent. VI of Makarios, no. 98. The role assigned here to Leo Phokas is more prominent than that given by Skyl. 278.66–67, who assigns the main responsibility to the emperor himself. F. Tinnefeld (*Kategorien der Kaiserkritik in der byzantinischen Historiographie von Prokop bis Niketas Choniates* [Munich, 1971], 116) suggests that Leo the Deacon is reflecting a positive bias toward Nikephoros II and thus here attempting to spread the blame.

money for the army, and he oppressed his subjects with these [taxes].[50] It is said that the emperor heard, either from one of those who examine the signs of the heavens, or from one of those who have chosen a solitary and celibate life, that he would end his life in the imperial palace, cut down by one of his own people. In his terror at this prophecy, he began to build a wall from one side of the palace, which sloped toward the sea, and brought it to the sea on the other side, and constructed a lofty and secure wall, which can be seen today, and protected the imperial palace, as he thought.[51]

7. On the feast of the Ascension of the Savior, when the emperor was in the usual manner taking part in a procession[52] outside the walls to the so-called Pege (where the very beautiful church was built in honor of the Virgin),[53] a fight broke out between some Byzantines and Armenians, [p. 65] in which many of the townspeople were injured by the Armenians.[54] Towards evening, as the emperor was returning to the palace,

---

[50] For the measures taken by Nikephoros II to support the army financially, see the more detailed lists at Skyl. 274.50–275.75 and Zonaras (*Ioannis Zonarae Epitomae historiarum*, ed. M. Pinder [Bonn, 1897], 3:505.16–506.10), trans. McGeer, *Warfare*, 196. For analysis see Morris, "Phokas," 87–88, 96–100; Lemerle, *Agr. Hist.*, 100–3, 128–31; and Treadgold, *Byz. State*, 502–3.

[51] Leo the Deacon's brief comment here is in sharp contrast to Skyl. 275.77–81, who observes that the construction of the wall was the most important source of the resentment of the populace against the emperor, as it required the destruction of many fine works around the palace and created a "tyrant's acropolis" (ἀκρόπολιν καὶ τυραννεῖον). The wall has recently been studied in detail by C. Mango (Mango, "The Palace of the Boukoleon"), who identifies extant portions and concludes that the sector enclosed by Nikephoros became the palace of the Boukoleon. See also J. Bardill, "The Great Palace of the Byzantine Emperors and the Walker Trust Excavations," *Journal of Roman Archaeology* 12 (1999): 216–30, esp. 216 and 226 and n. 54.

[52] The emperor traditionally celebrated the feast of the Ascension (forty days after Easter) at the church of the Pege monastery, just outside the walls of Constantinople; on the procession and ceremony, see *De cer.* 1, chaps. 8, 18, ed. Reiske, 54–58, 108–14.

[53] On the Pege monastery, see Janin, *Églises CP*, 223–28.

[54] The Armenians here are Phokas's soldiers: see J. Haldon, "Strategies of Defence, Problems of Security: The Garrisons of Constantinople in the Middle Byzantine Period," in *Constantinople and its Hinterland*, ed. C. Mango and G. Dagron (Aldershot, 1995), 150 and n. 29; and N. Garsoïan, "The Problem of Armenian Integration into the Byzantine Empire," in *Studies on the Internal Diaspora of the Byzantine Empire*, ed. H. Ahrweiler and A. Laiou (Washington, D.C., 1998), 59. For the role of Armenians in the Byzantine army, see above, Book I, n. 73. Skyl. 275.88–91 reports a similar battle at the preceding Easter between some sailors (πλώϊμοι) and Armenians, which resulted in many deaths.

the Byzantines began openly to hurl insults at him.[55] One woman and her daughter became so crazed as to lean from the roof and throw stones at the ruler. The next day she was arrested by the *praitor*,[56] and was punished together with her daughter, by being burned to death[57] in a suburb called Anaratai.[58] At that time I, who am writing these words, was a young man living in Byzantium,[59] as a student pursuing an education.[60] When I saw the emperor Nikephoros riding slowly on horseback through the town, unaffected by such insults, maintaining self-control, and acting as if nothing unusual were occurring, I was astonished at the imperturbable spirit of the man, how fearlessly he maintained the nobility of his spirit[61] in difficult circumstances. Approaching night, however, put an end to the unrest; and since the emperor, being very magnanimous, did not easily yield to anger, he considered the abuse hurled at him by the citizens on the previous

[55] Skylitzes (276.12–17) says that these were relatives of those who had lost their lives in the Hippodrome incident when the mock military battle led to a panic.

[56] Leo the Deacon in Book VI, chap. 2 describes the office of *praitor* (Lat. praetor) as among "the greatest offices of the state." H. Ahrweiler (*Bulletin de correspondance hellénique* 84 [1960]: 44) has suggested, based on these two references in Leo, that the office, in the sense of a high judicial official in Constantinople, was created by Nikephoros Phokas. See also *ODB* 3:1710, and R. Guilland, *Titres et fonctions de l'Empire byzantin* (London, 1976), no. XXV:80–84.

[57] On death at the stake as a possible punishment for rebellion, see *ODB* 3:1622, s.v. "Penalties." Genesios (*Iosephi Genesii regum libri quattuor*, ed. A. Lesmüller-Werner and I. Thurn [Berlin–New York, 1978], Book I, chap. 17) records that in the 9th c. Michael the Amorian was sentenced to be burned in the furnace of the palace baths for treason, although the execution was never carried out.

[58] A variant of τὰ Ὀνωράτου, a suburb on the Asian shore of the Bosporus: see Janin, *CP byz.*, 486.

[59] Reading ὁ . . . γράφων τῇ Βύζαντος for ὁ . . . γράφοντι Βυζάντιος, as conjectured by Hase and emended by Panagiotakes.

[60] The Greek here, συλλογὴ λόγων, is apparently a reference to the study of Aristotelian logic, particularly syllogisms; see Ammonius, *In Aristotelis Analyticorum priorum librum I commentarium*, ed. M. Wallies, CAG 4.6 (Berlin, 1899), 2.7–9; David the Philosopher, *Prolegomena et in Porphyrii Isagogen commentarium*, ed. A. Busse, CAG 18.2 (Berlin, 1904), 90.21–23; and Olympiodorus, *Prolegomena et in Categorias commentarium*, ed. A. Busse CAG 12.1 (Berlin, 1902), 8.13–14. It is notable that Leo uses a phrase associated with the Neoplatonists to describe this aspect of his studies. Below at 72.17–18 (Book IV, chap. 11), Leo indicates that he was pursuing the ἐγκύκλιος παίδευσις, that is, post-primary education, "most likely undertaken between ages 11 to 17" (thus μειράκιον here); for the ages and curriculum, see P. Lemerle, *Byzantine Humanism: The First Phase* (Canberra, 1986), 112–13 and n. 88.

[61] Reading ψυχῆς (as conjectured by Hase) or ψυχικὴν (as in E) for ψυχήν.

day to be an act of drunkenness, rather than the action of a disorderly crowd, and dismissed it from his mind. Then, after securely steadying with ballast[62] fire-bearing triremes, and filling large merchantmen with soldiers and weapons, he sent them to Sicily,[63] appointing as commander of the fleet the *patrikios* Niketas,[64] [p. 66] a God-fearing and venerated man, even though he was a eunuch. As commander of the cavalry he appointed his nephew Manuel,[65] who also had the distinguished rank of *patrikios*, a hot-headed and self-willed

[62] Leo here and below at 126.23 indicates this operation (ἑρματίζειν, an extremely rare verb in Byzantine Greek) specifically for the fire-bearing triremes (i.e., *dromones*), a notice not found in other sources. Presumably when used for this purpose, the *dromones* required secure stabilization. For an illustration from the Skylitzes manuscript of such a *dromon* in action, see Th. K. Korres, *Hygron Pyr*, 3rd ed. (Thessalonike, 1995), cover illustration, with discussion of such ships at 83–98.

[63] This ill-fated campaign, a Byzantine attempt to recover an island that had been almost completely taken over by the Arabs in the 9th c., has been variously dated to 964 or 965. In any case Leo has muddled the chronology of Book IV, placing the Sicilian campaign *after* Nikephoros's brief expedition to the Bulgarian frontier in 966 (above, chap. 5). Dölger ("Chronologie," 290 n. 1) dates the Byzantine attack on Sicily to October 964, following ibn al-Athir. Schlumberger (*Phocas*, 461 n. 1) rightly notes that Leo the Deacon, although a contemporary of the event, is not well informed about this expedition. For a list of Greek and Arab sources of the expedition, see V. von Falkenhausen, *Untersuchungen über die byzantinische Herrschaft in Süditalien vom 9. bis ins 11. Jahrhundert* (Wiesbaden, 1967), 26 n. 194; for scholarly accounts, see M. Amari, *Storia dei Musulmani di Sicilia* (Catania, 1935), 2:304–13, and J. Gay, *L'Italie méridionale et l'empire byzantin* (Paris, 1904), 2:290–91.

[64] Niketas was the brother of the *protovestiarios* Michael and thus known to the emperor. See Ringrose, *The Perfect Servant*, 136–37. Schlumberger (*Phocas*, 444) notes that he was a man of great piety, but incapable of exercising any military direction. After his capture by the Arabs in Sicily he was imprisoned in North Africa, where he spent his time copying religious texts in what now survives as MS Paris gr. 497 (H. Omont, *Inventaire sommaire des manuscrits grecs de la Bibliothèque Nationale* [Paris, 1886], 1:59–60). Hase (Leo diac. 444) prints Niketas's subscription to the manuscript, in which he identifies himself as the *droungarios* of the fleet and brother of the *protovestiarios* Michael and notes that he is imprisoned in Africa. See also Guilland, *Institutions*, 1:172, 184, 362, 539.

[65] To Leo the Deacon's characterization of him one may add Skylitzes' comment (267.65–68) that he was "worthy to be a soldier, not a general, and subject to many other vices and unwilling to listen to those offering better advice." On his fate in Sicily (beheaded), see Liudprand, *Relatio* 43.

Leo describes Manuel Phokas as the αὐτανέψιος of the emperor, an ambiguous term meaning both cousin and nephew; see above, Book III, n. 28. Cheynet ("Les Phocas," 306 and n. 53) argues that he was Nikephoros's nephew. He posits that, while Skyl. 261.11–12 clearly identifies him as the illegitimate son of the emperor's uncle Leo, Manuel's youth would make him much more likely the son of the emperor's brother Leo.

man, likely to yield to thoughtless impulse. After they crossed the Adriatic and reached Sicily, they disembarked from the transport ships and drew up into organized ranks. They enjoyed such good fortune at the beginning that they captured the renowned and celebrated cities of Syracuse and Himera at the first assault, and in addition subdued Tauromenium and Leontini without any bloodshed.[66] But in the end malicious fortune was not to send them a favorable breeze, but blew fiercely and violently against them, and submerged them [beneath the waves]. My narrative will now relate this clearly.

8. The Sicilians,[67] who were not able to withstand such an assault and the irresistible spirit of the Romans, abandoned their cities, retreated to rough terrain, and regrouped in strategic locations; for the island is, for the most part, craggy and forested, and able to provide natural defenses for anyone who wants them. As for Manuel, he should have guarded the cities he had captured, and whatever land was abounding in pasture and suitable for horses, and denied the[68] fugitives access to fodder and other foodstuffs (for thus exhausted by starvation, they would suffer one of two fates, either surrender to the Romans or die through lack of provisions). But being impetuous, and seething with youthful anger, and not especially endowed with effectiveness and intelligence, [p. 67] he was immoderately elated by the previous victories, and began to advance through those dangerous regions, seeking out the fugitives.

When the army broke ranks in the difficult terrain, and was proceeding in a disorganized fashion through rocky cliffs and hollows, the barbarians, who had been lying in wait for the men, leaped up from their places of ambush with great clatter and unintelligible shouts, and suddenly attacked them. [The Romans] were astonished by the unexpected assault, and,

---

[66] The Arab sources indicate that the impetus for the expedition was a request from the last Christian stronghold on the island, Rametta, in the mountains near Messina, for aid in relieving an Arab siege. They also suggest that the expedition landed first at Messina and the Byzantine land forces marched immediately toward Rametta. Notably, none of the other sources mentions Manuel's capture of these four Sicilian cities. Thus the accuracy of Leo's information here is questionable. See A. Metcalfe, *Muslims and Christians in Norman Sicily* (London, 2003), 21–22.

[67] The term here refers to the Arab masters of Sicily, on whom see *ODB* 3:1891–92. They are called Agarenes later in the chapter. See also A. Metcalfe, *Muslims and Christians in Norman Sicily* (London, 2003), 8–23; and J. Johns, *Arabic Administration in Norman Sicily* (Cambridge, 2002), 13–18, 22–30.

[68] Reading τοὺς for τὰς with Panagiotakes.

since they could not even see the sunlight because of the dense shade of the thicket, they turned to flight. The barbarians set upon them and slaughtered them mercilessly, like sacrificial victims; and they stopped killing the men only when their strength and rage were exhausted. Manuel himself was killed, and any Romans who escaped the sword were taken captive by the Agarenes. Then, after subduing the infantry, they hastened to the coast, where the Roman triremes were lying at anchor, and overwhelmed most of them by force. The *patrikios* Niketas was captured, and sent as a prisoner to the ruler of the Africans.[69] Thus out of such a large army, only a very few escaped and returned to the emperor Nikephoros. At the news of the destruction of such a great army, he was very disheartened and grieved in his soul at such a defeat and unaccountable misfortune. But as he reflected on the uncertainty of human affairs, he came to bear the disaster nobly, since he was of strong character, and knew how to hold his head high in difficult circumstances. [p. 68] So again he fit out an army against the Agarenes who inhabited Syria.

9. During the same year, when summer was just turning to autumn, God shook the earth greatly,[70] so that buildings and towns were destroyed. It happened then that Klaudioupolis, the most prosperous town of the Galatians,[71] was demolished by the irresistible quaking and trembling,

[69] The Fatimid caliph of North Africa, al-Mu'izz (954–75): see A. Tibi, "Byzantine-Fatimid Relations in the Reign of Al-Mu'izz Li-Din Allah (r. 953–75 A.D.) as Reflected in Primary Arabic Sources," *Graeco-Arabica* 4 (1991): 91–97; *EI²* 7:485–89; J. Johns, *Arabic Administration in Norman Sicily* (Cambridge, 2002), 20, 25; and Book V, n. 4.

[70] See Leo diac. 4.11–12 (Book I, chap. 1). Skyl. 277.37–40 dates the earthquake to 2 September of the 11th indiction (i.e., 967) and adds that it struck Honorias and Paphlagonia. Zonaras (ed. Pinder, 3:513.15–17) indicates that Constantinople was undamaged. Guidoboni (*Earthquakes*, 398–99) accepts Leo's reference to the fall equinox and dates the quake to late September 967.

[71] On Klaudioupolis, modern Bolu, about 90 km east-southeast of Constantinople, see K. Belke, *Paphlagonien und Honorias* (Vienna, 1996), 235–37. It was the metropolis of Honorias rather than of Galatia, so that Leo would seem to be in error here (see also Loretto, *Phokas*, 172 n. 68.2). Siuziumov et al., *Lev D'iakon*, 185 n. 54 suggest that Leo has confused it with Neoklaudiopolis. However, W. M. Ramsay (*The Historical Geography of Asia Minor* [London, 1890; repr. Amsterdam, 1962], 451) argued persuasively that there is no example of the use of "Neoklaudiopolis" (later Andrapa) in Byzantine times, and that it could not be described as "most prosperous." He concludes that Leo's reference is "a pure error, arising from forgetfulness of the old historical divisions, which had lost all political reality since the institution of the themes, though they were still kept up in the ecclesiastical arrangement."

Leo may be perhaps reflecting the naming convention found in the *De thematibus* of Constantine VII Porphyrogennetos (ed. A. Pertusi, *De Thematibus* [Vatican City, 1952],

and became a sudden grave for its inhabitants, and many visitors who happened to be there were also killed instantly. Mathematicians tell the tale that the cause of such a quake and trembling is certain vapors and fumes, confined in the bowels of the earth, which are then combined into a stormy wind; since the vapors cannot all escape together, because of the narrow outlets, they compress together, whirl about, and spin round the hollows [of the earth] with a violent movement, and shake everything that is covering and containing them, until they explode from their confined area, and after being blown outside are dispersed into the kindred air.[72] The foolish babbling of the Greeks has explained these things the way they want it; but I would go along with the holy David[73] and say that it is through the agency of God that such quakes happen to us, when, as He watches over our ways of life, [He sees] acts contrary to divine ordinance, in the hope that, terrified in this way, men may avoid base deeds, and strive[74] rather for [p. 69] praiseworthy ones.

In any case, all Klaudioupolis was at that time destroyed from its foundations by the force of the earthquake, and obliterated, *draining the cup of God's untempered wrath.*[75] Also during this year, around the middle of summer, just as the sun was entering the sign of Cancer,[76] a storm burst forth in Byzantium[77] and its environs, such as had never occurred before; for the disaster began as the day was drawing to a close (it was Friday), and ended at the ninth hour.[78] The rain poured down so vio-

---

71, VI.19–22) which has: εἰσὶ δὲ πόλεις αἱ συμπληροῦσαι τὸ θέμα τῶν Βουκελλαρίων τοσαῦται· πρώτη μὲν Ἄγκυρα, μητρόπολις τῶν Γαλατῶν, δευτέρα δὲ Κλαυδιούπολις, καὶ αὕτη μητρόπολις τῶν Μαριανδυνῶν . . . . However, just above at VI.7–8 it is noted, τὸ γὰρ οἰκεῖον ὄνομα τοῦ ἔθνους καὶ Ἑλληνικόν, Μαριανδυνοὶ ὀνομάζονται, ἐπεκλήθησαν δὲ Γαλάται, perhaps justifying Leo's usage. On the Mariandynoi, a people of Thracian origin, see F. Becker-Bertau, *Die Inschriften von Klaudiu Polis* (Bonn, 1986), 10 n. 68.

[72] Leo the Deacon here rephrases the theory of the cause of earthquakes (confined vapors, ἀναθυμιάσεις) found in Agath. 60.22–27; the core idea is presumably from Aristotle, *Meteorologica* 365a–370, which also credits vapors.

[73] See Ps. 103 (104):32: "[the Lord], Who looks upon the earth and makes it tremble."

[74] Leo here uses homoioteleuton, ἀφέξοιντο . . . ἀνθέξοιντο.

[75] Isa. 51:17 and Rev. 14:10.

[76] I.e., ca. 21 June 967.

[77] See Leo diac. 4.12–13 (Book I, chap. 1).

[78] Ca. 3:00 P.M. In 967, 21 June did indeed fall on a Friday.

lently that one could not see drops of rain as usual, but it was like streams overflowing with water. There was no church or renowned building that was not filled with water from above, through the roof, although the inhabitants laboriously drained it off into the streets; but as much as they poured out, poured in, and the flood was unconquerable. For three hours the rain poured down continually, and one could see overflowing rivers in the narrow streets of the city, destroying whatever living thing they carried along with them. The people wailed and lamented piteously, fearing that a flood like that fabled one of old[79] was again befalling them. But compassionate Providence, which loves mankind, thrust a rainbow through the clouds,[80] and with its rays dispersed the gloomy rain, and the structure of nature returned again to its previous condition. It so happened that there was a later downpour, which was turbid and mixed [p. 70] with ashes,[81] as in *the soot from a furnace*,[82] and it seemed lukewarm to those who touched it.

10. The emperor Nikephoros (for my narrative again returns to the point where it diverted its path) took the Roman forces, and hastened to Syrian Antioch,[83] where he set up camp. Because [the city] boasted of having sufficient provisions, and in its arrogance would not tolerate coming to terms right away, and since he did not want to destroy it with siege machines (for he knew that he would subdue it gradually with a

---

[79] See Gen. 6–8.

[80] See Gen. 9:13–14.

[81] Loretto (*Phokas*, 173 n. 70.1) tentatively suggests as the source of the volcanic eruption Bithynian Olympos or Mt. Argaios near Caesarea; specific identification does not appear possible.

[82] Exod. 9:8, 10.

[83] Antioch on the Orontes, the seat of a patriarchate, had fallen to the Arabs in 636–37: see *ODB* 1:113–16. Nikephoros Phokas led invasions of Syria in 966 and 968. Yahya of Antioch, *Histoire*, 805–6, says he attacked various cities in October 966, including Menbidj (Hierapolis), where he obtained the *keramion* and unsuccessfully besieged Antioch for eight days. Yahya also indicates (814–15) that in October 968 Phokas again arrived at Antioch, proceeded south to attack various cities, including Tripolis and Arqah, returned to Antioch, and stationed troops under Peter the *stratopedarch* nearby at Baghras to make incursions against Antioch and its environs. Halkin, "Translation," 259.5–6 indicates that Phokas brought the *keramion* to Constantinople on 24 January in the year 6475 (= 967). Leo the Deacon has apparently conflated these two campaigns in what follows into 968. See also Skylitzes (270.45–271.63), who as well seems to conflate the two campaigns, but into 966. See also Schlumberger, *Phocas*, 704–6 n. 5.

combination of force[84] and stratagems), he besieged it for a while, terrifying its inhabitants greatly with his divisions and display of weapons.[85] He then departed from there and traversed the interior, called Palestine,[86] which is all fertile and *flowing with milk and honey*,[87] just as in the Holy Scriptures; on his right he had Cilicia and the coast. After capturing Edessa,[88] and entering the church of the Holy Confessors[89] to give thanks to the divin-

---

[84] The text reads τροπαίοις, which presents difficulties. An anonymous reader has suggested the emendation to τρόποις (and translation as "with devices"); see the *Chronicon* of George Sphrantzes, 35.6.1–2, ed. V. Grecu, *Georgios Sphrantzes. Memorii 1401–1477* (Bucharest, 1966), 96.11. In Leo diac. 81.17–18 (Book V, chap. 4), we are told how the Byzantines harassed Antioch with daily raids (καταδρομαῖς).

[85] Use of such displays to terrify the enemy are recommended by Maurikios and Leo VI: see Sullivan, "Prescriptions," 186–87.

[86] Leo's statement that Nikephoros Phokas traversed Palestine has prompted much discussion. As is evident from a later passage (Leo diac. 166.14–16), he erroneously defined Palestine as the area of Syria east of Mt. Lebanon, i.e., far to the north of its traditional placement. Another geographical error occurs just below in the apparent use of Edessa for Hierapolis. Whether Nikephoros ever reached the former Roman provinces of Palaestina is doubtful; just below Leo gives Tripolis as the southern limit of the Byzantine advance, while Skyl. 271.69–70 says that Nikephoros brought Tripolis and Damascus under tribute (ὑποφόρους). The error may reflect the Byzantine desire to recover Jerusalem. Skyl. 271.66–67 also states that Nikephoros took cities and fortresses of Cilicia, Syria, and "Lebanese Phoenicia," which Hase (Leo diac. 446) takes as the region of Phoenicia around Emesa. On the problem see also Schlumberger, *Phocas*, 706 n. 5; J. Starr, "Notes on Byzantine Incursions into Syria and Palestine (?)," *Archiv Orientální* 8 (1936): 91–95 and Loretto, *Phokas*, 173 n. 70.2.

[87] Exod. 3:8, 13:5, etc.

[88] For Edessa see *ODB* 1:676. The text here indicates that Nikephoros II found the Holy Tile (*keramion*) in Edessa, but this is problematic. Traveling from Antioch with the coast on the right would lead south away from Edessa; the transition below (71.13) from the story of the Holy Tile, "After he took Mempetze," is without any preparation; and Skyl. 271.60–63 states that Nikephoros found the tile (and the hair of John the Baptist) at Hierapolis (Mempetze). Unless text has been lost here (see n. 90 below), Leo the Deacon may have inadequately blended conflicting traditions about the *keramion* (on which see *ODB* 2:1123) or be confusing the *keramion* with the *mandylion* found at Edessa in 944. E. von Döbschutz's (*Christusbilder* [Leipzig, 1899], 172 and n. 1) suggestion of emending Edessa to Emesa, not accepted by Panagiotakes, would fit with movement south, but not with the subsequent reference to the church of the Confessors and the various traditions regarding the *keramion*. Further confounding the issue, Leo records below (Book X, chap. 4) that John Tzimiskes found the sandals of Christ and the hair of John the Baptist at Mempetze. On the confusion see also Schlumberger, *Phocas* 704–6 and n. 5.

[89] On the church of the Confessors of Edessa (Ss. Shmona, Gurya, and Habib), built by Bishop Abraham after 345, see J. B. Segal, *Edessa "The Blessed City"* (Oxford, 1970), 174, 182.

ity, he allowed his army to rest a while * * *.[90] For he had heard that the image of our Savior God that was imprinted on a tile[91] was kept in this fortified city. They say the imprint was made in the following manner. The apostle Thaddeus was sent by the Savior to Abgar, the ruler of Edessa,[92] to cure him by means of the theandric image from the paralysis that afflicted him. While he was passing by there, he hid the cloth, on which Christ had ineffably imprinted the image of His face, [p. 71] among some tiles lying outside the town, so that the next day he could retrieve it from there. And it came to pass that the tiles were illuminated all night long by an inexplicable light. In the morning, when Thaddeus retrieved the cloth to continue the rest of his journey, the tile that the cloth happened to have touched had received the immaculate impression of the theandric image of our Savior. The barbarians took it, and preserved it in their fortress with great wonder and reverence.

At that time the emperor Nikephoros, after capturing the town, took this very sacred tile away; later he had a case adorned with gold and gems,[93] reverently set the tile in it, and dedicated it to the church of

---

[90] A lacuna was proposed here by Panagiotakes. He noted that other sources indicate that Phokas found the Holy Tile in Hierapolis (Mempetze) and that the various place references in Leo's subsequent narrative in this chapter—τῷδε τῷ φρουρίῳ, ἐνταῦθα, τοῦ ἄστεος, τὸ φρούριον, τὸ ἄστυ, ἐκεῖθεν—must all refer to Hierapolis (Mempetze), which, however, is not mentioned until later in the text and then unexpectedly. B. Flusin "Didascalie de Constantin Stilbès sur le mandylion et la sainte tuile (BHG 796m)," REB 55 (1997): 53–79, at 61 suggests: "il semble que Léon le Diacre anticipe quand il localise la sainte tuile à Édesse, alors qu' il parle de la relique conservée à Hiérapolis-Mabboug (Membidj), ville citée aussitôt après."

[91] On the Holy Tile and the various legends of its origin, see ODB 2:1123, s.v. "Keramion," and Halkin, "Translation." On the mandylion see ODB 2:1282–83 and for an English translation of the Narratio de imagine Edessena (PG 113:421–54) attributed to Constantine VII Porphyrogennetos see Ian Wilson, The Turin Shroud (London, 1978), 235–51. See also A.-M. Dubarle, "L'homélie de Grégoire le Référendaire pour la réception de l'image d'Édesse," REB 55 (1997): 5–51.

Leo uses the term πέπλος to describe the mandylion; for other terms used for it, see C. Walter, "The Abgar Cycle at Mateić," in Studien zur byzantinischen Kunstgeschichte. Festschrift für Horst Hallensleben zum 65. Geburtstag, ed. B. Borkopp et al. (Amsterdam, 1995), 221–31, at 223.

[92] For possible identifications of the Abgar of the legend, see ODB 1:676 s.v. "Edessa."

[93] For speculation on the possible form of the box, see A. Frolow, Les reliquaires de la vraie croix (Paris, 1965), 193 n. 4.

Book IV

the Mother of God, which is in the imperial palace.[94] After he took the fortress of Mempetze,[95] he crossed Mt. Lebanon[96] diagonally to reach Tripolis.[97] Seeing that it was well defended and much more difficult to capture than other cities, and since his ships were delayed, as they had been held back by adverse winds, he passed it by and decided to besiege the fortress of Arka,[98] which had untold quantities of wealth within. After encircling it with three palisades, he besieged it most vigorously, and, after demolishing its towers with his siege machines, he plundered it for nine whole days, and carried off from there untold wealth; and many other fortresses he captured as well with the first assault. [p. 72]

11. While the emperor was thus engaged in Syria, about the time of the winter solstice an eclipse of the sun[99] took place, such as had never occurred before, except for the one that took place at the time of the

---

[94] The church of the Virgin of the Pharos: see Janin, Églises CP, 232–36, esp. 235, and I. Kalavrezou, "Helping Hands for the Empire," in H. Maguire, Byzantine Court Culture from 829 to 1204 (Washington, D.C., 1997), 53–79, at 55–57.

[95] On Mempetze, Arabic Manbij, ancient Hierapolis in Syria, 78 km northeast of Aleppo, see ODB 2:928–29; EI² 6:377–83 (s.v. "Manbidg"); Der Neue Pauly 2:429–30, s.v. "Bambyke"; and R. Burns, Monuments of Syria: A Historical Guide (New York, 1992), 153–54. Leo indicates below (see Book X, n. 35) that Mempetze is the "Syrian" (i.e., Arabic) form of the name. Skyl. 271.61 has ἐν Ἱεραπόλει, indicating that Nikephoros found the Holy Tile and the hair of John the Baptist there; Leo attributes the acquisition of the latter to Tzimiskes below in Book X, chap. 4.

[96] On Mt. Lebanon see also below, Book X, chap. 4, where Leo describes it as the huge, rugged mountain separating Phoenicia from Palestine. For the mountain as a point of Arab-Byzantine confrontation, see EI² 5:789–90, s.v. "Lubnan."

[97] The distance from Hierapolis to Tripolis, a port on the Phoenician coast, was ca. 115 km. Below, in Book X, chap. 6, Leo notes that John Tzimiskes also made an unsuccessful attempt to take Tripolis. On the city see ODB 3:2119–20. Its excellent natural defenses are attested by the fact that the Crusaders needed eight years (1101–9) to take the town by siege.

[98] For Arka, located between Tripolis and Antarados, see RE 2:1117–18; Schlumberger, Phocas, 703; and Chronicon Paschale, ed. L. Dindorf (Bonn, 1832), 63.1–2: κλίματος τετάρτου Συρίας κοίλης, Ἀντιόχεια, Ἄρκα, Ἱεράπολις. . . . The siege is also described by Yahya of Antioch, Histoire, 815–16.

[99] The eclipse of 22 December 968 is recorded in a number of other sources, including Skyl. 279.85 and Liudprand (Relatio 64; from Corfu). For a full listing, see Schove, Chronology, 234–36, who comments that totality at Constantinople would have been at about 11:15 AM, which he equates to the end of the fifth hour of the day. See also Grumel, Chronologie, 464. F. Richard Stephenson, Historical Eclipses and Earth's Rotation (Cambridge, 1997), 390, comments: "Leo's splendid account contains the earliest known reference to the corona which is definitely datable."

Passion of the Lord[100] on account of the madness of the Jews, when they committed the great sin of nailing the Creator of all things to the Cross. The nature of the eclipse was as follows. On the 22nd of December, at the fourth hour of the day, in calm, clear weather, darkness covered the earth, and all the brighter stars were visible.[101] One could see the disk of the sun dark and unlighted, and a dim and faint gleam, like a delicate headband, illuminating the edge of the disk all the way around. Gradually the sun passed by the moon (for the latter could be seen screening off the former in a direct line),[102] and sent out its own rays, which again filled the earth with light. People were terrified at the novel and unaccustomed sight, and propitiated the divinity with supplications, as was fitting. At that time I myself was living in Byzantium, pursuing my general education.[103]

After the emperor easily captured the enemy fortresses (for the narrative should now return again to him, after digressing from its sequence), he proceeded with all his forces to Antioch. After setting up camp before its walls, he summoned the generals and captains, and, standing in a place of vantage in the open, he spoke as follows: [p. 73]

"My fellow soldiers, as you know, with the help of Providence and as a result of your experience, combined with your innate bravery, we have captured the fortresses located beyond this city, contrary to all expectation. I express my very great gratitude to you, because you looked to me as your leader, and did not slacken at the many unpleasant and disagreeable [labors] that war usually brings, but you fought with eagerness and calculated strength, so that none of the fortresses that we attacked was a match for your valor, and remained uncaptured. I am aware of your desire to destroy this city, how you, the army, are excited and eager to demolish it and ravage it with fire. But a kind of pity for this city has gradually come over me, that the city that is third in the

---

[100] See Matt. 27:45, Luke 23:44, etc.

[101] Skyl. 279.86 also says that stars appeared. On the phenomenon, see Schove, *Chronology*, xi.

[102] On the relative positions of the moon and sun, see Aetius citing pseudo-Thales (H. Diehls, *Doxographi Graeci* [Berlin, 1879] 353–354): πρῶτος ἔφη ἐκλείπειν τὸν ἥλιον τῆς σελήνης αὐτὸν ὑπερχομένης κατὰ κάθετον, οὔσης φύσει γεώδους, βλέπεσθαι δὲ τοῦτο κατοπτρικῶς ὑποτιθέμενον τῷ δίσκῳ. For the translation of κατὰ κάθετον as "in a direct line," see A. Fairbanks, *The First Philosophers of Greece* (London, 1898), 6.

[103] On Leo's education, see above, n. 60, and Introduction, 23–24.

Book IV

world,[104] on account of the beauty and size of its walls (for you see to what height they rise), and also because of the multitude of its people and the extraordinary construction of its buildings, should be reduced to rubble, like some poor fortress. To me it seems senseless to exhaust the Roman army in the sacking of this city, and to destroy and ravage again what we have subdued with warfare. For I would call that man a particularly provident general who ravaged and destroyed the land of the enemy with a combination of attacks and stalling tactics; but I would not hesitate to call foolish, or indeed criminally stupid, the man who destroyed and ravaged his own land with repeated raids and sallies by his army up and down the country.[105] [p. 74] He is acting like the dogs ridiculed in the proverb, who ought to scare the wolves off from the sheep, to protect the flocks from attack, but, in addition to not scaring off [the wolves], they themselves tear apart [the sheep] and rend them in pieces even more than the wild animals.[106] If then you are willing to listen to me, since this hill appears particularly secure,[107] and is well-watered, as you see, it should be fortified immediately, and a squadron of cavalry and a cohort of infantry should be left on it, so that by daily attacks and raids, and by plundering of provisions, they may bring Antioch to its knees, reduce it to dire straits, and force it, albeit unwilling, to become tributary to the Romans."[108]

[104] Treadgold (Byz. State, 573, 954 n. 36), citing this passage, observes that Antioch was the largest city conquered by the Byzantines, and after resettlement would have ranked behind Constantinople and Thessalonike. Siuziumov et al., Lev D'iakon, 187 n. 74, suggest as the second city Alexandria, which was no longer under Byzantine control. Loretto, Phokas, 175 n. 73.1, suggests either Alexandria or Rome. From the Byzantine perspective Treadgold's suggestion seems the most plausible, although certainty is not possible. On Thessalonike as the second city of the empire, see R. Browning, "Byzantine Thessalonike: A Unique City?" Dialogos 2 (1995): 91–104, esp. 91 and n. 1; and J.W. Barker, "Late Byzantine Thessalonike: A Second City's Challenges and Responses," DOP 57 (2003): 5–34.

[105] Leo's attribution of motive should be contrasted with Skyl. 272.83–87, who reports that Nikephoros could have taken Antioch at the time, but feared to do so because of a prophecy that when Antioch was taken the emperor would die.

[106] See Plato, Republic 416a; K. Krumbacher, Mittelgriechische Sprichwörter (Munich, 1893), 125, no. 88.

[107] The hill has been identified as Baghras, about 26 km north of Antioch. See Yahya of Antioch, Histoire, 816–17 [118–19]. See also Schlumberger, Phocas, 708; Canard, H'amdanides, 831–32; and W. Saunders, "Qal'at Seman: A Frontier Fort of the Tenth and Eleventh Centuries," in Armies and Frontiers in Roman and Byzantine Anatolia, ed. S. Mitchell (Oxford, 1983), 291–303, esp. 294–95.

[108] C. Holmes argues that Byzantium may have followed a policy of controlling "the eastern frontier through tribute-raising arrangements with local populations": see "'How

Book IV

This was the emperor's speech; then he put a rock on his shoulder[109] (for he was of humble nature and did not disdain to do such things), and climbed up the hill, ordering all the army to do the same. Thus one could see built on the hill in three days a town that was well-walled and very secure. He left behind in the fortress a unit of five hundred cavalry and a cohort of a thousand infantry,[110] furnishing them with sufficient provisions, with orders to attack Antioch every day, and to put to the sword or plunder anything that came their way. He himself departed from there to return to the imperial city, where he stayed after being welcomed magnificently by the citizens.[111]

---

the East was Won' in the Reign of Basil II," in *Eastern Approaches to Byzantium*, ed. A. Eastmond (Aldershot, 2001), 41–56, at 48.

[109] See the vita of St. Nikon (D. Sullivan, *The Life of Saint Nikon* [Brookline, 1987], chap. 35.24–25) where the saint puts three stones on his shoulders and carries them to the site of the proposed new church of Christ, the Theotokos, and the martyr Kyriake, as an impetus to the citizens of Sparta to supply construction materials.

[110] McGeer, *Warfare* 203, n. 14, suggests that Leo's thousand-strong "cohort" is to be equated with the contemporary taxiarchy, while the five-hundred-man cavalry "phalanx" conforms exactly with the strength of a regular cavalry division (παράταξις) in the *Praecepta militaria*.

[111] Nikephoros must have returned to Constantinople early in 969 since he was still in Syria at the time of the eclipse of 22 December 968.

Book V

[anno 969]

THE EMPEROR NIKEPHOROS RAIDED SYRIA AND ITS COASTLINE in this way, as I have already related,[1] driving off all opposition, plundering with impunity,[2] and capturing a great many towns; then, after constructing in three days and garrisoning a secure fortress in the most advantageous location[3] in the vicinity of great Antioch, he returned to Byzantium. Thence he dispatched messengers to the ruler of the Carthaginians,[4] [p. 76] sending him as a gift the sword of the most accursed and impious Muhammad,[5] which he had taken as plunder

---

[1] For the campaign of 968–69 to which Leo refers, see Book IV, chaps. 10–11.

[2] Lit. "collecting Mysian plunder," a proverb going back to the Homeric age, when Telephus was king of Mysia (Bulgaria); cf. CPG 1:122, 2:38, 538, and esp. 762–63.

[3] I.e., at Baghras; see Book IV, chap. 11 and n. 107.

[4] I.e., the Fatimid ruler al-Mu'izz, previously mentioned in Book IV, chap. 8 (Leo diac. 67.16) and there called "ruler of the Africans." Leo uses the term "Carthaginians" for the Arabs of North Africa and Egypt for the first time in this passage; for subsequent usages see Leo diac. 76.11 and 103.3 (Book V, chap. 1 and Book VI, chap. 8). Theoph. Cont. (288.16, 289.5, 296.11, 304.22, 309.11) also uses "Carthaginians" for the Arabs of North Africa, in this case the Aghlabids. The Fatimids, based in Tunisia since 909, began their conquest of Egypt in 969, and posed as the successors to the Hamdanids as the defenders of Islam.

[5] It may be assumed that the sword of Muhammad mentioned here was the famous sword the Prophet wielded on the battlefield of Badr (624). It was called Dhu'l-fakar (the Cleaver of Vertebrae). The sword was closely associated with Ali, the Prophet's son-in-law. Since Ali was the patron of the Hamdanids, it seems that the offer of the sword of Muhammad to the Fatimids was a serious political mistake on the part of Nikephoros. The reason is that the Fatimids, once established in Cairo, tried to promote their influence among the Muslim populations in Palestine and Syria. If this were the real sword of the Prophet, then Nikephoros might have offered his enemies a major symbolic weapon against him in the contest for the lands of Syria and Palestine. This may also be the reason why no other Byzantine source for Nikephoros's reign mentions this detail. Dhu'l-fakar is purported to be one of the Muslim relics preserved at the Topkapi palace in Istanbul. See EI² 2:233.

Prof. Irfan Shahîd (personal communication) has informed us that a variant of this tale is found in the 13th-c. historian Ibn al-Athīr (Al-Kamīl [Beirut, 1966], 8:557), who recounts that during a Fatimid battle in Sicily against the Byzantines an Indian sword was captured from the Greeks, and sent to Al-Mu'izz together with the prisoners of war. Al-Athīr states, however, that this was a sword "often used in battles within sight of the Prophet Muhammad," not the Prophet's own sword.

from one of the fortresses he had captured in Palestine;[6] and he demanded [the release of] the *patrikios* Niketas,[7] who had previously been taken prisoner at the time of the Roman defeat in Sicily and had been sent to this ruler of the Africans, as my narrative has related.[8] In the accompanying letter he warned him that, if he hesitated over the return of the *patrikios* and did not immediately release from imprisonment and send this man to him, he should expect a relentless[9] war and the destruction of all his territory by ravaging Roman troops.

The Carthaginian, frightened by these messages, as if by the proverbial Scythian saying,[10] sent as a gift to the emperor Nikephoros the *patrikios* Niketas, as well as the prisoners who had been captured with him and all the Roman captives from different areas whom he was detaining in prison. For he was gripped with fear, when he heard about [the threat of] a land and sea campaign by this man.[11] For all the peoples feared and marveled at Nikephoros's invincibility, the way he could not be withstood or attacked in battle, and how quickly and easily he subdued every foe, as if with the aid of some divine influence,[12] and they were eager to have him, not as an enemy, but as a friend and master. Thus the *patrikios* Niketas and the other Roman captives were rescued from prison and their chains, and returned to Byzantium. The emperor Nikephoros was delighted, [p. 77] as was fitting, and held a day of celebration to render prayers of thanksgiving to God for His deliverance of his fellow countrymen.

---

[6] On Leo the Deacon's definition of Palestine, see Book IV, n. 86.

[7] On Niketas, see Book IV, n. 64.

[8] See above, Book IV, chap. 8.

[9] Lit. "unheralded," ἀκήρυκτον. On this expression, see Book II, n. 55.

[10] On the meaning of the expression "Scythian saying," see Book III, n. 45.

[11] The implication is that although al-Muʿizz had recently won a victory over the Byzantines in Sicily, he had great respect for the military prowess of Nikephoros Phokas, and feared a different outcome from this expedition led by the emperor himself. Cf. the assessment of Yahya of Antioch, *Histoire*, 825–26: "No one doubted that Nikephoros would conquer the whole of Syria. . . . He went where he wished and devastated as he pleased without one of the Muslims or anyone else to turn him back or block his way," trans. J. Forsyth, "The Byzantine Arab Chronicle (938–1034) of Yahya b. Saʾid al-Antaki" (Ph.D. diss., Univ. of Michigan, 1977), 334–35 with n. 66, who also cites M. Siuziumov, "Ob Istochnikakh Leva D'iakona i Skilitsii," *Vizantiiskoe Obozrenie* 2 (1916): 123 on the possibility that Yahya and Leo the Deacon may have shared a common pro-Phocan source.

[12] Cf. Leo diac. 18.16–17, where the same phrase is used of his brother, Leo Phokas.

Book V

While the emperor was accomplishing these things in Syria and Byzantium, the *patrikios* Kalokyres,[13] who had been sent to the Tauroscythians by imperial command, arrived in Scythia and developed friendly relations with the ruler of the Taurians.[14] By seducing him with gifts and enticing him with tempting words (since all the Scythians are exceptionally greedy and particularly gluttonous, they are susceptible to the promising and taking of bribes), he persuaded him to muster a powerful army and march against the Mysians;[15] and once he had defeated them, to reduce their land, and keep it for his own dwelling-place, and then to help him attack the Romans, so that he might become emperor and attain the Roman imperial power. He promised to pay him vast and indescribable sums of money, which he would take out of the imperial treasury.

2. After hearing these words Sphendosthlavos[16] (for this was what the Taurians called him) could not restrain himself, but was buoyed up with hopes of wealth, and dreamed of possessing the land of the Mysians. Since in any case he was hot-headed and bold, and a brave and active man, he urged all the Taurians, from youths upwards, to join the campaign.

After thus assembling an army of sixty thousand men in their prime, not counting the service unit, he set off against the Mysians together with

---

[13] On Kalokyres and his embassy to Rus', probably to be dated to 966 or 967, see Book IV, n. 44. Kalokyres' embassy must have lasted a long time, since Leo makes the embassy contemporaneous with the Syrian campaign of 968–69. W. Hanak suggests, following G. Vernadsky (*Kievan Russia* [New Haven, 1966], 45), that this meeting took place in the northern Crimea rather than in Kiev: see Hanak, "The Infamous Svjatoslav," 141 n. 9.

[14] On Tauroscythians (also Taurians) as a term for the Rus', see Book IV, n. 45. The ruler of Kiev at this time was Sviatoslav, on whom see n. 16 below.

[15] The Bulgarians.

[16] Sviatoslav, ruler of Kiev, from ca. 945. A major figure in early Russian history, with ambitions of empire, he appears prominently in Leo's subsequent narrative, particularly in Book VI, chap. 10 in negotiations with Tzimiskes (he tells Tzimiskes' envoys that the Byzantines "should quickly withdraw from Europe, which did not belong to them, and move to Asia") and Book IX, chap. 7–12, when Tzimiskes defeats him in the siege of Dorystolon. Leo's detailed physical description of Sviatoslav at Book IX, chap. 11—Leo's only other such descriptions are of the emperors Phokas and Tzimiskes—is particularly striking. His campaign against Bulgaria was launched in 967, according to Stokes, "Balkan Campaigns of Svyatoslav," 52, 57, and D. Obolensky, "The Empire and its Northern Neighbors, 565–1018," in *Cambridge Medieval History*, vol. 4 (Cambridge, 1966), chap. 11, 513 n. 3; but see also Stephenson (*Balkan Frontier*, 48), who dates it to 968, as does Kazhdan, following Karyshkovskii. He died at the Dnieper rapids in the early spring of 972. See *ODB* 3:1979, and Hanak, "The Infamous Svjatoslav."

the *patrikios* Kalokyres, [p. 78] whom he also took as a brother by the bonds of friendship.[17] While he was sailing along the Istros and was hastening toward a landing-place on the shore, the Mysians perceived what was going on, and, after organizing themselves into an army composed of thirty thousand men, they went out to meet them. But the Taurians disembarked from their transport ships, and, after vigorously presenting their shields and drawing their swords, they cut down the Mysians on all sides. Since the latter were unable to withstand the first wave of assault, they turned to flight, and ignominiously shut themselves up in Dorystolon (this was a strong Mysian fortress).[18] It is said that then Peter, the Mysian ruler,[19] a pious and respected man, in his extreme distress at the unexpected rout, suffered an attack of epilepsy, and departed this world,[20] after lingering a short while. But these things occurred later in Mysia.

Meanwhile, when the Roman emperor Nikephoros learned about the situation with the Taurians, since he was always careful and vigilant throughout his entire life, and was never drowsy, nor did he become enslaved by certain pleasures (for no one could say that he had seen him indulging in revelry even during his youth), he then seemed to be everywhere at once. He began to equip the infantry, to arm the companies, to draw up the cavalry regiment in depth, and to display the ironclad horsemen. In addition, he had artillery engines made and set them up on the walls of the city. He also secured to the tower that is usually called Kentenarion[21] a very heavy chain made of iron, [p. 79] attached it to enormous logs, stretched it next to the Bosporos,[22] and fastened it to

---

[17] Hanak ("The Infamous Svjatoslav," 141 n. 10) comments that 60,000 men must be an inflated figure. As for "the bonds of friendship," a ritual brotherhood relationship between a Rus' and a Greek was highly unusual: see Siuziumov et al., *Lev D'iakon*, 189 n. 11. On Byzantine traditions of ritual brotherhood see *ODB* 1:19–20, and C. Rapp, "Ritual Brotherhood in Byzantium," *Traditio* 52 (1997): 285–326.

[18] Dorystolon or Dorostolon (ancient Durostorum, medieval Slavic Dristra, present-day Silistra) was a city and military stronghold on the south bank of the river Danube in modern Bulgaria: see *ODB* 1:653.

[19] On Peter, tsar of Bulgaria (927–69), see *ODB* 3:1639.

[20] 30 January 969.

[21] This tower was situated on the south side of the entrance to the Golden Horn in τὰ Εὐγενίου; see Berger, *Untersuchungen*, 676 and 743.

[22] Most scholars (e.g., R. Guilland, "La chaîne de la Corne d'Or," *EEBS* 25 [1955]: 88–120, at 90, and additional bibliography in n. 23 below) have assumed that, since the Kastellion tower is in Galata, Leo is here referring to a chain stretching across the entrance

a tower of the Kastellion on the other side.[23] Since he was more effective and wiser than anyone we know of, he did not think it expedient to war against both peoples. Therefore he decided it would be a good idea to win over one of the peoples, for thus he thought he could prevail over the other very easily and subdue it in a shorter time.

3. Hence, since he despaired of negotiating with the Taurian[24] (for he knew that, once the *patrikios* Kalokyres had swerved from the straight [path],[25] rebelled against his authority, and acquired great influence with Sphendosthlavos, he would not readily yield to his will), he determined to send an embassy instead to the Mysians, who were of the same religion. So he sent to them as envoys the *patrikios* Nikephoros, whose surname was Erotikos,[26] and Philotheos, who presided over [the see of]

---

to the Golden Horn. Guilland's article includes a review of all instances when such a chain was used. For maps showing the placement of the chain, see map 2, Müller-Wiener, *Bildlexikon*, 25 and 27, and H. Magoulias, *O City of Byzantium: Annals of Niketas Choniates* (Detroit, 1984), 419.

In a recent article, however, Berger and Bardill argue that the chain was fastened across the Bosporos to the so-called Kızkulesi near the Asiatic shore: A. Berger and J. Bardill, "The Representations of Constantinople in Hartmann Schedel's *World Chronicle*, and Related Pictures," *BMGS* 22 (1998): 5–6. However, this chain across the Bosporos was first deployed by the emperor Manuel I Komnenos (1143–80), who had the two towers that held the second chain built; see *Nicetae Choniatae Historia*, ed. J. von Dieten (Berlin, 1975), 1: 205–6.

[23] On the tower of the Kastellion, the principal fortress of Galata, see Berger, *Untersuchungen*, 689–91 (but see also n. 22 above for his revised opinion); Müller-Wiener, *Bildlexikon*, 320ff; and Janin, *CP byz.*, 460–61, s.v. "Kastellion." Niketas Choniates (ed. J. van Dieten, *Nicetae Choniatae Historia* [Berlin, 1975], 1:542.77–78) calls it a fortress (φρούριον) ἐν ᾧ εἴθισται Ῥωμαίοις σιδηρᾶν ἀποδέειν βαρυτάλαντον ἄλυσιν, ἡνίκα πλοίων πολεμίων ἐνσταίη τις ἔφοδος.

[24] Reading παρὰ τὸν Ταῦρον for παρὰ τῶν Ταύρων; cf. p. 75.6–7, παρὰ τὸν τῶν Καρχηδονίων ἀγὸν διεκηρυκεύετο.

[25] At the suggestion of Matina McGrath we have supplied ὁδοῦ after εὐθείας, following the parallel of Symeon the New Theologian, *Oration* 7.95, ed. B. Krivochéine and trans. J. Paramelle, *Catéchèses* (Paris, 1964), 2:54.

[26] Nikephoros Erotikos is probably to be identified with the *patrikios* of the same name who held the chair of geometry at the "University of Constantinople": see Guilland, *Institutions*, 2:185, and *Theoph. Cont.* 446.12–14. He was the son-in-law of Theophilos Erotikos, eparch under Constantine VII.

Nikephoros Erotikos is not mentioned by Skylitzes in his account of the embassy. Elsewhere (323.5, 10, 15, 26) he does refer to another member of the family, Manuel Erotikos, a general of Basil II who fought against the rebel Bardas Skleros ca. 978.

Euchaita,[27] to remind them of their common religion (for the Mysians undeniably profess the Christian faith), and to ask for maidens from the royal family, that he might marry them to the sons of the emperor Romanos,[28] in order to confirm by marriage an unbreakable alliance and friendship between the Romans and Mysians. After a cordial reception of the embassy, the Mysians put maidens of royal blood [p. 80] on wagons (it is customary for Mysian women to ride on wagons),[29] and sent them to the emperor Nikephoros, imploring him to come to their defense as quickly as possible, to turn aside and render harmless the Taurian *axe that was pressing against their necks.*[30]

And he would have come to their defense, and would have won victories over the Taurians, as in the case of all[31] those against whom he turned the Roman forces; but human fortunes *are raised up by a small shift of the scale,*[32] and are as if suspended from a *slender thread,*[33] and are wont to turn also in the opposite direction. For some people rightly believe that *a certain divine wrath and human envy* attack *the most prominent* and valorous *men,* tripping them up, overthrowing them, and driving them to extinction.[34] This is the sort of fate that then befell the emperor Nikephoros, when his fortunes were prospering, more so than for any of those who ruled before him. And I will say this: that it is through the unfathomable forethought of the Almighty that mankind's prospering affairs change to the opposite, so that they may thus be taught that they

---

[27] On Euchaita and Philotheos, see Book III, n. 43. The embassy is variously dated to 968 (Stokes, "Balkan Campaigns of Svyatoslav," 54) and 969 (Dölger, *Regesten,* no. 718). According to Darrouzès (*Epistoliers byzantins du Xe siècle* [Paris, 1960], 274), Philotheos is probably to be identified with Theophilos, metropolitan of Euchaita, sent by Tzimiskes on missions to the Bulgarians and Petchenegs in 971; see Dölger, *Regesten,* nos. 739–40. Skylitzes (310.49–50) also calls him Theophilos instead of Philotheos.

[28] On Basil (II) and Constantine (VIII), the sons of Romanos II, see above Book II, chap. 10 and n. 64.

[29] See Herodotus 4.114 and 121, where Scythian women are said to live in wagons.

[30] Parallels to this phrase can be found in Herodian and Constantine Porphyrogennetos; see Book III, chap. 1 and n. 11 (36.23–24), where Leo uses a similar expression.

[31] The Greek phrase, which reads ἐπεὶ καὶ κατὰ πάντων, without a verb, is an example of brachylogy.

[32] Dionysius of Halicarnassus, *Roman Antiquities* 8.52.1.

[33] See Lucian, *Ploion* 26 (ed. M. D. Macleod [Oxford, 1987]: 4.109.16–18).

[34] See, e.g., Dionysius of Halicarnassus, *Roman Antiquities* 8.52.1, and Herodotus 7.10, trans. A. D. Godley (Cambridge, Mass., 1922), esp. p. 319.

are mortal and ephemeral beings, and should not puff up more than is fitting. For already certain men, who have met with success and have distinguished themselves in battle, have not hesitated to declare themselves gods, insulting Providence itself. Examples of such men are the sons of Aloeus, Otos and Ephialtes, who, according to legend, tried to ascend into the heavens,[35] and Nebuchadnezzar the Babylonian, [p. 81] who set up an image of himself,[36] and Alexander the son of Philip, who demanded to be called the son of Ammon.[37] Thus it is understandable that men's fortunes are subject to changes and reverses. This is what then happened to the Romans, who soon lost their ruler, a man the likes of whom the Roman empire had not had before. For if their fortunes had not been reversed through his murder, then nothing would have prevented them, if he had lived, from establishing the boundaries of their territory where the sun rises in India, and again where it sets, at the very ends of the world. But my narrative must return to the point where it began to digress from its sequence.

4. And so the Mysians were spreading open their hands in supplication, entreating the emperor to come to their defense. While he was preparing for the campaign, word arrived of the capture of Antioch the Great,[38] which was taken in accordance with the instructions[39] that he had given to the soldiers whom he left behind to subject it to constant raids.[40] For it is said that, when the city had been reduced to great hardship and dire lack of provisions as a result of the daily attacks, the *patrikios* and *stratopedarches* Peter,[41] a eunuch, but still extremely active and robust,

---

[35] See Homer, *Odyssey* 11.308–16.

[36] See Dan. 3:1–18.

[37] See Arrian, *Anabasis of Alexander* 4.9.9, 7.8.3.

[38] Antioch fell to the Byzantines on 28 October 969.

[39] Leo seems to contradict himself here. Nikephoros's orders (see here and above, Book IV, chap. 11) were to reduce Antioch to submission by daily raids, not to enter by ladders. On a possible reason for Nikephoros's hesitance about the conquest of Antioch, see n. 42.

[40] Λεηλατεῖν normally has the meaning of "plunder" in Leo the Deacon, but it here it seems to mean "harry," "subject to constant raids." On this "strategy of attrition," making it impossible to work the lands and interdicting supplies, see J. Howard-Johnston, "Studies in the Organization of the Byzantine Army in the Tenth and Eleventh Centuries" (D.Phil. diss., University of Oxford, 1971), chap. 4 and esp. 244–49.

[41] Peter was made *stratopedarches* of Cilicia in 967, according to Oikonomides, *Listes*, 334; he reluctantly joined Michael Bourtzes (on whom see next footnote) in the conquest

who was raiding Syria, arrived there with his army, and sent the *taxiarches* Michael, whose surname was Bourtzes,[42] to reconnoiter the city. When he and other picked men drew near, they carefully observed where the wall might be scaled, [p. 82] hastened back to the camp, and constructed ladders of exactly the same height as the towers.[43] Then they loaded them on beasts of burden, and together with a troop[44] of very brave soldiers, when it was already the middle of the night, again reached the circuit wall of Antioch, quietly set the ladders against the wall, climbed up by means of them, and dispatched with their swords the Agarene guards, who were fast asleep. After the Romans gained control of the walls in this way, they descended from the towers and set fire to all four corners of the town. The inhabitants of Antioch, stupefied at the unexpected event, turned to wailing and lamentation, and were at a terrible loss, wondering what they should do. While they were deciding to resist bravely and robustly to withstand the enemy in close combat, as the eastern sky began to dawn brightly, the *stratopedarches* Peter beat them to the attack, and with his army entered the city through the gates that

---

of Antioch. After Tzimiskes seized the throne, he sent Peter on the expedition against the Rus' in 970 (Book VI, chap. 11). Peter was killed in 976 at the battle of Lapara, while fighting against the rebel Bardas Skleros (Book X, chap. 7). On him see also McGrath, "Aristocracy," 212–13; Guilland, *Institutions*, 1:172–73, 392, 499; Kühn, *Armee*, 265; and Ringrose, *The Perfect Servant*, 133, 137–38.

On the high military position of *stratopedarches*, created by Nikephoros Phokas to allow Peter, a eunuch, to serve as a commander (the rank of *domestikos* was not open to eunuchs), see Cheynet, "Les Phocas," 306, and *ODB* 3:1966–67.

[42] Michael Bourtzes, who was soon to join the murderous conspiracy against Nikephoros II, was *patrikios* and *strategos* of the Black Mountain in 969 (Skyl. 271.76–77). According to Skylitzes, Bourtzes and Peter the *stratopedarches* captured Antioch against Nikephoros's orders, for there was a popular belief that the emperor who conquered Antioch would soon die. Thus Bourtzes was demoted and placed under house arrest; this punishment no doubt explains his resentment of the emperor and willingness to participate in his murder: see Skyl. 272–273; McGrath, "Aristocracy," 115–16 and n. 103; Guilland, *Institutions* 1:172–73, 499, 539; Kühn, *Armee*, 171–72, 275–76; J.-C. Cheynet, and J. F. Vannier, *Études prosopographiques* (Paris, 1986), 18–24.

In the 10th c. *taxiarches* (*-os*) came to mean the commander of a 1000-man unit composed of 500 heavy infantrymen, 300 archers, and 200 light infantrymen: see *ODB* 3:2018.

[43] For the careful measurement of various siege devices, see the treatise of "Heron of Byzantium" in Sullivan, *Siegecraft*, 115–51 and the citations at 236 n. 14.

[44] Lit. "legion," λεγεών.

were opened for him by the Romans who had already occupied the town. The Antiochenes, who were unable even to face such an army, threw down their arms and turned to supplication. The *stratopedarches* took them captive and extinguished the fire; then, after choosing the first spoils of the booty, he took complete possession of the city and strengthened the vulnerable sections of the walls.

5. Thus the celebrated and great Antioch was taken and plundered by the Romans. At the news of its capture, the emperor rejoiced and [p. 83] offered thanks to the Almighty. It so happened that the service of commemoration of the Archangels fell at that time,[45] during which a certain hermit monk is said to have given a letter to the emperor and to have immediately departed; he unrolled it and read its contents. The text was as follows: "O emperor, it has been revealed by Providence to me, who *am but a worm*,[46] that you will depart from this world in the third month after the September that has now elapsed." The emperor made many inquiries, but did not find the monk. Then he lapsed into dejection and melancholy, and from that time was not at all willing to sleep in a bed, but used to spread on the floor a leopardskin[47] and a scarlet felt cloth, on which he would sleep, covering his body above with a cloak that belonged to his uncle, the monk Michael, whose surname was Maleinos.[48] It had been his custom to sleep on these whenever one of the feast days of the Lord came round and he wanted to partake of the immaculate sacrament of Christ.

During these days it happened that the caesar Bardas, the father of the emperor Nikephoros, departed this life, after living more than ninety years,[49] after growing old in the military ranks [where he had served] since his youth, and after crowning himself with many triumphs and victories through his heroic feats in war.[50] The emperor mourned him

[45] The feast of the Archangels, 8 November (969).

[46] See Ps. 21 (22):6.

[47] Skylitzes (280.10) calls it a bearskin.

[48] On the saintly Michael Maleinos and his monastery on Mt. Kyminas, see *ODB* 2:1276–77, and A. E. Laiou, "The General and the Saint: Michael Maleinos and Nikephoros Phokas," in *EYΨYXIA. Mélanges offerts à Hélène Ahrweiler* (Paris, 1998), 2:399–412.

[49] On Bardas Phokas, see Book III, n. 53. At his death in the fall of 969 he may well have been more than ninety years of age. The previous year Liudprand of Cremona noted that he looked one hundred and fifty years old: see Liudprand, *Relatio*, chap. 28, 190.2–4.

[50] Although the caesar Bardas Phokas may have won some victories over the Muslims, his forces were severely defeated in 953, 954, and 955, and he was forced to resign: see Dennis, *Treatises*, 139.

after his death in the proper manner, and escorted his body from the palace as far as his home (which was located on the south side of the town, next to the steep part of the street that leads to the sea, [p. 84] where the harbor of Sophia spreads out),[51] and laid it in its coffin.

A few days later, when the emperor's mourning for his father had abated, the augusta Theophano seized an opportunity to approach him in private. She spoke very persuasively, petitioning without pause on behalf of the *magistros* John, whose sobriquet was Tzimiskes; she entreated and implored, and put forward a presumably justifiable pretext, saying: "O emperor, since you manage everything with due proportion and balance, so that you yourself are an exact standard and most upright model of prudence, why do you overlook the fact that such a brave and vigorous man, who has distinguished himself in battles and is invincible, is *wallowing in the mire*[52] of pleasures and leading a dissipated and idle existence,[53] when he is bursting with strength and in the prime of life, and moreover is your majesty's nephew, possessed of a brilliant ancestral lineage?[54] If you agree, bid him leave immediately the place where he is staying and come to us, to be married to a wife of a noble family. For as you know, bitter and limb-relaxing death[55] has already mowed down his previous lawful wife.[56] Yield then, O emperor, be

---

[51] On the harbor of Sophia, on the southern shore of Constantinople, see Janin, *CP byz.*, 231–33; Berger, *Untersuchungen*, 570–78; and A. Cameron, "Notes on the Sophiae, the Sophianae and the Harbour of Sophia," *Byzantion* 37 (1967): 11–20.

On the house of Bardas Phokas, see P. Magdalino, "The Maritime Neighborhoods of Constantinople: Commercial and Residential Functions, Sixth to Twelfth Centuries," *DOP* 54 (2000): 216–17.

[52] See 2 Pet. 2:22.

[53] When last mentioned by Leo, in Book IV, chap. 3, the *doux* John was *domestikos* of the East, and appointed to lead the left wing in the battle against the Tarsians in 965. As we learn from Skylitzes (Skyl. 279.89–91), sometime thereafter Nikephoros II, suspicious of his loyalty, had removed him from his military command and placed him under house arrest. During the assassination (at Leo diac. 88.13–15, Book V, chap. 7), Leo describes Tzimiskes as bitterly reproaching Nikephoros for dismissing him from his military post and banishing him to the countryside, probably his country estates.

[54] Tzimiskes was a member of the Kourkouas family (on which see *ODB* 2:1156–57); his mother was the sister of emperor Nikephoros. For a family tree, see p. 224 and Cheynet, *Pouvoir*, 270; for a recent analysis of Tzimiskes' usurpation of the throne, see Morris, "Succession and Usurpation."

[55] Euripides, *Suppliants* 47.

[56] Maria Skleraina, sister of Bardas Skleros. She is also mentioned below in Book VI, chap. 11 (Leo diac. 107.14) and Book VII, chap. 3 (Leo diac. 117.3).

persuaded by one who is advising you on the proper course, and do not let a man of your family, who is praised by everyone for his brave deeds in war, be exposed to the ridicule and sarcasm of unbridled tongues."

6. After beseeching the emperor with these words, and, [p. 85] in all likelihood, beguiling him (for he granted her more favors than was fitting, since he was absolutely overwhelmed by her beauty), she persuaded him to summon John to come quickly to Byzantium. Upon his arrival at the imperial city, he presented himself before the emperor and, since he received instructions to visit the palace every day, he first went home, and subsequently did not fail to visit the imperial court frequently. Since he was hotheaded by nature, more daring[57] than anyone else, and most venturesome at attempting unusual endeavors, he found a way to slip in through certain secret passages, prepared by the augusta, in order to have conversations with her and plan the removal of the emperor Nikephoros from the palace. From then onwards he kept sending her[58] at intervals strong men, who were vigorous warriors, whom she received and kept near her in a secret room. When their conspiracy, having conceived a wicked deed, had labored to bring forth terrible wrongdoing, and was eager *to give birth to the* wicked *crime,*[59] they met again in their customary way, and decided to remove the emperor Nikephoros by force from his rulership. Then John went home, summoned Michael Bourtzes[60] and Leo Pediasimos,[61] and behind closed doors began to plot with them the murder of the emperor Nikephoros. It was then the tenth day of the month of December.

It is said [p. 86] that during the evening, about the time of the vesper hymns,[62] a certain priest of the imperial court handed the emperor a note, on which this was written: "Let it be known to you, O emperor, that a terrible death is being prepared[63] for you tonight. Because this is true, order a search of the women's quarters, where armed men will be

---

[57] Reading τολμητίας with Panagiotakes for τολμήσας.

[58] Reading αὐτὴν for αὐτὸν as suggested by Hase and adopted by Panagiotakes.

[59] See Ps. 7:14.

[60] On Bourtzes, see n. 42 above.

[61] Cheynet (*Pouvoir*, 23 n. 4 and 328) conjectures that Pediasimos was a military officer who had worked under Tzimiskes. He is the first individual recorded with this family name: see *ODB* 3:1615. Pediasimos is not specifically named in Skylitzes' list of the conspirators (Skyl. 279.4–5), but is apparently one of the ἕτεροι δύο mentioned there.

[62] On the vespers, celebrated at sundown, see *ODB* 3:2161–62.

[63] Ἐπικαττύεται, lit. "stitched" or "cobbled together," a quite rare verb.

apprehended who are planning to carry out your murder." After the emperor read the note, he ordered the chamberlain Michael[64] to make a careful search for the men. But either out of respect for the augusta, or because he procrastinated, or was led astray by divine madness, he left unsearched the room in which the band of murderers[65] was sitting. As night had already fallen, the empress, as was her custom, went in to the emperor, and spoke of the maidens who had recently arrived from Mysia, saying, "I am leaving to give some instructions[66] about their care, and then I will come back to you. But leave the bedchamber open and don't lock it now; for I will lock it when I come back." With these words she left. During a whole watch of the night the emperor made his usual prayers to God and devoted himself to study of the Holy Scriptures. When the need for sleep came upon him, he lay down on the floor, upon the leopardskin and scarlet felt cloth, before the holy icons of the theandric image of Christ and of the Mother of God and of the Holy Forerunner and Herald.[67] [p. 87]

7. Meanwhile John's retainers, who had been admitted by the augusta, had emerged from the room, armed with swords, and were awaiting his arrival, watching closely from the terrace of the upper rooms of the palace. The clock was just indicating the fifth hour of the night,[68] a fierce north wind filled the air, and snow was falling heavily. Then John arrived with his fellow conspirators, sailing along the shore in a light boat and disembarking on land where the stone lion is seizing the bull (traditionally

---

[64] The Greek phrase is τῷ τοῦ κοιτῶνος κατάρχοντι, literally, "the one in charge of the bedchamber," which should be equivalent to chamberlain, the *parakoimomenos*. Apparently Leo is referring to Michael, the former *protovestiarios*, promoted to chamberlain (to whom the *protovestiarios* was subordinate) and brother of the *droungarios* Niketas; see above, Book IV, n. 64, and Guilland, *Institutions*, 1:172, 184, 220 and esp. 362. Skylitzes (Skyl. 281.36) says he gave the order to the *protovestiarios*.

[65] Reading φονώντων for φόνων τῶν, as suggested by Panagiotakes.

[66] Reading ἐπισκήψουσα for ἐπισκήψασα, as suggested by Panagiotakes.

[67] Note that this assemblage of three icons forms a Deesis scene, on which see *ODB* 1:599–600.

[68] The Greek term translated as "clock" is γνώμων, literally "indicator," used specifically of the pointer on a sundial. In this case it must refer to a waterclock, on which see *ODB* 2:947, s.v. Horologion. For a parallel to Leo's usage see Athenaeus, *Deipnosophists* 2.42b (G. Kaibel, ed., *Athenaei Naucratitae deipnosophistarum libri xv*, 3 vols. [Leipzig: 1887, 1890; repr. Stuttgart, 1965–66]): ἐν τοῖς γνώμοσι ῥέον <ὕδωρ> οὐκ ἀναδίδωσι τὰς ὥρας ἐν τῷ χειμῶνι, apparently the only other such usage. The fifth hour of the night was about 11:00 P.M.

the place is called Boukoleon);[69] whistling to his retainers, who were leaning out from the terrace above, he was recognized; for this was the signal he had given to the murderers. They let down from above a basket attached to ropes, and hauled up first all the conspirators one at a time, and then John himself. After thus ascending without being detected, they entered the imperial bedchamber with swords drawn. When they reached the bed and found it empty with no one sleeping in it, they were petrified with terror and tried to hurl themselves into the sea [from the terrace]. But a dastardly[70] fellow[71] from [the staff of] the women's quarters led them and pointed out the sleeping emperor; they surrounded him and leapt at him and kicked him with their feet.

When Nikephoros was awakened and propped his head on his elbow, Leo, called Balantes,[72] struck him violently with his sword. And the emperor, in severe pain [p. 88] from the wound ([for] the sword struck his brow and eyelid, *crushing the bone*,[73] but not injuring the brain), cried out in a very loud voice, "Help me, O Mother of God!";[74] and he was covered all over with blood and stained with red. John, sitting on the imperial bed, ordered [them] to drag the emperor over to him. When he was dragged over, prostrate and collapsing on the floor (for he was not even able to rise to his knees, since his gigantic strength had been sapped by the blow of the sword), [John] questioned him in a threatening manner, saying, "Tell me, you most ungrateful and malicious tyrant, wasn't it through me that you attained the Roman rule and received such power? Why then did you disregard such a good turn, and, driven by envy and evil frenzy, did not hesitate to remove me, your benefactor, from the

---

[69] The Boukoleon palace had its own small port on the Sea of Marmara. It took its name from a statue of a lion attacking a bull that survived until the earthquake of 1532: see Janin, *CP byz.*, 101; R. Guilland, "Le palais du Boukoléon. L'assassinat de Nicéphore II Phokas," *BSl* 13 (1952/53): 101–36; Berger, *Untersuchungen*, 258–60; and Mango, "The Palace of the Boukoleon."

[70] Reading ἰταμόν with Panagiotakes instead of the ἰταμῶν of the Hase ed.

[71] Ἀνδράριον, literally "little man"; elsewhere in Leo (7.4, 39.4) the word is always used of a eunuch, and surely that is the implication here. See Ringrose, *The Perfect Servant*, 35–39.

[72] In Skylitzes (Skyl. 279.4, 280.17, 285.30) his name is twice rendered Abalantes and he is called a *taxiarch*. The Balantai were an aristocratic family from Asia Minor: see Cheynet, "Les Phocas," 309, and idem, *Pouvoir*, 328.

[73] See Homer, *Iliad* 16.324.

[74] On the prayer, cf. Theoph. 1:442.30–31: καὶ εἴ πού τις συμπίπτων ἢ ἀλγῶν τὴν συνήθη Χριστιανοῖς ἀφῆκε φωνήν, τὸ θεοτόκε βοήθει. . . .

command of the troops? Instead you dismissed me to waste my time in the countryside with peasants, *like some alien without any rights,*[75] even though I am more brave and vigorous than you; the armies of the enemy fear me, and there is no one now who can save you from my hands. Speak then, if you have any grounds of defense remaining against these charges."

8. The emperor, who was already growing faint and did not have anyone to defend him, kept calling on the Mother of God for assistance. But John grabbed hold of his beard and pulled it mercilessly, while his fellow conspirators cruelly and inhumanly smashed his jaws with their sword handles [p. 89] so as to shake loose his teeth and knock them out of the jawbone. When they had their fill of tormenting him, John kicked him in the chest, raised up his sword, and drove it right through the middle of his brain, ordering the others to strike the man, too. They slashed at him mercilessly, and one of them hit him in the back with an *akouphion*[76] and thrust it right through to the breast. This is a long iron weapon that very much resembles a heron's beak. But it differs from the beak in its shape, inasmuch as nature bestowed a straight beak on the bird, whereas the *akouphion* gradually extends in a moderate curve, ending in a rather sharp point.

Such was the end of the life of the emperor Nikephoros, who lived fifty-seven years, but held the imperial power for only six years and four months.[77] He was a man who unquestionably surpassed every man of his generation in courage and physical strength, and was very experienced and energetic in warfare; unyielding in every kind of undertaking, not softened or spoiled by physical pleasures, a man of magnanimity and of genius in affairs of state, a most upright judge and steadfast legislator, inferior to none of those who spend all their lives on these matters; he was strict and unbending in his prayers and all-night standing vigils[78] to God, and kept his mind undistracted during the singing of hymns,

---

[75] See Homer, *Iliad* 9.648 and 16.58–59, where the angry Achilles indicates his view of how Agamemnon had treated him.

[76] According to Trapp, *LBG*, s.v. (no doubt following Kolias, *Waffen*, 172) the *akouphion* is a *Hakenhammer*, a hooked hammer. M. Parani, on the other hand, has suggested that it may have been a curved saber: see Parani, *Reconstructing the Reality of Images*, 131–32.

[77] Leo is evidently calculating the length of Nikephoros's reign from August 963, when he entered Constantinople (after being proclaimed emperor by his troops in Cappadocia the previous month), until December 969.

[78] A common ascetic practice; see *ODB* 1:203, s.v. "Asceticism."

Book V

never letting it wander off to worldly thoughts. Most people considered it a weakness in the man that he wanted everyone to preserve virtue uncompromised, [p. 90] and not to debase the scrupulousness of justice. Therefore he was relentless in the pursuit of these [goals], and seemed implacable and harsh to wrongdoers, and annoying to those who wanted to lead an unprincipled life. But I say that, if some malicious fortune had not begrudged his prospering affairs and suddenly snatched away this man's life, the Roman empire would have obtained greater glory than ever before. But Providence, which abhors *harsh and overweening spirits* in men, curtails and checks them and reduces[79] them *to nothing*,[80] with its incomprehensible decisions steering the transport ship of life on an expedient course.

9. After John had accomplished this unholy and abominable deed, loathsome to God, he went to the splendid hall of the imperial palace (they call the structure the Chrysotriklinos),[81] put the scarlet boots on his feet, sat on the imperial throne, and began to devote his attention to affairs of state, so that he might gain control of them and so that none of the emperor's relatives would rebel against him. When Nikephoros's bodyguards heard, too late, about his murder, they rushed to defend him, in the belief that the man was still among the living, and they tried to force open the iron gates with all their strength. But John ordered that Nikephoros's head be brought in and [p. 91] shown to his bodyguards through a window. A man named Atzypotheodoros[82] came and cut off the head and showed it to the turbulent group of men. When they saw the monstrous and unbelievable sight, they let their swords fall from their hands, *changed their tune*,[83] and with one voice proclaimed John as

[79] Lit. "propels."

[80] For a similar sentiment, see Dionysius of Halicarnassus, *Roman Antiquities* 8.25.3, and Herodotus 7.10, as cited above in n. 34. See Introduction, 18–19.

[81] On the Chrysotriklinos (lit. "golden hall"), a reception chamber in the imperial palace, see *ODB* 1:455–56 and Janin, *CP byz.*, 115–17.

[82] Skylitzes (279.5) describes Atzypotheodoros as one of Tzimiskes' most loyal followers. When the patriarch Polyeuktos imposed a penance on Tzimiskes for the murder of Nikephoros II, Tzimiskes asserted that not he, but Atzypotheodoros and Balantes had struck the fatal blow (Skyl. 285.21–34). As a consequence Atzypotheodoros was sent into exile. According to an interpolation in one manuscript of Skylitzes (see 336.95), Atzypotheodoros was executed at Abydos, probably in 989 at the time of the defeat and death of the rebel Bardas Phokas. The sobriquet *atzypo-* seems to derive from ἀτζυπάς, a variant form of ἀτζουπάς, a bodyguard; see Trapp, *LBG*, s.v. ἀτζυπάδες.

[83] See *CPG* 2:210, 766.

emperor of the Romans. Nikephoros's body lay outside in the snow all day long (it was Saturday, the eleventh of December), until late in the evening John ordered that it be carried off for the funeral service. After placing it in a hastily improvised wooden coffin, in the middle of the night they carried it secretly to the holy church of the Apostles, and buried it in one of the imperial sarcophagi in the *heroon*,[84] where the body of the holy and celebrated Constantine[85] is laid to rest.

Justice, however, did not nod at the murderous act of those wretched men, but later pursued all of them with vengeance; everyone who was personally involved in his murder had his property confiscated, was reduced to the direst poverty, and departed this life in miserable circumstances.[86]

But I think I have said enough about the deeds of the emperor Nikephoros and about his life and death; for I believe that to spend excessive time on a narrative and to stretch it out at length is characteristic of excessively detailed and verbose writers, those who do not leave even a chance occurrence unexamined. Therefore I think I should bring to an end this account of him [p. 92] and his deeds, and relate to the best of my ability the subsequent accomplishments of John, whose sobriquet was Tzimiskes (this is a name in the Armenian dialect, which translated into Greek means "mouzakitzes";[87] he received this name because he was

[84] Adjacent to the church of the Holy Apostles were two imperial mausolea, which served as the burial place of emperors until 1028: see *ODB* 2:940 and P. Grierson, "The Tombs and Obits of the Byzantine Emperors (337–1042)," *DOP* 16 (1962): 3–63, esp. 29. According to a note preserved in several manuscripts of Skylitzes, Nikephoros's sarcophagus was later moved to the Peribleptos monastery. The epitaph on Nikephoros by John, metropolitan of Melitene, is also preserved in these manuscripts; see Skyl. 282–83.

[85] Constantine I the Great.

[86] Leo's statement here is questionable since in fact most of the murderers did not come to a bad end. At least two of the conspirators are known from other sources to have been politically involved in later events, Michael Bourtzes as *doux* (990–95); see Morris, "Succession and Usurpation," 212.

[87] Loretto (*Phokas*, 178) comments that the Armenian (and Persian) term meant "slipper, shoe." The word μουζακίτζης, a hapax legomenon, is of uncertain meaning. Ducange lists the word μουζάκιον, meaning "shoe," of which μουζακίτζης might well be the diminutive, but s.v. Τζιμισκῆς, where he interprets the name as meaning "youth," evidently seeing a derivation from μοιρακίτζης (μειρακίτζης). According to Sophocles, *Lexicon*, s.v. μουζακίτζης, the word means "mannikin." See also Ph. Koukoules, "Περὶ τῆς ὑποκοριστικῆς καταλήξεως -ιτσιν," *Hellenika* 4 (1931): 363.

The link to Tzimiskes' apparent short stature (see also Leo diac. 59.11–13 and 178.17) is not clear and Leo may have misinterpreted the significance of the sobriquet. Cf. (with Loretto) "Caligula" ("Little Boot"), a nickname he was given as a child by his father's troops. The earliest reference to the sobriquet Τζιμισκῆς is apparently *Theoph. Cont.* 428.17.

extremely short in stature), so that deeds useful in life that deserve to be remembered *may not pass away into the depths of oblivion.*[88]

[88] See Gregory of Nazianzus, *Or.* 44.1 (PG 36:608). Note that a very similar expression is used in Book I, chap. 1 (4.8). This "ring formation" is yet another indication that the first five books of Leo's *History* form a separate unit.

Book VI
[annis 969–970]

AFTER THE EMPEROR NIKEPHOROS WAS MURDERED in the manner that I have recounted, John, whose sobriquet was Tzimiskes, took in his hands the reins of empire. The fourth watch of the night[1] was just beginning, and Saturday was dawning,[2] that eleventh day of the month of December, in the thirteenth indiction, of the year 6478,[3] when a corps of picked men passed through the streets of the town, [p. 94] proclaiming John as emperor of the Romans, together with the sons of the previous emperor Romanos.[4] They were followed at a distance by Basil, the bastard son of the emperor Romanos the elder[5] by a Scythian woman, who held the distinguished rank of *proedros*[6] (Nikephoros alone among other emperors[7] invented this rank to honor the man); although he happened to be a eunuch, he was still an exceptionally *energetic and shrewd* man,[8] able to adapt himself cleverly to the circumstances at times of crisis. Since he had conspired with John, and was extremely well disposed towards him, he first pretended to be ill,[9] then fell ill in reality and took to his bed. When he learned during the night of the murder of Nikephoros, he followed the aforementioned corps of men with a cohort

[1] The night was divided into four watches of three hours each: see *ODB* 2:952, s.v. "Hour." Thus the beginning of the fourth watch was in the early morning hours before dawn, ca. 3:00 A.M.

[2] Reading διαφανούσης for διαφανούσης as suggested by Hase.

[3] Saturday, 11 December 969.

[4] I.e., Basil [II] and Constantine [VIII], sons of Romanos II.

[5] Reading παλαιτάτου as in E. This was Romanos I Lekapenos (920–44). Basil was castrated as an infant; on him, see *ODB* 1:270; and above, Book III, n. 56.

[6] On the dignity of *proedros*, see Book III, n. 76. Skyl. 284.2–5 agrees that this title was first conferred by Nikephoros II. The term could also be used in an ecclesiastical context to mean bishop, as in Leo diac. 79.16.

[7] Lit. σεβαστοί or *augusti*.

[8] The phrase δραστήριος καὶ ἀγχίνους is also used of Nikephoros Phokas in Book I, chap. 5 (10.18–19), and of Hamdan at Book II, chap. 1 (17.8); also of the Persian Kabades by Prokopios, *Persian Wars* 1.6.19.6. See Ringrose, *The Perfect Servant*, 40.

[9] Basil, as *parakoimomenos*, may have feigned illness to avoid having to attend upon Phokas in his palace bedchamber on the night of his assassination; see Brokkaar, "Basil Lacapenus," 220–21.

of brave youths, and proclaimed John as august emperor of the Romans. Then he returned to the palace, to assist John with affairs of state, after receiving from him the title of *parakoimomenos*.[10] After taking counsel about what course would be expedient for them, they immediately sent commands and decrees through the whole town that it was forbidden for anyone to rebel or turn to looting; for anyone who attempted anything of the sort ran the risk of losing his head.[11] This proclamation thoroughly terrified the inhabitants of Byzantium, and no one dared stir up any trouble in defiance of the decree; usually, at the time of such changes, the idle and indigent members of the populace used to turn to looting property and destroying houses, and even sometimes [p. 95] to murdering their fellow citizens, as happened when Nikephoros was proclaimed emperor.[12] John's edict, however, anticipated[13] and checked this irresistible impulse of the common mob.

2. Meanwhile, with matters hanging in suspense, Leo the *kouropalates*,[14] Nikephoros's brother, was asleep at home. Since he possessed vast amounts of gold, at the news of his brother's murder he should have scattered it in the streets to win the favor of the citizens, and should have exhorted them to take vengeance on the usurpers (for if he had thought of this he would quickly have driven John from the palace[15] without any bloodshed, because the men entrusted with government positions had received them from Nikephoros, and because a combat-ready army of men under his command were in [the city of] Byzantium, all of whom would have joined him if he had desired and embarked on resistance and rebellion); but, startled out of his wits by the magnitude of the misfortune, he did not even think of this, but ran as fast as he could to reach the celebrated church of the Wisdom of God,[16] leaving his domestic affairs[17] to fortune and the course of events. In any case, before the sun spread its rays brightly over the earth, John appointed

---

[10] Actually Basil retained the title of *parakoimomenos* which he previously held (see Brokkaar, "Basil Lacapenus"). On the office of imperial chamberlain, see Book II, n. 68.

[11] On this decree of 11 December 969, see Dölger, *Regesten*, 1: no. 725.

[12] There is nothing further about such happenings in Leo, but see Skyl. 257–58.

[13] Reading προφθάσαν, as emended by Panagiotakes, for προφθάσας of Hase ed.

[14] On Leo Phokas, see Book II, n. 9.

[15] For the use of τὰ ἀρχεῖα to mean "palace," see Nicetas Choniates, *Historia*, ed. J. L. van Dieten (Berlin–New York, 1975), 12, 347, 384.

[16] I.e., Hagia Sophia.

[17] Reading τὰ τῆς ἑστίας with Panagiotakes (following E) instead of ταῦτα of Hase ed., emended from ταύτης ἐστί of P.

his own men to the most important government positions—*praitor*,[18] *droungarios* of the fleet,[19] and of the watch,[20] and the person whom they call "night prefect,"[21]—after dismissing Nikephoros's appointees. [p. 96] He sent the latter and Nikephoros's relatives to live on their estates. After giving assurances of physical safety to Leo the *kouropalates*, brother of the emperor Nikephoros, and to the *patrikios* Nikephoros,[22] son of this Leo, he exiled them to Methymna,[23] located on the island of Lesbos, and removed the governors[24] of all the districts and replaced them with his own men. At that time he also relieved of his command Bardas,[25] the son of Leo the *kouropalates*, who was a *patrikios* with the rank of *doux*[26] living within the boundaries

[18] On *praitor*, see Book IV, n. 56.

[19] The *droungarios* of the fleet was the commander of the navy, stationed in Constantinople: see *ODB* 1:663–64, and R. Guilland, "Le drongaire de la flotte, le Grand drongaire de la flotte, le Duc de la flotte, le Mégaduc," in *Institutions*, 1:535–62.

[20] The *droungarios* of the watch (*vigla*) was the commander of the tagma of the *vigla*, stationed in the capital: see Kühn, *Armee*, 104–6; *ODB* 1:663.

[21] On this position, see R. Guilland, "Études sur l'histoire administrative de l'Empire Byzantin—l'Éparque. II. Les éparques autres que l'éparque de la ville," *BSl* 42 (1981): 193.

[22] On Nikephoros Phokas, son of Leo the *kouropalates* and nephew of the emperor Nikephoros II, see Cheynet, "Les Phocas," 307.

[23] Methymna was the second city on Lesbos, after Mytilene: see *ODB* 2:1219, s.v. "Lesbos."

[24] Leo uses τοπάρχης, a general term indicating an independent ruler and, sometimes, a Byzantine provincial governor: see J.-C. Cheynet, "Toparque et topotèrètès à la fin du XIe siècle," *REB* 42 (1984): 215–24, and *ODB* 3:2095.

[25] Bardas Phokas, nephew of the emperor, was one of the two major figures (with Bardas Skleros) in the civil wars that followed the death of Nikephoros Phokas. He led a rebellion against John Tzimiskes in 970 and was defeated by Tzimiskes' designate, the general Bardas Skleros (described by Leo in Book VII, chaps. 1–6 and 8). When Skleros himself later rebelled against the emperors Basil II and Constantine VIII in 976–79, Bardas Phokas was recalled from exile, appointed *domestikos*, and defeated Skleros (described by Leo in Book X, chap. 7). Phokas himself led a rebellion against Basil and Constantine in 987–89 and died confronting them on the battlefield at Abydos on 13 April 989 (described by Leo in Book X, chap. 9). On Bardas Phokas's career see Cheynet, "Les Phocas," 307–8. For an analysis of the various sources see C. Holmes, "Basil II and the Government of Empire (976–1025)" (D.Phil. diss., University of Oxford, 1999), Chapter 3, "The Revolts of Bardas Skleros and Bardas Phokas: Historiographical Traditions."

[26] For δούξ used here to indicate the military commander of a large district (here Chaldia), a usage specific to the second half of the tenth century, see *ODB* 1:659. This is "the first mention of the position of *doux* in a frontier context"; see C. Holmes, "Basil II and the

of Chaldia,[27] and banished him to Amaseia.[28] After he thus gained sufficient security for himself and his government, and purged the state of
every suspicious element, he spent his time in the palace. He was in his
forty-fifth year when he assumed the imperial rule.[29]

3. His appearance was as follows:[30] he had a fair and healthy complexion, and blond hair that was thin at the forehead; his eyes were
manly and bright,[31] his nose narrow and well-proportioned; his upper
facial hair was red, falling into an oblong shape,[32] whereas his beard was
of moderate length and appropriate size, with no bare spots. He was
short in stature, even though he had a broad chest and back. His strength
was gigantic, and there was great dexterity and irresistible might in his
hands. He also had a heroic [spirit],[33] fearless and imperturbable, [p. 97]
which displayed supernatural courage in such a small frame; for he was
not afraid of attacking single-handed an entire enemy contingent, and
after killing large numbers he would return again with great speed un-
scathed to his own close formation. He surpassed everyone of his generation in leaping, ball-playing, and throwing the javelin, and in drawing
and shooting a bow. It is said that he used to line up four riding horses in
a row, and would leap from one side and land on the last horse like a
bird.[34] When he shot an arrow, he aimed so well at the target that he

---

Government of Empire (976–1025)" (D.Phil. diss., University of Oxford, 1999),
290–91.

[27] Chaldaia or Chaldia was a theme and, from the 8th–10th c., a *doukaton* in northeast
Asia Minor, under the command of a *doux*; see *ODB* 1:404.

[28] Amaseia, modern Amasya, capital of the Armeniakon theme, was strategically located
on the Lykos River in Pontos: see *ODB* 1:74.

[29] Thus he must have been born ca. 925.

[30] For surviving portraits of Tzimiskes, see N. Thierry, "Un portrait de Jean Tzimiskès
en Cappadoce," *TM* 9 (1985): 479, 481, figs. 2 and 5; and Treadgold, *Byz. State*, 506, fig.
122. For another translation of and brief comment on the description that follows, see
McGeer, *Warfare*, 219–21. Leo's description of Tzimiskes is also translated by J. Wortley,
"John Skylitzes: A Synopsis of Histories (811–1057 A.D.): A Provisional Translation"
(typescript, University of Manitoba, 2000), 169. R. Morris ("Succession and Usurpation,"
210) argues that this description is idealized.

[31] Or perhaps "bluish-gray"; see LSJ, s.v. χαροπός, 2 and 3.

[32] Εἰς πλαίσιον, a very rare expression apparently describing a mustache; perhaps Leo is
making a pun on the fact that John's mustache resembled a military formation? Leo uses
πλαίσιον specifically of a military formation above in Book II, chap. 6 (24.18).

[33] Ψυχή was added in brackets by Panagiotakes.

[34] On this feat see discussion in Book III, n. 82.

could make it pass through the hole in a ring; by so much he surpassed the islander celebrated by Homer, who shot the arrow through the axeheads.[35] He used to place a ball made of leather on the base of a glass cup, and, goading his horse with his spurs to quicken its speed, he would hit the ball with a stick to make it leap up and fly off; and he would leave the cup remaining in place, undisturbed and unbroken. He was more generous and bountiful than anyone; for no one who petitioned him ever went away disappointed of his hopes. He treated everyone kindly and graciously, *lending the mercy*[36] of good deeds mentioned by the prophet, and, if Basil the *parakoimomenos*[37] had not restrained his insatiable urge to benefit his fellow countrymen, he would soon have emptied the imperial treasuries with donations to the needy. John had the following fault, [p. 98] that sometimes he used to drink more than he should when he was carousing, and he was unable to resist physical pleasures.

4. After thus gaining control in seven days over the state and acquiring the imperium for himself, as no one ever thought he would (for at times of great changes in government, usually a lot of unrest and tumult flares up, but at that time, I don't know how,[38] it so happened that good order and deep quiet prevailed over the people, and only the emperor Nikephoros and one of his bodyguards were killed, no one else receiving so much as a slap in the face), he went to the holy and great church of the Wisdom of God to be crowned by the hierarch with the imperial diadem in the usual manner.[39] For it is customary for those who have newly embarked upon the Roman rule to ascend the ambo[40] of the church to be blessed by the current patriarch and have the imperial crown placed on their heads. Since Polyeuktos,[41] who occupied the patriarchal throne at that time, was a holy man with fervent spirit, although advanced in

---

[35] The islander is Odysseus; see Homer, *Odyssey* 21.420–23. For a summary of the various interpretations of Odysseus's feat, see J. Russo et al., *A Commentary on Homer's Odyssey*, vol. 3, *Books XVII–XXIV* (Oxford, 1992), 141–47.

[36] Reading ἔλεον instead of ἔλαιον of Hase ed.; see Ps. 111 (112):4–5.

[37] See above, chap. 1, and Book III, n. 57.

[38] Leo seems to forget that just above in chap. 1 he has stated that Tzimiskes' decree forbidding rebellion and looting kept the populace quiet.

[39] For the coronation of an emperor in the 10th c., see *De cer.* 1.38, ed. Reiske, 1:191–96, and *ODB* 1:533–34.

[40] The ambo was a platform or pulpit that stood in the nave between the chancel barrier and the west wall: see *ODB* 1:75.

[41] On Polyeuktos, see above, Book II, chaps. 10–11 and n. 62.

age, he declared to the emperor that he could not enter the church until he banished the augusta[42] from the palace, pointed out the murderer of the emperor Nikephoros, whoever he might be, and furthermore returned to the synod the powers that by decree Nikephoros had improperly revoked. For Nikephoros, wishing either to restore in the way he thought best ecclesiastical affairs that were disturbed by certain members of the clergy, or to have authority over ecclesiastical matters, too (which was a violation), had forced the prelates to draw up a decree [p. 99] that they would not take any action in church affairs without his approval.[43] Polyeuktos proposed these conditions to the emperor, for otherwise he could not allow him to enter the holy precincts. Upon receiving this ultimatum, he removed the augusta from the palace and banished her to the island of Prote,[44] returned Nikephoros's decree to the synod, and pointed out Leo Balantes,[45] affirming that he, and no other, was the perpetrator and planner of the murder of Nikephoros. Thus John was admitted into the holy church to be crowned by Polyeuktos,[46] and then returned to the imperial palace, acclaimed by all the host of soldiers and the people.

5. Then he took advantage of a brief respite and period of leisure to divide in half his ancestral property (and a lot was left to him by his ancestors—for John was descended from a very distinguished family, *of noble birth* on his father's side, *from the east*,[47] and, through his mother, was nephew of the emperor Nikephoros[48]—and [he also had land] from

---

[42] Theophano, the widow of Nikephoros Phokas.

[43] See Skyl. 274.51–62, and Morris, "Phokas," esp. 88. The decree is not included in *Les regestes des actes du patriarcat de Constantinople*, vol. 1, fasc. 2–3, rev. ed. J. Darrouzès (Paris, 1989) under the patriarchate of Polyeuktos.

[44] Prote (modern Kenaliada) was one of the larger of the Princes' Islands in the Sea of Marmara, noted as the site of several monasteries and as a place of exile: see Janin, *CP byz.*, 511. According to Skyl. 285.35–39, Theophano was first exiled to Prokonnesos, and subsequently banished to the convent of Damideia in the Armeniakon theme.

[45] In Book V, chap. 7, Leo Balantes is named as the conspirator who struck the first blow against Nikephoros II, as he lay sleeping on the floor of his bedchamber. For further information on him and his family, see Book V, n. 72, and Morris, "Succession and Usurpation," 212.

[46] John Tzimiskes was crowned on 25 December 969; see Skyl. 286.46–48.

[47] See Job 1:3. As stated earlier in Book V, n. 54, Tzimiskes was a member of the Kourkouas family.

[48] Leo has already stated in Book III, chap. 3 that John's mother was sister of Nikephoros Phokas.

Book VI

imperial grants, which he received in abundance because of his triumphs in battle). He let half of it be distributed to adjacent and neighboring farmers, and granted the rest to the hospital for lepers[49] opposite Byzantium, adding to the old structures new buildings for those suffering from the holy disease [of leprosy], and increasing the number of patients. [p. 100] And he used to go over to visit them, would distribute gold to them, and did not disdain to treat as best he could their ulcerated limbs, which were ravaged by the disease, even though he was an aesthete of quite delicate sensibilities. He was so compassionate and sympathetic toward victims of physical suffering when he chanced to meet them that he disdained the weight of majesty and the pomp engendered by the wearing of the purple. He also granted immunity from taxation [and corvée labor][50] to the Armeniac theme,[51] for he came from there. And when it was time for the stipends[52] that the senate and the noble and reputable citizens receive from the hand of the emperor, of his own accord, impelled by his generous and kindly spirit, he increased the stipend for everyone who was entitled to this payment.

6. Since Antioch the Great, on the Orontes, which had just been captured by the emperor Nikephoros,[53] was bereft of a hierarch (for its former Agarene ruler had killed the patriarch Christopher,[54] an apostolic and divinely inspired man, by thrusting a javelin though his chest, holding

[49] St. Zotikos founded a leprosarium in the second half of the 4th c. outside the walls on a hill across the Golden Horn from Constantinople (in the region later termed Pera), at a location called Elaiones (Olive Trees). See T. Miller, "The Legend of St. Zotikos according to Constantine Akropolites," *AB* 112 (1994): 339–76; M. Aubineau, "Zoticos de Constantinople, nourricier des pauvres et serviteur des lépreux," *AB* 93 (1975): 67–108; Janin, *Églises CP*, 566–67.
[50] After ἀτέλειαν Panagiotakes has supplied from the Paris manuscript ἐργάσιον, omitted by Hase, and suggested emendation to <καὶ> ἐργασιῶν, meaning ἀγγαρειῶν.
[51] The Armeniakon theme was a large and important province in eastern Asia Minor: see *ODB* 1:177.
[52] On such stipends (ῥόγαι), see *ODB* 3:1801.
[53] Antioch had been taken by the armies of Nikephoros II on 28 October 969; see above, Book V, chap. 4.
[54] Christopher, named Melkite patriarch of Antioch in 960, was murdered on 22 May 967 according to Yahya of Antioch (*Histoire*, 806–9) and Abraham the Protospatharios: see W. Saunders, "Qalʿat Semʿan: A Frontier Fort of the Tenth and Eleventh Centuries," in *Armies and Frontiers in Roman and Byzantine Anatolia*, ed. S. Mitchell (Oxford, 1983), 291; see also Papadopoulos, Ἱστορία, 807–10. The phrase "its former Agarene ruler" would seem to refer to Sayf ad-Dawla, but he predeceased Christopher in 967. According

against the man the crime of reverence for Christ the Savior), the emperor John, deeming it of great importance to find a bridegroom for this [city], zealously devoted much attention to finding a man worthy of this high-priestly position.[55] While he was *brooding over and thinking*[56] about this, there came to mind Theodore of Koloneia,[57] a man who had chosen the solitary and contemplative life from childhood,[58] and had subdued his flesh with many ascetic labors. For he used to wear a ragged hair tunic, [p. 101] concealing with it the iron that he wore to torment his body,[59] and did not remove the tunic until it completely fell to pieces and became useless. This monk is said to have prophesied the proclamation of first Nikephoros, and then John, as emperor. Since Theodore was in Byzantium at that time, John brought him to Polyeuktos, who, together with the resident bishops,[60] examined the man; after finding that his secular[61] education was not very advanced, but that he was thor-

---

to Yahya, Christopher was killed by Khorasanians in the home of Ibn Manik, an Arab whom he had rescued from prison. Other sources give a date of 969 for Christopher's murder; see Saunders ("Qal'at Sem'an," 291–92), who prefers 967.

[55] The usual procedure for the election of a patriarch in the Byzantine Empire was that the permanent (*endemousa*) synod in Constantinople (see below, n. 60) presented the emperor with three names, from which he chose one, or someone not on the list: see Beck, *Kirche*, 95–97, and *ODB* 1:520. The procedure here seems more streamlined, and underlines the important role of the emperor in the selection of patriarchs.

[56] See Agath. 21.16.

[57] Theodore, abbot of the monastery of Kyr Antonios in the Armeniac theme, was elected patriarch of Antioch on 23 January 970 and was in office until 28 May 976. See Papadopoulos, Ἱστορία, 825–27, 829–31.

[58] Although the normal expression is ἐξ ἁπαλῶν ὀνύχων, both here and at 102.14 Leo uses the abbreviated phrase ἐξ ὀνύχων to express "from childhood."

[59] The wearing of iron weights or rings was a common ascetic practice; see, e.g., *Vie de Théodore de Sykéôn*, ed. A.-J. Festugière (Brussels, 1970), 1: chap. 28. For some middle Byzantine examples, see Ch. van de Vorst, "La vie de s. Evariste, higoumène à Constantinople," *AB* 41 (1923): 312.1–3, 314.34–35, 318.31–33; I. van den Gheyn, "Acta graeca ss. Davidis, Symeonis et Georgii Mitylenae in insula Lesbo," *AB* 18 (1899): 220.23–25, trans. D. Domingo-Forasté, in *Byzantine Defenders of Images*, ed. A.-M. Talbot (Washington, D.C., 1998), 143–241, here 167.

[60] These are the members of the *synodos endemousa* or permanent synod, comprised of bishops who were in or near the capital at the time; it served as an advisory board to the patriarch and had some decision-making authority: see Beck, *Kirche*, 42–44; Hussey, *Orthodox Church*, 318–25; and *ODB* 1:697, s.v. "Endemousa Synodos."

[61] Θύραθεν, lit. "from outside," i.e., secular education as opposed to "ours," that is, Christian or religious education.

oughly versed in our [Christian] divine studies, he anointed him as patriarch of Antioch. Polyeuktos lived on a few days after the selection of Theodore, and then departed this life,[62] leaving to the church as a memorial the images of the virtues, as well as the knowledge of divine and human wisdom and learning that he cultivated to the utmost. After Polyeuktos, who guided the reins of the patriarchate for thirteen years, departed to his blessed repose, the emperor John was eager to appoint to the hierarchal throne[63] a man who surpassed most men in virtue and character. Thus the next day he summoned the bishops and the senate to the imperial court, and spoke as follows:

7. "I recognize One Authority, the highest and foremost, which *brought into being from non-being the structure of the visible and invisible world*.[64] But I know that in this life and in the earthly sphere here below there are two [authorities], priesthood and imperial rule;[65] to the former [p. 102] the Creator granted responsibility for our souls, to the latter the guidance of our bodies, so that no part of these [i.e., body and soul] would be defective, but would be preserved whole and undamaged. Therefore, since the one who guides the church has paid his debt, it is the work of *the Eye that nothing escapes*[66] to promote to the ministry of divine affairs the man who surpasses all others, to whom men's ways are known even before they are conceived;[67] and I myself am raising to the ecclesiastical throne this man, of whom I have indisputable knowledge for a long time, so

---

[62] On 5 February 970.

[63] This statement that John I had the power to appoint the patriarch reflects reality; see n. 55 above.

[64] A conflation of two citations. The first part, "brought into being from non-being," is found in the "preface" to the anaphora of the liturgy of John Chrysostom, ed. F. E. Brightman, *Liturgies, Eastern and Western* (Oxford, 1896), 322. The second part of the phrase may derive from Gregory of Nazianzus, *Ep.* 101.38.4 in P. Gallay, *Grégoire de Nazianze. Lettres théologiques* (Paris, 1974). The whole phrase also subtly echoes the opening of the Nicene Creed, "I believe in One God, maker ... of all things visible and invisible."

[65] As suggested by G. Dagron (in *Evêques, moines et empereurs [610–1054]* [Paris, 1993], 207–8), these sentiments are reminiscent of the *Eisagoge* (or *Epanagoge*): see *Epanagoge aucta*, Tit. 2, chap. 8, in *Ecloga privata aucta*, ed. K. E. Zachariä von Lingenthal [*Jus graecoromanum* 6] (Athens, 1931), 59–60.

[66] See Book II, n. 74.

[67] This translation follows the order of the text in the Hase edition, and the interpretation of E. Barker, *Social and Political Thought in Byzantium* (Oxford, 1957), 96, that ᾧ refers to τὸν κατευμεγεθοῦντα and alludes to Basil's foresight, which is described a few lines below. The text and punctuation of this passage is problematic, however, and Panagiotakes

Book VI

that a man celebrated for all sorts of virtues, to whom God has granted the gift of foresight, may not spend his life in an obscure corner; for he has proclaimed to me *with a divinely inspired voice*[68] many future events, which came to pass in their time." So spoke the emperor, and brought out in their midst the monk[69] Basil,[70] who had chosen the solitary life from childhood, and performed many feats of ascetic discipline on the slopes of Mt. Olympos.[71] He bade him come to the patriarchal palace, and the next day (it was the Sunday on which the holy fathers affirmed the orthodox belief about the veneration of holy icons)[72] Basil was anointed with the high priesthood, and proclaimed ecumenical patriarch.[73]

8. The mind of the emperor John was torn with many concerns, and he was assailed by doubt[74] as to which he should give his attention to first, and not be diverted from the proper course. For lack [p. 103] of provisions and increasing famine had been ravaging the Roman empire for three years; there was also the invasion of the Rus',[75] which did not afford many grounds for optimism, and the attack of the Carthaginians and Arabs against Syrian Antioch,[76] which had just been occupied by the Romans. He put an end to the relentless evil of famine by the importation

---

suggested that the phrase ᾧ ... διέγνωσται should be placed before τὸν ... παραγαγεῖν, taking ᾧ as referring to the ἀλάθητος ὀφθαλμός; he also proposed a lacuna before αὐτὸς δέ. This would increase the force of the biblical allusion, to Pss. 22:9–10, 71:6, 139:13.

[68] See Homer, *Iliad* 2.41; *Odyssey* 3.215, 16.96.

[69] Reading μοναχὸν as abbreviated in P, rather than ἀναχωρητήν, erroneously supplied by Hase.

[70] Basil I Skamandrenos became patriarch on 13 February 970, according to Grumel, *Chronologie*, 436, and J. Darrouzès, "Sur la chronologie du patriarche Antoine III Stoudite," *REB* 46 (1988): 55–60. See also below, Book X, nn. 20 and 23.

[71] Mt. Olympos in Bithynia, a center of monasticism in the middle Byzantine era: see Janin, *Grands centres*, 127–91, and *ODB* 3:1525.

[72] I.e., the Sunday of Orthodoxy, celebrated on the first Sunday in Lent: see *ODB* 3:2122–23.

[73] By the end of the 6th c. this term was used by the patriarch of Constantinople to declare that he was the superior bishop in the empire: see Beck, *Kirche*, 63–64; *ODB* 1:675–76.

[74] Lit. ἐν τριόδῳ, "at a crossing of three roads"; see *CPG* 1:76, 241; 2:111, 404.

[75] This refers to Sviatoslav's successful campaigns in Bulgaria and his capture of Preslav in 969.

[76] Yahya of Antioch, *Histoire*, 350, mentions a five-month siege of Antioch in 970/71 by an army sent from Damascus by Jafar ibn Jalah. The term "Carthaginians" may refer to the Fatimids; see Book V, n. 4.

of grain, which he collected quickly [and] with forethought from markets everywhere, stopping the spread of such a calamity. He checked the
attack of the Agarenes by marshaling the troops in the east, under the
command of the *patrikios* Nicholas,[77] who was one of the emperor's
household eunuchs and had obtained experience from much training in
many[78] battles. As for Sphendosthlavos, the leader of the Rus' army,[79] he
decided to negotiate with him; and he sent ambassadors to tell him that
he should take the pay promised by the emperor Nikephoros for attacking
the Mysians, and should return to his own territory and the Cimmerian
Bosporos,[80] abandoning Mysia, since it belonged to the Romans and
was a part of Macedonia from of old. For it is said that the Mysians, who
were colonists of the Hyperborean Kotragoi,[81] Khazars,[82] and
Khounaboi,[83] migrated from their own territory, wandered into Europe,
and occupied and settled this land, when Constantine, with the sobriquet

---

[77] According to Skylitzes (Skyl. 287.85–90) Tzimiskes sent Nicholas, a eunuch in his
household, as ἄρχων τοῦ ὅλου στρατοῦ: see Guilland, *Institutions*, 1:172 and Ringrose,
The Perfect Servant, 138. On the title *patrikios*, see above, Book I, n. 33.

[78] Hase omitted πολλῶν before ἀγώνων.

[79] On Sviatoslav, see Book V, chap. 2 and n. 16.

[80] The ancient name of the Straits of Kerč, the passage from the Black Sea to the Sea of
Azov: see *ODB* 1:313.

[81] The Koutrigurs or Cotrigurs were a Hunnish people north of the Black Sea who
came under Avar rule in the 6th c.: see Moravcsik, *Byzantinoturcica*, 2:171–72; *ODB*
1:540. The patriarch Nikephoros I (Nikeph., *Short History*, chap. 35.4–5) says the Kotragoi
are "of the same stock" (ὁμόφυλοι) as the Bulgarians. Theophanes (Theoph. 1:356) also
mentions them in relation to the early Bulgarians.

The Hyperboreans were a legendary people who were supposed to live in the far
north; see LSJ, s.v.

[82] The Khazars were a Turkic people who ruled over the region north of the Caucasus
from the 7th through the 10th c. and who, for most of their history, were allies of
Byzantium: see D. M. Dunlop, *The History of the Jewish Khazars* (Princeton, 1954); *ODB*
2:1127. The patriarch Nikephoros (Nikeph., *Short History*, chap. 35.28–34) says the Khazars
subjected one of the early subdivisions of the Bulgarians to tributary status. Theophanes
(p. 358) gives the same information.

[83] Panagiotakes retained the manuscript reading (Χουνάβων) here against Hase's
conjecture of Χουμάνων. As the "Cumans" (properly Κούμανοι) did not appear in the
east European steppe until 1050–60 (see *ODB* 1:563), the manuscript reading is also
retained in the translation. On the "Khounaboi" see Moravcsik, *Byzantinoturcica*, 2:347.
While the Kotragoi and Khazars are mentioned in the accounts of the proto-Bulgarians
by Theophanes and Patriarch Nikephoros I, those authors do not mention the Khounaboi.
The source of Leo's inclusion of them here is not clear.

Pogonatos, was emperor of the Romans; they called the land Bulgaria after the name of their chieftain, Boulgaros.[84] [p. 104]

9. Another tale is told about these people, approximately as follows: when the Roman emperor Justinian, who had his nose slit by Leontios[85] and was exiled to Cherson,[86] managed to escape from there in a wily manner, he came to Maeotis[87] and made an agreement with the Mysian people, that if they restored his empire to him they would receive great rewards. And so they followed him, and received from him, once he again obtained imperial rule, the land that the Istros borders within Macedonia.[88] After moving there, they constantly waged wars against the Romans and took them prisoner, always anxious to make war and raiding the Thracian regions. When the Romans went out to oppose them, they were not [able to] withstand the Romans' power, but withdrew to densely thicketed areas so as to fight them in difficult terrain. Thus from that time many wars broke out, brave generals were slain, and the emperor Nikephoros the elder was killed in battle[89] by the Mysians. The Mysians are said to have been defeated only by Constantine Kopronymos[90] and again by his grandson Constantine,[91]

[84] The Bulgarians first settled in Europe during the reign of Constantine IV Pogonatos ("the bearded") (641–68): see Runciman, *Bulgarian Empire*, 3–43; Moravcsik, *Byzantinoturcica*, 2:100–106; G. Cankova-Petkova, "Bulgarians and Byzantium during the First Decades after the Foundation of the Bulgarian State," *BSl* 24 (1963): 41–53, at 52.

[85] The emperor Justinian II (685–95 and 705–11) was deposed in 695 by the general Leontios (who reigned 695–98), and had his nose mutilated (hence his epithet *rhinotmetos*, "cut-nose"). He regained the imperium in 705 with the aid of the Bulgarians. See Theoph. 368–69, 372–74; and Nikeph., *Short History*, 40.33–36, 42.35–61.

[86] Cherson was a city in the Crimea; see *ODB* 1:418–19.

[87] The Sea of Azov.

[88] The ceding of land is not mentioned among the rewards for Bulgarian aid in the earliest sources (Theophanes and Nikephoros), but first only by George the Monk, who reports: Ἰουστινιανὸς τὴν βασιλείαν τὸ δεύτερον ἀπολαβών, δῶρα πολλὰ τῷ Τερβελι δοὺς καὶ χώραν τῶν Ῥωμαίων ἐκκόψας, δίδωσιν αὐτῷ, τὰ λεγόμενα νῦν Ζαγόρια. It seems likely that Leo is following an incorrect tradition: see C. Head, *Justinian II of Byzantium* (Madison, Wisc., 1972), 123 and n. 1, which cites V. Beševliev, "K voprosu o nagrade, polučennoj Tervelem ot Justiniana II v 705 g," *Vizantiiskii Vremenik* 16 (1959): 12–13.

[89] The emperor Nikephoros I was slain in battle against the Bulgarian khan Krum on 26 July 811: see *ODB* 2:1159, s.v. "Krum."

[90] Constantine V (741–75). Theophanes (Theoph. 1:432–33) describes his victory over the Bulgarians at Anchialos in 763, and his subsequent triumphal procession with Bulgarian captives.

[91] Leo seems to be in error here. The only attested expedition against the Bulgarians by Constantine VI (790–97) resulted in his own severe defeat at Markellai in 792: see *ODB*

the son of the augusta Irene, and now by the emperor John, who subdued the cities of the Mysians by force. No other Roman is recorded who prevailed against them in their own land. But enough about this. [p. 105]

10. Sphendosthlavos was very puffed up by his victories over the Mysians and swaggered insolently with barbarian arrogance (for he already held the land securely). And since he had reduced the Mysians to terror and stunned submission with his innate cruelty (for they say that, when he took Philippopolis[92] by force, he cruelly and inhumanly affixed to a stake[93] twenty thousand of the men captured in the town, thus terrifying all his enemies and making them come to terms), he delivered arrogant and insolent responses to the Roman envoys: that he would not renounce his claim to this fertile land, except in return for the payment of vast sums of money and the ransom of the cities and prisoners that he had taken in warfare; if the Romans were not willing to pay this, then they should quickly withdraw from Europe, which did not belong to them, and move to Asia; and they should not think that Tauroscythians would come to terms with Romans on any other conditions. When the emperor John received such responses from the Scythian, he made the following reply through the previous messengers:

"We do not think it is right to break the peace that God mediated and has come down to us intact from our fathers, since we believe that there is a Providence that guides everything and we honor Christian traditions. Therefore we advise and counsel you as friends to depart immediately, without any delay or hesitation, from the land that does not belong to you in any way, in the knowledge that if you do not obey this expedient advice, it is not we, but you, who will be breaking the

---

2:1300, s.v. "Markellai." For an interesting sidelight on the battle, see D. Sullivan, "Was Constantine VI Lassoed at Markellai?" *GRBS* 35 (1994): 287–91.

[92] Philippopolis (modern Plovdiv) is located in northern Thrace on the Marica River; it fell to the Rus' in late fall of 969: see *ODB* 3:1654–55.

[93] In middle Byzantine Greek the verb ἀνασκολοπίζω means "hang on a *phourka*" rather than "impale"; see Trapp, *LBG*, s.v. ἀνασκολοπισμός, etc. The *phourka* (Lat. *furca*) was a forked stake to which offenders were affixed and exposed to ridicule; they might also subsequently be executed by strangulation. See W. Smith, *A Dictionary of Greek and Roman Antiquities* (London, 1875), 562–63; P. Speck, "Der Tod an der Furca," *JÖB* 40 (1990): 349–50; and idem, "Eine Quelle zum Tod an der Furca," *JÖB* 42 (1992): 83–85, with earlier bibliography. Another instance of ἀνασκολοπισμός is found at Leo diac. 174.6. See also *Theoph. Cont.* 303.16–18 for an additional passage demonstrating the linkage between the *phourka* and ἀνασκολοπισμός, not noted by Speck.

[p. 106] treaties formulated of old.[94] I hope we do not seem to be making these replies in a boastful spirit; for we have confidence in Christ, the immortal God, that, if you do not leave the land, then willing or not you will be driven from it by us. For I think you are well aware of the mistake of your father Igor,[95] who, making light of the sworn treaties, sailed against the imperial city with a large force and thousands of light boats,[96] but returned to the Cimmerian Bosporos with scarcely ten boats, himself the messenger of the disaster that had befallen him.[97] I will pass over the *wretched fate*[98] that befell him later, on his campaign against the Germans, when he was captured by them, tied to tree trunks, and torn in two.[99] And I think that you too will fail to return to your own country, if

---

[94] This passage is noteworthy as the sole hint in Greek sources of the agreements of Oleg with the Byzantines in 907 as reported in the *Russian Primary Chronicle* (trans. Cross, 64–65): see A. A. Vasiliev, *History of the Byzantine Empire* (Madison, Wisc., 1952), 1:321, and *ODB* 3:2111–12.

[95] Igor, ruler of Kiev, led an unsuccessful naval attack against Constantinople in 941: see *Theoph. Cont.* 423–26, and *ODB* 2:984–85, s.v. "Igor." For another reference by Leo to this attack, see Book IX, chap. 2. Zuckerman "Chronology," 258, has pointed out the value of Leo's independent verification of the role of Igor in the attack of 941.

[96] The σκάφη are presumably wooden dugouts, boats made from hollowed-out tree trunks, the *monoxyla* described in the *De administrando imperio*: see *Constantine Porphyrogenitus. De administrando imperio*, ed. G. Moravcsik, trans. R. J. H. Jenkins (Washington, D.C., 1967), chap. 9, line 17, where they are called σκαφίδια. The Rus' are said to drag and carry the *monoxyla* on their shoulders where necessary (chap. 9.53–54). See also *De administrando imperio*, vol. 2, *Commentary*, ed. R. J. H. Jenkins (London, 1962), 23–25.

Cf. the thousands (lit. "myriads") of boats mentioned here, and the μυριόστολον στρατόν in Book IX, chap. 2 (n. 6). Leo is exaggerating in both passages.

[97] Siuziumov et al. (*Lev D'iakon*, 200 n. 68) comment that this passage proves that Leo the Deacon was familiar with the vita of St. Basil the Younger, in which we read with regard to the Rus' attack: "A few of them got safely away to their homeland, narrating there what had befallen them." See A. N. Veselovskii, "Razyskaniia v oblasti russkogo duchovnogo sticha," *Sbornik Otdeleniia russkogo iazyka i slovesnosti Imperatorskoi Akademii nauk* 46 (1889–90): supp. 68 (and 66). On the Cimmerian Bosporos, see n. 80 above.

[98] See 2 Macc. 9:28.

[99] In 944 or 945 Igor was captured near the city of Iskorosten, and killed by the Derevliane, a people living west of the middle Dnieper. As suggested in Siuziumov et al., *Lev D'iakon*, 200 n. 69, Leo's "Germanoi" seem to be a garbled rendering of the Βερβιανοί (or better Δερβιανοί) of *De administrando imperio*, chap. 9.107–8, referring to the Derevliane. About them, see D. Obolensky in *De administrando imperio*, vol. 2, *Commentary*, ed. R. Jenkins (London, 1962), 60. See also *Russian Primary Chronicle*, 78.

No other source corroborates the sensational manner of Igor's death as described by Leo. D. Sullivan has suggested that Leo may have invented this gory scenario, borrowing

you force the Roman army to march against you, but you will be killed there with all your troops, so that not even a fire-bearing [priest][100] will return to Scythia, to announce the dreadful fate that overtook you."

Sphendosthlavos became furious at this response, and, carried away by barbarian frenzy and rage, made the following reply: "I see no urgent need for the emperor of the Romans to come to us. Therefore let him not tire himself out by coming to this land; for we will soon pitch our tents before the gates of Byzantium, will surround this [city] with a mighty palisade, and will meet him bravely when he sallies forth, if he should dare to undertake such a great struggle.[101] [p. 107] We will teach him with very deeds that we are not mere *manual laborers who live by the work of our hands*,[102] but *bloodthirsty warriors*[103] who fight our foes with weapons, although the emperor believes in ignorance that Rus' soldiers are like pampered women, and tries to frighten us with these threats, as if we were suckling infants to be frightened by hobgoblins."

11. Upon hearing these insane words of the Scythian,[104] the emperor decided not to delay, but to prepare for war with utmost zeal, so that he might anticipate the Scythian's attack against him, and check his assault against the imperial city. Thus he immediately selected a squadron of brave and vigorous men, calling them "Immortals,"[105] whom he bade remain at his side. Then [he chose] the *magistros* Bardas, surnamed

---

from Diodorus Siculus's description of Sinis, who lived near the Isthmus of Corinth, and used to tie his victims to two bent-down pine trees, and then release the trees so that the bodies were torn asunder; see Diodorus Siculus, *Bibliotheca historica* 4.59.3. See, however, Zuckerman, "Chronology," 268 and n. 118, who accepts Leo's account as factual.

[100] See *CPG* 1:134–35, 289; 2:44, 580, 582. This proverbial expression was derived from the ancient tradition that a victorious enemy would normally spare the priests who carried sacred fire for sacrifices. If even these priests were slaughtered, it meant the total destruction of an army.

[101] Reading τοσοῦτον πόνον for τοσούτων πόνων as Hase suggests and Panagiotakes emends.

[102] See Lucian, *Somnium sive vita Luciani*, sect. 9.19. This is meant to reflect the warrior ethic of despising lowly craftsmen.

[103] Pss. 5:6; 25 (26):9; 54 (55):23; et alibi.

[104] Reading Σκύθου with Panagiotakes instead of ἐκεῖθεν of Hase ed.

[105] The "Immortals" were an elite cavalry regiment created by John Tzimiskes in 970; their commander had the title of *domestikos*. Their last recorded action was in 1094: see Kühn, *Armee*, 243–47 and McGeer, *Warfare*, 199, 221, 316, 343. Treadgold (*Byz. State*, 949 n. 18) presumes, following Skylitzes (Skyl. 295.22), that they numbered 4,000. The name echoed that of Alexander's Immortals.

Skleros,[106] the brother of Maria, the deceased wife of the emperor, an energetic and extremely powerful man, and the *patrikios* Peter, who had been appointed *stratopedarches*[107] by the emperor Nikephoros because of his inherent valor and heroic feats in battle (for it is said that once, when the Scythians were raiding Thrace, it came about that Peter, although a eunuch, met them in pitched battle with the corps that was following him. The Scythian commander, an enormous man, who was securely protected with armor, rode out on the battlefield, brandishing a long lance, and challenged anyone who wished to fight with him;[108] [p. 108] and Peter, filled with inconceivable valor and spirit, impetuously urged his horse on with his spurs, and, after brandishing his spear mightily, thrust it with both hands at the Scythian's chest. The force of it was so great that it bore right through and pierced all the way to the broad of his back, his chainmail breastplate failing to stop it. That enormous man was dashed to the earth without a sound, and the Scythians turned to flight, amazed at this novel and strange sight). The emperor ordered these generals to take his troops and march to the region that adjoins and borders Mysia; to spend the winter there, drill the army, and watch over the region vigilantly, so that it would not suffer any damage from Scythian raids; and to send bilingual men, clothed in Scythian garb, to the camps and abodes of the enemy, to learn their plans, and communicate them to the emperor. After receiving these orders from the emperor, they crossed over to Europe.

12. At the news of their crossing, the Tauroscythians separated off a portion of their army, to which they added a multitude of Huns[109] and Mysians, and sent them to march against the Romans.[110] As soon as the

[106] On Bardas Skleros, brother of Maria, first wife of John Tzimiskes, see Seibt, *Skleroi*, 29–58, no. 10, and *ODB* 3:1911–12. See also above, Book VI n. 25.

[107] On Peter, who had captured Antioch in 969, see Book V, chap. 4 and n. 41.

[108] On such single combats (see also below, Book VI, chap. 13, and Book IX, chap. 6) as a reflection of the contemporary values of the military élite and of a new approach to the representation of warfare in literature, see Haldon, *Warfare*, 244. This combat is described in Ringrose, *The Perfect Servant*, 137–38, part of a section on eunuchs as military commanders (131–41).

[109] The term "Huns" was applied to various peoples; probably the Magyars are meant here. See Book II, n. 14.

[110] The battle reported here is also described in Skyl. 288.23–291.4, with English translation and analysis in McGeer, *Warfare*, 294–300. One of the major differences in Skylitzes' account is that John Alakas (Alakasseus in Skylitzes) is also ordered to and uses feigned retreats to lure the enemy into an ambush.

magistros Bardas[111] learned of their approach, since he was an extremely brave and active man, and at that time was incited by anger and a surge of strength, [p. 109] he assembled the picked men with him, and urged them to engage the enemy. He summoned John Alakas[112] and sent him out as a scout to observe the Scythians, estimate the size of the host, and see where they were camped and what they were doing. He was then to send him a full report as quickly as possible, so that he might prepare and deploy the army for battle. Taking the picked men who were following him, John rode off quickly toward the Scythians; and the next day he sent to the *magistros*, urging him to come with the army, for the Scythians were encamped not far away but nearby. When he heard this message, he deployed the army in three sections, ordering one to follow him in the van, the others to lie in wait in the thickets on either side. They were to sally forth from the place of ambush when they heard the trumpet sound the call to battle.

After giving these orders to the captains, he marched straight against the Scythians, fighting valiantly. The enemy army had superior numbers, over thirty thousand, while the men following the *magistros*, including those lying in ambush, did not come to more than ten thousand.[113] When the battle began, the mightiest men fell on both sides. It is said that here one of the Scythians, who boasted of his courage and the size of his body, drew apart from his unit, rode out and attacked Bardas, striking him with his sword on the helmet; but the sword blow was in vain [p. 110] since the blade was deflected by the helmet, glancing off to the side as a result of its resistance.[114] Then the *patrikios* Constantine,[115] Bardas's brother, whose face was just sprouting its first growth of down, but who had an enormous body, with irresistible and invincible strength, drew his sword and went to strike the Scythian. The latter, however, perceived his assault, and avoided the blow by bending back toward the haunches of his horse. The horse received the blow on its neck, which was cut through; and the Scythian tumbled down together with his horse and was slain by Constantine.

---

[111] Bardas Skleros; see n. 106 above.

[112] The form of the name should probably be emended to Alakaseus. The family was of Petcheneg origin: see A. Savvides, "Ὁ βυζαντινός οἶκος τῶν Ἀλακάδων-Ἀλακασέων," *Byzantiaka* 11 (1991): 231–38.

[113] Skyl. 288.24 gives 12,000.

[114] This incident is described in Skyl. 290.80–81; see also McGeer, *Warfare*, 297.

[115] On Constantine, Bardas Skleros's younger brother, see Seibt, *Skleroi*, 58–60, no. 11.

Book VI

13. As the course of the battle was turning this way and that, with frequent and indecisive shifts of the scale in both directions, Bardas ordered the call to battle to sound, and the drums to roll continuously. At the signal the army sallied forth from the places of ambush, and appeared to the rear of the Scythians, who were struck with terror and turned to flight. The rout was not yet in full sway, when one of the prominent Scythians, distinguished from the others by the size of his body and the gleam of his armor, went around the battlefield, encouraging his companions to fight bravely. Bardas Skleros rode out on his horse and struck him on the head. The sword went right through to his waistguard,[116] neither his helmet nor his breastplate being strong enough to withstand the strength of his arm or the slash of his sword. When he was cut in two and dashed to the ground, the Romans shouted for joy and were encouraged to brave deeds, while the Scythians, terrified by the novel and extraordinary blow, broke their close formation with lamentation, and turned to flight.[117] [p. 111] The Romans pursued them until late in the evening, slaughtering them mercilessly. Fifty-five Romans[118] are said to have died in this battle, many were wounded, and most of the horses were slain, while more than twenty thousand Scythians were killed.

This was the final outcome of the Romans' struggle with the Scythians at that time. Then the emperor John ordered the troops from Asia to cross over to Europe by way of the Hellespont, to spend the winter in the region of Thrace and Macedonia, drill daily with their weapons (so that they would not be out of training at the campaign season and be unfit for battle with the enemy), and wait for springtime. For when [spring] began to emerge from *the gloom of winter*[119] and brought

---

[116] The ζωστήρ, a term found in Homer, apparently describes a wide belt that protected the upper abdomen: see G. S. Kirk, *The Iliad: A Commentary* (Cambridge, 1985), 1:344. Earlier in Book III, chap. 7, Leo used the term μίτρα apparently of a "waistguard" (see Book III, n. 60). The relation between the ζωστήρ and the μίτρα, both Homeric terms, neither found in Byzantine military manuals, is difficult to understand even in the Homeric context, and their application to 10th-c. Byzantine military equipment is uncertain.

[117] On Bardas Skleros's great victory over the Rus', which took place at Arkadioupolis (modern Lüleburgaz) in the spring of 970, see Seibt, *Skleroi*, 31.

[118] Skyl. 291.4 gives the figure of 25.

[119] See Gregory of Nyssa, *Commentarius in Canticum canticorum*, Or. 5 (*Gr. Nys.* 6:155.16). The same phrase is used by Leo at 51.6 and 128.1.

the state of the world[120] into steady fair weather, then the emperor would come to them, leading his own troops, in order to attack the Tauroscythians with all his forces.

---

[120] See *Vettii Valentis Antiocheni Anthologiarum libri novem*, ed. D. Pingree (Leipzig, 1986), 188.23.

Book VII

[anno 970]

W HILE THE EMPEROR JOHN WAS OCCUPIED WITH THESE ACTIONS against the Rus', the *doux* Bardas, who was son of Leo the *kouropalates* and nephew of the emperor Nikephoros, secretly turned to rebellion,[1] and fled from Amaseia,[2] where he had been banished. He was joined by the brothers Theodore, Bardas, and Nikephoros,[3] who were *patrikioi* and had the sobriquet Parsakoutenoi after the city of their birth, Parsakouta,[4] and were cousins of the *doux* Bardas. [p. 113] After the *doux* escaped secretly from Amaseia in the middle of the night, he arrived at Caesarea in Cappadocia[5] after several prearranged relays of horses.[6] He made encampment there for a few days, and, as his relatives and friends arrived daily, he assembled a host of foolish men inclined to revolt; for *men* tend *to rejoice* exceedingly *at novel situations*,[7] misled by dreams and hopes of glory, and of awards of dignities and distributions of money. The rebellion was also supported by the above-mentioned Parsakoutenoi, who mustered troops with great zeal, and by Symeon, a

---

[1] This rebellion occurred in 970; on Bardas Phokas, see Book VI, n. 25.

[2] On Amaseia, see Book VI, n. 28.

[3] Panagiotakes has added a comma before Bardas, thus indicating that there were three Parsakoutenos brothers. This seems better than the punctuation of Hase with no comma, since Bardas Parsakoutenos is mentioned later by Leo in Book X, chap. 7. Cheynet ("Les Phocas," 311) and Mark Whittow ("Rural Fortifications in Western Europe and Byzantium, Tenth to Twelfth Century," *ByzF* 21 [1995]: 64 and n. 35) concur that there were three brothers. Skylitzes (Skyl. 291.13–14) adds that Theodore and Nikephoros were the sons of the *patrikios* Theodoulos Parsakoutenos, and were exarchs in Cappadocia. See also Guilland, *Institutions*, 2:193.

[4] The village (*kome*) of Parsakouta was on the road between Nymphaion and Sardis in the Thrakesian theme: see H. Ahrweiler, "L'histoire et la géographie de la région de Smyrne entre les deux occupations turques (1081–1317), particulièrement au XIIIe siècle," *TM* 1 (1965): 71–72.

[5] On Caesarea, modern Kayseri, see Book III, n. 21.

[6] For such relay systems, cf. Prokopios, *Historia arcana*, ed. J. Haury [*Procopii Caesariensis opera omnia*, III] (Leipzig, 1963), chap. 30.5 (181.18–21): συχναῖς δὲ ἵππων δοκιμωτάτων ὄντων διαδοχαῖς ἐλαύνοντες ἀεὶ οἷσπερ ἐπίκειται τὸ ἔργον τοῦτο, δέκα τε, ἂν οὕτω τύχοι, ὁδὸν ἡμερῶν ἀμείβοντες ἐν ἡμέρᾳ μιᾷ.

[7] See Gregory of Nazianzus, *Or.* 43.58 (PG 36:572B).

cultivator of vineyards, who took his sobriquet from his work and was called Ambelas [Vinedresser],[8] a man of obscure and low-born origins, but who, on account of his courage and physical strength, was second to none among men celebrated for their force and might.

When Bardas saw assembled around him a corps sufficient to be arrayed in unbroken close formations, and capable of fighting the enemy in pitched battle,[9] he removed his dark-hued boots, immediately exchanged them for scarlet ones,[10] and was publicly proclaimed emperor of the Romans by the rebels. He also began to promise distributions of money, and to offer awards of dignities, appointing taxiarchs[11] and generals, and the glorious positions that an emperor is accustomed to offer generously to his supporters. The rebellion was also supported by Leo [p. 114] the *kouropalates*, the father of Bardas, who was under guard on the island of Lesbos.[12] Through Stephen, the bishop of Abydos,[13] he promised money and honors to the Macedonians,[14] urging them to receive him when he left the island, and to join and cooperate with him in the removal of the emperor John from the palace.

2. At the news of this rebellion, the emperor was seriously distressed, as was reasonable, and with great speed had the bishop Stephen brought from Abydos,[15] and delivered to the lawcourts. When the matter was investigated and the deed clearly exposed, he had [Stephen] brought before the synod of bishops to be deprived of his priestly rank.[16] However, when the judges condemned Leo the *kouropalates* and his son

---

[8] Symeon Ambelas is also mentioned by Skylitzes (Skyl. 291.14–292.1), who calls him a *patrikios*. Leo the Deacon relates below in chap. 5 (120.13–14) that he later abandoned the rebellion of Bardas Phokas and went over to the emperor. On the sobriquet Ambelas, see Kazhdan, "Byzantine Family Names," 108.

[9] Or: "on an equal footing" (ἐξ ἀντιπάλου). See below, n. 34.

[10] I.e., the boots reserved for the emperor. See Book III, n. 30.

[11] On taxiarchs, see Book V, n. 42.

[12] See Book VI, chap. 2.

[13] Stephen does not seem to be otherwise attested. See n. 16 below.

[14] These must be the Macedonian *tagmata*: see Book III, chap. 7 and n. 49.

[15] On Abydos, see Book III, n. 42.

[16] As Leo the Deacon indicates here, Stephen was evidently convicted of treason by a civil tribunal and then deposed from his bishopric by the synod: on this incident see *Les regestes des actes du Patriarcat de Constantinople*, 2nd ed., vol. 1, fasc. 2–3 (Paris, 1989), 308, no. 797a.

Nikephoros[17] to the sentence of death, the emperor, swayed by mercy, did not execute them, but sent [men] to Lesbos and put out the eyes of both.[18] This was the outcome of the crossing over to Europe planned at that time by the *kouropalates*, ending in this punishment for himself, and depriving of money and homes many of his friends who were involved in his plot for the deposition of the emperor. But as for Bardas, once he became involved in rebellion, he clung fast to it, exulting in the large number of troops around him, priding himself on his regiments, and dreaming that very soon he would possess the empire. Thus he ravaged Asia, burning the homes of those who did not surrender to him and plundering them with impunity.[19] [p. 115]

Then the emperor wrote to him as follows: "When we heard about the rebellion that took place recently in the east, we thought that this was not so much the result of *your* initiative, but was rather a consequence of the folly and barbarous character of your supporters, who were completely struck by divine madness. For they did not hesitate to thrust themselves into such peril, even though they were aware that, for those who undertake to revolt and insolently to raise a hostile hand against the Roman emperors themselves, there is no pretext left for pardon, once they have been subdued by force and handed over for punishment. For our part we are loath to defile the land with kindred blood.[20] For if we wanted to retaliate against the rebels with force of arms, we would soon (with the help of God, let it be said) slaughter them in a pitiful manner. For who is so tough as to withstand the weight of our attack, and does not straightway turn to flight in terror? Therefore we counsel you to choose a safe course rather than a fatal one; while there is still a chance for forgiveness, cast aside your weapons and yield to our imperial majesty, who, with God as our witness, grants you irrevocable amnesty and pardon for this rash endeavor; and your property will be left absolutely untouched and inviolate. So we urge you to recover from the state of intoxication, and seek instead without delay the

[17] On Nikephoros Phokas, son of Leo the *kouropalates*, see Book VI, n. 22.

[18] According to Skylitzes (Skyl. 292.26–31), the emperor's henchmen only pretended to blind them and left their eyes unharmed. Leo himself later states (145.14ff) that the blinding was not in fact carried out (Book IX, chap. 3), but they were blinded later after their second attempt at rebellion (Book IX, chap. 4).

[19] Lit. "making Mysian plunder"; for this proverbial expression, see Book V, n. 2.

[20] Cf. the advice of Leo VI, in *Leonis imperatoris Tactica*, ed. R. Vári, 1 (Budapest, 1917), II, chap. 45.522–23.

chance of safety that is offered you. But if you [insist on] fighting in vain and give your support to the rebellion, then you will repent [p. 116] your stupidity, when you are led to the punishment of death by decision of the laws."

3. When Bardas Phokas received this letter, he did not deign to send an answer to the emperor, but reviled him, calling him a blackguard and wretch and stigmatizing him as an abominable murderer of his kin, and bade him step down from his usurped throne; for, he said, the imperial power belonged rather to him, since he could boast that his grandfather was a caesar and his uncle emperor;[21] whom [John], unafraid of the vigilant *eye of justice*,[22] had slaughtered like a sheep on his bedding on the floor; that, on unclear and unproven grounds, he had deprived of sweetest sight his father and dearest brother,[23] who suffered the worst of fates; and that he would by all means wreak avenging justice on their behalf, exacting *sevenfold retribution*[24] for his kindred blood from the man who plotted the destruction of a noble and heroic family. When the emperor John heard of these ravings, he realized that the man was incurably ill and anxious to proceed to cruel and inhumane plunder and murder together with the conspirators who were following him. He resolved, therefore, not to delay or hesitate any longer, lest through such negligence the rebel faction might have an opportunity to lay siege to cities and might slip into even greater insanity; but wherever practicable he would resist mightily as best as he could under the circumstances and [p. 117] would retaliate against the brigands.[25]

---

[21] Bardas Phokas was the grandson of the caesar Bardas Phokas (d. 969) and the nephew of Nikephoros II Phokas. See Book VI, n. 25.

[22] *CPG* 2:366, 423. For a comparable expression, ἀλάθητος ὀφθαλμός, used by Leo, see Book II, chap. 11 (33.4) and Book VI, chap. 7 (102.4–5).

[23] Leo and Nikephoros Phokas; see above, n. 18.

[24] See Sirach 32:11 (ed. Brenton) and 35:10 (ed. Rahlfs); and above, Book I, chap. 6, n. 66.

[25] Panagiotakes has suggested the emendation of πελάτης to ἐπελάτας or ἀπελάτας here and at 140.3. If one accepts the emendation, the term, while apparently used of irregular troops (cf. *De cer.* 696.4 with Sophocles, *Lexicon*, ἀπελάτης, citing that passage: "2. In the plural, ἀπελάται, a body of soldiers so called" and Suda *mu*, 1225 at Μονόζωνοι—ἔφοδοι βάρβαροι, ἢ ἀπελάται μάχιμοι and Μονόζωνοι—οἱ τίμιοι τῶν στρατιωτῶν, οἱ μὴ τὸν αὐτὸν τοῖς ἄλλοις ζωστῆρα φοροῦντες· οἱ ἀσύντακτοι καὶ ὡσανεὶ λησταί), is perhaps used pejoratively here. See J. Mavrogordato, *Digenes Akrites* (Oxford, 1956), xxxvi–xxxvii: "Brigands . . . means simply drivers-away, reivers, rustlers, cattle-drivers, or horse-thieves." Loretto (*Phokas*, 186 n. 140.1) uses ἀπελάτης at the second occurrence and translates "Späher" ("scouts"), suggesting a second possibility "Partisanen" ("guerillas").

Book VII

Thus the emperor sent for Bardas, by surname Skleros,[26] an extremely vigorous and energetic man, whose sister Maria, *greatly celebrated*[27] for her beauty and virtue, had formerly been married to John (but bitter death had already laid her low). He was a *magistros* and commander of the troops in Thrace, and was nobly checking the violent attack of the Rus' against the Romans, after the victory that he recently won by routing the Scythians, as I have already related.[28] The emperor summoned this man, appointed him as supreme commander,[29] and sent him to Asia against the rebels, ordering him, if possible, not to defile the land with the blood of fellow countrymen,[30] unless it was absolutely necessary, but to seduce the followers of the rebel with promises of honors, gifts of money, and pledges of amnesty. He also entrusted to him documents sealed with the imperial seals of gold,[31] in which were written appointments of taxiarchs, generals, and *patrikioi*, ordering him to use these to bribe the men who changed their minds, renounced the authority of the usurper, and acknowledged their submission to the emperor. After crossing the Bosporos, the supreme commander Skleros arrived at Dorylaion,[32] where he mustered the army, organized it into a unit, and drilled it with daily exercises. Seeing that the assembled army was already sufficiently numerous to be able[33] to meet the enemy in pitched battle[34] when the occasion arose, [p. 118] he sent the following message to the *doux* Bardas, his brother-in-law (for the *patrikios* Constantine, Skleros's brother,[35] was married to Phokas's sister):[36]

---

[26] On him, see Book VI, n. 106.

[27] See Homer, *Iliad* 6.446, 10.212, and passim.

[28] In Book VI, chap. 11–13.

[29] On the Greek term here, στρατηλάτης, see Oikonomides, *Listes*, 332; Guilland, *Institutions*, 1:387; and *ODB* 3:1965.

[30] For similar wording, see Leo diac. 115.10 and n. 20 above.

[31] These were chrysobulls, solemn documents bearing the emperor's gold seal.

[32] Dorylaion (modern Eskişehir), a city in northwestern Phrygia that was a major military post: see *ODB* 1:655.

[33] Hase emended the ἐξικάνην of P to εἶναι ἱκανὴν, a conjecture accepted by Panagiotakes. Even better would be the emendation to ἐξικάνειν, as proposed by Alexander Alexakis.

[34] Or: "on equal terms." See above, n. 9.

[35] On Constantine Skleros, see Book VI, n. 115.

[36] Her name was Sophia: see Skyl. 294.87.

4. "You have devised a perilous and extremely dangerous scheme, as you speak boldly against the emperors, plan a deadly usurpation, take up arms against your fellow countrymen, and defile the precincts of holy buildings with the plundering of your boorish fellow rebels. In vain, O *patrikios*, have you been deluded into *provoking* a sleeping *lion*,[37] the invincible emperor; for you know that when this man has appeared on the battlefield, he has put large armies to flight by his reputation alone. How then were you persuaded by the counsels of corrupt men to hurl yourself onto such a destructive course? But, if you will, listen to me, as a brother-in-law and friend and one who is giving you better advice: renounce this wicked usurpation and grasp instead a chance of safety, by seeking forgiveness for your misguided ways (and I personally guarantee that you will suffer no unpleasant fate, either at the hands of the emperor or from anyone else, but a full pardon for this rash endeavor will also be granted to the corps that is following you); do not attempt to muster against yourself the imperial wrath, which is implacable toward those who are not willing to show a conciliatory spirit. Come to your senses then, do not let go the *final anchor*,[38] but while there is a chance for mercy, take advantage of it, since you will not find it again if you look for it, and you will lament loudly, as you blame yourself for your stupidity."

After Bardas Phokas [p. 119] read through the contents of the letter, he made the following reply: "I realize that *advice is a* good and *holy thing*,[39] since I myself have read books of olden times, but I think it is useful only at a time when conditions admit of a solution. But when affairs are on the brink of disaster and are being driven to the worst of fates, then I think that advice is of no value whatever. For when I reflect on the fortunes in which my family has been ensnared by the impious and accursed John, who mercilessly killed *a sleeping lion*,[40] the emperor, my uncle, who was his benefactor, and exiled me to no purpose, and cruelly and inhumanly blinded my father and brother for no good reason, I consider *life not worth living*.[41] Do not tire yourself out, therefore,

---

[37] See *CPG* 1:189, 2:483.

[38] See *CPG* 1:256, 537.

[39] See *CPG* 1:96, 2:34, 174.

[40] Leo here uses a variant of the proverbial expression just used by Skleros, "to provoke a [sleeping] lion" (*CPG* 1:189, 2:483); see n. 37 above.

[41] See Aristophanes, *Plutus* 969 et alibi; Leo has used the same expression previously at 36.20 (Book III, chap. 1).

urging me to deliver my life into the hands of an abominable foe; for you will not persuade me. But since I am a man and have girded on my sword, I will fight for the departed members of my family. And since fortune swings between two poles, one of two things will happen in any case: either I will attain imperial glory and will exact complete vengeance from the murderers, or I will bravely accept my fate, and be delivered from an accursed and impious tyrant."

5. Upon receiving this letter, Bardas Skleros despaired that he would ever dissuade through advice this man who was plunging headlong from an act of folly into madness; so he organized the army into squadrons [of cavalry] and cohorts [of infantry] [p. 120] to march to Dipotamos.[42] Upon his arrival there, he immediately sent spies disguised as beggars to the camp of Bardas Phokas, to disclose to the leaders of the army the emperor's promises and his pardon for their rash endeavor, and to tell them furthermore that, if they did not quickly forsake the rebel and surrender to the emperor, the supreme commander [Skleros] would watch for an opportunity to attack with his troops, and deal with them as enemies. After they heard these words, and reflected that it was better to take the honors offered by the emperor rather than to shadowfight with an uncertain outcome, at nightfall they abandoned their alliance with Phokas, and deserted to the supreme commander; and the most eminent of them were the patrikios Adralestos,[43] Phokas's nephew, and Symeon Ambelas.[44] When Bardas learned of their flight and how they abandoned him without any hesitation, he was distressed, as was reasonable, and entreated with supplications those who remained behind, saying that they should not betray him and God, Whom they had made witness and overseer of their oaths, but should rather fight to the utmost of their ability and cooperate with a man who had suffered terribly; for Skleros,

[42] An imperial estate, also known as Mesanakta, south or west of the lake of the Forty Martyrs (present day Akşehir gölü), exact location unknown: see Belke and Mersich, *Phrygien und Pisidien*, 338–39.

[43] Panagiotakes prefers the reading "Adralestos" to the "Andralestos" of P and the Hase ed.; see H. Moritz, *Die Zunamen bei den byzantinischen Historikern und Chronisten*, Programm K. Human. Gymn. in Landshut, 1896/97, 2:51. Skylitzes (Skyl. 292.43) also gives the form Adralestos, plus a first name, Diogenes. See Cheynet, "Les Phocas," 311 and n. 74 for possible ways in which Diogenes was related to Bardas Phokas. Ph. Koukoules (Βυζαντινῶν βίος καὶ πολιτισμός 6 [Athens, 1955], 485) notes that the name means "coarse" or "crude."

[44] See above, chap. 1, n. 8.

he said, would not be able to contend with them in close combat, unless they went into battle in a sluggish and careless fashion. Despite these entreaties and supplications, however, they gradually slipped out of the camp to join the supreme commander Skleros.

It is said that in the depths of the night [p. 121] Phokas became violently agitated about the flight of his fellow rebels; in his distress he was unable to sleep, and propitiated the divinity with prayers, repeating those words of David, "*Judge thou, O Lord, them that injure me.*"[45] Suddenly a voice came out of the air and hummed around his ears, bidding him not to continue with the psalm,[46] because the supreme commander Bardas [Skleros] had already used the same words of the psalm against him in his prayers. After this voice echoed in his ears three times, he was astounded by the strange prophecy, and leapt from his bed in great terror to await daybreak.

6. When the day had dawned for sure, he mounted his horse and proceeded through the army [encampment], with his gaze fixed on his boots; and as he stared, he experienced a strange illusion, for they did not seem to be scarlet,[47] but of a pure dark color. When he asked his retainers how they had made such a mistake, and given him ordinary boots instead of the imperial ones, they replied that they were scarlet, and advised him to look at them carefully. Casting his eye on them, he perceived that they were indeed scarlet, just as they had been before. Phokas considered this portent as a second bad omen, and, seeing that his army was dissident and rebellious, he decided to save his skin in any way possible.

So in the middle of the night he took thirty[48] of his most trusted men, [p. 122] securely armed, secretly left the camp, and took the road leading to the fortress of the Tyrants,[49] called Antigous,[50] which, suspecting

[45] Ps. 34 (35):1.

[46] The psalm continues (vv. 1–3) "Fight against them that fight against me. Take hold of shield and buckler, and arise for my help. Bring forth a sword, and stop the way against them that persecute me." In the liturgy this psalm is recited at the third hour of Good Friday, so the overtones are clear. (We thank Aristeides Papadakis for this reference.)

[47] I.e., the color reserved for imperial boots. See above, Book III, n. 30.

[48] Panagiotakes prefers the reading τριάκοντα found in P to the τριακοσίους of E adopted by Hase.

[49] Panagiotakes suggested an emendation to τῶν Τυάνων, "of Tyana." But Hild in *Kappadokien*, 142, states that this Cappadocian fortress that belonged to the Phokas family had no connection with Tyana. Skyl. (293.55) writes Τυροποιόν.

[50] For Antigous (modern Altunhisar) in Cappadocia, see Hild and Restle, *Kappadokien*, 142.

the reverses of fortune, he had been strengthening for a long time, by supplying it abundantly with grain and all kinds of fodder. And the place where Bardas Phokas's army broke close formation had from of old been called Bardaetta.[51] When the supreme commander Bardas [Skleros] learned of Phokas's flight, he rode out in pursuit of him, together with picked men. He failed to catch him, however, since he had already found refuge in the fortress, but he put out the eyes of his fellow rebels whom he took captive, as this was the command of the emperor. And it is said that the place where this misfortune befell the wretched men is called Typhlovivaria.[52] To me it seems marvelous how men in olden times were moved by some inspiration to give to places names that were fitting and appropriate to the course of subsequent events. For it is said that when Leo Phokas, Bardas's great-uncle, had his eyes cruelly put out,[53] the place in which he suffered this punishment had the name Oeleon, but was called Goleon in the rustic idiom.[54] Thus places of punishment had received such names from of old. And perhaps it will not seem a digression to recount briefly the manner of Leo's blinding.

7. When the emperor Leo had recently died of consumption[55] [p. 123] and his brother Alexander followed him soon after,[56] the Roman empire was ruled precariously by his son Constantine,[57] who was still in the care of nurses, and by the augusta Zoe.[58] Then Symeon, the ruler of the

---

[51] Bardaetta (modern Sarayönü), which literally means "defeat of Bardas," was north of Ikonion. Its original name may have been Παρέθθων, demoticized into Bardaetta, which took on a new meaning with the defeat of Bardas: see Belke and Mersich, *Phrygien und Pisidien*, 205.

[52] A place on the border between Phrygia and Lykaonia, exact location unknown: see Belke and Mersich, *Phrygien und Pisidien*, 409. Its name means "enclosure (holding pen) of the blind."

[53] This Leo Phokas (b. ca. 875/80), son of Nikephoros the Elder, was the brother of Bardas Phokas's grandfather Bardas Phokas: see Cheynet, "Les Phocas," 296–97. He was appointed *domestikos* of the Schools in 917, and was blinded after his unsuccessful rebellion against Romanos I in 919; see Skyl. 211.19–20.

[54] The form Ὠἠ Λέων ("Woe, Leo") is found in Skyl. 211.16 (with variants in apparatus) and Γωηλέοντι in *Theoph. Cont.* 396.21. See H. Grégoire, "Goeléonta–Golanta," *Byzantion* 11 (1936): 537–39.

[55] Leo VI died on 11 May 912: see *ODB* 2:1210.

[56] On Alexander, who died on 6 June 913, see *ODB* 1:56–57.

[57] Constantine VII (b. 905) was seven years old when his father died.

[58] Zoe Karbonopsina, the fourth wife of Leo VI, became regent for her young son Constantine after the deaths of Leo and Alexander: see *ODB* 3:2228, and above, Introduction, 1.

Mysians,[59] a venturesome man, audacious in warfare, who had been chafing at the bit for a long time and longed painfully to fight the Romans, seized the opportunity to ravage Macedonia and Thrace ceaselessly, and, puffed up with the customary Scythian madness, bade the Romans to declare him emperor. These latter could not endure the open arrogance and insolence of the Scythian, and decided to wage war against him. They chose as commander of the army Leo Phokas,[60] who at that time surpassed the other generals in his courage and victories, proclaiming him as *domestikos* of the Schools, and appointed Romanos[61] as admiral of the fireships (they give the title of *droungarios* of the fleet[62] to the man who receives this command), and they sent them to attack the Mysians, one by land, the other by sea. They say that when Leo completed the march and arrived in Mysia, he fought marvelously, cutting down countless multitudes of the enemy, so that Symeon was driven to dire straits and was at a loss as to what he should do, and how he might escape such a bold and invincible man.

When the rest of the Mysians were already exhausted and turning to flight, a message is said to have been brought to Leo by one of his bodyguards, that the *droungarios* Romanos had departed under full sail, [p. 124] *with the wind at his stern*,[63] and was returning to the city of Byzantium with the desire of seizing the throne; Leo was very distressed at the inauspicious news, broke up his close formation, and, turning his back to the Mysians, hastened back to the imperial city, in the hope that he might arrive before Romanos's fleet and seize control of the Roman imperial power. When Symeon saw the inexplicable and strange retreat of the Romans, he wondered for a moment if there was not some trick and the Mysians would be destroyed if they pursued, but when he learned that they were retreating as fast as they could, he pursued them and mercilessly slaughtered countless multitudes. Today one can still see heaps of bones next to Anchialos, where the retreating Roman troops were

---

[59] On Symeon, tsar of Bulgaria (893–927), who invaded the Byzantine Empire in 916, see *ODB* 3:1984.

[60] On this Leo Phokas, see n. 53, above.

[61] This was Romanos Lekapenos, the future emperor Romanos I. On him, see Runciman, *Romanus.*

[62] See Book VI, n. 19.

[63] A common expression in patristic Greek; see, for example, Basil of Caesarea, *Homilia in principium proverbiorum*, PG 31:417.48.

ingloriously cut down at that time.[64] After Leo arrived too late at
Byzantium and was deceived of his hopes (for Romanos reached the
imperial palace first and was proclaimed "father of the emperor"),[65] he
crossed over to Asia by way of Abydos,[66] turned to rebellion, and caused
many problems for Romanos and the state, as he laid waste [the land],
carried off the annual revenues, and overpowered those who opposed
him. But when in the course of time his robbers' band was dispersed and
he changed his mind and turned to flight, he was caught and his eyes
were cruelly put out.

8. And this is the way it was. As Bardas Phokas was hastening at that
time [p. 125] toward the fortress[67] and bringing up the rear of his troops,
one of his pursuers,[68] who was bold and arrogant, rode ahead on his
horse to attack him, brandishing his sword, spouting threats, and attempting to strike him. Bardas urged him to retreat as quickly as possible, out of pity for the fate that had befallen him; and that, since he was
mortal, he should in any case be wary of the vicissitudes and uncertainty
of fortune, and not add *suffering to the sufferings*[69] of a man in distress; for
sufficient were the troubles that overwhelmed him, putting him, a former
commander of the Roman army, in such straits as he was in now, reduced to a fugitive. The man, however, considered these words to be idle
nonsense, and went closer, trying to strike him. Bardas grabbed the mace[70]

[64] The battle of the Achelous, a river (or, according to Skyl. 203.95, a fortress) in Thrace
near the Black Sea coastal town of Anchialos, where Symeon defeated the Byzantines on
20 August 917; see *ODB* 1:13, 90, s.vv. "Achelous" and "Anchialos." Piles of bones are
also mentioned in Book II, chap. 5 (23.8) in a different context.
 Leo the Deacon presents here a version of the defeat more favorable to Leo Phokas.
The battle is also described in *Theoph. Cont.* 388–90, who notes that Leo Phokas was
more courageous than skilled in strategy; he makes no mention of a deliberate retreat to
arrive at Constantinople before Romanos, only complete defeat by the Bulgarians and
subsequent flight. Skylitzes gives both versions, perhaps using both Theophanes
Continuatus and the same pro-Phokas source as Leo the Deacon.
[65] Romanos married his daughter Helen to Constantine VII in May 919, and thus
became the emperor's father-in-law. On his high-ranking title, the "father of the emperor"
or *basileopator*, see P. Karlin-Hayter, "The Title or Office of Basileopator," *Byzantion* 38
(1968), 278–80, and *ODB* 1:263–64.
[66] On Abydos, see Book III, n. 42.
[67] The fortress of the Tyrants; see chap. 6 and n. 49 above.
[68] Skylitzes (Skyl. 293.61) gives his name, Constantine Charon.
[69] See Euripides, *Alcestis* 1039 and *Trojan Women* 596.
[70] On the κορύνη, see Kolias, *Waffen*, 178, 181 n. 49; and above, Introduction, 39 n. 134.

hanging at his side, and, turning suddenly, struck the man on his helmet. Both his helmet and skull were crushed, he was dashed wordlessly to the ground, and thus Phokas was able to reach the fortress safely.

After surrounding the fortress, Bardas [Skleros], the supreme commander and *magistros*, urged Bardas Phokas to beg the emperor for clemency and to come out of the fortifications as quickly as possible. Since he was caught in a most hopeless position and was in dire straits, he thought and reflected at length, and decided to yield to fortune and surrender to the emperors, if he would receive amnesty for himself and his loved ones. Therefore he immediately asked for pledges that he would not suffer any unpleasant fate, and, when he received them from Skleros, he came out of the fortress with his wife and children.[71] After [Skleros] received them, [p. 126] he kept them free from harm, reported to the emperor what had happened, and asked him what he should do. The emperor John declared that he should banish Bardas Phokas with his wife and children to the island of Chios, after he received the tonsure of a cleric,[72] and that he [Skleros] should take his troops, cross over to Europe by way of the Hellespont, and spend the winter there in winter quarters; and that, as soon as spring came, the emperor himself would campaign with his elite guard[73] against the Scythians,[74] for he could not endure their unchecked insolence any longer.

9. For when the Scythians heard about the departure from Europe of the supreme commander Bardas [Skleros], when he was sent to Asia by the emperor on account of the rebellion recently kindled by Bardas Phokas, as I have already related, they began to harass the Romans terribly; they made sudden incursions, plundering and ravaging Macedonia unsparingly, since the *magistros* John, surnamed Kourkouas,[75] who was entrusted with the command of the army there, had turned to immoderate indolence and

---

[71] This failed rebellion occurred in 970: see Cheynet, "Les Phocas," 307.

[72] Banishment to a monastery was a typical form of punishment: see *ODB* 3:1622, s.v. "Penalties." In this case, however, Bardas Phokas is described as receiving *clerical* tonsure, and being sent into exile with his family, with no mention of a monastery. Skylitzes also reports that he was made a κληρικός (Skyl. 294.91).

[73] Lit. "bodyguards," ὑπασπισταί, probably a reference to the Immortals, on whom see Book VI, n. 105. In Book VIII, chap. 4 (132.18 and 133.22), John's command of the Immortals against the Rus' is specifically mentioned.

[74] I.e., the Rus'.

[75] John Kourkouas belonged to a distinguished military family of Armenian origin, on which see *ODB* 2:1156–57; McGrath, "Aristocracy," 169–70; Cheynet, *Pouvoir*, 270; Runciman, *Romanus*, 135–50; and A. Kazhdan, *Armiane v sostave gospodstvujushchego klassa*

drink, and handled the situation in an inexperienced and stupid manner; therefore the spirits of the Rus' were raised to insolence and boldness. Because the emperor could not endure their overweening insolence and downright arrogance, he was anxious to curtail and break it with all his might by fighting them in close combat. Thus he ordered that the fire-bearing triremes be steadied with ballast,[76] and that a large quantity of grain, fodder for the beasts of burden, and sufficient weapons for the army be transported to Adrianople[77] in supply [p. 127] ships, so that the Romans would not run short of any of these while they were engaged in war.

While these preparations were being made, John took in marriage Theodora,[78] the daughter of the emperor Constantine Porphyrogennetos, who was not exceptionally distinguished for her beauty and physical grace, but indisputably surpassed all other women in prudence and in every kind of virtue. The wedding celebration took place in the month of November, in the second year of his reign.[79] The people were overcome with tremendous rejoicing, because the emperor governed his subjects with a gracious disposition and equitable manner; he was especially admired because,[80] even though he was distinguished and possessed the temperament of a ruler, he also revealed himself as gentle and reasonable toward his subjects, and readily granted mercy to those who asked for it. Then he entertained the people with largesse and contests in the Hippodrome, and spent the winter in Byzantium, awaiting the spring season, drilling his select troops daily in *whirling about* in both directions *while fully armed*,[81] and in every military skill that has been devised for warfare by the most valiant of men.

Vizantiiskoi imperii v XI–XII vv. (Erevan, 1975), 13–14. This John was son of Romanos Kourkouas, *domestikos* of the Schools in the West. He reappears later in Leo's history in Book IX, chap. 5, at the siege of Dorystolon (971), in which he was killed by the Rus'.

[76] On this ballasting, see Leo diac. 65.19; Book IV, n. 62; and Introduction, 40.

[77] Adrianople (modern Edirne) was a strategically located city in central Thrace. The ships must have been small enough to sail up the Hebros River, since Adrianople is far from the sea.

[78] On Theodora, see Garland, *Empresses*, 134.

[79] I.e., November 970. Leo is in error in assigning the wedding to the second rather than the first year of Tzimiskes' reign. The error presumably resulted from conflation of items in his source: see Dölger, "Chronologie," 282–83, and H. Grégoire, "La dernière campagne de Jean Tzimiskès contre les Russes," *Byzantion* 12 (1937): 267–76, at 267–70.

[80] Reading ὅτι with P for ὅτε of Hase ed.

[81] See Agath. 40.6. Leo uses a similar phrase in Book III, chap. 1 (36.5). On the nature of this training, see above, Introduction, 39.

Book VIII
[anno 971]

A S SOON AS *THE GLOOM OF WINTER*[1] CHANGED to the fair weather of springtime,[2] the emperor raised the standard of the cross and prepared to march against the Tauroscythians. And so he left the palace and went to the venerated church of Christ the Savior at the Brazen Gate[3] to offer prayers to the Divinity. Observing that it was a narrow chapel, scarcely able to hold fifteen men inside, and that the way up to it was crooked and difficult of access, like a winding maze[4] or hiding place, he immediately [p. 129] ordered that it be rebuilt from the foundations in a more splendid and sacred fashion; and he personally laid out the circumference of the walls,[5] and, as a result of his inspired zeal and instructions, its construction achieved the beauty and size that is apparent today.[6] Then, after he went to the holy and celebrated church of the Wisdom of God,[7] and prayed that he be granted an angel to go before the army and *make straight the road*,[8] he made a prayerful procession to the venerated church of the Mother of God at Blachernai.[9] And after propitiating the Divinity here, too, with prayers of supplication, as

[1] See Gregory of Nyssa, *Commentarius in Canticum canticorum, Or.* 5 (Gr. Nys. 6:155.16). The same phrase is used by Leo at 51.6 and 111.13.

[2] April of 971: see Dölger, "Chronologie," 275–92.

[3] On the church at the Chalke Gate, see Mango, *Brazen House*, 150–52; Janin, *Églises CP*, 529–30; J. Kostenec, "Studies on the Great Palace in Constantinople: II. The Magnaura," *BSl* 60 (1999): 170; and Berger, *Untersuchungen*, 269–70. The original chapel was built by Romanos I Lekapenos (920–44).

[4] Mango interprets this as a "spiral staircase" (*Brazen House*, 152).

[5] For γεῖσα with the meaning of "walls," see also Leo diac. 11.9 and 26.1. For discussion of this method of building design (σχηματίσας τὸν περίμετρον), with examples of similar personal involvement by other church patrons, see R. Ousterhout, *Master Builders of Byzantium* (Princeton, 1999), 58–64.

[6] The rebuilt church was served by fifty clergy (Mango, *Brazen House*, 150), so it must have been substantially larger than the original chapel.

[7] I.e., Hagia Sophia.

[8] See Ps. 5:8, Isa. 40:3, and 1 Thess. 3:11.

[9] On the celebrated church of the Virgin at Blachernai, see Janin, *Églises CP*, 161–71, and *ODB* 1:293.

was fitting, he went to the palace there[10] to survey the fire-bearing triremes that were riding at anchor in orderly fashion in the inlet[11] of the Bosporos; here is a safe and calm harbor for cargo vessels, extending in a gentle curve as far as the bridge and the river that flows under it.[12]

After the emperor observed the experienced and orderly rowing and racing[13] of the triremes (of which there were over three hundred, together with swift and light vessels, which these days are colloquially called galleys and patrol boats),[14] he rewarded the oarsmen and marines on them with gifts of money. Then he sent them to the Istros to guard its passageway, so that the Scythians would not be able to sail away to their own country and the Cimmerian Bosporos,[15] if they should turn to flight. The Istros is said to be one of the rivers that originate in [the garden of] Eden, the so-called Phison, which has its source in the east, and goes underground through the infinitely great wisdom of the Creator and [p. 130] springs up again in the Celtic mountains; then it winds through Europe, and, after dividing into five mouths, empties its streams

[10] On the palace at Blachernai, see Janin, *CP byz.*, 123–128. Located in the northwestern-most corner of the city, it afforded an excellent view over the Golden Horn. In the 10th c. the palace was a simple structure, and served primarily as a resting-place for the emperor when he visited the church at Blachernai.

[11] I.e., the Golden Horn.

[12] Evidently a reference to the bridge at the northern end of the Golden Horn that crossed the Barbyzes River; it is variously called the bridge "of Justinian," "of St. Kallinikos," and "of St. Panteleemon": see Janin, *CP byz.*, 240–41 and map VIII, and A. van Millingen, *Byzantine Constantinople* (London, 1899), 174–77.

[13] For parallels to the meaning of ἄμιλλα as "race," see Isocrates, *Oration* 9.189, in *Isocrates*, trans. L. van Hook (Cambridge, Mass., 1945), 4.1, and *Pausanias: Description of Greece*, trans. W. H. S. Jones (London, 1918), 1:438, *Corinth*, xxxv.1.

[14] A γαλέα was a light and swift warship (δρόμων) of medium size, while the μονέριον (usually μονήρης) was smaller, with one bank of oars: see Ahrweiler, *Mer*, 413–14, 416–17; and A. Failler, "Petite note lexicographique sur la monère et l'hénère," *REB* 58 (2000): 269–71. See also *Taktika* of Leo VI, Const. 19, chap. 74 (PG 107:1013A–B): ἔχειν δὲ καὶ μικροὺς δρόμωνας καὶ ταχεῖς, οὐ πρὸς πόλεμον ἐξωπλισμένους, ἀλλὰ πρὸς τὰς βίγλας, καὶ τὰ μανδάτα, καὶ τὰς ἄλλας ἀπαντώσας ὁμοίως χρείας. καὶ ἔστι τά τε μονήρια λεγόμενα, καὶ τὰς γαλέας, πλὴν καὶ αὐτοὺς ἐνόπλους, διὰ τὰ τυχηρῶς συμπίπτοντα. "You should also have small and fast dromons, not fitted out for combat, but for scouting and communication and other needs likely to occur. These are the so-called *moneria* and the galleys, except that they may be armed in situations that may arise" (We thank G. Dennis, who provided this translation). Galleys are also mentioned in *De cer.* 657.4 and 665, in connection with the expedition against Crete of 949.

[15] Ancient name for the straits of Kerč, on which see Book VI, n. 80.

into the Pontos, which is called the Euxine.[16] But some people say that Phison is the [river] that divides the land of India, usually called Ganges,[17] where emeralds are found.[18]

2. In any case the triremes were despatched to the Istros in this manner. After the emperor John departed from Byzantium, he arrived with all his army at Adrianople. The story goes that it was built by Orestes, the son of Agamemnon, when he was reduced to wandering after he killed Clytemnestra, his own mother, and that the city was originally called Orestias after him; but later the emperor Hadrian, who was fighting the Scythians, was attracted by the situation of the site, and fortified it with strong walls and called it the city of Hadrian.[19] Upon the emperor's arrival there, he learned from scouts that the difficult and narrow paths leading to Mysia (which they call *kleisourai* because they are so closed in)[20] were not guarded by the Scythians; and he assembled the captains and taxiarchs[21] and spoke as follows: "My fellow soldiers, I thought that the Scythians, who have been expecting our arrival in their land for a

[16] The same equation of Phison with Istros (Danube) is found in Ps.-Kaisarios, *Dial.* I (int. 68) and III (int. 144), PG 38:936, 1093. As pointed out by Panagiotakes, Leo's identification of the Phison, one of the four rivers of Paradise (Gen. 2:11), with the Danube is very similar to the description of the Danube found in an anonymous Byzantine excerptor (ed. M. Treu, "Excerpta anonymi byzantini ex codice Parisino suppl. gr. 607A," in *Städtisches Gymnasium zu Ohlau* 8.2 [Ohlau, 1880], 42–43); the same text is also published in PG 106:1056–57, under the title Περὶ τεσσάρων τοῦ παραδείσου ποταμῶν. The only difference is that Leo has the river reappear in the "Celtic Mountains," whereas the anonymous Byzantine author states that the river reemerges in the Apennine Mountains. Leo's "Celtic Mountains" are the Pyrenees: see Herodotus 2.33, and *Critobuli Imbriotae Historiae*, ed. D. R. Reinsch (Berlin–New York, 1983), 2.7.1 [= p. 95.6–7].

[17] The anonymous Byzantine excerptor states that the Phison is called the Ganges in the east; this is a much more common tradition, found, for example, in Kosmas Indikopleustes (ed. W. Wolska-Conus, *Topographie chrétienne* [Paris, 1968], 2:81) and *Eusebius. Onomastikon der biblischen Ortsnamen*, ed. E. Klostermann (Leipzig, 1904), 80.24, 166.7.

[18] For emeralds by the Phison, see Gen. 2:11–12 (ed. Rahlfs): ὄνομα τῷ ἑνὶ Φισων. οὗτος ὁ κυκλῶν πᾶσαν τὴν γῆν Ευιλατ, ἐκεῖ οὗ ἐστιν τὸ χρυσίον· τὸ δὲ χρυσίον τῆς γῆς ἐκείνης καλόν· καὶ ἐκεῖ ἐστιν ὁ ἄνθραξ καὶ ὁ λίθος ὁ πράσινος.

[19] Adrianople. As Panagiotakes pointed out, this information on the origin of the names Adrianople and Orestias is very similar to that provided in such 10th-c. chronicles as ps.-Symeon Magister (686.16–687.2) and Theophanes Continuatus (*Theoph. Cont.* 387.16–22): see A. Diller, "Excerpts from Strabo and Stephanus in Byzantine Chronicles," *TAPA* 81 (1950): 248.

[20] The Greek verb is κατακεκλεῖσθαι.

[21] On taxiarchs, see Book V, n. 42.

long time, would have with all their might closed off the most strategic and narrow and inaccessible portions of the paths with walls and stock-ades,[22] so that we could not easily proceed further. But the approach of Holy Easter has deterred them from securing the roads and [p. 131] preventing our passage, since they do not believe that we would give up the ceremonies attendant on the great festival, the splendid attire and processions and luxuries and spectacles, and become involved in the toils and tribulations of warfare. Thus I think the best course of action is to seize the opportunity immediately, and, equipping ourselves as quickly as possible, proceed along the narrow path before the Tauroscythians become aware of our approach and rush in force to the rough terrain. For if we manage to pass through the dangerous ground first and attack them unexpectedly, I think that (with the aid of God, let it be said) we will capture at the first assault the city of Preslav[23] itself, where the Mysians have their royal palace; and setting forth from there, we will very easily subdue the insolent Rus'."

3. This was the advice of the emperor, but to the commanders and taxiarchs at any rate these words seemed to be ill-timed recklessness and purposeless rashness verging on senseless insanity, to recommend thought-lessly that the Roman forces proceed into foreign territory by a precipi-tous path full of cavernous hiding places. Therefore, since they remained silent for quite a long time, the emperor again resumed speaking, swol-len with rage: "Since I have engaged from my youth in warfare, and, as you know, have crowned myself with many triumphs and victories, I myself am well aware that to go into battle without due deliberation, but in a bold and arrogant manner, is particularly likely to result in danger and ruinous destruction. On the other hand, when the situation is, as [p. 132] it were, *on a razor's edge*,[24] and does not give an opportunity to act according to one's wishes, then I think you too will agree with me that it is necessary to seize first this moment and take good care of our own affairs, since you have acquired great experience of the varying and

---

[22] On such stockades, mentioned also by Kekaumenos and Skylitzes (as τὰ δέματα), see McGeer, *Warfare*, 342 and n. 15; and cf. Anna Komnene, *Alexiad* 13.5.1 (ed. Leib, 3:104.12–13): διὰ τῶν καλουμένων ξυλοκλασιῶν.

[23] Great Preslav (located just south of modern Preslav in northeastern Bulgaria) was founded by Tsar Symeon in the late 9th c. as the second capital of Bulgaria. Excavations there have uncovered substantial remains of the medieval city: see *ODB* 3:1715–16.

[24] See *CPG* 1:238; 2:28, 166, 392, 753.

shifting fortunes of battles. If then you will heed me as I counsel a better course of action, while the Scythians have lapsed into indolence, as yet unaware of our approach, let us seize the opportunity and victory will follow upon our passage through the gorge. For if they should perceive us when we were about to pass through, and should deploy themselves into ranks to oppose us in the narrow defile, the situation would not turn out well for us, but would lead to dire straits and difficulties. Therefore pluck up your courage, and, remembering that you are Romans,[25] who have overwhelmed all your enemies by force of arms in the past, follow as quickly as possible, displaying your valor by means of your deeds."

4. After making this speech and putting on shining armor, he mounted a proud and mettlesome horse and shouldered a very long spear, and set off on the road, having in the van the company of so-called "Immortals,"[26] suitably sheathed in armor. He was followed by fifteen thousand of the most valiant heavy-armed infantry, and by thirteen thousand cavalrymen;[27] the rest of the soldiers and the service unit, who were transporting the siege machinery and all kinds of siege engines, followed slowly behind with the *proedros* Basil,[28] to whom the emperor entrusted responsibility for these [machines]. After he marched them through dangerous and precipitous areas without [p. 133] anyone taking notice, he checked the intense pace of the march, and allowed the cavalry and infantry to rest on a secure hill that had a river flowing past on both sides, promising an abundance of water. As soon as full light dawned, he roused the soldiers and deployed them into deep formations,[29] and advanced on Preslav, ordering the trumpets to sound the call to battle frequently, and the cymbals to clash and the drums to roll. And thus an indescribable clamor burst forth, as the mountains there echoed the drums, and the weapons clanked in response, and the horses whinnied, and the men shouted and encouraged each other for the battle, as was fitting.

[25] The same exhortation is used by Nikephoros Phokas in Crete (above, Book I, chap. 6), by the general Leo (Book II, chap. 3), and again by John Tzimiskes (below, chap. 10). The patriarch Polyeuktos uses it in Book II, chap. 12.

[26] On the "Immortals," an elite cavalry regiment, see Book VI, chap. 11 and n. 105.

[27] For comments on these figures, see Treadgold, *Byz. State*, 949 n. 18.

[28] On Basil the Nothos, see Book III, n. 56.

[29] See Book II, chap. 6, n. 34.

The Tauroscythians, on the other hand, when they saw the approach of the disciplined army towards them, were seized with panic and terror, in their astonishment at the unexpected turn of events. But they quickly seized their weapons and shouldered their shields (these were very strong, and made so that they reached to their feet,[30] for greater protection), and drew up into a strong close formation and advanced against the Romans on the plain before the town (which is suitable for cavalry), roaring like wild beasts and uttering strange and weird howls. The Romans came to blows with them, and fought stoutly and accomplished worthy feats of warfare. When the battle was evenly balanced on both sides, at this point the emperor ordered the Immortals to attack the left wing of the Scythians with a charge. So they held [p. 134] their spears[31] before them and violently spurred on their horses, and advanced against them. Since the Scythians were on foot (for they are not accustomed to fight from horseback, since they are not trained for this),[32] they were not able to withstand the spears of the Romans, but turned to flight and shut themselves up within the walls of the town; the Romans pursued them and killed them mercilessly.[33] For they say that in this attack eight thousand five hundred Scythians were killed.

5. The survivors shut themselves up in the town, and vigorously hurled missiles from the battlements above. It is said that at that time the *patrikios* Kalokyres[34] was staying at Preslav, the man who, as I have already related, previously incited the Rus' army against the Mysians; and that when he heard about the arrival of the emperor (for it was impossible for him to miss it, since the bright gold of the imperial insignia was gleaming incredibly), he secretly slipped out of the town in the middle of the night and went to Sphendosthlavos, who was staying with all his army somewhere near Dorystolon (which is now called

---

[30] On these full-length shields, see Book IX, n. 9.

[31] The Greek here is ἄκοντας, which is usually used by Leo to describe javelins, light throwing spears. Here they are clearly heavier cavalry spears, and just below (134.5) δορατισμός is used to describe the same spears.

[32] Leo is evidently exaggerating here (and at 140.22–23 and 143.16) the inexperience of the Rus' with cavalry: see Siuziumov et al., *Lev D'iakon*, 206 n. 21, and Book IX, n. 4. For another view, however, see Terras, "Ethnology of Kievan Rus'," esp. 397.

[33] For another translation of this passage, see McGeer, *Warfare*, 316.

[34] On Kalokyres, an imperial envoy to the Rus' under Nikephoros II, see Book IV, chap. 6, n. 44. Ambitious for imperial power, he hoped the Rus' would help him rebel against the empire (Book V, chap. 1).

Dristra).[35] So Kalokyres escaped in this way, and oncoming darkness made the Romans desist from battle. The next day, when the rest of the army came up with the siege machines (the day was the so-called Holy Thursday,[36] on which the Savior, on His way to the Passion, instructed the disciples in lessons of salvation after the Last Supper),[37] the emperor John rose early, [p. 135] and organized the units into unbroken close formations, and, after ordering the trumpets to sound the charge, he attacked the fortified wall in the hope of capturing the city at the first assault. As for the Rus', after they were encouraged by their general (this was Sphengelos,[38] who ranked third among the Scythians after Sphendosthlavos, for the latter ruled over everyone), they resisted from the battlements and warded off the attacking Romans as best they could, hurling javelins and missiles and fist-sized stones from above. The Romans, shooting constantly from below with bows and stone-throwing devices, and with slings and javelins, forced the Scythians back, by pressing hard and not allowing them to lean out from the battlements with impunity. And the emperor shouted in quite a loud voice and ordered them to set ladders against the circuit wall, and gave new vigor to the siege with his shouting; and everyone fought bravely under the gaze of the emperor, and hoped soon to receive from him rewards commensurate to their labors.

6. While the Romans were pressing hard and setting the ladders up against the walls, at this point a brave young man, whose face had just begun to be downy with reddish fuzz, a native of the Anatolic [theme] whose name was Theodosios, with the surname Mesonyktes,[39] drew his

[35] On Sviatoslav (Sphendosthlavos), see Book V, chap. 2 and n. 16. On Dorystolon, see Book V, n. 18. Panagiotakes changed the Δρίστα of the Hase ed. (δρήστα in P) to Δρήστρα.

[36] I.e., 13 April 971.

[37] See John 13:31–17:26. Note the play on words, ὁ Σωτὴρ and τὰ σωτήρια.

[38] Σφέγγελος (Σφάγγελος in Skyl. 296.51) is identified by M. Hrushevsky (*History of Ukraine-Rus'* [Edmonton, 1997], 1:360) as Sveneld (Sviatold), mentioned in the *Russian Primary Chronicle* (trans. Cross, 89) in the text of the treaty of 971. In Skyl. 296.51–52 he is described as commander of the Rus' army at Preslav, and as ranked *second* after Sviatoslav. The *Russian Primary Chronicle* (trans. Cross, 90) states, however, that Sveneld survived the later Petcheneg ambush (see Book IX, chap. 12) and made it back to Kiev. The second-ranked Rus' was Ikmor; see Leo diac. 149.2–3 (Book IX, chap. 6).

[39] Theodosios Mesonyktes (called Mesanyktes in Skylitzes), a hero of the capture of Preslav, later joined the rebellion of Bardas Phokas of 987–89, and was taken prisoner at the battle of Abydos (Skyl. 338.33).

sword with one hand and with the left raised his shield over his head, so that he would not be hit from above by the Scythians, and climbed up the ladder. When he got near the battlements, he aimed at the Scythian who was leaning out and defending himself against [Mesonyktes] [p. 136] with his spear, and struck him in the neck tendon; his head was swept off together with his helmet and rolled to the ground outside the walls. The Romans cheered loudly at the novel deed, and many of them ran up the ladders, emulating the courage of the man who had climbed up first. When Mesonyktes got up on the wall and gained control of the battlement, he smote great numbers of the defending Rus' on all sides and threw them headlong from the walls. And after many men quickly climbed up the circuit walls everywhere, and cut down the enemy with all their might, the Scythians abandoned the battlements and ignobly rushed into the stoutly walled royal palace, where the Mysians' treasure was stored, but inadvertently left a gate open.

While this was happening, the host of the Romans, attacking from outside the walls, broke through and smashed the pivots and bolts of the gates, and entered within the town, inflicting incredible slaughter upon the Scythians. And it is said that then Boris,[40] the king of the Mysians, whose face was thickly covered with reddish [hair],[41] was captured with his wife and two infant children, and brought before the emperor. The latter received him and treated him honorably, calling him ruler of the Bulgarians, and saying that he came to avenge the Mysians, who had suffered terribly at the hands of the Scythians.

7. As soon as the Romans got inside the town, they spread through the streets, slaying the enemy and carrying off loot. Then they attacked the royal palace, [p. 137] where the host of the Rus' was crowded together. But the Scythians inside resisted mightily and slew them as they slipped in through the gate, and killed up to a hundred and fifty vigorous men. When the emperor learned of this disaster, he quickly rode out on his horse, and urged his followers to throw themselves into the battle

---

[40] Boris II, tsar of Bulgaria 969–71.

[41] Hase suggested and Panagiotakes accepted the emendation of οὕτω 136.17 to οὕπω, meaning "whose face was not yet thickly covered with reddish [hair]." But this seems a strange description for a man probably born ca. 930, who would have been 40 in 971. Πυρσοῖς should probably be emended to πυρσαῖς with θριξίν understood, as in Leo diac. 135.19. There may have been a textual confusion with the description at the beginning of this chapter.

with all their strength. But since he was not able to achieve any glorious result (for the Tauroscythians were waiting for those who entered through the narrow gate, and easily killed most of them with their swords), he restrained the senseless headlong onslaught of the Romans, and ordered them to set fire to the palace on all sides with flaming arrows.[42]

Since the fire was burning fiercely and quickly reducing the underlying [structures] to ashes, the Rus', more than seven thousand in number, came out of the buildings and crowded together in the open courtyard, and prepared to defend themselves against their assailants. Against them the emperor deployed the *magistros* Bardas Skleros[43] with a vigorous company of men; Skleros surrounded them with the unit of most valiant men who were following him and set to work. Once the struggle began, the Rus' fought bravely, not turning their backs to the enemy, but the Romans shot them all down by virtue of their valor and experience of warfare, and most of the Mysians also fell in this battle; for they joined with the Scythians, and were hostile to the Romans, because they were the cause of the Scythians' coming to them. [p. 138] Sphengelos escaped to Sphendosthlavos, finding safety in flight together with a few men; but then he was killed, as I will soon recount.[44] Thus Preslav was captured in two days and made subject to the Romans.[45]

8. The emperor John rewarded the army, as was fitting, and let them rest, and celebrated there the Holy Resurrection of the Savior.[46] Then he selected some of the Tauroscythian prisoners, and sent them to Sphendosthlavos to announce to him the capture of the city and the slaughter of his comrades, and to tell him not to hesitate, but to choose immediately one of two options: either to lay down his weapons and yield to a stronger force and beg forgiveness for his rash deeds, and to depart immediately from the land of the Mysians; or, if he was unwilling to do this, but was inclined rather to his customary insolence, then he should *defend himself with all his might*[47] against the advancing Roman

---

[42] Reading πυροβόλων for περιβόλων.

[43] On Bardas Skleros, see Book VI, n. 106.

[44] See Book IX, chap. 2.

[45] For a very different account of the battle of Preslav, more favorable to the Rus', see *Russian Primary Chronicle*, 87–88.

[46] Easter fell on 16 April in 971: see Grumel, *Chronologie*, 310.

[47] See Agath. 23.3, 41.17.

forces. He ordered them to make these declarations to Sphendosthlavos; and then, after spending a few days in the city and restoring
the damaged fortifications and leaving behind a sufficient garrison,
and calling it Johannoupolis after his own name, he went off with all
his army to Dorystolon (which was built from the foundations by
Constantine,[48] celebrated among emperors, who constructed it with
the beauty and size that is apparent today, at the time when he saw
the sign of the cross placed among the stars in heaven, and subdued
the Scythians who were hostilely disposed to him and attacked him
in a frenzy).[49] Along the way the emperor captured the city called
Pliskova[50] [p. 139] and Dineia[51] and many of the cities that rebelled against
the Scythians and came over to the Romans. When Sphendosthlavos
learned of the disaster at Preslav, he was distressed and sorely grieved,
considering this a bad omen for the future; but, incited by the Scythian
madness and exultant at his victories over the Mysians, he thought he
could easily defeat the Roman forces.

9. When he saw that the Mysians were rebelling against their alliance with him, and going over to the emperor, he deliberated at length
and reflected that, if the Mysians sided with the Romans, affairs would
not turn out well for him. So he selected three hundred of the Mysians
who were of distinguished ancestry and power, and devised a cruel and
inhuman fate for them: for he had all their throats cut and killed them;
and he put the rest in chains and confined them in prison. Then he
mustered the Tauroscythian army, which came to sixty thousand men,
and deployed it against the Romans. And while the emperor was approaching them at a deliberate pace, certain bold souls, spurred on by

[48] Constantine I the Great.

[49] The site of Constantine's vision of the heavenly cross was transferred from the battle
of the Milvian Bridge to a battle on the Danube against invading barbarians in an
anonymous text on the "Vision of Constantine" preserved in two 11th-c. manuscripts:
see J. B. Aufhauser, *Konstantins Kreuzesvision in ausgewählten Texten* (Bonn, 1912), 19–21
(reference provided by Panagiotakes). The text makes no mention, however, of
Constantine's foundation of Dorystolon, which in fact came under Roman authority in
the reign of Domitian.

[50] Pliskoba or Pliska in northeastern Bulgaria was the first capital of the Bulgarian
kingdom. It was gradually abandoned in the 10th c. after the establishment of a new
capital at Preslav: see *ODB* 3:1685–86.

[51] Perhaps to be identified with the Dardanian fortress of Dinion mentioned in Prokopios,
Buildings, 4.4, p. 120.33.

reckless courage, separated off from the Rus' army, set up an ambush, and then attacked some of the advance scouts from their hiding place and killed them. When the emperor saw their bodies tossed alongside the path, he reined in his horse, and in anger at the death of fellow-countrymen [p. 140] ordered that the perpetrators of this deed be tracked down. After the footsoldiers zealously searched the copses and thickets and captured those attackers,[52] and led them in chains into the presence of the emperor, he ordered that they be put to the sword immediately. And they did not hesitate at all, but cut them completely to pieces with their swords.

As soon as the troops assembled in the area before Dorystolon,[53] which they were accustomed to call Dristra, the Tauroscythians closed their ranks with spears and shields and, as it were, made them into a tower, and awaited the enemy on the battlefield. After the emperor deployed the Romans in the van and placed ironclad horsemen on both wings, and assigned the archers and slingers to the rear and ordered them to keep up steady fire, he led out the army.[54]

10. As soon as the troops came to grips with each other, the battle broke out fiercely, and during the first assault the contest was equal on both sides for a while. For the Rus' fought furiously, considering it a terrible and shocking thing, if, when they had the reputation with neighboring peoples of always prevailing over their enemies in battle, they were now to be shamefully defeated by the Romans and lose this [reputation]. The Romans, on the other hand, were overcome by shame and anger, lest they, who prevailed over every enemy by force of arms and their own valor, should now have to withdraw, as if inexperienced in battle, overwhelmed by a people who fought on foot, and knew nothing of riding on horseback, and [p. 141] lest their great glory should vanish in a moment. So the soldiers fought valiantly, nourishing in their hearts such concerns for their reputation. The Rus', who were directed by their habitual ferocity and passion, attacked the Romans with a charge,

---

[52] On πελάτης, defined by LSJ as "neighbor," "one who approaches," but here with the apparent meaning of "attacker," see Book VII, n. 25.

[53] On the battle of Dorystolon, see S. McGrath, "The Battles of Dorostolon (971): Rhetoric and Reality," in Miller-Nesbitt, *Peace and War*, 152–64. The article compares the descriptions of the battles by Leo the Deacon and John Skylitzes. See also above, n. 35.

[54] On the battle tactics employed here, see McGeer, *Warfare*, 316.

bellowing as if possessed, but the Romans rushed to meet them with discipline and practical skill; and many men fell on both sides.

Until late afternoon victory appeared to be in the balance, as the course of battle swayed this way and that. The sun was already setting, when the emperor threw the cavalry against them in force, and bolstered the men's spirits, shouting that, since they were Romans, they should display their prowess by means of their deeds. So they pressed forward with an extraordinary assault and the trumpeters sounded the call to battle, and a shout arose from the Romans in a body. And the Scythians were not able to withstand their attack, and turned to flight and rushed to the fortifications, losing many of their men in this battle. The Romans chanted the songs of victory, and acclaimed the emperor, and he then rewarded them with awards of dignities and with banquets, and made them even more zealous for battle.

Book IX

[anno 971]

S SOON AS DAY BROKE, THE EMPEROR FORTIFIED the camp with a secure palisade in the following manner. A low hill rises from the plain some distance from Dorystolon. He had the army pitch its tents there and ordered them to dig a trench all round. They were to carry the dirt to the [p. 143] edge of the ditch that encircled the camp and deposit it, and when the dirt was piled up to a sufficient height, they were to plant spears firmly on top, and to lean against them shields touching each other, so that the army could use the ditch and heaped-up dirt as a wall, and the enemy would be unable to get inside, but their attack would be thwarted when they approached the trench. And it was customary for the Romans to set up their camp in this way in enemy territory.[1] After strengthening the palisade in this manner, the next day he drew up the army in battle order and began attacking the wall.[2]

The Scythians leaned over the towers and hurled missiles and stones and other far-darting weapons[3] against the Roman army; and they in turn defended themselves from below against the Scythians with slings and arrows, and the fighting on both sides consisted of this sort of skirmishing. Then the Romans went to their palisaded camp for their evening meal; but the Scythians, as the day was coming to a close, emerged from

[1] A similar description of this "shield-cover" is found in the 10th-c. *Taktika* of Nikephoros Ouranos, chap. 62.31–33 (ed. McGeer, *Warfare*, 136; see also 350–54, with illustrations of such "shield-covers" from the Madrid Skylitzes). Yahya of Antioch remarks that the use of a ditch and shield-cover was standard practice at a Byzantine camp: see M. Canard, "Les sources arabes de l'histoire byzantine aux confins des Xe et XIe siècles," *REB* 19 (1961): 284–314.

[2] The walls of Dorystolon were 4.7 meters thick, according to C. Lisitsov, *Kreposti i zaščitni sorženija na prvnata Bŭlgarska država* (Sofia, 1974), 37.

For another English translation of the above passage, with comments, see McGeer, *Warfare*, 353–54.

[3] The adjective ἐκηβόλος is Homer's epithet for Apollo as archer (e.g., *Iliad* 1.14). Arrian (*Tactica* 3.3.3; 15.1.2, ed. A. G. Roos and G. Wirth, *Flavii Arriani quae extant omnia*, 2 [Leipzig, 1968]) uses the adjective for bows, javelins, slings, and hand-thrown stones, while Anna Komnene (*Alexiad* 2.8.5 [ed. Leib, 1:90.19]; 10.8.6 [2:217.11]) uses ἐκηβόλος to refer to troops and crossbows.

the fortress on horseback, making at that time their first appearance riding on horses.[4] For they had always been accustomed to advance into battle without cavalry, since they were untrained in mounting on horses[5] and fighting the enemy. The Romans quickly protected themselves with armor and mounted their horses, and after snatching up lances (they use very long ones in battle), they rode out against them with a vigorous and mighty charge. And since [the Scythians] did not even know how to guide their horses with reins, they were cut down by the Romans, and turned to flight and shut themselves up inside the walls. [p. 144]

2. Then the Romans' fire-bearing triremes and the grain transports appeared sailing up the Istros; and when the Romans saw them, they were filled with unspeakable joy, but the Scythians were seized with fear, since they were afraid of the "liquid fire" that they transported. For they had heard from the elders of their people how the immense army of Igor,[6] the father of Sphendosthlavos, had been reduced to ashes by the Romans in the Euxine by means of this Median fire.[7] Therefore they quickly collected their own light boats,[8] and dragged them in front of the town wall, where the Istros as it flows by washes one side of Dorystolon. The fire-ships surrounded them and kept watch so that the Scythians would not be able to embark on them and escape to their own land.

The next day the Tauroscythians slipped out of the town and arrayed themselves on the plain, protecting themselves with shields that reached to their feet and chainmail breastplates;[9] and the Romans also emerged

---

[4] At Preslav the Rus' were still fighting on foot according to Leo diac. 133–134 (Book VIII, chap. 4 and n. 32). On the military equipment and tactics of the Rus', see Schreiner, "Ausrüstung," 226.

[5] Reading ἐφ' ἵππων with Panagiotakes for τῶν ἐφίππων of the manuscript, in preference to τῶν ἐφιππίων proposed by Hase. Cf. Book III, n. 82.

[6] When Igor, prince of Kiev, led a small naval expedition against Constantinople in 941 (see also above, Book VI, chap. 10), the Rus' were kept away from the capital by the patrikios Theophanes. After two months of plundering the Bithynian coast, their boats were destroyed by Greek fire on 15 September. Note Leo's exaggeration in referring to τὸν μυριόστολον στρατόν.

[7] "Median fire," an alternative term for "Greek fire," probably derived its epithet from the origins of naphtha, called "Median oil" by Prokopios (Gothic Wars 4.11.36). The term "Median fire" was also used by Attaleiates, Skylitzes, and Kinnamos. See Th. Korres, Hygron pyr, 31, 57, 67, 76, 78 n. 25, 80 n. 29, 96, 104, 105, 127.

[8] On the monoxyla of the Rus', see Book VI, n. 96.

[9] Ποδηνεκεῖς θυρεούς, a term perhaps borrowed from Homer, Iliad 15.645–46: ἀσπίδος … τὴν … ποδηνεκέ'. These full-length shields are also mentioned as typical of Scythian

from their camp completely sheathed in armor. Both sides fought valiantly, and it was unclear who would be victorious, as both sides pushed
each other back in turn. But then one of the Romans broke away from
the formation and struck down Sphengelos, a huge and vigorous man,
who was ranked third after Sphendosthlavos by the Tauroscythians,[10]
and was fighting furiously at that time; and the Tauroscythians were
thrown into disarray by his death, and gradually retreated from the plain
and hastened back to the town. At that time, too, Theodore Lalakon,[11] a
man who was hard to withstand and invincible in the might and strength
of his body, [p. 145] killed great numbers of the enemy with an iron
mace;[12] for he wielded it with such force in his arm that he would crush
at the same time the helmet and the skull protected by it. Thus the
Scythians then turned to flight and retreated to the town;[13] and the emperor ordered the signal for withdrawal to be sounded, and summoned
the Romans back to camp, and rewarded them with gifts and drinking
bouts, [thus] encouraging them to go into battle with robust spirits.

    3. While the situation was still uncertain, and the war was in progress,
Leo the *kouropalates*, the brother of the emperor Nikephoros, who was
confined at Methymna on Lesbos together with his son Nikephoros, as
I have already related,[14] bribed his guards with gold, and turned to rebellion, since the pupils of his eyes were undamaged. For the man who
was previously enjoined to destroy his eyesight,[15] acting either at the
command of the emperor (and there is good reason for this suspicion,
proof being that the man was not punished after the discovery of his
deed), or moved by pity at such misfortune, burned [only] his eyelids,

---

protective gear at Leo diac. 133.15–16; see also Terras, "Ethnology of Kievan Rus',"
398–99. On the chainmail breastplates, see Terras, "Ethnology of Kievan Rus'," 398 and
Schreiner, "Ausrüstung," 226.

[10] On the Rus' commander Sphengelos (Sveneld), see Book VIII, n. 38.

[11] A member of a family of the military aristocracy, Theodore is apparently attested only
here. An ancestor, Leo Lalakon, was *strategos* of the Armeniakon theme under Leo VI
(Treadgold, *Byz. State*, 466). On the family, see A. Kazhdan and S. Ronchey, *L'aristocrazia
bizantina dal principio dell' XI alla fine del XII secolo* (Palermo, 1997), 367.

[12] On the κορύνη, see Book VII, n. 70.

[13] The Greek reads διὰ τοῦ ἄστεος, literally "through the city," but this phrase seems to
repeat a phrase a few lines above, where the Scythians "retreated from the plain and
hastened back to the city (πρὸς τὸ ἄστυ)."

[14] See above, Book VI, chap. 2.

[15] On blinding as punishment for rebellion, see *ODB* 1:297.

but left his pupils undamaged and unhurt.[16] Then the *kouropalates* embarked on a light boat, and landed unperceived on the shore opposite Byzantium, and hid in a monastery that is called Pelamys.[17] From there he sent one of his men to inform his friends and acquaintances of his arrival. They agreed to assist him with all their might, and to assemble a host of armed men, [p. 146] and to steal the keys to the imperial palace, by means of which he could easily gain entrance to the palace. So they set to work, and made no delay in attempting to accomplish in deeds what they had promised in words. Thus they won over with bribes one of the imperial key-keepers,[18] and persuaded him to make a wax impression of the keys, and to give them the wax. And he did not hesitate, but made the wax impression and handed it over; and they hired an artisan, and quickly had the keys forged in a hearth.[19]

4. Since everything was going according to their plans, as they thought, they bade the *kouropalates* cross the Bosporos and land at Byzantium. So he embarked on a boat in the middle of the night and put in at the acropolis, and from there slipped into the town through a gate that was beneath the sanctuary of St. Phokas,[20] dreaming that he already held in his hands the imperial power. But instead of the brilliant purple mantle and golden scepters and absolute power that he improperly sought, fortune devised for him bitter blindness and distant exile and confiscation of his property, mocking the man's hopes, so that they did not lie assured, but turned out contrary to his plans and heaped up a grievous affliction of misfortune.

For while he was sitting in the house of one of his retainers in the quarter of Sphorakion[21] and was waiting for the conspirators to assemble,

---

[16] See Book VII, n. 18.

[17] Pelamys or Pelamydion was a monastery on the Asiatic shore of the Bosporos, probably near Hiereia: see Janin, *Grands Centres* 35. Skylitzes (Skyl. 303.54–55) calls it an estate (προάστειον).

[18] We have found no other reference to an imperial official called a κλειδοῦχος, though a κλειδοφύλαξ is attested in a third-century papyrus. On keys in Byzantium, see *ODB* 2:1125, and G. Vikan and J. Nesbitt, *Security in Byzantium* (Washington, D.C., 1980), 2–9.

[19] Although in Leo the Deacon the phrase ἐφ' ἑστίας normally means "at home," here it seems to have the more literal meaning of "in a hearth."

[20] The postern gate in the maritime wall surrounding the acropolis and the church of St. Phokas are known only from this passage: see Janin, *Églises CP* 497–98.

[21] A neighborhood of Constantinople north of Hagia Sophia, about halfway between the Milion and the Forum of Constantine, to the right of the Mese: see Janin, *CP byz.*, 428–29.

one of his followers slipped out of the house and approached one of his friends, who was in charge of the imperial weaving establishment,[22] [p. 147] and informed him of the arrival of the *kouropalates*, and revealed the plot and beseeched him and the body of workers in the weaving establishment to help them. He promised to help immediately and got up and went off as if to summon[23] his fellow [workers]. But instead he went to the *patrikios* Leo, the *droungarios* of the fleet,[24] who was at that time entrusted by the emperor with responsibility for the city of Byzantium, and told him everything: that the *kouropalates* had come back from exile, and now that he had returned and was staying in someone's house, he was plotting to seize the throne soon. Leo the *patrikios* was astounded by the unexpected news, but then recovered (for he was calm at times of crisis and effective at devising the proper solution to difficulties), and took his men and immediately attacked the building where the *kouropalates* was staying. When the *kouropalates* realized that his plot was discovered and revealed, he slipped out through a window with his son Nikephoros, and sought refuge in the holy and great church,[25] and could be seen as a *pitiful suppliant* instead of as an *arrogant*[26] and boastful usurper. The *droungarios*'s men dragged him away from there[27] and put him on a small boat together with his son Nikephoros, and exiled him to the island called Kalonymos,[28] and then, in accordance with the imperial command that came from the emperor in Mysia, they blinded them both and confiscated their property.

---

[22] This passage in Leo is a unique textual allusion to the existence of a guild (σύστημα) of imperial weavers in the 10th c.: see A. Christophilopoulou, "Σύστημα βασιλικῶν ἱστουργῶν: ἕνα σωματεῖο κρατικῶν ὑφαντουργῶν τὸν ι´ αἰῶνα," in *Βυζάντιον· Ἀφιέρωμα στὸν Ἀνδρέα Ν. Στράτο* (Athens, 1986), 1:65–72.

[23] Reading καλέσων with Panagiotakes for καλέσας of Hase ed.

[24] On Leo, *protovestiarios* and *patrikios*, see Guilland, *Institutions*, 1:173, 220, 432, 499, 539. On the *droungarios* of the fleet, see Book VI, chap. 2, n. 19.

[25] I.e., Hagia Sophia. On asylum, see Book III, n. 53.

[26] See Gregory of Nazianzus, *Or.* 43.57 (PG 36:569); the same phrase is used in Book III, chap. 7 for Joseph Bringas when he too sought asylum at Hagia Sophia.

[27] Violation of the privilege of asylum met with strong censure by church officials. See the 8th-c. case when the patriarch Tarasios excommunicated the soldiers who had dragged away from Hagia Sophia a *spatharios* who had taken refuge there (S. Efthymiadis, *The Life of the Patriarch Tarasios by Ignatios the Deacon* [Aldershot, 1998], chap. 34–37).

[28] An island in Lake Apollonias in Bithynia that has had many names over the course of its history, including Kalolimno, Hagios Konstantinos, and Amraliadasi. It was the site of a monastery founded by St. Theophanes the Confessor. See F. W. Hasluck, "Bithynica,"

Book IX

5. Thus the attempted usurpation by the *kouropalates* Leo had a terrible and disastrous end. Meanwhile the Rus' [p. 148] drew up in serried ranks (for again my narrative picks up where it left off), and marched out on the plain, endeavoring with all their might to burn the Romans' siege machinery; for they were unable to withstand the whizzing missiles the latter discharged, and many of the Scythians were killed each day by the stones that were hurled. The *magistros* John Kourkouas,[29] who was related to the emperor and was keeping guard over these machines, saw the bold attack of the enemy and, although he was drowsy from wine and nodding off (for it was after lunch), he mounted his horse and attacked them with picked followers. But his horse fell in a hole and threw the *magistros* off his back. When the Scythians caught sight of his gleaming armor and the horse's cheek-pieces and other trappings, which were magnificently wrought (for they were lavishly gilded), they thought that he was the emperor, and attacked him in a body with their weapons, and cruelly cut him to pieces with swords and axes; and they stuck his head on a spear and attached it to the towers, jeering at the Romans that they had butchered their emperor like a sheep. To fall victim to the wrath of barbarians was the price that the *magistros* John paid for his drunken violence against holy churches; for he is said to have plundered many of the [churches] in Mysia and to have refashioned their furnishings and holy vessels into personal valuables.

6. Elated by this victory, the Rus' issued forth from the city the next day, and drew up their ranks on the battlefield; and the Romans also [p. 149] were arrayed in close order and in a deep formation and went to meet them. At this point Anemas, one of the imperial bodyguards and son of the leader of the Cretans,[30] caught sight of Ikmor, second in command of the Scythian

---

Annual of the British School at Athens 13 (1906–7): 301–5; Janin, *Grands centres*, 157. Skylitzes (303.61) states that Leo and his son were banished to Prote, one of the Princes' Isles (on which see Book VI, n. 44). Loretto (*Phokas*, 187 n. 147.3) tentatively suggests emending to Kalymnos, between Samos and Rhodes.

[29] On John Kourkouas, see Book VII, n. 75. It should be noted that a drinking problem is mentioned in both passages.

[30] Anemas, son of the last Arab emir of Crete, ʿAbd al-ʾAziz (called Kouroupas in the Byzantine sources), became a loyal Byzantine subject after Nikephoros Phokas's recovery of Crete, and was appointed an imperial bodyguard and army commander: see Skyl. 250.42, 304.92. His heroic death on the battlefield is described later in Book IX, chap. 8. On him, see further G. Miles, *The Coinage of the Arab Amirs of Crete* (New York, 1970), 82–84.

army after Sphendosthlavos and ranked immediately after him,[31] a huge and vigorous man, who was frenziedly attacking with a company of infantry following him and killing large numbers of Romans; and Anemas was incited by his innate prowess, and drew the sword which was hanging at his side and turned his horse this way and that, and goaded it with his spurs, and headed toward Ikmor. And he overtook him and struck him in the neck; and the Scythian's head and right arm were severed and dashed to the ground. As he fell, a cry mingled with lamentation arose from the Scythians; and the Romans attacked them. They could not withstand the enemy assault, but, grievously distressed by the death of their general, raised their shields, covering their shoulders, and withdrew to the town; and the Romans pursued them and slaughtered them.

When night fell, since the moon was nearly full, they [the Rus'] came out on the plain and searched for their dead; and they collected them in front of the city wall and kindled numerous fires and burned them, after slaughtering on top of them many captives, both men and women, in accordance with their ancestral custom.[32] And they made sacrificial offerings by drowning suckling infants and chickens in the Istros, plunging them into the rushing waters of the river.[33] For they are said [p. 150] to be addicted to Hellenic mysteries,[34] and to make sacrifices and libations to the dead in the Hellenic fashion, having been initiated in these things either by their

---

[31] Skylitzes (304.87–91) describes the Rus' commander Ikmor as "most distinguished among the Scythians, . . . second in honor after Sphangelos (Sveneld) who had been killed, highly regarded by them not because of his lineage, nor out of compassion, but respected by all solely on account of his bravery. . . ."

[32] This statement may derive from Herodotus 4.62, who states that the Scythians sacrifice one man in every hundred captives. The 10th-c. Arab traveler Ibn Fadlan described a Rus' funeral on the Volga ca. 921, which involved the sacrifice of a rooster, the ritual killing of a concubine, and the cremation of the corpses of the Rus' chief and his concubine by making a funeral pyre of his wooden ship: see Eng. trans. of this text in G. Jones, *A History of the Vikings*, rev. ed. (Oxford, 1984), 425–30. See also T. Lewicki, "Les rites funéraires païens des slaves occidentaux et des anciens russes d'après les relations—remontant surtout aux IXe–Xe siècles—des voyageurs et des écrivains arabes," *Folia orientalia* 5 (1963): 1–74; A. P. Kovaleskii, *Kniga Akhmeda ibn-Fadlana o ego puteshestvii na Volgu v 921–922 gg.* (Khar'kov, 1956), 143; V. N. Zakhoder, *Kaspiiskii svod svedenii o Vostochnoi Evrope*, (Moscow, 1967), 2:113; and Terras, "Ethnology of Kievan Rus'," 400–401.

[33] The account of Ibn Fadlan (see note above) alludes to the sacrifice of chickens, dogs, cows, and horses, but not of suckling infants.

[34] Leo probably derived this notion from Herodotus 4.76–78, who repeats several times that the Scythians tended to adopt Greek rituals and usages.

own philosophers, Anacharsis and Zamolxis,[35] or by the comrades of Achilles. For Arrian says in the *Periplous* that Achilles, son of Peleus, was a Scythian, from a small town called Myrmekion located by Lake Maeotis;[36] and that he was banished by the Scythians because of his harsh, cruel, and arrogant temperament, and then went to live in Thessaly.[37] Clear proofs of this story are the style of his clothing with a brooch, and his fighting on foot, and his red hair and grey eyes, and his reckless and passionate and cruel temperament, on account of which Agamemnon reproached and mocked him, speaking as follows: "*Always is strife dear to you and wars and battles.*"[38] For the Tauroscythians are still acccustomed to settle their disputes with killing and bloodshed. That this people is reckless and warlike and mighty, and attacks all the neighboring peoples, is attested by many people, among them the holy Ezekiel, who alludes to them when he says as follows: "*Behold, I will bring upon you Gog and Magog, the ruler of the Ros.*"[39] But this is enough about the sacrifices of the Taurians.

7. Then, since day was already dawning, Sphendosthlavos assembled a council of nobles, called a *komenton*[40] in their language. When they were

---

[35] Anacharsis (Herodotus 4.76–78) was a hellenized Scythian sage who lived ca. 600 B.C. (*Oxford Classical Dictionary*, s.v.). Zamolxis, better known as Zalmoxis or Salmoxis, was a Getan deity of the dead sometimes identified with a slave of Pythagoras: see Herodotus, 4:94–96. Herodotus states that he was very familiar with Ionian Greek customs. Photius (*Lexicon*, s.v. "Zamolxis") also uses Zamolxis as the form of his name. Leo may have gotten this from Agath. 4.2.

[36] The Sea of Azov, connected to the Black Sea by the Cimmerian Bosporos (Straits of Kerč). The likely source for Myrmekion and the rest is Strabo (*Geography* 7.4.5, 11.2.6), who refers to a small city named Myrmekion 20 stades from Lake Maeotis, with the village of Achilleion on the opposite shore. Leo refers to the same passage from Strabo (11.2) in chap. 12 of Book IX: see nn. 65–66 below.

[37] The *Periplous* of Arrian has no information on the Scythian origins of Achilles; perhaps Leo drew his information from the anonymous *Periplus Ponti Euxini*: see A. Diller, *The Tradition of the Minor Greek Geographers* (Oxford, 1952), 7 and n. 29.

[38] Homer, *Iliad* 1.177.

[39] See Ezek. 38:2–4. Leo follows Theodoret's version of Ezekiel, which inserts a reference to Magog from v. 2 into vv. 3 and 4, and he omits the reference to Mosoch and Thobel. On the connection of Magog with the "Scythians," first found in Josephus (*Antiquitates Judaicae* 1.123.3, ed. B. Niese, *Flavii Josephi opera* [Berlin, 1887], 1:29.10–13), see A. Anderson, *Alexander's Gate, Gog and Magog, and the Inclosed Nations* (Cambridge, Mass., 1932), esp. 8 and n. 2.

[40] The Greek κομέντον (variant forms κόμβενδος, κόμβεντον, κομμέντον) derives from the Latin *conventus*, although Leo believes it to be a word of Slavic origin, while Skylitzes (460.6) thinks it is Petcheneg. See Moravcsik, *Byzantinoturcica*, 2:163 and Terras, "Ethnology of Kievan Rus'," 399–400.

all gathered round him, and [p. 151] had been asked by him what the course of action should be, some advised that they should embark on their boats in the middle of the night and steal away by any means whatsoever; for they were not able to contend with ironclad horsemen, and besides they had lost their best warriors, who had encouraged the army and sharpened their mettle. Others counseled, on the contrary, that they should come to terms with the Romans, and receive pledges in return, and thus save the remaining army. For they could not easily escape by ship, since the fire-ships were keeping watch over the transports on both sides of the Istros, so that they could immediately set fire to all of them, if they attempted to sail out on the river. Sphendosthlavos groaned deeply and bitterly, and said: "If we now yield ignobly to the Romans, gone will be the glory that has attended upon the arms of the Rus', as they have effortlessly over-whelmed neighboring peoples, and enslaved whole lands without blood-shed. Rather, let us again manifest the valor of our ancestors, and, remembering that up till now the might of the Rus' has been unvanquished, let us fight ardently for our safety. For it is not our custom to return to our fatherland as fugitives, but either to be victorious and live, or to die gloriously, after displaying deeds [worthy] of brave men." Such was the advice of Sphendosthlavos.

8. This also is said about the Tauroscythians, that never up until now had they surrendered to the enemy when defeated; but when they lose hope of safety, they drive their swords into their vital parts, [p. 152] and thus kill themselves. And they do this because of the following belief: they say that if they are killed in battle by the enemy, then after their death and the separation of their souls from their bodies they will serve their slayers in Hades. And the Tauroscythians dread such servitude, and, hating to wait upon those who have killed them, inflict death upon themselves with their own hands. Such is the belief that prevails among them.[41] But then, after listening to the words of their leader, out of love for life[42] they decided to choose danger for the sake of their own safety, and spiritedly drew up to oppose the Roman forces.

---

[41] G. Moravcsik argues that there is no evidence for such a belief among the Slavs, but such beliefs are found among Hungarians, Mongols, and Tatars: see "Zum Bericht des Leon Diakonos über den Glauben an die Dienstleistung im Jenseits," in *Studia antiqua Antonio Salač septuagenario oblata* (Prague, 1955), 74–76. Terras ("Ethnology of Kievan Rus'," 401) agrees with Moravcsik, and thinks Leo was misinformed on this point.

[42] Φιλόψυχος often has the connotation of "cowardly" or "fainthearted," but here it must mean just the opposite.

Book IX

Thus the next day (it was Friday, the twenty-fourth of July),[43] around sunset, the Tauroscythians emerged from the city with all their forces, and, having decided to run every risk with all their might, they drew up into a strong formation and presented their javelins.[44] And the emperor organized the Romans and led them out of camp. Once the battle broke out, the Scythians stoutly attacked the Romans, harassing them with javelins and wounding their horses with arrows, and hurling their riders to the ground. At this point Anemas, who had distinguished himself the previous day by killing Ikmor, saw Sphendosthlavos charging the Romans in a frenzied rage and encouraging his regiments; and he spurred on his horse (for he was accustomed to doing this, and had previously killed many Scythians in this way), and giving the horse free rein, he rode up to him [p. 153] and struck him on the collarbone with his sword, and knocked him flat, but did not kill him; for he was protected by his coat of mail and the shield with which he was equipped, out of fear of the Roman spears. And although Anemas was surrounded by the Scythian army, and his horse was brought down by numerous spear thrusts, he killed many of the [Scythians], but then was himself killed, a man surpassed by no one his age in brave feats in battle.

9. Therefore the Rus' took courage at his fall, and shouted loudly and fiercely, and pushed back the Romans. And they began to retreat at headlong speed,[45] to avoid the extraordinary assault of the Scythians. At this point, when the emperor perceived that the Roman army was giving way, he was afraid that in its terror at the extraordinary onslaught of the Scythians it might fall into mortal danger, so he encouraged his companions[46] and brandished his spear mightily, and advanced against the enemy; and the

---

[43] Either the day of the week or the date is in error, since in 971 the 24th of July fell on a Monday. Dölger ("Chronologie," 290–91) suggested that Leo may have conflated two dates that he found in his common source with Skylitzes, the day of the actual battle and the day of the end of the fighting and the agreement of capitulation.

[44] Although the same phrase, προβαλόντες τοὺς ἄκοντας, is translated at 134.1 as "holding their *spears* before them," here it seems that ἄκοντες must have its usual meaning of "javelin," especially since ἀκόντια is used just below to describe the same weapons.

[45] Leo has not understood that this was a feigned retreat: see J. Howard-Johnston, "Studies in the Organisation of the Byzantine Army in the Tenth and Eleventh Centuries," (D. phil. thesis, Oxford, 1971), 278–79.

[46] Τοῖς ἀμφ᾽ αὐτὸν: a select contingent of elite soldiers who accompanied the emperor into battle. See Leo diac. 108.23–109.1 and 127.17, where the soldiers are termed λογάδας. On this passage in chap. 9, see McGeer, *Warfare*, 318.

drums beat, and the trumpets sounded the battle call. The Romans were put to shame by the emperor's assault, and wheeled round their horses, and fiercely attacked the Scythians. At the same time a wind and rainstorm broke out, pouring down heavily from the sky, and struck the enemy,[47] and the dust that was stirred up irritated their eyes.

And it is said that there appeared a man on a white horse, who went ahead of the Romans and encouraged them to advance against the Scythians; and he [p. 154] broke through the enemy regiments in a wondrous fashion, and threw them into disarray. And they say that the men[48] in the camp had not seen this man previously, nor did they see him again after the battle, although the emperor looked for him, so that he might present him with suitable gifts, and reward him with compensation for his labors. But despite the search he was not found. Therefore a definite suspicion was aroused that it was the great martyr Theodore,[49] whom the emperor used to beseech for help in battle, and to protect and preserve him together with all the army. And they say that the following occurred on the evening before the battle. In Byzantium a virgin dedicated to God[50] thought that she saw in a dream the Mother of God, escorted by men in the form of flames.[51] And She said to them, "Summon for me the martyr Theodore"; and immediately there appeared a brave young man in armor. And the Mother of God

---

[47] For a similar storm, sent by the Theotokos, which also affected only the enemy forces, see Theoph. 315.19–21. For the emphasis on the supernatural element here and below— the mysterious storm, the participation of St. Theodore, the vision of the Virgin—as well as the renaming of Dorystolon as Theodoroupolis, and many aspects of the subsequent triumph as propaganda by Tzimiskes to give the appearance of celestial approval for the assassination of Nikephoros Phokas, see McCormick, *Eternal Victory*, 170–76. For similar propaganda, see also the gold nomisma depicting the Virgin crowning John, with the "hand of God" just above them (*DOC* 3.2:592 and pl. XLII, 1a).

[48] Reading τοὺς with Panagiotakes (following E) rather than τις of Hase ed.

[49] St. Theodore Stratelates, a military saint, who is often depicted as a mounted warrior (*ODB* 3:2047); Leo later specifies this identification at 158.1–2.

[50] I.e., a nun.

[51] The φλογοειδεῖς ἄνδρες are probably angels, more specifically seraphim (cf. the αἱ φλογοείκελοι ἀξίαι τῶν ἀγγέλλων of Eustathios of Antioch, *De engastrimytho contra Origenem* 10, ed. E. Klostermann in *Origenes, Eustathius von Antiochien, und Gregor von Nyssa über die Hexe von Endor*, Kleine Texte 83 [Bonn, 1912], 31.4); the term is extremely rare, attested only three times by the *TLG* for 10th-c. authors. Perhaps this vision was inspired by a verse in the *Akathistos Hymnos*, "Hail, Perfect Dwelling of the One above the Seraphim," ed. C. Trypanis, *Fourteen Early Byzantine Cantica* (Vienna, 1968), p. 36, ιε΄ line 11. See L. M. Peltomaa, *The Image of the Virgin Mary in the Akathistos Hymn* (Leiden, 2001), 183–84.

said to him, "Lord Theodore, your John, who is fighting the Scythians at Dorystolon, is now in very difficult straits. Make haste to help him. For if you are not in time, he will be in danger." He in turn replied that he was ready to obey the Mother of God his Lord; and after saying this he departed immediately, and thus sleep vanished from the eyes of the virgin. And the virgin's dream was fulfilled in this way.

10. The Romans, following the divine personage who led the way, [p. 155] came to grips with the enemy. And when fierce fighting broke out, the Scythians could not withstand the assault of the cavalry, and were surrounded by the *magistros* Bardas, whose surname was Skleros (for he made the encircling movement with his accompanying host),[52] and turned to flight, and were trampled right up to the city wall and fell ignobly. Sphendosthlavos himself narrowly escaped capture, since he had *lost a lot of blood and had been stricken by many arrows*,[53] but he was saved by the approach of darkness. And it is said that in this battle fifteen thousand five hundred Scythians were killed, and that twenty thousand shields and a vast number of swords were captured; while three hundred fifty of the Romans were killed, and many wounded. Such was the victory that the Romans won in this battle.

Although Sphendosthlavos grieved all night over the decimation of his army, and was distraught and seething with rage, since he was not able to prevail over an invincible army, he recognized that it was the task of an intelligent general not to fall into despair when caught in dire straits, but to endeavor to save his men in any way possible. And so at dawn he sent envoys to the emperor John, and asked for sworn agreements, that, on the one hand the Tauroscythians would hand Dorystolon over to the Romans, and release the prisoners, and depart from Mysia, and return to their own country; while the Romans were to allow them to sail away and were not [p. 156] to attack with their fireships while they were setting sail[54] (for they were terribly afraid of Median fire,[55] which can reduce even stones to ashes), and were to supply them with provisions, and to consider

---

[52] Encirclement (κύκλωσις) of the enemy formation by outflanking troops was a tactic recommended by 10th-c. military manuals: see *Praecepta Militaria* IV.185 and *Taktika* of Nikephoros Ouranos, 61.37, 136, 260, in McGeer, *Warfare*, 48.185, 118.37, 124.136, 130.260.

[53] See Book I, n. 55.

[54] Reading ἀναγομένοις with Panagiotakes for ἐναγομένοις of Hase ed.

[55] See n. 7 above.

them as friends when they journeyed to Byzantium to trade, just as was their previous custom.[56]

11. The emperor readily accepted such a reconciliation (for he very much preferred peace to warfare,[57] since he was aware that the former preserves the people, whereas the latter, on the contrary, destroys them), and he concluded the agreements and treaties,[58] and gave grain to each man, measuring out two *medimnoi*[59] apiece. And they say that the men who received the grain were twenty-two thousand in number, who, out of the sixty thousand men in the Rus' army, had escaped death; for the Roman spears struck down thirty-eight thousand.

After the treaties were arranged, Sphendosthlavos asked to come and speak with the emperor. And the latter came without delay on horseback to the bank of the Istros, clad in armor ornamented with gold, accompanied by a vast squadron of armed horsemen adorned with gold.[60] Sphendosthlavos arrived sailing along the river in a Scythian light boat, grasping an oar and rowing with his companions[61] as if he were one of them. His appearance was as follows: he was of moderate height, neither taller than average, nor particularly short; his eyebrows were thick; he had grey eyes and a snub nose; [p. 157] his beard was clean-shaven, but he let the hair grow abundantly on his upper lip where it was bushy and long; and he shaved his head completely, except for a lock of hair that hung down on one side, as a mark of the nobility of his ancestry; he was solid in the neck, broad in the chest and very well articulated in the rest of his body; he had a rather angry and savage appearance; on one ear was fastened a gold earring, adorned with two pearls with a red gemstone[62] between them; his clothing was white, no different from that of his companions except in

[56] On the Russo-Byzantine treaties of 911 and 944, which dealt in part with the privileges and responsibilities of Rus' merchants in Constantinople, see *ODB* 3:2111–12 (s.v. "Treaties, Russo-Byzantine") and the relevant bibliography.

[57] See Herodotus 1.87; Euripides, *Suppliants* 488.

[58] The text of the treaty, as preserved in the *Russian Primary Chronicle* (trans. Cross, 89–90), does not include any trade agreements; they may have been in a separate document.

[59] A *medimnos*, a classicizing term for *modios*, was a unit of measurement for grain, of varying quantity.

[60] This seems to be the same elite contingent (the "Immortals") noted above in chap. 9 (Leo diac. 153.15).

[61] Reading ἑταίροις with Panagiotakes (as conjectured by Hase) for ἑτέροις of P.

[62] The Greek word ἄνθραξ can mean a ruby, garnet, or carbuncle.

cleanliness.[63] After talking briefly with the emperor about their reconciliation, he departed sitting on the helmsman's seat of the boat. Thus the war
of the Romans with the Scythians came to an end.

12. After Sphendosthlavos abandoned Dorystolon and handed over
the captives in accordance with the treaties, he sailed away with his remaining comrades, eager to return to their fatherland. But in the course of
their voyage they were ambushed by the Patzinaks[64] (they are a very numerous nomadic people, who eat lice[65] and carry their houses with them,[66]
living for the most part in wagons), who killed almost all of them and
slaughtered Sphendosthlavos himself along with the rest, so that out of
such a large army of Rus' only a few returned safely to their native abodes.

After the emperor John fought the Rus' forces for four whole months,
as my narrative has just related, and saved Mysia for the Romans, [p. 158]
he changed the name of Dorystolon to Theodoroupolis in honor of the
warrior and martyr Theodore the Stratelates,[67] and he left a substantial
garrison there and returned to Byzantium with great trophies of victory;
and on his arrival he found the citizens before the walls, welcoming him
with crowns and scepters wrought of gold and precious stones. And they
brought a chariot decorated with gold and drawn by a white horse, and
demanded that he ride on it and lead the customary triumphal procession.[68]

---

[63] See the description of Attila in *Prisci excerpta de Legationibus Romanorum*, ed. C. de
Boor in *Excerpta historica iussu imp. Constantini Porphyrogeniti confecta* (Berlin, 1903), 1:144.
On this portrait of Sviatoslav, see Terras, "Ethnology of Kievan Rus'," 401–5; also I.
Ševčenko, "Sviatoslav in Byzantine and Slavic Miniatures," *Slavonic Review* 24 (1965):
709–13.

[64] The Patzinaks or Petchenegs were a nomadic people who moved from Central Asia
into the Volga basin in the late 9th c. Although previously the Petchenegs had helped
Sviatoslav against the Byzantines, the latter were eventually able to purchase their support,
and they killed Sviatoslav in 972 at the cataracts of the Dnieper. See *ODB* 3:1613–14,
and E. Malamut, "L'image byzantine des Petchenegues," *BZ* 88 (1995): 117, who cites
this passage from Leo.

[65] Strabo (*Geography* 11.2.1) places a people called the lice-eaters (φθειροφάγοι) near
Lake Maeotis, indicating that they are so named because of their squalor and filthiness
(11.2.19). It was apparently Leo the Deacon who first gave this epithet to the Patzinaks.

[66] Herodotus (4.46) uses the same epithet φερέοικοι of the Scythians, while Strabo
(*Geography* 11.2.1) calls the Scythians νομάδες καὶ ἁμάξοικοι.

[67] See n. 49 above. Note, however, the suspicions of Oikonomides about the veracity of
Leo's account of the renaming of Dorystolon; see N. Oikonomides, "Le dédoublement
de Saint Théodore et les villes d'Euchaïta et d'Euchaneia," *AB* 104 (1986): 330 n. 10.

[68] On this triumph of 971, see McCormick, *Eternal Victory*, 170–74. As McCormick
points out, the description of the chariot is borrowed from Plutarch's *Camillus*, 7.1. See

While he accepted the crowns and scepters and rewarded them many times over with gifts, he refused to mount on the chariot, but placed on the chariot's golden throne the icon that he brought from Mysia of the Mother of God, holding in Her arms the theanthropic Word,[69] and placed beneath it the purple garments of the Mysians and the crowns. And he followed behind, mounted on a fine steed, his head encircled with a diadem and carrying the crowns and scepters in his hands. Thus he led the triumphal procession through the middle of the city, which was everywhere decorated with purple cloths and, like a bridal chamber, was thickly bedecked with laurel branches and with fabric interwoven with gold,[70] and entered the great church of the Wisdom of God. And after offering up prayers of thanksgiving, and dedicating to God the splendid crown of the Mysians as a gift from the first spoils, he went to the palace, and brought forth Boris, the king of the Mysians, and made him take off the royal insignia (they were a tiara with purple border, studded with gold and pearls, [p. 159] and a purple robe and scarlet boots), and honored him with the rank of *magistros*. Thus, after the emperor John achieved such triumphs in an unbelievably short time, overwhelming and casting to the ground the insolence of the Rus' and their arrogant tempers through his experience in warfare and his daring and calculated courage, and making Mysia subject to the Romans, he returned to Byzantium for the winter[71] and, as was fitting, rewarded his subjects with gifts and entertained them with sumptuous banquets.

McCormick's fig. 10 for a reproduction of a miniature from the Madrid Skylitzes depicting Tzimiskes' triumphal entry.

[69] The icon is usually identified as the Hodegetria: see A. W. Carr, "The Mother of God in Public," in *Mother of God: Representations of the Virgin in Byzantine Art*, ed. M. Vassilaki (Milan, 2000), 332 and fig. 207.

[70] This passage resembles Constantine VII's descriptions of the decoration of Constantinople for the triumphal entries of Theophilos and Basil I after successful campaigns, where the ornamented city is also compared to a bridal chamber: see J. Haldon, *Constantine Porphyrogenitus. Three Treatises on Imperial Military Expeditions* (Vienna, 1990), 140, 146–48.

[71] The winter of 971/72.

Book X

W HEN SUMMER ARRIVED AND CONSISTENT FAIR WEATHER spread over the earth, the emperor set forth from Byzantium, to campaign against the Agarenes who inhabited Upper Syria.[2] And so after traversing the interior regions, he crossed the Euphrates; this is the biggest of the rivers that cut across Asia [p. 161] and one of those that rise in Eden, as we have learned from the Holy Scriptures.[3] To his misfortune a certain secretary named Niketas,[4] an extremely knowledgeable and intelligent man, and in the prime of life, accompanied the emperor on this campaign, even though his father entreated him at length not to do this, but urged[5] him rather to stay at home and look after his father in his old age and care for him to the best of his ability, since he was

---

[1] The absolute dates of the events described by Leo in Book X, particularly the eastern campaigns of Tzimiskes against the Arabs, have been much discussed. Most modern historians are now agreed that there were three Byzantine campaigns against the Arabs: in 972, 974, and 975. Problems arise because Leo the Deacon seems to have conflated the campaigns of 972 and 974, and the principal Arab historian, Yahya of Antioch, does not mention the campaign of 974. This has led to great confusion. Valiant attempts to sort out the chronology have been made by Dölger, "Chronologie," Canard, "Expéditions mésopotamiennes," and Grégoire, "Amorians and Macedonians," among others, with somewhat differing conclusions.

[2] This would seem to be the summer of 972, immediately following upon the winter of 971/72 described at the very end of Book IX: see Dölger, "Chronologie," 285. Grégoire agrees that there was a campaign in 972, but mistakenly states that Leo placed it in 973: see "Amorians and Macedonians," 164. On the evidence of Arab sources for the campaign of 972, see Canard, "Expéditions mésopotamiennes," 101–7.
  Leo proceeds, however, to describe events of the campaign of 974, omitting, for example, the capture of Nisibis in 972 and Melias's siege of Amida in 973. Hase (Leo diac. 488) states that Book X covers the years 973–74, since Leo is silent about the beginning of the war in 972.

[3] Gen. 2:14. For more on Leo's understanding of the four rivers that originate in Eden, see Book VIII, n. 16.

[4] Not otherwise known. The term ὑπογραφεύς was often used for imperial scribes or secretaries: see, e.g., *The Life of the Patriarch Tarasios by Ignatios the Deacon*, ed. S. Efthymiadis (Aldershot, 1998), chap. 6.9; C. de Boor, *Nicephori archiepiscopi Constantinopolitani opuscula historica* (Leipzig, 1880), 144.8, 189.30–31.

[5] Reading προσειπόντος for προσέποντος of the manuscripts; Panagiotakes proposes an emendation to προτρέποντος .

on the threshold of old age[6] and would soon move into *the sunset of life.*[7] But he ignored his father's bidding, as he should not have, and disregarded his admonitions, and, equipping himself as best he could,[8] went off to the army encampment. But while he was crossing the river, he was made dizzy by the depth of the water, and slipped off his horse and fell into the river, and was carried off by the current, and drowned wretchedly, receiving a watery death in the Euphrates as the price of his disobedience.

The emperor began to raid Syria with all his army, but none of the enemy came out to oppose him, since they were all confounded by the report of his invasion and shut themselves up in their fortresses and towns. And he captured Emet[9] (this is a strong and famous city) and brought it to terms, and took countless tribute; and setting forth from there he went to Miefarkim;[10] this is a famous and splendid town, superior in wealth and livestock to the other cities in the same region. [p. 162] And he brought it to terms and carried off numerous beautiful gifts in gold and silver and cloth woven with gold, which he demanded from its inhabitants; then he went to Nisibis,[11] which the great Jacob, after taking the helm of the

[6] See Homer, *Odyssey* 15.246, 348, 23.212, etc.

[7] See Aristotle, *Poetics* 1457b.

[8] It is not clear whether the phrase ὡς εἶχεν ἐνσκευασάμενος implies that he was equipping himself at his own expense.

[9] As noted in n. 2 above, here Leo seems to jump two years ahead to 974, the date of the capitulation of Amida according to Matthew of Edessa: see Canard, "Expéditions mésopotamiennes," 107. Emet/Amida (= Diyarbakir in present-day southeastern Turkey) was under the control of the Hamdanids (see J. Sourdel-Thomine, in *EI²* 2:344–45) when it was forced to pay tribute to the Byzantines to avoid sack and pillage: see Grégoire, "Amorians and Macedonians," 167; Treadgold, *Byz. State*, 511.

[10] Miefarkim is Leo's rendering of Meyyafariqin (= Silvan in present-day Turkey), the Arabic name for ancient Martyropolis, located northeast of Amida; like Amida, it was in the hands of the Hamdanids in 974 (see *EI²* 6:929–30), when it was forced to pay tribute to the Byzantines: see Grégoire, "Amorians and Macedonians," 167; Treadgold, *Byz. State*, 511. In 972 it had been unsuccessfully besieged by Tzimiskes: see Canard, "Expéditions mésopotamiennes," 107.

[11] A city in Mesopotamia much disputed in late antiquity between the Romans and Persians; it is now Nusaybin in present-day Turkey. See *ODB* 3:1488; E. Honigmann and C. E. Bosworth, in *EI²* 7:983–84; and J. M. Fiey, *Nisibe, métropole syriaque orientale et ses suffragants des origines à nos jours* (Louvain, 1977). Tzimiskes had taken the city and burned it in 972: see Grégoire, "Amorians and Macedonians," 164; M. Canard, "Byzantium and the Muslim World to the Middle of the Eleventh Century," in *The Cambridge Medieval History*, 4.1 (Cambridge, 1966), 722–23. In 974 Tzimiskes found Nisibis deserted: see Grégoire, "Amorians and Macedonians," 167.

bishopric, had defended against the Persians who attacked Nisibis with a great army, fighting them with swarms of gnats and mosquitoes and making them instantly turn to flight and in this way overcoming the enemy.[12] The emperor found the city deserted, since the inhabitants had left in their fear of the Roman expedition and had fled to the interior.

2. Therefore he raided the surrounding region and made it subject to the Romans, and then went off toward Ekbatana,[13] where the palace of the Agarenes was, containing fabulous silver and gold and every sort of wealth, anxious to take it, too, by assault. For it is said that the city of Ekbatana has more wealth and gold than any other cities under the sun; and the reason is that it extracts wealth from many lands, but has never yet suffered invasion by any of its enemies. But his invasion was checked by the lack of water and scarcity of provisions in the area; for the desert called Karmanitis[14] extends through those regions, providing *a rugged and steep route*, and it neither produces any water nor bears any vegetation,[15] [p. 163] but is sandy and dry. Therefore he packed up the gifts[16] brought him by the Agarenes, which amounted to three million [nomismata?] in gold and silver, and returned to Byzantium; there he displayed in a triumphal procession through the marketplace[17] the gold and silver and the cloths and perfumes from the Seres[18] and the other gifts that he received from the Agarenes, and the

[12] This miraculous rescue of Nisibis was effected by its bishop Jacob in 338. See Theodoret of Cyrus, *Historia ecclesiastica* 167–69; see also P. Canivet and A. Leroy-Molinghen, *Théodoret de Cyr. Histoire des moines de Syrie* (Paris, 1977), 1:186.40.

[13] Ekbatana, the former capital of Media in central Iran, is present-day Hamadan. Loretto (*Phokas*, 190) plausibly thinks that Baghdad is meant, as does Honigmann (*Ostgrenze*, 98); see n. 72 below. On this campaign, see also W. Kaegi, "Challenges to Late Roman and Byzantine Military Operations in Iraq (4th–9th Centuries)," *Klio* 73 (1991): 592–93.

[14] Again Leo's geography seems to be confused and he may intend to refer to the "Syrian desert" west of the Euphrates. Karmania is the area of Iran southwest of the great desert (the Dasht-i-Lut), a region into which it is unlikely that Tzimiskes led his troops: see Honigmann, *Ostgrenze*, 99, and Grégoire, "Amorians and Macedonians," 168. Leo may have known about Karmania from Strabo (15.2.14).

[15] Note the use of paronomasia in the Greek, βλυστάνουσα ... ἀναβλαστάνουσα. For the "rugged and steep route," see Plato, *Republic* 364d.

[16] Perhaps add τὰ after διὰ ταῦτα, as suggested by Hase and Panagiotakes.

[17] Guilland (*Topographie*, 2:73–76) has shown that ἀγορά in a Constantinopolitan context usually referred to the Mese, along which there were market stalls and shops.

[18] I.e., the Chinese (see LSJ, s.v. Σήρ), the people from whom silk was obtained; on the medieval silk route, see *ODB* 3:1898, and A. A. Ierusalimskaia and B. Borkopp, *Von China nach Byzanz: Frühmittelalterliche Seiden aus der Staatlichen Ermitage Sankt Petersburg* (Munich,

citizens watched and marveled at their quantity, and welcomed him with honor and escorted him with acclamations to the palace, extolled with praises for these victories.[19]

At that time, on account of the envy of the bishops, a slanderous charge was made to the emperor about the patriarch Basil,[20] that he was making use of his authority like the magnates[21] and was not administering the Church as is laid down by the holy canons, and he was summoned before the imperial tribunal. Since he did not present himself, but in response asserted that an ecumenical council should be convoked and then the charges would be dismissed (for this was the intent of the divinely inspired precepts of the Fathers, that an ecumenical council should be summoned for the deposition of a patriarch),[22] he was banished by the emperor to the monastery that he himself had built on the Skamandros River;[23] he was an emaciated man and almost devoid of flesh, since he had disciplined himself since childhood with superhuman feats of asceticism, and he wore only one garment summer and winter and did not remove it until it fell apart and became useless, and he tasted no food or drink except water and fruit juices.[24] [p. 164] And it is said that he did not sleep in a bed,

---

1996). Chinese fabrics are also mentioned in *Ioannis Caminiatae De Expugnatione Thessalonicae*, ed. G. Böhlig (Berlin–New York, 1973), 11.83, where it is stated that these fabrics were valued in Thessalonike as low as woolen ones.

[19] For this triumph, see McCormick, *Eternal Victory*, 175; he dates the triumph to late 972 or 973, as does Dölger ("Chronologie," 285). We would place it, however, in 974, following Grégoire, "Amorians and Macedonians," 169.

[20] Basil I Skamandrenos. For his dates, see above, Book VI, n. 70, and n. 23 below.

[21] Reading ὡς δίκην with Panagiotakes for ὡς δή τινι of Hase ed. If the reading of the manuscript is retained, then one could translate "that he was purportedly lending his authority to one of the magnates."

[22] On the deposition of patriarchs by the synod, see J. Darrouzès, *Recherches sur les ὀφφίκια de l'église byzantine* (Paris, 1970), 492. No documents at all survive from the patriarchate of Basil: see *Les Regestes des actes du patriarcat de Constantinople*, ed. V. Grumel, 2nd ed., 1.2–3 (Paris, 1989), 308.

[23] Basil was deposed ca. 13 August 973, according to a new chronology established by J. Darrouzès, "Sur la chronologie du patriarche Antoine III Stoudite," *REB* 46 (1988): 55–60. The traditional date of 974 (Grumel, *Chronologie*, 436) seems to fit better, however, with the chronology of Leo the Deacon as we have interpreted it, following Grégoire. Basil's monastery was located on the Skamandros River (the Küçük Menderes), near Kyzikos: see Janin, *Grands centres*, 212–13.

[24] The precise translation of τῶν ἐξ ἀκροδρύων χυμῶν is uncertain. Ἀκρόδρυα usually are interpreted as hard-shelled fruits that grow on trees, like nuts and pomegranates (see,

but on the ground during all the time of his ascetic discipline. And they say that the man had only one fault, that he was excessively concerned with prying into men's conduct and behavior, and was a busybody and more inquisitive than he should be.

3. Thus Basil was sentenced to exile, and the helm of the patriarchate was entrusted to Antony,[25] a man who from his youth had chosen the ascetic discipline and led an apostolic life in the monastery of Stoudios.[26] He never wore more clothes than necessary [to cover] his flesh, even though he was generously rewarded by notables and the emperors themselves for his inherent virtue; and in addition he took the remuneration for his official position (for he was previously honored with the office of *synkellos*),[27] and gave it all to the poor, *imitating the mercy of God*,[28] and was wealthier than anyone else in divine and human knowledge. A marvelous grace shone in his face and manner in his great old age; for no one of those who live luxuriously, and vaunt themselves greatly on the vanity of life, ever approached him and did not go away immediately edified, having learned that *life is but a shadow*[29] and a dream; nor, on the other hand, was there anyone leading an unhappy existence, because of *unbearable misfortunes*,[30] who did not leave in good spirits, having learned *not to lose heart at afflictions*, but to throw himself *on the One Who can save him from affliction*[31] and to seek salvation from Him. [p. 165] Such was Antony in his life and discourse, in short an angelic and divine man.

e.g., H. Beckh, *Geoponica sive Cassiani Bassi scholastici De re rustica eclogae* [Leipzig, 1895], 309, Book X, chap. 74), but sometimes seem to be a generic term for fruit; see LSJ, s.v. and Lampe, *PGL*, s.v. Ἀκρόδρυα are regularly included among the food of ascetics: see, e.g., vita B of Athanasios of Athos, ed. J. Noret, *Vitae duae antiquae sancti Athanasii Athonitae* (Turnhout, 1982), 139, chap. 13.18.

[25] Antony III Stoudites. The traditional dates of his patriarchate are 974–79 (see Grumel, *Chronologie*, 436). A revised chronology of December 973–ca. June 978 is proposed by J. Darrouzès (see n. 23 above), but 974 seems to work better with Leo's chronology as we have interpreted it here.

[26] On this celebrated Constantinopolitan monastery, see Janin, *Églises CP*, 430–40.

[27] The advisor of a patriarch, who by the 10th c. was viewed as the successor designate: see *ODB* 3:1993–94.

[28] See Gregory of Nazianzus, *Or.* 14.26 (PG 35:892.43).

[29] See Job 8:9, 1 Chron. 29:15, Wisd. of Sol. 2:5, Pindar, *Pythian Odes* 8.95.

[30] See Thucydides 5.111.3, Agath. 41.22–23.

[31] See Eph. 3:13, Heb. 5:7, Sirach 2:11.

At this time male twins, who came from the region of Cappadocia, were wandering through many parts of the Roman Empire; I myself, who am writing these lines, have often seen them in Asia, a monstrous and novel wonder. For the [various] parts of their bodies were whole and complete, but their sides were attached from the armpit to the hip, uniting their bodies and combining them into one.[32] And with their adjacent arms they embraced each other's necks, and in the others they carried staffs, on which they supported themselves as they walked. They were thirty years old and well developed physically, appearing youthful and vigorous. On long journeys they used to ride on a mule, sitting [sideways] on the saddle in the female fashion, and they had indescribably sweet and good dispositions. But enough about this.

4. When spring appeared once again, the emperor John mustered the Roman troops and equipped them thoroughly, and, after departing from the imperial city, marched through Palestine,[33] a prosperous land, *flowing with milk and honey*,[34] in the words of the prophet. There he attacked the fortress that is called Mempetze in the Syrian tongue.[35] After he brought it to terms by means of warfare and all sorts of siege machines, [p. 166] he discovered there the sandals of Christ the Savior and the hair

---

[32] On an unsuccessful attempt by Byzantine surgeons to separate conjoined twins from Armenia in the 10th c., see Skyl. 232.73–78, *Theoph. Cont.* 433.1–11, and G. E. Pentogalos and J. G. Lascaratos, "A Surgical Operation Performed on Siamese Twins during the Tenth Century in Byzantium," *Bulletin of the History of Medicine* 58 (1984): 99–102.

[33] John departed on this Syrian campaign in spring of 975 (Grégoire, "Amorians and Macedonians," 169); for a comparison of the Arabic and Byzantine sources, see P. E. Walker, "The 'Crusade' of John Tzimisces in the Light of New Arabic Evidence," *Byzantion* 47 (1977): 301–27. Dölger ("Chronologie," 285) places the first part of this campaign in 974. On Leo's use of the term Palestine for the region east of Mt. Lebanon, see below in this chapter (Leo diac. 166.14–16), and Book IV n. 86.

[34] Exod. 3:8 et passim.

[35] Probably Arabic. On Mempetze, Leo's Greek rendering of the Arabic Manbij, the ancient Hierapolis, see Book IV, n. 95. For different spellings of the place name see *Narratio de imagine Edessena* (E. von Döbschutz, *Christusbilder* [Leipzig, 1899], 51**; PG 113:432): εἰς τὸ κάστρον Ἱεραπόλεως ἔφθασεν, ὃ τῇ μὲν Σαρακηνῶν φωνῇ Μεμβὶχ (other mss. have Μεμμίχ) λέγεται, τῇ δὲ τῶν Σύρων Μαβούκ. The same phrasing is repeated in one version (ms. Paris Coislin 296) of the text on the translation of the Holy Tile: see Halkin, "Translation," 257 n. 1.

N. Elisséeff, *EI*² 6:377–383, dates the Byzantine capture of the city to AH 363/AD 974 (379). Grégoire, however, claims that Leo is in error about the capitulation of Mempetze, having confused this campaign of Tzimiskes with Nikephoros Phokas's expedition of 966: see "Amorians and Macedonians," 169. Walker ("The 'Crusade' of

of the holy Forerunner and Herald,[36] and carried them off as a gift from heaven. And he dedicated the former as a priceless treasure in the famous church of the Mother of God that was built in the imperial palace,[37] and the latter in the church of the Savior, which he constructed from the foundations.[38] After leaving there he attacked Apameia[39] (this is a strong fortress and difficult to capture), but he captured it, too, in a few days and destroyed it, and then headed for Damascus[40] with his army. The inhabitants of this city went to meet the emperor in front of[41] the market, carrying very precious gifts in their hands, attempting to placate his anger and to propitiate him with gifts. And after he imposed specified tribute on them and made them subject to the Romans, he set forth from there and moved diagonally across the Lebanon (the Lebanon is a rugged and huge mountain that extends through that region and separates Phoenicia and Palestine from each other),[42] and when he reached its ridge he took by storm

---

John Tzimisces," [as in n. 33 above] 315 n. 43) observes that Hierapolis did not lie on the route of Tzimiskes' army in the campaign of 975 and suggests that the capture may have taken place the previous year.

[36] As Mango notes (*Brazen House*, 150), Leo seems to be mistaken in his statement that the sandals of Christ and the hair of John the Baptist came from Hierapolis/Manbij, since John Tzimiskes himself wrote in his letter to the Armenian king Ashot III that he found these relics at the town of Gabaon (Gabala) on the coast of Phoenicia. The accuracy and authenticity of this letter continues, however, to be a matter of dispute. According to Skyl. 271.62–63 it was Nikephoros II who found a lock of the hair of John the Baptist at Hierapolis. Obviously, the tradition about the discovery of these relics is confused; see Book IV, n. 88.

[37] On the church of the Virgin of the Pharos, the repository of many Passion relics, see Book IV, n. 94.

[38] The church of the Savior at Chalke; Mango (*Brazen House*, 150 and n. 7) remarks that several different shrines reportedly housed hair from the head of St. John the Baptist.

John Tzimiskes began to rebuild the church of the Savior at Chalke in 971 (see Leo Diac. 128–29; Book VIII, chap. 1), with construction materials acquired from the palace bath of the Oikonomeion, the demolition of which he ordered: see *Patria*, ed. Preger, *Scriptores*, 145, and Mango, *Brazen House*, 149.

[39] Apameia on the Orontes River, former capital of the province of Syria Secunda; its ruins are to be seen in the Arab village of Qal'at al-Mudiq in modern Syria: see *ODB* 1:127. Grégoire (see n. 35 above) argues that Leo may be in error about Tzimiskes' capture of Apameia, as he was about Mempetze.

[40] Damascus, former capital of the Umayyad dynasty (661–750), was under Fatimid suzerainty in 975.

[41] Reading πρὸ for πρὸς with Panagiotakes (as conjectured by Hase).

[42] On Mt. Lebanon, see Book IV n. 96. This passage provides crucial evidence for Leo's use of the term Palestine; see Book IV, n. 86.

Borzo,[43] a strongly fortified city. Upon his departure from there he went on to Phoenicia and captured the fortress of Balanaiai[44] and laid siege to Berytos,[45] where he found an icon of the Crucifixion of the Savior[46] and carried it away from there, and sent[47] it to the church of the Savior, which he constructed from the foundations.[48]

5. An extraordinary miracle is said to have occurred in connection with this sacred icon. For they say that a man who professed the Christian religion lived in a house in Berytos [p. 167] in which he set up the above-mentioned icon and revered it. Later he moved to another house and, by some divine providence, was overcome by forgetfulness and left the icon in the first house. A Jew took over this house as his residence, and the next day he entertained some of his fellow believers. When they entered the house and saw set up in front of them [an icon of] the Crucifixion of the Savior, they bitterly reproached the Jew as a violator of their religion and as a believer in Christianity. He assured them with oaths that most certainly he had not seen the icon until that moment; and then those murderous people said to him, "If you do not practice Christian rites, then prove it to us with deeds, by taking up this lance, and piercing the image

---

[43] Borzo is the Greek name for Arabic Barzuya, a castle the ruins of which still stand, west of the Orontes and south of Apameia. In 975 the fortress was in Hamdanid hands: see *EI²* 1:1073.

[44] Balanaiai is medieval Arabic Bulunyas, modern Arabic Baniyas on the Phoenician coast, 50 km south of Laodikeia: see *EI²* 1:1016–17.

[45] According to *EI²* 1:1137, the Fatimids soon recaptured Beirut from the Byzantines.

[46] See Ps.-Athanasios, *Sermo de miraculo Beryti*, PG 28:798–812; E. von Döbschutz, *Christusbilder. Untersuchungen zur christlichen Legende* (Leipzig, 1899) 280★★ff; *Bibliotheca hagiographica graeca* 3, ed. F. Halkin (Brussels, 1957), 3:108–10 (780–88b); Mango, *Brazen House*, 150–51.

[47] Dölger ("Chronologie," 286) interprets the verb παρεκπέμπω here (166.22) and παραπέμπω at 168.3 as meaning "escort" rather than "send," and argues that this proves that Tzimiskes returned to Constantinople at this time (which he believes is 974), and that the campaign of 975 begins in chap. 6. No other historian seems to have followed his argumentation on this point, and παραπέμπω normally has the meaning of "send" in Leo; see e.g., Leo diac. 43.11, 53.17, and 96.2.

[48] I.e., the church of Christ the Savior in Chalke; see above, n. 38. The icon of the Crucifixion is also mentioned in the *Patria*, ed. Preger, *Scriptores*, 282. Mango (*Brazen House* 151 n. 14) proposes emending the text of the *Patria* to τὴν τε τιμίαν σταύρωσιν τῆς ἁγίας εἰκόνος τῆς Βηρυτοῦ. Mango also suggests (150) that Leo erred in stating that John found the image of Christ at Beirut. Finally, he points out that the Crucifixion icon must be different from the original "Beirut icon of Christ," which is described as a full-length standing figure in the *narratio* of ps.-Athanasios.

of the Nazarene in the side just as our forefathers of old stabbed Him when they crucified Him." He angrily seized the lance, and in his particular desire to reassure them, and in his eagerness to repudiate the charge leveled against him, he pierced the side of the image.[49] As soon as the point struck, a quantity of blood and water flowed forth, and the impious Jews were transfixed with horror at the sight. After the rumor spread, Christians burst into the Jew's house and carried off the holy [icon of the] Crucifixion of the Savior, still spurting holy [p. 168] blood,[50] and dedicated it in a holy church, and revered it with great honor. It was this representation of the God-Man that the emperor carried off from there and sent to Byzantium, as I have already explained.

6. After he took Balanaiai and Berytos by force, he attacked Tripolis,[51] and, since he was not able to take it with a siege attack[52] (for it was spread out on a steep hill and surrounded by strong walls by land, and on both sides was washed by the sea, which afforded a harbor and bay with good mooring and protected in winter), he left there, and, as he proceeded, besieged the coastal towns and forced them to capitulate.[53] At this time

[49] This assault on the icon took place in 765, according to Mango, *Brazen House*, 151. The incident is placed in 320 by H. R. Hahnloser, *Il Tesoro di San Marco*, vol. 2, *Il Tesoro e il Museo* (Florence, 1971), 117, no. 128. This kind of incident is a frequent hagiographic topos: in some of the stories the Jew who wounds an icon is converted to Christianity, but here he is not.

[50] A portion of this holy blood was carried off to Constantinople by Nikephoros Phokas in 962 (or more likely in 966) and placed in the church of All Saints. After the Fourth Crusade of 1204 it was taken to Venice, where it was preserved in the Treasury of St. Mark in a silver-gilt reliquary: see Hahnloser, *Il Tesoro di San Marco* (as in n. 49), 116–18, no. 128; Mango, *Brazen House*, 151 and n. 20; *The Treasury of San Marco, Venice*, ed. D. Buckton (Milan, 1984), 237, no. 33; H. C. Evans and W. D. Wixom, *The Glory of Byzantium* (New York, 1997), 251, no. 176; Halkin, "Translation" and B. Flusin, "Didascalie de Constantin Stilbès sur le mandylion et la sainte tuile (BHG 796m)," *REB* 55 (1997): 53–79, at 60.

[51] On Tripolis, see Book IV, n. 97.

[52] The Greek phrase is πολιορκεῖν ἐξ ἐπιδρομῆς. Normally Leo uses the phrase ἐξ ἐπιδρομῆς to mean "by assault" or "by storm" in contrast with a slow besieging process, but here he has combined the two notions in a curious fashion.

[53] According to J. Starr, "Notes on the Byzantine Incursions into Syria and Palestine (?)," *Archiv Orientální* 8 (1936) 94–95, the furthest south Tzimiskes went was Sidon, despite his claim in his letter to Ashot III of Armenia (of questionable accuracy) that he captured several towns in Palestine. Walker (see n. 33 above), who was unfamiliar with Starr's article, came to similar conclusions. See also Book IV, n. 86.

(it was the beginning of August) there appeared a comet,[54] a marvelous and novel sight exceeding human understanding; for nothing of the sort had been seen in our time, nor had one shone previously for so many days. It rose in the northeast and reached its greatest elevation, lofty as a cypress,[55] [and] then, gradually curving down, it inclined toward the south, burning with immense flames and shooting forth far-ranging and brilliant rays, an object that filled men who saw it with awe and terror. After making its appearance at the beginning of the month of August, as I have said, it continued to rise for a full eighty days, rising in the middle of the night and remaining visible until full daylight.

When the emperor saw the unusual portent, he asked scholars of astronomy[56] for their [p. 169] opinion on the significance of such a phenomenon. And they interpreted the appearance of the comet, not as their technical knowledge would lead them to conclude, but in accordance with the wishes of the emperor, and declared that he would be victorious over his enemies and live a long life. The men who made these false interpretations were Symeon the *logothetes* and *magistros*,[57] and Stephen, bishop of Nikomedeia,[58] who were held in higher regard than any of the scholars of that time. But the appearance of the comet did not foretell these events, which the men told the emperor to please him, but bitter revolts, and invasions of foreign peoples, and civil wars, and migrations from cities

[54] The comet appeared from August to October 975: see Skyl. 311.84–88 (where it is termed πωγωνίας, "bearded"); Grumel, *Chronologie*, 472; and Schove, *Chronology*, 297. Schove calls it the "Great Comet" and notes that it was visible in both Europe and Asia.

[55] Both Michael Psellos and Anna Komnene use the simile of a cypress tree to express height: see Psellos, *Chronographia* 7.80.4 (ed. Renauld, 132.4), and Anna Komnene, *Alexiad* 3.2.4 (ed. Leib, 1:107.29).

[56] On the sciences of astronomy and astrology in Byzantium, see *ODB* 1:214–17. On the numerous horoscopes during the reign of Basil II and their millennial significance, see Magdalino, "The Year 1000 in Byzantium," in idem, *Year 1000*, 261.

[57] For the second half of the 10th c. there are numerous references to writers and scholars called Symeon the *magistros* and *logothetes*: the evidence is summarized by I. Ševčenko, "Poems on the Deaths of Leo VI and Constantine VII in the Madrid Manuscript of Scylitzes," *DOP* 23–24 (1969–70): 216–18. See also *ODB* 3:1982–83.

[58] Stephen, metropolitan of Nikomedeia and synkellos, was sent by Basil II in 976 as an envoy to the rebel Bardas Skleros, who was marching on Constantinople (Dölger, *Regesten*, no. 756). He may have still been alive in 1011, according to the vita of St. Symeon the New Theologian, ed. I. Hausherr, *Un grand mystique byzantin. Vie de Syméon le Nouveau Théologien* (Rome, 1928), li–lvi, xc. See also J. Darrouzès in *DictSpir* 4 (1961) 1514–15. For his seals, see Laurent, *Corpus* V, 1, no. 378, and *DOSeals*, 3 (Washington, D.C., 1996), no. 83.8.

and the countryside, famines and plagues and terrible earthquakes, indeed almost the total destruction of the Roman empire, all of which I witnessed as the events unfolded.[59]

7. For after the death of the emperor John[60] the *magistros* Bardas, surnamed Skleros, who was afflicted with lust for power and insatiable greed, and deceived and hoodwinked the gullible masses, planned a great rebellion against the emperors,[61] and laid waste Asia for four years,[62] ravaging the countryside with fire and destroying cities, cruelly defeating and slaughtering in a pitched battle the Roman forces that were deployed against him. [One army] was led by the *patrikios* and *stratopedarches* Peter,[63] when battle broke out on the plain of Lapara[64] (this is on the boundary of Armenian territory), at which time even the *patrikios* Peter himself was hit by a spear and knocked from his horse, [p. 170] and breathed his last right in the line of battle, while most of his bodyguards were killed along with him. [Another army was led] by the *magistros* Bardas Phokas,[65] who, after receiving from the emperors the office of *domestikos* of the Schools,[66] drew up in battle order to oppose Skleros at Pankaleia[67] (this is a plain near Amorion[68] that is suitable for cavalry action), at which time Phokas was struck on the skull with a staff on the battlefield and was knocked from his horse and brought to the ground; and he would have been captured by his foes[69] and died ingloriously, if he had not

---

[59] See above Book I, chap. 1, for a similar list of contemporary calamities that Leo claims to have seen.

[60] Here Leo begins a digression into the reign of Basil II that continues through chap. 10.

[61] I.e., Basil II and Constantine VIII.

[62] The rebellion of Bardas Skleros (ca. 920–91) against Basil II and Constantine VIII began in 976 and lasted until 979. The most detailed study of this figure is by Seibt, *Skleroi*, 29–58. Skleros is previously mentioned by Leo at 107.13 and 117.1.

[63] On Peter, see Book V, n. 41, and on his death, Ringrose, *The Perfect Servant*, 137.

[64] On this site in Cappadocia (= Lykandos), see *ODB* 2:1178 and Hild and Restle, *Kappadokien*, 224. The battle took place in late 976.

[65] On Bardas Phokas see above, Book VI, n. 25. On his death at Abydos, see the more detailed account of Psellos, *Chronographia*, 1.15–17.

[66] On the office of *domestikos* of the Schools, see Book I, n. 38 and Book II, n. 11. Apparently Leo forgot to specify here "*domestikos* of the Schools of the East."

[67] A plain near Amorion where either one or two battles took place in 978–79: see *ODB* 3:1571; Belke, *Galatien*, 212. Seibt (*Skleroi*, 43) dates the battle to 19 June 978.

[68] Amorion (now Hisar in modern Turkey) was the capital of the Anatolikon theme.

[69] Reading <πρὸς> τῶν ἐναντίων as emended by Panagiotakes.

been overlooked as one of the rank and file by the enemy, who did not recognize him, and been saved by the approach of night.

Skleros was puffed up and elated at these victories and considered himself irresistible and invincible. Thereupon he forced Nicaea and Abydos and Attaleia to surrender, and subdued[70] all Roman territory in Asia. And he acquired numerous triremes and gained control of the sea, and caused great harm to the merchants and the imperial city itself, by not allowing the grain transports to sail to it as they did previously; until the emperors secretly dispatched from Byzantium fireships, under the command of the *magistros* Bardas Parsakoutenos,[71] who landed suddenly at Abydos and set fire to the usurper's triremes and destroyed his army of soldiers and seized the fortress. Then Phokas attacked Skleros, after assembling about him a large band of soldiers; and he defeated him and forced him to seek refuge at Ekbatana with the Agarenes.[72] [p. 171]

8. Then, when Bardas Skleros's robber band of conspirators was completely dispersed, the emperor Basil mustered his troops and marched against the Mysians.[73] For those arrogant and cruel people, who breathed murder, were harassing Roman territory and mercilessly plundering Macedonia, killing everyone from youth upwards. Therefore he was roused to greater anger than was proper or provident, and hastened to destroy them at the first assault, but he was deceived of his hopes through the intervention of fortune. For after he traversed the narrow and steep tracks and reached the vicinity of Sardica, which the Scythians are accustomed to call Tralitza,[74] he set up camp here for the army and settled down and kept watch over [the city] for twenty days. But he was not able to accomplish anything, since the army fell into indolence and sluggishness as a result of the incompetence of the commanders. Thus the Mysians ambushed them first, when they left

---

[70] Reading ὑπεποιήσατο for ἐπεποιήσατο with Panagiotakis, following the conjecture of Hase.

[71] Bardas Parsakoutenos and his brothers had supported the rebellion of Bardas Phokas (their cousin) in 970; see Book VII, chap. 1.

[72] Skleros was defeated by Phokas on 24 March 979 and fled to Arab territory. Leo has confused Ekbatana (modern Hamadan) with Baghdad, at this time under Buyid control, where Bardas Skleros spent several years: see n. 13 above, and Seibt, *Skleroi*, 47–48.

[73] This was the disastrous Bulgarian campaign of 986 against Tsar Samuel, who had invaded Macedonia and Thessaly in the early 980s.

[74] Sardica (or Serdica) is Sofia in modern Bulgaria; Tralitza is apparently a corrupt form from Triaditza, as suggested by Panagiotakes. For Triaditza as an alternative name for Sardica, see also Michael Glycas, *Annales*, ed. I. Bekker (Bonn, 1836), 465.16–17.

Book X

the camp for forage and fodder, and killed many of them, and carried off a large number of their pack animals and horses. Then, after the siege machines and the other contrivances accomplished nothing, because of the inexperience of the men who brought them up against the walls, and they [the machines] were set on fire by the enemy, and when lack of supplies began to overwhelm the army, since the provisions they brought with them were already exhausted because they did not consume them sparingly but greedily, he and the army packed up and headed back to Byzantium. And after marching all day he pitched camp in a thicket [p. 172] and allowed the army to rest.

The first watch of the night[75] was not yet concluded, when suddenly an enormous star[76] darted from the eastern side of the camp and illuminated the tents with boundless light, and then dropped into the trench on the west side and was extinguished after disintegrating in a burst of sparks. The sinking of the star foretold the imminent destruction of the army; for wherever something of this sort has occurred, it has meant the total destruction of whatever lay below. Clear proof of this is the star that descended upon the Trojan host, when Pandaros was shooting at Menelaus;[77] for there on the same day the Trojan army was forced into ignoble flight by the Achaeans. And if one were to peruse the history of the Roman wars, he would find that this has been a frequent occurrence and that the army has been destroyed when the phenomenon appeared. And we ourselves saw such [a star] descending upon the house of the *proedros* Basil, and, after only a short time passed, he departed this life and his property was plundered and looted.[78] But this is enough about the apparition of the star.

The next day, then, the army was traversing a wooded defile, which was full of caves, and as soon as they passed through it they came to steep terrain, filled with gullies. Here the Mysians attacked the Romans, killing huge numbers of men and seizing the imperial headquarters[79] and

[75] The first night watch lasted from approximately 6:00 P.M. to 9:00 P.M.; see Book VI, n. 1.

[76] Perhaps a meteorite.

[77] See Homer, *Iliad* 4.85ff. Pandaros, son of Lykaon, was a Trojan who shot at Menelaus, thus breaking the truce.

[78] Basil the Nothos, illegitimate son of Romanos I; on him, see above, Book III, chap. 7 and n. 56. On the location of Basil's house, see Brokkaar, "Basil Lacapenus," 233 n. 1. In 985 the emperor Basil II sent Basil into exile: see ibid., 232–33. The precise date of his death is unknown.

[79] Τὴν βασίλειον ἀρχήν. Perhaps it means the imperial command tent.

riches, and plundering all the army's baggage. I myself, who tell this sad tale, [p. 173] was present at that time, to my misfortune, attending the emperor and performing the services of deacon. And *my steps had well nigh slipped*[80] and I would have fallen victim to a Scythian sword, if I had not been led away from this danger by some divine providence, which made me gallop off quickly before the enemy arrived at the steep slope, and [allowed me] to pass over it and quickly reach the ridge. The remains of the army, going through [nearly] impassable mountains, barely escaped the Mysian attack, losing almost all their horses and the baggage they were carrying, and returned to Roman territory.[81]

9. Before the effects of this disaster had completely passed, the *magistros* Bardas Phokas rebelled against the emperors[82] and defeated the Roman forces in Asia and captured all the ports and towns along the coast except for Abydos; and after hauling numerous triremes [onto shore],[83] he kept guard over the straits of the Hellespont, and did not allow cargo ships to proceed to the imperial city; and he established most of his army, under the command of the *magistros* Leo Melissenos,[84] on land near Abydos, to protect their own triremes and to besiege Abydos. Then he erected a secure palisaded encampment opposite Byzantium on the hill of

---

[80] Ps. 72 (73):2.

[81] The Byzantine defeat occurred at the pass of Trajan's Gate on 16/17 August 986: see *ODB* 3:2103.

[82] In 987 Bardas Phokas joined forces in rebellion with Bardas Skleros (recently returned from Baghdad) and was proclaimed emperor at Caesarea in Cappadocia: see Cheynet, "Les Phocas," 308.

[83] The verb νεωλκέω, used only here in Leo, seems to have this meaning consistently; see Skyl. 267.52. Perhaps Leo means that they hauled the boats, sterns first, onto land and lined the beach ready to sail out.

[84] For Leo Melissenos, who joined the rebellion of Bardas Phokas, together with his kinsman Theognostos Melissenos, see I. Jordanov, "Les sceaux de deux chefs militaires byzantins trouvés à Preslav: le magistros Léon Melissenos et le patrice Theodorakan," *Byzantinobulgarica* 8 (1986): 183–87. Leo had a distinguished military career: in 976 he was either *doux* of Thrace and Macedonia or *doux* of Thessalonike, and in 985 he was named *doux* of Antioch. In 986 he besieged Balanaiai and captured it; later the same year he took part in Basil II's Bulgarian campaign just described in chap. 8. He commanded the right wing of Bardas Phokas's rebel army at the battle of Abydos of 13 April 989, but seems to have escaped punishment after Phokas's defeat (Skyl. 338.35–44). He is last mentioned in 993, when he made an unsuccessful expedition to Aleppo. One of his seals was found at Preslav; it terms him *magistros* and *domestikos* of the Schools of the West, a position Jordanov hypothesizes that he held ca. 987.

Chrysopolis,[85] and despatched [there] large numbers of cavalry and infantry, and appointed as commanders of this army his brother, the *patrikios*
Nikephoros,[86] and the *patrikios* Kalokyres, surnamed Delphinas.[87] Then
the emperor Basil [p. 174] crossed the Bosporos with a sufficient force
and defeated these men in a pitched battle and took them prisoner;[88]
Nikephoros, the brother of Phokas, was put in fetters and confined in
prison, whereas Kalokyres Delphinas was affixed to a stake[89] right there
on the hill of Chrysopolis, where his tent was pitched.

When Bardas Phokas heard about the destruction of his army at
Chrysopolis, and the capture and imprisonment of his brother and the
hanging of Delphinas on a stake, he mustered his troops and went to
Abydos, to try to take the fortress there by siege and cross over to Europe so he could conquer it too. But the emperor Basil learned about
the usurper's march on Abydos, and, after assembling his army and fitting out the fire-bearing triremes, got ready to oppose him. After crossing the Hellespont, he pitched the imperial tent on the plain before
Abydos, and drew up his troops daily and drilled them and debated how
he should attack the rebel. Thus one night he organized the army into
companies, and he attacked the enemy on the path beside the sea, and, as
soon as day broke, he burned all their triremes and did not leave off
killing the enemy. Bardas Phokas, astounded by the emperor's sudden
arrival and attack, sallied forth from the camp to meet him. And as he
confronted him on the battlefield, he suddenly fell from his horse, and
his neck was severed by a sword.[90] His [p. 175] gigantic body was buried

---

[85] Chrysopolis is a port on the Asian shore of the Bosporos and a suburb of Chalcedon:
see *ODB* 1:455, and Janin, *CP byz.*, 494–95.

[86] On Nikephoros Phokas, brother of Bardas Phokas, see above, Book VI, chap. 2 and
n. 22, and Cheynet, "Les Phocas," 307. As Cheynet notes, Nikephoros Phokas had been
blinded in 971 (see Book IX, chap. 4).

[87] Kalokyres Delphinas was *patrikios, anthypatos,* and *katepano* of Italy before joining
Bardas Phokas's rebellion; see V. von Falkenhausen, *Untersuchungen über die byzantinische
Herrschaft in Süditalien vom 9. bis ins 11. Jahrhundert* (Wiesbaden, 1967), 84. Skylitzes
(Skyl. 336.85–88) adds that the emperor Basil II begged Delphinas to desist from the
rebellion and withdraw from Chrysopolis. See also Guilland, *Institutions,* 2:72 on Delphinas,
who probably joined the revolt of Bardas Phokas in 987.

[88] This battle at Chrysopolis took place early in 988 (according to Thurn in Skyl. 336)
or early in 989 according to Treadgold, *Byz. State,* 518.

[89] On ἀνασκολοπισμός meaning being hanged on a *phourka,* see Book VI, n. 93; see also
Skylitzes (336.92), who states that Delphinas "was hanged on a piece of wood."

[90] Bardas Phokas was killed on 13 April 989: see Cheynet, "Les Phocas," 308.

in the earth at Abydos, while his head was sent to the imperial city, fixed on a spear, paraded triumphantly through the streets, and sent to the rebels in Asia. Thus a period of rebellion was transformed into a stable calm.

10. Still other calamities were portended by the rising of the star that appeared and again by the fiery pillars that were manifested in the north[91] in the middle of the night and terrified those who saw them; for these portended the capture of Cherson by the Tauroscythians[92] and the occupation of Berrhoia by the Mysians.[93] Then there was the star that rose in the west at sunset, which, as it made its evening appearances, did not remain fixed on one point, but emitted bright and far-reaching beams and frequently changed its position, now visible in the north, now in the south;[94] and sometimes during a single appearance[95] it would change its place in the sky and make a clear and rapid shift in position, so that people who saw it were amazed and astonished and suspected that the peculiar movement of the comet did not bode well; and indeed this came to pass in accordance with the suspicions of the many.

For on the eve of the day when traditionally the memory of the great martyr Demetrios is celebrated, a terrible earthquake occurred,[96]

[91] Evidently an aurora borealis; Obolensky, "Cherson," 250–51, agreed with O. M. Rapov's rejection ("O date prinyatiya khristianstva knyazem Vladimirom i Kievlyanami," *Voprosy Istorii* [1984, no. 6]: 37) of the suggestion by A. Poppe (see next note) that the "columns of fire" were a phenomenon observed in Cairo in April 989 and described by Yahya of Antioch.

[92] The date and circumstances of Vladimir's capture of Crimean Cherson are under dispute, but must have occurred in 989 or 990; see A. Poppe, "The Political Background to the Baptism of Rus': Byzantine-Russian Relations between 986–989," *DOP* 30 (1976): 195–244, at 211–13; and Obolensky, "Cherson." This is the only mention of the event by a Byzantine source.

[93] The date of the capture of Macedonian Berrhoia by Samuel of Bulgaria is disputed; for the various proposals, see G.C. Chionides, Ἱστορία τῆς Βεροίας (Thessalonike, 1970), 2:20–23. Most scholars accept the date 989, which Leo seems to imply by his linking of the conquest with other events securely dated to 989; but see Obolensky, "Cherson," 250 and n. 25.

[94] This is Halley's Comet, which was observed in August and September 989 in Europe and Asia: see Grumel, *Chronologie* 472 and Schove, *Chronology* 297.

[95] Reading κατ' αὐτὴν τὴν μίαν ἐπιτολὴν for καὶ αὐτὴν τὴν μίαν ἐπιτολὴν with Panagiotakes and as conjectured by Hase.

[96] I.e., 25 October 989: see Grumel, *Chronologie*, 480. C. Mango, *Materials for the Study of the Mosaics of St. Sophia at Istanbul* (Washington, D.C., 1962), 77, and Guidoboni, *Earthquakes*, 404–5, give the date of 26 October, evidently interpreting ἑσπέρας in Leo as "evening" rather than "eve."

the likes of which had not happened in this generation, and demolished to the ground the fortifications of Byzantium [p. 176] and destroyed most of the houses, turning them into tombs for their inhabitants,[97] and razed to the ground the districts near Byzantium and caused much loss of life among the peasants. Furthermore, it brought down and knocked to the ground the half-dome of the upper part of the Great Church, together with the west apse[98] (these were rebuilt by the emperor Basil in six years).[99] And the harsh famines and plagues, droughts and floods and gales of violent winds (when the column in the quarter of Eutropios[100] was knocked over by the force of the waves and the monk [who lived] on it[101] was cruelly drowned in the currents of the sea), and the barrenness of the earth and calamities that occurred, all came to pass after the appearance of the star. But my history will describe these in detail in their place.[102]

11. The emperor John then departed from Syria (for I am returning to the point where I began to digress)[103] and headed back to Byzantium. When en route he saw Longinias[104] and Drize,[105] fertile and prosperous places that the Roman army had previously recovered for the empire with much sweat and blood, but then were taken over by the *proedros* and *parakoimomenos* Basil,[106] he was distressed and annoyed, as was rea-

[97] For a parallel to this phrase, τάφον ... τοῖς οἰκοῦσιν, see Leo diac. 68.7–8 (Book IV, chap. 9), τῶν οἰκητόρων τάφον, with regard to the earthquake at Klaudioupolis.

[98] For the collapse of the great western arch of Hagia Sophia, together with part of the dome, see Mango, *Materials* (see n. 96 above), and idem, "The Collapse of St. Sophia, Psellus and the *Etymologicum Genuinum*," in *Gonimos: Neoplatonic and Byzantine Studies presented to Leendert G. Westerink at 75* (Buffalo, N.Y., 1988), 168.

[99] This phrase was secluded by Siuziumov, who suspected it was a later addition; see Siuziumov et al., *Lev D'iakon*, 223 n. 73. Yahya of Antioch states that the rebuilding was completed in 993, i.e., in only four years: see Mango, "The Collapse of St. Sophia" (see previous footnote).

[100] The column in the region of Eutropios on the Asiatic coast of the Bosporos, just south of Chalcedon, on which St. Luke the Stylite (d. 979) spent over four decades.

[101] This anonymous monk seems to have been the successor to St. Luke.

[102] An indication that Leo intended to continue his history into the reign of Basil II.

[103] Here Leo ends his digression into the reign of Basil II, which began in chap. 7, and returns to John Tzimiskes' Syrian expedition of 975.

[104] An estate in Cilicia near Tarsos: see Hild and Hellenkemper, *Kilikien*, 334.

[105] A site in Cappadocia northwest of Tyana: see Hild and Restle, *Kappadokien*, 172–73, s.v. Δρίζιον.

[106] On Basil the Nothos as "the only really successful individual predator in the borderlands," with reference to this passage of Leo the Deacon, see J. Howard-Johnston,

sonable, and censured the man's greed-driven use of force. He [Basil] in turn could not openly protest, since he feared the emperor's wrath, but in secret he sneered at his words and plotted to get rid in some way or other of this man, who had now become an *oppressive master*[107] for him. [p. 177] When the emperor arrived at the plain of Atroa,[108] which is located next to [Mount] Olympos, he went to stay at the house of the *patrikios* Romanos, who also held the distinguished rank of *sebastophoros*.[109]

It is said that here a eunuch who attended upon the emperor, either on his own account, because he was ill-disposed towards him, or because he was led astray by one of those people[110] who hold a grudge against good fortune[111] and long to see changes in the situation, and was deceived by promises of bribes (this reason is more frequently mentioned and given greater credence than the first), mixed poison and gave it to the emperor in his drink; and he was not on his guard against something of the sort and drank the poison as a saving draught.[112] At all events the next day his limbs became numb and his whole body paralyzed, and the skill of doctors was revealed to be futile and useless against the sudden affliction, since it could not make an accurate diagnosis of such symptoms. When the emperor realized that he had suddenly lost his previous gigantic strength, he hurried to reach Byzantium; and he

"Crown Lands and the Defence of Imperial Authority," *ByzF* 21 (1995): 75–100, here 93 and n. 63. See also above, n. 78.

[107] See Gregory of Nazianzus, *Or.* 7.20 (PG 35:780C).

[108] A plain at the foot of Bithynian Mt. Olympos, 7 km southwest of Prousa.

[109] Romanos, *patrikios* and *sebastophoros*, was the grandson of emperor Romanos I Lekapenos, son of Stephen Lekapenos (emperor 944–45), and nephew of Basil the Nothos. He was castrated after his family's downfall in 944/45. He was apparently the first person to bear the honorific title of *sebastophoros*, created sometime between 963 and 975. It was a dignity usually reserved for eunuchs. See R. Guilland, "Etudes sur l'histoire administrative de l'empire byzantin. Le sébastophore," *REB* 21 (1963): 199–201; and *ODB* 3:1862.

[110] Reading πρός του τῶν with Panagiotakes for πρὸς τούτων of Hase ed. (cf. πρόστου των of P).

[111] Or: "envy the successful." For parallels to the phrase τοῖς καλοῖς βασκαινούντων, see Eusebius, *Vita Constantini* 3.1.1, ed. F. Winkelmann, GCS 57 (Berlin, 1975), 80.1; idem, *De laudibus Constantini* 16.7.2, ed. I. A. Heikel, GCS 7 (Leipzig, 1902), 250.8; idem, *Commentaria in Psalmos*, PG 23:1384B. See M. W. Dickie, "The Fathers of the Church and the Evil Eye," in *Byzantine Magic*, ed. H. Maguire (Washington, D.C., 1995), 9–34.

[112] Skylitzes (312.13–20) specifically states that the poison was administered by a supporter of Basil the Nothos. See Ringrose, *The Perfect Servant*, 130.

Book X

made haste to complete as quickly as possible the tomb that was being
fabricated for his remains in the church of the Savior, which he himself
had constructed.[113] Hastening his journey, he arrived at the imperial
city, and was cordially welcomed by the citizens, but was already quite
feeble, and drawing and exhaling deep breaths with difficulty.

As soon as he arrived at the imperial palace, he had to take to his
bed, exhausted by the effect of the poison. And in the realization that he
would not recover from such an affliction (for the insidious evil was
severely ravaging his vital organs), [p. 178] he began to draw lavishly on
the imperial treasuries and to make distributions to the poor, especially
to those who were maimed and whose bodies were consumed with the
holy disease [of leprosy],[114] whom he treated more generously than
other poor people. And he summoned Nicholas, the bishop of
Adrianople,[115] a holy and reverend man, and confessed to him his sins of
omission in the course of his life,[116] shedding streams of tears from his
eyes and with their water washing away the shame and filth of his sins,
and calling on the Mother of God to help him on the Day of Judgment,
when mortals' deeds are weighed in the impartial scales and balance by
her Son, our God. After the emperor made such a confession with un-
hesitating purpose and contrite soul, he departed this world and went
to his repose in the next, on the tenth of January, the fourth indiction,
in the year 6485,[117] and was buried in the church of the Savior at Chalke,
which he had constructed magnificently from the foundations. Such
was the end of the life of the emperor John, a man who was short in
stature, but possessed of heroic strength, brave and invincible in war and

---

[113] According to some manuscripts of the *Patria* (ed. Preger, *Scriptores*, 283, apparatus),
the sarcophagus was made of gold and enamel, ὁλόχρυσον μετὰ χυμεύσεως καὶ ἐγκαύσεως
χρυσοχικῆς (*sic*) ἐντέχνου. . . . The "church of the Savior" is the church at the Chalke
Gate in the palace; for its reconstruction by Tzimiskes, see Book VIII, chap. 1.

[114] This is the second time that Leo singles out Tzimiskes' special concern for lepers; see
also Book VI, chap. 5.

[115] Nicholas, metropolitan of Adrianople, is called a saint (ἁγιωτάτου . . . νέου ἐλεήμονος
καὶ μυροβλύτου) in the Synodikon of Adrianople (V. Laurent, "La liste épiscopale du
synodicon de la métropole d'Andrinople," *EO* 38 [1939]: 8 [no. 2], 14), but must have
had a purely local cult. His seal is preserved: see Laurent, *Corpus*, V.1, no. 717.

[116] This is an odd deathbed confession, that does not contain sins of commission. Might
this be a subtle reference to Tzimiskes' involvement in the murder of Phokas, at the least
his complicity in allowing others to commit the murder?

[117] This date needs to be emended to 6484, equivalent to AD 976.

courageous and daring in the face of danger, after living a total lifespan of fifty-one years, and ruling the empire for six years and thirty days.[118]

---

[118] I.e., 11 December 969 to 10 January 976. He must have been born ca. 925.

PARTIAL GENEALOGY OF THE MACEDONIAN DYNASTY

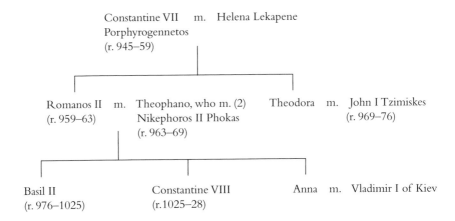

Constantine VII   m.   Helena Lekapene
Porphyrogennetos
(r. 945–59)

Romanos II   m.   Theophano, who m. (2)   Theodora   m.   John I Tzimiskes
(r. 959–63)   Nikephoros II Phokas   (r. 969–76)
                          (r. 963–69)

Basil II   Constantine VIII   Anna   m.   Vladimir I of Kiev
(r. 976–1025)   (r.1025–28)

Based on Grumel, *Chronologie*, 363

Partial Genealogy of the Phokas Family

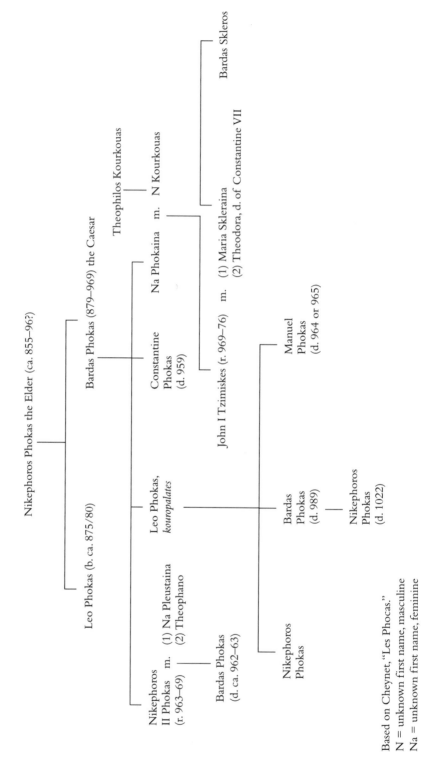

Based on Cheynet, "Les Phocas."
N = unknown first name, masculine
Na = unknown first name, feminine

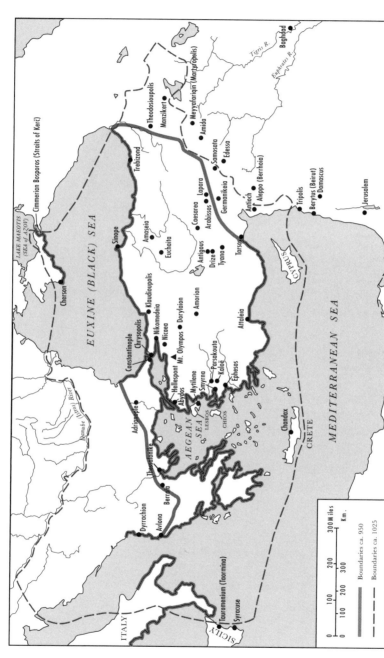

Map 1. The Byzantine Empire in the Tenth and Eleventh Centuries (after G. Ostrogorsky, *History of the Byzantine State* [New Brunswick, 1969] and G. Schlumberger, *Un empereur byzantin au dixième siècle. Nicéphore Phocas* [Paris, 1890], between pp. 324 and 325).

Church of Virgin
at Blachernai

Chora Monastery

GOLDEN HORN

GALATA

Kastellion

Lykos R.

Holy Apostles

Mese

Kentenarion

BOSPOROS

Forum Bovis

Forum of
Theodosios

SPHORAKION
QUARTER

Hagia Sophia

Mese

Pege Monastery

Forum of
Constantine

Forum of
Arkadios

Hippodrome

Great
Palace

Stoudios
Monastery

Harbor of Sophia

SEA of MARMARA

Golden Gate

0   Mile   1/2

0   500

---·---·---   Wall of Constantine
················   Sea Walls
::::::::::::::::   Theodosian Walls
······················   Chain

CONSTANTINOPLE
in the Tenth Century

Map 2. Constantinople in the Tenth Century (after *ODB* 1:509)

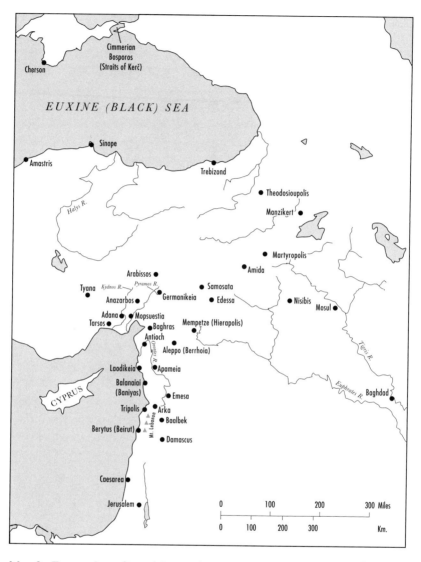

Map 3. Eastern Anatolia and Syro–Palestine (after G. Ostrogorsky, *History of the Byzantine State* [Oxford, 1968])

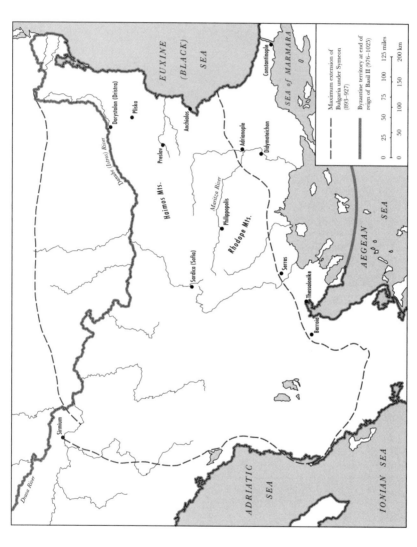

Map 4. Bulgaria in the Tenth and Eleventh Centuries (after R. Browning, *Byzantium and Bulgaria* [Berkeley, 1975])

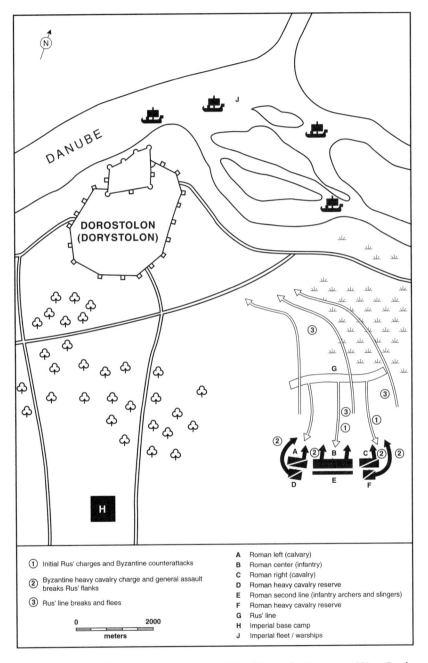

N

DANUBE

DOROSTOLON
(DORYSTOLON)

G

H

① Initial Rus' charges and Byzantine counterattacks

② Byzantine heavy cavalry charge and general assault breaks Rus' flanks

③ Rus' line breaks and flees

0   2000

meters

A   Roman left (calvary)
B   Roman center (infantry)
C   Roman right (cavalry)
D   Roman heavy cavalry reserve
E   Roman second line (infantry archers and slingers)
F   Roman heavy cavalry reserve
G   Rus' line
H   Imperial base camp
J   Imperial fleet / warships

Map 5. The Battle of Dorystolon (after J. Haldon, *The Byzantine Wars: Battles and Campaigns of the Byzantine Era* [Stroud–Charleston, 2001], 102, with modfications. Reproduced with permission of the author)

Bibliography

Primary Sources

Editions and Translations of Leo the Deacon

Hase, C. B., ed. *Leonis diaconi Caloënsis Historiae libri decem*. Bonn, 1828.

Karales, B., trans. Λέων Διάκονος. Ἱστορία. Athens, 2000.

Loretto, F., trans. *Nikephoros Phokas "Der bleiche Tod der Sarazenen" und Johannes Tzimiskes: Die Zeit von 959 bis 976 in der Darstellung des Leon Diakonos*. Graz, 1961.

Popov, D., trans. *Istoriia Lva D'iakona Kaloiskago*. St. Petersburg, 1820.

Siuziumov, M. I. A. et al., trans. *Istoriia: Lev D'iakon*. Moscow, 1988.

Turtledove, H., trans. "The *History* of Leo the Deacon." Unpublished typescript, n.d.

Other Medieval Authors

Agathias. *Historiarum libri quinque*. Edited by R. Keydell. Berlin, 1967.

————. *The Histories*. Translated by J. D. Frendo. Berlin, 1975.

Byzantine Defenders of Images. Edited by A.-M. Talbot. Washington, D.C., 1998.

Constantine Porphyrogenitus: Three Treatises on Imperial Military Expeditions. Edited by J. Haldon. CFHB 28. Vienna, 1990.

De cerimoniis aulae byzantinae. Edited by J.J. Reiske. 2 vols. Bonn, 1829–30.

De obsidione toleranda. D. Sullivan, "A Byzantine Instruction Manual on Siege Defense: The *De obsidione toleranda*," in *Byzantine Authors: Literary Activities and Preoccupations: Texts and Translations Dedicated to the Memory of Nicholas Oikonomides*, ed. J. Nesbitt (Leiden, 2003), 139–266.

Epistoliers byzantins du Xe siècle. Edited by J. Darrouzès. Paris, 1960.

Holy Women of Byzantium: Ten Saints' Lives in English Translation. Edited by A.-M. Talbot. Washington, D.C., 1996.

Jus graecoromanum. Edited by J. and P. Zepos. 8 vols. Athens, 1931. Reprint, Aalen, 1962.

Komnene, Anna. *Anne Comnène. Alexiade*. Edited by B. Leib and P. Gautier. 4 vols. Paris, 1937–76.

The Life of Saint Nikon. Edited and translated by D. Sullivan. Brookline, Mass., 1987.

The Life of the Patriarch Tarasios by Ignatios the Deacon. Edited and translated by S. Efthymiadis. Aldershot, 1998.

Liudprand of Cremona. *Antapodosis; Homelia paschalis; Historia Ottonis; Relatio de legatione Constantinopolitana*. In *Liudprandi Cremonensis opera*, edited by P. Chiesa. Turnhout, 1998.

Bibliography

Nikephoros, Patriarch of Constantinople: Short History. Edited and translated by C. Mango. Washington, D.C., 1990.

Nikephoros Phokas. *Le traité sur la guérilla (De velitatione) de l'empereur Nicéphore Phocas (963–969)*. Edited by G. Dagron and H. Mihaescu. Paris, 1986.

Procopii Caesariensis opera omnia. Edited by J. Haury and P. Wirth. 4 vols. Leipzig, 1962–64.

Psellos, Michael. *Michel Psellos. Chronographie*. Edited by E. Renauld. 2 vols. Paris, 1926–28.

Russian Primary Chronicle. Laurentian Text. Translated by S. H. Cross, O. P. Sherbowitz-Wetzor. Cambridge, Mass., 1953.

Scriptores originum Constantinopolitanarum. Edited by T. Preger. Leipzig, 1901–7. Reprint, New York, 1975.

Siegecraft: Two Tenth-Century Instructional Manuals by "Heron of Byzantium." Edited and translated by D. Sullivan. Washington, D.C., 2000.

Skylitzes, John. *Ioannis Scylitzae Synopsis historiarum*. Edited by I. Thurn. CFHB 5. Berlin–New York, 1973.

Sylloge Tacticorum. Edited by A. Dain. Paris, 1938.

Theodosii Diaconi, De Creta capta. Edited by H. Criscuolo. Leipzig, 1979.

Theophanes Continuatus. Edited by I. Bekker. Bonn, 1838.

Theophanis Chronographia. Edited by C. de Boor. Leipzig, 1883.

Three Byzantine Military Treatises. Edited by G. Dennis. Washington, D.C., 1985. Reprint, 2000.

Skylitzes Continuatus. *Ἡ συνέχεια τῆς Χρονογραφίας τοῦ Ἰωάννου Σκυλίτζη*. Edited by E. Tsolakes. Thessalonike, 1968.

Vitae duae antiquae Sancti Athanasii Athonitae. Edited by J. Noret. Turnhout, 1982.

Yahya of Antioch. *Histoire de Yahya-ibn-Said d'Antioche, continuateur de Said-ibn-Bitriq*. Edited and translated by I. Kratchkovsky and A. A. Vasiliev. PO 18 (Paris, 1924): 705–833; 23 (Paris, 1932): 349–520; 47.4 (Turnhout, 1997).

Secondary Literature

Ahrweiler, H. *Byzance et la mer*. Paris, 1966.

———. *Études sur les structures administratives et sociales de Byzance*. London, 1971.

Apostolopoulou, S. "Ἡ "Ἅλωση τῆς Μοψουεστίας (±965) καὶ τῆς Ταρσοῦ (965) ἀπὸ βυζαντινὲς καὶ ἀραβικὲς πηγές." *Graeco-Arabica* 1 (1982): 157–67.

Bardill, J. "The Great Palace of the Byzantine Emperors and the Walker Trust Excavations." *Journal of Roman Archaeology* 12 (1999): 216–30.

Barker, E. *Social and Political Thought in Byzantium*. Oxford, 1957.

Barker, J. W. "Late Byzantine Thessalonike: A Second City's Challenges and Responses." *DOP* 57 (2003): 5–34.

Bartusis, M. *The Late Byzantine Army: Arms and Society, 1204–1453*. Philadelphia, 1992.

Beck, H.-G. *Kirche und theologische Literatur im byzantinischen Reich*. Munich, 1959.

Bibliography

Belke, K., *Galatien und Lykaonien. TIB* 4. Vienna, 1984.

―――. *Paphlagonien und Honorias.* Vienna, 1996.

Belke, K., and N. Mersich. *Phrygien und Pisidien. TIB* 7. Vienna, 1990.

Bellinger, A. R., P. Grierson, and M. F. Hendy. *Catalogue of the Byzantine Coins in the Dumbarton Oaks Collection and in the Whittemore Collection.* 5 vols. Washington, D.C., 1966–99.

Berger, A. *Untersuchungen zu den Patria Konstantinupoleos.* Bonn, 1988.

Berger, A., and J. Bardill. "The Representations of Constantinople in Hartmann Schedel's *World Chronicle,* and Related Pictures." *BMGS* 22 (1998): 2–37.

Brokkaar, W. G. "Basil Lacapenus. Byzantium in the 10th Century." In *Studia Byzantina et Neohellenica Neerlandica,* edited by W. F. Bakker et al., 199–234. Leiden, 1972.

Browning, R. "Homer in Byzantium." *Viator* 6 (1975): 15–33.

Bury, J. B. *The Imperial Administrative System in the Ninth Century.* London, 1911. Reprint, New York, n.d.

Cameron, A. *Agathias.* Oxford, 1970.

―――. "Notes on the Sophiae, the Sophianae and the Harbour of Sophia." *Byzantion* 37 (1967): 11–20.

―――. *Procopius.* Berkeley, 1985.

Canard, M. "Byzantium and the Muslim World to the Middle of the Eleventh Century." In *The Cambridge Medieval History,* vol. 4.1, edited by J. M. Hussey, 696–735. Cambridge, 1966.

―――. *Histoire de la Dynastie des H'amdanides de Jazíra et de Syrie.* Alger, 1951.

―――. "La date des expéditions mésopotamiennes de Jean Tzimiscès." *AIPHOS* 10 (1950), 99–108.

―――. "Les sources arabes de l'histoire byzantine aux confins des Xe et XIe siècles." *REB* 19 (1961): 284–314.

Cheynet, J.-C. "Les Phocas." In *Le traité sur la guérilla (De velitatione) de l'empereur Nicéphore Phocas (963–969),* edited by G. Dagron and H. Mihaescu, 289–315. Paris, 1986.

―――. *Pouvoir et contestations à Byzance (963–1210).* Paris, 1990.

―――. "Toparque et topotèrètès à la fin du XIe siècle." *REB* 42 (1984): 214–24.

Cheynet, J.-C. and J. F. Vannier. *Études prosopographiques.* Paris, 1986.

Chionides, G. C. Ἱστορία τῆς Βερροίας. 2 vols. Thessalonike, 1970.

Christides, V. *The Conquest of Crete by the Arabs (ca. 824), a Turning Point in the Struggle between Byzantium and Islam.* Athens, 1984.

―――. "Naval History and Naval Technology in Medieval Times: The Need for Interdisciplinary Studies." *Byzantion* 58 (1988): 309–32.

―――. "The Raids of the Moslems of Crete in the Aegean Sea: Piracy and Conquest." *Byzantion* 51 (1981): 76–111.

Christophilopoulou, A. "Σύστημα βασιλικῶν ἱστουργῶν· Ἕνα σωματεῖο κρατικῶν ὑφαντουργῶν τὸν ι´ αἰῶνα." In Βυζάντιον: Ἀφιέρωμα στὸν Ἀνδρέα Ν. Στράτο, edited by N. A. Stratos, 1:65–72. Athens, 1986.

Bibliography

Dagron, G. "Minorités ethniques et religieuses dans l'Orient byzantin à la fin du Xe et au XIe siècle: L'immigration syrienne." *TM* 6 (1976): 177–216.

Darrouzès, J. *Recherches sur les ὀφφίκια de l'église byzantine.* Paris, 1970.

———. "Sur la chronologie du patriarche Antoine III Stoudite." *REB* 46 (1988): 55–60.

Dennis, G. "Byzantine Battle Flags." *ByzF* 8 (1982): 51–59.

———. "Byzantine Heavy Artillery: The Helepolis." *GRBS* 39 (1998): 99–115.

———. "The Byzantines in Battle." In *Τὸ ἐμπόλεμο Βυζάντιο, 9–12 αἰ.* [*Byzantium at War (9th–12th c.)*], edited by K. Tsiknakes, 165–78. Athens, 1997.

———. "Religious Services in the Byzantine Army." In ΕΥΛΟΓΗΜΑ: *Studies in Honor of Robert Taft, SJ*, edited by E. Carr et al., 107–17. Rome, 1993.

Diehl, C. "De la signification du titre de 'proèdre' à Byzance." In *Mélanges offerts à M. Gustave Schlumberger*, 1:105–17. Paris, 1924.

Dölger, F., *Beiträge zur Geschichte der byzantinischen Finanzverwaltung, besonders des 10. und 11. Jahrhunderts.* Leipzig, 1927. Reprint, Hildesheim, 1960.

———. "Die Chronologie des grossen Feldzuges des Kaisers Johannes Tzimiskes gegen die Russen." *BZ* 32 (1932): 275–92.

Dölger, F., and P. Wirth. *Regesten der Kaiserurkunden des oströmischen Reiches.* Munich–Berlin, 1924–.

Dubarle, A.-M. "L'homélie de Grégoire le Référendaire pour la réception de l'image d'Edesse." *REB* 55 (1997): 5–51.

The Encyclopedia of Islam. 2nd ed. Leiden–London, 1960–.

Fiey, J. M. *Nisibe, métropole syriaque orientale et ses suffragants des origines à nos jours.* Louvain, 1977.

Fischer, W. "Beiträge zur historischen Kritik des Leon Diakonos und Michael Psellos." *Mitteilungen des Instituts für Österreichische Geschichtsforschungen* 7 (1886): 353–77.

Flusin, B. "Didascalie de Constantin Stilbès sur le mandylion et la sainte tuile (BHG 796m)." *REB* 55 (1997): 53–79.

Forsyth, J. "The Byzantine Arab Chronicle (938–1034) of Yaḥyā b. Saʿīd al-Anṭākī." Ph.D. diss., University of Michigan, 1977.

Garland, L. *Byzantine Empresses: Women and Power in Byzantium, AD 527–1204.* London, 1999.

Garsoian, N. "The Problem of Armenian Integration into the Byzantine Empire." In *Studies on the Internal Diaspora of the Byzantine Empire*, edited by H. Ahrweiler and A. Laiou, 53–124. Washington, D.C., 1998.

Gaul, N. "Eunuchs in the Late Byzantine Empire, c. 1250–1400." In Tougher, *Eunuchs in Antiquity and Beyond*, 199–219.

Grégoire, H. "The Amorians and Macedonians, 842–1025." *Cambridge Medieval History*, vol. 4.1, edited by J. M. Hussey, 105–92. Cambridge, 1966.

———. "La dernière campagne de Jean Tzimiscès contre les Russes." *Byzantion* 12 (1937): 267–76.

Bibliography

———. "Goeléonta–Golanta." *Byzantion* 11 (1936): 537–39.

Gregoriou-Ioannidou, M. "Οι Ούγγροι και οι επιδρομές τους στον Δυτικό-Ευρωπαϊκό και στον Βυζαντινό χώρο (τέλη 9ου–10ος αἰ.)." *Byzantina* 20 (1999): 65–135.

Grosse, R. "Die Fahnen in der römisch-byzantinischen Armee des 4.–10. Jahrhunderts." *BZ* 24 (1923/24): 359–72.

Grumel, V. *La chronologie.* Paris, 1958.

Guidoboni, E. *Catalogue of Ancient Earthquakes in the Mediterranean Area up to the 10th Century.* Rome, 1994.

Guilland, R. "La chaîne de la Corne d'Or." *EEBS* 25 (1955): 88–120.

———. "Le drongaire de la flotte, le Grand drongaire de la flotte, le Duc de la flotte, le Mégaduc." In *Recherches sur les institutions,* 1:535–62. Amsterdam, 1967.

———. *Études de topographie de Constantinople byzantine.* 2 vols. in 1 pt. Amsterdam, 1969.

———. "Études sur l'histoire administrative de l'Empire byzantin—l'Éparque." II. Les Éparques, autres que l'Éparque de la Ville." *BSl* 42 (1981): 186–96.

———. "Études sur l'histoire administrative de l'empire byzantin. Le sébastophore." *REB* 21 (1963): 199–207.

———. "Études sur l'histoire administrative de l'Empire byzantin: L'ordre (τάξις) des Maîtres (τῶν μαγίστρων)." *EEBS* 39–40 (1972–73): 14–28.

———. "Le palais du Boukoléon. L'assassinat de Nicéphore II Phokas." *BSl* 13 (1952/53): 101–36.

———. *Recherches sur les institutions byzantines.* 2 vols. Amsterdam, 1967.

Haldon, J. F. *The Byzantine Wars: Battles and Campaigns of the Byzantine Era.* Stroud, Gloucestershire, 2001.

———. *Recruitment and Conscription in the Byzantine Army c. 550–950: A Study of the Origins of the Stratiotika Ktemata.* Vienna, 1979.

———. "Some Aspects of Byzantine Military Technology from the Sixth to the Tenth Centuries." *BMGS* 1 (1975): 11–47.

———. "Strategies of Defence, Problems of Security: The Garrisons of Constantinople in the Middle Byzantine Period." In *Constantinople and its Hinterland,* edited by C. Mango and G. Dagron, 143–55. Aldershot, 1995.

———. "Theory and Practice in Tenth-Century Military Administration: Chapters II, 44 and 45 of the *Book of Ceremonies.*" *TM* 13 (2000), 201–352. [Greek text, English translation, and commentary]

———. *Warfare, State and Society in the Byzantine World, 565–1204.* London, 1999.

Haldon, J. F., and M. Byrne. "A Possible Solution to the Problem of Greek Fire." *BZ* 70 (1977): 91–99.

Haldon, J. F., and H. Kennedy. "The Arab-Byzantine Frontier in the Eighth and Ninth Centuries: Military Organisation and Society in the Borderlands." *ZRVI* 19 (1980): 79–116.

Bibliography

Hammond, N. G. L. "The Speeches in Arrian's *Indica* and *Anabasis.*" *Classical Quarterly* 49 (1999): 238–53.

Hanak,W. "The Infamous Svjatoslav: Master of Duplicity in War and Peace?" In Miller and Nesbitt, *Peace and War,* 138–51.

Hansen, M. H. "The Battle Exhortation in Ancient Historiography." *Historia* 42 (1993): 161–80.

Hasluck, F. W. "Bithynica." *Annual of the British School at Athens* 13 (1906–7): 285–308.

Hild, F., and H. Hellenkemper. *Kilikien und Isaurien. TIB* 5. Vienna, 1990.

Hild, F., and M. Restle. *Kappadokien: Kappadokia, Charsianon, Sebasteia und Lykandos. TIB* 2. Vienna, 1981.

Holmes, C. "'How the East Was Won' in the Reign of Basil II." In *Eastern Approaches to Byzantium,* edited by A. Eastmond, 41–56. Aldershot, 2001.

Honigmann, E. *Die Ostgrenze des byzantinischen Reiches von 363 bis 1071.* Brussels, 1935. [= A. Vasiliev, *Byzance et les Arabes,* 3]

Howard-Johnston, J. "Crown Lands and the Defence of Imperial Authority." *ByzF* 21 (1995): 75–100.

———. "Studies in the Organization of the Byzantine Army in the Tenth and Eleventh Centuries." D.Phil. diss., Oxford, 1971.

Hrushevsky, M. *History of Ukraine-Rus'.* Vol. 1. Edmonton, 1997.

Hunger, H. *Die hochsprachliche profane Literatur der Byzantiner.* 2 vols. Munich, 1978.

Hussey, J. *The Orthodox Church in the Byzantine Empire.* Oxford, 1986.

Ivanov, S. A. "Polemicheskaia napravlennost'Istorii'L'va D'iakona." *Viz Vrem* 43 (1982): 74–80.

Janin, R. *Constantinople byzantine: Développement urbain et répertoire topographique.* 2nd ed. Paris, 1964.

———. *La géographie ecclésiastique de l'empire byzantin.* Vol. 1, *Le siège de Constantinople et le patriarcat oecuménique.* Pt. 3, *Les églises et les monastères.* 2nd ed. Paris, 1969.

———. *La géographie ecclésiastique de l'empire byzantin.* Vol. 2, *Les églises et les monastères des grands centres byzantins.* Paris, 1975.

Jenkins, R. J. H. *Byzantium: The Imperial Centuries, A.D. 610–1071.* London, 1966.

———. ed. *Constantine Porphyrogenitus, De Administrando Imperio.* Vol. 2, *Commentary.* London, 1962.

Johns, J. *Arabic Administration in Norman Sicily.* Cambridge, 2002.

Jordanov, I. "Les sceaux de deux chefs militaires byzantins trouvés à Preslav: Le magistros Léon Melissenos et le patrice Theodorakan." *Byzantinobulgarica* 8 (1986): 183–87.

Karlin-Hayter, P. "The Title or Office of Basileopator." *Byzantion* 38 (1968): 278–80.

Bibliography

Kazhdan, A. "The Aristocracy and the Imperial Ideal." In *The Byzantine Aristocracy, IX to XIII c.*, edited by M. Angold, 43–57. Oxford, 1984.

———. "The Armenians in the Byzantine Ruling Class Predominantly in the Ninth through Twelfth Centuries." In *Medieval Armenian Culture*, edited by T. J. Samuelian and M. E. Stone, 439–51. Chico, Calif., 1984.

———. *Armiane v sostave gospodstvuiushchego klassa Vizantiiskoi imperii v XI–XII vv.* Erevan, 1975.

———. "Certain Traits of Imperial Propaganda in the Byzantine Empire from the Eighth to the Fifteenth Centuries." In *Prédication et propagande au Moyen-Age*, edited by G. Makdisi et al., 13–18. Paris, 1983.

———. "The Formation of Byzantine Family Names in the Ninth and Tenth Centuries." *BSl* 58 (1997): 90–109.

———. "Iz istorii vizantiiskoi khronografii X v. 2. Istochniki L'va D'iakona i Skilitsy dlia istorii tretei chetverti X stoletiia." *VizVrem* 20 (1961): 106–28.

———. "*Polis* and *Kastron* in Theophanes and Some Other Historical Writers." In *EYΨYXIA. Mélanges offerts à Hélène Ahrweiler*, 2:345–60. Paris, 1998.

Kazhdan, A., and S. Ronchey. *L'aristocrazia bizantina dal principio dell' XI alla fine del XII secolo.* Palermo, 1997.

Kazhdan, A., et al., eds. *Oxford Dictionary of Byzantium.* 3 vols. New York, 1991.

Kolias, T. *Byzantinische Waffen.* Vienna, 1988.

Korres, Th. K. Ύγρὸν πῦρ: Ένα όπλο της βυζαντινής ναυτικής τακτικής. 3rd ed. Thessalonike, 1995.

Kostenec, J. "Studies on the Great Palace in Constantinople. II. The Magnaura." *BSl* 60 (1999): 161–82.

Kresten, O. "Sprachliche und inhaltliche Beobachtungen zu Kapitel I 96 des sogenannten 'Zeremonienbuches'." *BZ* 93 (2000): 474–84.

Krumbacher, K. *Geschichte des byzantinischen Litteratur von Justinian bis zum Ende des oströmischen Reiches (527–1453).* 2nd ed. Munich, 1897.

Kühn, H.-J. *Die byzantinische Armee im 10. und 11. Jahrhundert.* Vienna, 1991.

Laiou, A. "The General and the Saint: Michael Maleinos and Nikephoros Phokas." In *EYΨYXIA: Mélanges offerts à Hélène Ahrweiler*, 2:399–412. Paris, 1998.

Laurent, V. *Corpus des sceaux de l'empire byzantin.* 2 vols. in 5 pts. Paris, 1963–81.

Lemerle, P. *The Agrarian History of Byzantium from the Origins to the Twelfth Century.* Galway, 1979.

Lewickii, T. "Les rites funéraires païens des slaves occidentaux et des anciens russes d'après les relations—remontant surtout aux IXe–Xe siècles—des voyageurs et des écrivains arabes." *Folia Orientalia* 5 (1963): 1–74.

Lisitov, C. *Kreposti i zashchitni sorzheniia na prvnata Bŭlgarska drzhava.* Sofia, 1974.

Liubarskii, I. "John Kinnamos as a Writer." In *Polypleuros Nous. Miscellanea für Peter Schreiner zu seinem 60. Geburtstag*, edited by C. Scholz and G. Makris, 164–73. Leipzig, 2000.

———. "Nikephoros Phokas in Byzantine Historical Writings." *BSl* 54 (1993): 245–53.

Bibliography

————. "Writers' Intrusion in Early Byzantine Literature." In *XVIIIe Congrès international des études byzantines. Rapports pléniers*, 433–56. Moscow, 1991.

————. "Zamechaniia ob obrazakh i khudozhestvennoi prirode 'Istorii' L'va D'iakona." In *Vizantiiskie Ocherki: Trudy sovetskikh uchenykh k XVIII mezhdunarodnomu kongressu vizantinistov, 8–15 avgusta 1991 g. Moskva*, 150–62. Moscow, 1991.

Macrides, R. "The Byzantine Godfather." *BMGS* 12 (1987): 139–62.

————. "The Historian in the History." In *Φιλέλλην: Studies in Honour of Robert Browning*, edited by C. N. Constantinides et al., 205–24. Venice, 1996.

————. "Killing, Asylum and the Law in Byzantium." *Speculum* 63 (1988): 509–38.

Magdalino, P., ed., *Byzantium in the Year 1000*. Leiden, 2003.

————. "The History of the Future and Its Uses: Prophecy, Policy and Propaganda." In *The Making of Byzantine History: Studies Dedicated to Donald M. Nicol*, edited by R. Beaton and C. Rouéche, 3–34. Aldershot, 1993.

————. "The Maritime Neighborhoods of Constantinople: Commercial and Residential Functions, Sixth to Twelfth Centuries." *DOP* 54 (2000): 209–26.

————. "Paphlagonians in Byzantine High Society." In *Byzantine Asia Minor (6th–12th cent.)*, 141–50. Athens, 1998.

————. "The Year 1000 in Byzantium." In idem, *Byzantium in the Year 1000*, 233–70.

Malamut, E. "L'image byzantine des Petchenegues." *BZ* 88 (1995): 105–47.

Maliaras, N. "Die Musikinstrumente im byzantinischen Heer vom 6. bis zum 12. Jahrhundert." *JÖB* 51 (2001): 73–104.

Mango, C. *The Brazen House: A Study of the Vestibule of the Imperial Palace of Constantinople*. Copenhagen, 1959.

————. "The Collapse of St. Sophia, Psellus and the Etymologicum Genuinum." In *Gonimos: Neoplatonic and Byzantine Studies Presented to Leendert G. Westerink at 75*, edited by J. Duffy and J. Peradotto, 167–74. Buffalo, N.Y., 1988.

————. "The Palace of the Boukoleon." *Cahiers archéologiques* 45 (1997): 41–50.

Markopoulos, A. "Byzantine History Writing at the End of the First Millennium." In Magdalino, *Year 1000*, 183–97.

————. "Le témoignage du Vaticanus gr. 163 pour la période entre 945–963." *Symmeikta* 3 (1979): 83–119.

————. "Ζητήματα κοινωνικοῦ φύλου στὸν Λέοντα τὸν Διάκονο." In *Ἐνθύμησις Νικολάου Μ. Παναγιωτάκη*, edited by S. Kaklamanes, A. Markopoulos, et al., 475–93. Herakleion, 2000.

————. "Zu den Biographien des Nikephoros Phokas." *JÖB* 38 (1988): 225–33.

McCormick, M. *Eternal Victory: Triumphal Rulership in Late Antiquity, Byzantium and the Early Medieval West*. Cambridge–Paris, 1986.

Bibliography

McGeer, E. "Byzantine Siege Warfare in Theory and Practice." In *The Medieval City Under Siege*, edited by I. Corfis and M. Wolfe, 123–29. Woodbridge, 1995.

———. *The Land Legislation of the Macedonian Emperors.* Toronto, 2000.

———. "The Legal Decree of Nikephoros II Phokas Concerning the Armenian *Stratiotai.*" In Miller and Nesbitt, *Peace and War*, 123–37.

———. "Menaulion—Menaulatoi." *Diptycha* 4 (1986–87), 53–57.

———. *Sowing the Dragon's Teeth: Byzantine Warfare in the Tenth Century.* Washington, D.C., 1995.

McGrath, S. F.-P. "The Battles of Dorostolon (971): Rhetoric and Reality." In Miller and Nesbitt, *Peace and War*, 152–64.

———. "A Study of the Social Structure of Byzantine Aristocracy as Seen through Ioannes Skylitzes' Synopsis Historiarum," Ph.D. diss., Catholic University of America, Washington, D.C., 1996.

Metcalfe, A. *Muslims and Christians in Norman Sicily.* London, 2003.

Miles, G. C. "Byzantium and the Arabs: Relations in Crete and the Aegean Area." *DOP* 18 (1964): 1–32.

———. *The Coinage of the Arab Emirs of Crete.* New York, 1970.

Miller, T. S., and J. Nesbitt, eds. *Peace and War in Byzantium: Essays in Honor of George T. Dennis, S.J.* Washington, D.C., 1995.

Moravcsik, G. "Zum Bericht des Leon Diakonos über den Glauben an die Dienstleistung im Jenseits." In *Studia antiqua Antonio Salač septuagenario oblata*, 74–76. Prague, 1955.

———. *Byzantinoturcica.* 2nd ed. 2 vols. Berlin, 1958.

Morris, R. "Succession and Usurpation: Politics and Rhetoric in the Late Tenth Century." In *New Constantines: The Rhythm of Imperial Renewal in Byzantium, 4th–13th Centuries*, edited by P. Magdalino, 199–214. Aldershot, 1994.

———. "The Two Faces of Nikephoros Phokas." *BMGS* 12 (1998): 83–115.

Müller-Wiener, W. *Bildlexikon zur Topographie Istanbuls.* Tübingen, 1977.

Mullett, M. "Theophylact of Ochrid's *In Defence of Eunuchs.*" In Tougher, *Eunuchs in Antiquity and Beyond*, 177–98.

Obolensky, D. "Cherson and the Conversion of Rus': An Anti-Revisionist View." *BMGS* 13 (1989): 244–57.

Oikonomides, N. "L'évolution de l'organisation administrative de l'empire byzantin au XIe siècle (1025–1118)." *TM* 6 (1976): 125–52.

———. *Les listes de préséance byzantines du IXe et Xe siècle.* Paris, 1972.

———. "L'organisation de la frontière orientale de Byzance aux Xe–XIe siècles et le *Taktikon* de l'Escorial." In *Actes du XIVe congrès international des études byzantines*, 1:285–302. Bucharest, 1974. Reprint as no. XXIV in idem, *Documents et études sur les institutions de Byzance (VIIe–XVe s.).* London, 1976.

Oikonomides, N., and J. Nesbitt, eds. *Catalogue of Byzantine Seals at Dumbarton Oaks and in the Fogg Museum of Art.* Washington, D.C., 1991–.

Bibliography

Ousterhout, R. *Master Builders of Byzantium*. Princeton, 1999.

Panagiotakes, N. "Ἡ Βυζαντινὴ οἰκογένεια τῶν Πλευστῶν· Συμβολὴ στὰ γενεαλογικὰ τῶν Φωκάδων." *Dodone* 1 (1972): 243–64.

———. *Θεοδόσιος ὁ διάκονος καὶ τὸ ποίημα αὐτοῦ "Ἅλωσις τῆς Κρήτης*. Heraklion, 1960.

———. *Λέων ὁ Διάκονος*. Athens, 1965.

Papadopoulos Ch. *Ἱστορία τῆς Ἐκκλησίας Ἀντιοχείας*. Alexandria, 1951.

Parani, M. *Reconstructing the Reality of Images: Byzantine Material Culture and Religious Iconography (11th–15th Centuries)*. Leiden, 2003.

Partington, J. R. *A History of Greek Fire and Gunpowder*. Cambridge, 1960.

Patlagean, E. "Le basileus assassiné et la sainteté impériale," in *Media in Francia . . . Recueil de mélanges offert à Karl Ferdinand Werner*, 345–61. Paris, 1989.

Platon, N. "Νέα στοιχεῖα διὰ τὴν μελέτην τῶν Βυζαντινῶν τειχῶν τοῦ Χάνδακος." *Κρητικὰ Χρονικά* 6 (1952): 439–59.

Polemis, D. *The Doukai: A Contribution to Byzantine Prosopography*. London, 1968.

Poppe, A. "The Political Background to the Baptism of Rus'. Byzantine-Russian Relations between 986–989." *DOP* 30 (1976): 195–244.

Pryor, J. H. "The Transportation of Horses by Sea During the Era of the Crusades: Eighth Century to 1295 A.D." *The Mariner's Mirror* 68 (1982): 9–27, 103–25.

Ramsay, W. M. *The Historical Geography of Asia Minor*. London, 1890. Reprint, Amsterdam, 1962.

Rapp, C. "Ritual Brotherhood in Byzantium." *Traditio* 52 (1997): 285–326.

Ringrose, K. *The Perfect Servant: Eunuchs and the Social Construction of Gender in Byzantium*. Chicago, 2003.

Runciman, S. *The Emperor Romanus Lecapenus and his Reign: A Study of 10th-Century Byzantium*. Cambridge, 1929. Reprint, 1988.

———. *A History of the First Bulgarian Empire*. London, 1930.

Saunders, W. "Qalʿat Semʿan: A Frontier Fort of the Tenth and Eleventh Centuries." In *Armies and Frontiers in Roman and Byzantine Anatolia*, edited by S. Mitchell, 291–303. Oxford, 1983.

Savvides, A. "Ο βυζαντινός οἶκος των Αλακάδων-Αλακασέων." *Byzantiaka* 11 (1991): 231–38.

Schlumberger, J. *Un empereur byzantin au dixième siècle: Nicéphore Phocas*. Paris, 1890.

Schove, D. J. and A. Fletcher. *Chronology of Eclipses and Comets AD 1–1000*. Woodbridge, Suffolk, 1987.

Schreiner, P. "Zur Ausrüstung des Kriegers in Byzanz, im Kiewer Russland und in Nordeuropa nach bildlichen und literarischen Quellen." In *Les pays du Nord et Byzance*, edited by R. Zeitler, 215–36. Uppsala, 1981.

Scott, R. "The Classical Tradition in Byzantine Historiography." In *Byzantium and the Classical Tradition*, edited by M. Mullett and R. Scott, 61–74. Birmingham, 1981.

Seibt, W. *Die Skleroi: Eine prosopographische-sigillographische Studie*. Vienna, 1976.

Ševčenko, I. "Poems on the Deaths of Leo VI and Constantine VII in the Madrid

Manuscript of Scylitzes." *DOP* 23–24 (1969–70): 185–228.

———. "Sviatoslav in Byzantine and Slavic Miniatures." *Slavonic Review* 24 (1965): 709–13.

———. "Unpublished Texts on the End of the World about the Year 1000 A.D." In *Mélanges Gilbert Dagron* [*TM* 14], 561–78. Paris, 2002.

Sidéris, G. "'Eunuchs of Light': Power, Imperial Ceremonial and Positive Representations of Eunuchs in Byzantium (4th–12th Centuries AD)." In Tougher, *Eunuchs in Antiquity and Beyond*, 161–75.

Simeonova, L. "In the Depths of Tenth-Century Byzantine Ceremonial: The Treatment of Arab Prisoners of War at Imperial Banquets." *BMGS* 22 (1998): 75–104.

———. "The Short Fuse. Examples of Diplomatic Abuse in Byzantine and Bulgarian History." *ByzF* 23 (1996): 55–73.

Siuziumov, M. I. A. "Mirovozzrenie L'va D'iakona." *Antichnaia Drevnost' i Srednie Veka* 7 (1971): 127–48.

———. "Ob istochnikakh L'va D'iakona i Skilitsy." *Vizantiiskoe obozrenie* 2 (1916): 106–66.

Snipes, K. "Notes on Parisinus Graecus 1712." *JÖB* 41 (1991): 141–61.

Speck, P. "Eine Quelle zum Tod an der Furca." *JÖB* 42 (1992): 83–85.

———. "Der Tod an der Furca." *JÖB* 40 (1990): 349–50.

Starr, J. "Notes on Byzantine Incursions into Syria and Palestine (?)." *Archiv Orientální* 8 (1936): 91–95.

Stephenson, F. R. *Historical Eclipses and the Earth's Rotation.* Cambridge, 1997.

Stephenson, P. *Byzantium's Balkan Frontier.* Cambridge, 2000.

Stokes, A. D. "The Background and Chronology of the Balkan Campaigns of Svyatoslav Igorevich." *SEER* 40 (1961–62): 44–57.

Sullivan, D. "A Byzantine Instructional Manual on Siege Defense: The *De obsidione toleranda*." In *Byzantine Authors: Literary Activities and Preoccupations*, edited by J. W. Nesbitt, 139–266. Leiden, 2003.

———. "Byzantium Besieged: Prescription and Practice." In Βυζάντιο κράτος και κοινωνία: Μνήμη Νίκου Οικονομίδη, ed. A. Avramea, A. Laiou, and E. Chrysos, 509–21. Athens, 2003.

———. "Tenth Century Byzantine Offensive Siege Warfare: Instructional Prescriptions and Historical Practice." In Τὸ ἐμπόλεμο Βυζάντιο, 9–12 αἰ. [*Byzantium at War, 9th–12th c.*], edited by K. Tsinakes, 179–200. Athens, 1997.

Sykoutres, I. "Λέοντος τοῦ Διακόνου ἀνέκδοτον ἐγκώμιον εἰς Βασίλειον τὸν Β΄." *EEBS* 10 (1933): 425–34.

Tarver, W. T. S. "The Traction Trebuchet: A Reconstruction of an Early Medieval Siege Engine." *Technology and Culture* 36 (1995): 136–67.

Terras, V. "Leo Diaconus and the Ethnology of Kievan Rus'." *Slavic Review* 24 (1965): 395–406.

Bibliography

Thierry, N. "Un portrait de Jean Tzimiskès en Cappadoce." *TM* 9 (1985): 477–84.

Tibi, A. "Byzantine-Fatimid Relations in the Reign of Al-Mu'izz Li-Din Allah (R. 953–975 A.D.) as Reflected in Primary Arabic Sources." *Graeco-Arabica* 4 (1991): 91–97.

Tinnefeld, F. *Kategorien der Kaiserkritik in der byzantinischen Historiographie von Prokop bis Niketas Choniates.* Munich, 1971.

Tougher, S., ed. *Eunuchs in Antiquity and Beyond.* London, 2002.

———. "In or Out? Origins of Court Eunuchs." In idem, *Eunuchs in Antiquity and Beyond*, 143–59.

Treadgold, W. *Byzantium and its Army.* Stanford, 1995.

———. *A History of the Byzantine State and Society.* Stanford, 1997.

Tsougarakis, D. *Byzantine Crete. From the 5th Century to the Venetian Conquest.* Athens, 1988.

Van Millingen, A. *Byzantine Constantinople.* London, 1899.

Vannier, J.-F. *Familles byzantines: Les Argyroi (IXe–XIIe siècles).* Paris, 1975.

Vasiliev, A. A. *Byzance et les Arabes.* Vols. 1, 2.1, 2.2. Brussels, 1935, 1968, 1950.

———. "Medieval Ideas of the End of the World: West and East." *Byzantion* 16 (1942–43): 462–502.

Von Dobschütz, E. *Christusbilder.* Leipzig, 1899.

Von Falkenhausen, V. *Untersuchungen über die byzantinische Herrschaft in Süditalien vom 9. bis ins 11. Jahrhundert.* Wiesbaden, 1967.

Walker, P. E. "The 'Crusade' of John Tzimisces in the Light of New Arabic Evidence." *Byzantion* 47 (1977): 301–27.

Wartenberg, G. "Das Geschichtswerk des Leon Diakonos." *BZ* 6 (1897): 106–11.

Westerink, L. G. "Nicetas the Paphlagonian on the End of the World." In *Μελετήματα στὴ μνήμη Βασιλείου Λαούρδα*, 177–95. Thessalonike, 1975.

Wheeler, E. "*Hoplomachia* and Greek Dances in Arms." *GRBS* 23 (1982): 223–33.

Whitby, M. *The Emperor Maurice and his Historian.* Oxford, 1988.

———. "Greek Historical Writing after Procopius: Variety and Vitality." In *The Byzantine and Early Islamic Near East*, edited by A. Cameron and L. I. Conrad, 1:25–80. Princeton, 1992.

Whittow, M. "Rural Fortifications in Western Europe and Byzantium, Tenth to Twelfth Century." *ByzF* 21 (1995): 57–74.

Zuckerman, C. "On the Date of the Khazars' Conversion to Judaism and the Chronology of the Kings of the Rus Oleg and Igor." *REB* 53 (1995): 237–70.

INDEX OF PROPER NAMES

Index of Proper Names

Index of Proper Names

Index of Proper Names

Index of Proper Names

Index of Proper Names

Index of Proper Names

Index of Proper Names

Index of Proper Names

Index of Proper Names

Index of Proper Names

Index of Proper Names

General Index

adventus, imperial, 98 n. 67
akouphion, 139 n. 76
ambassadors
  Bulgarian, to Byzantines, 16, 20, 109–10 and n. 38
  Byzantine
    to Bulgarians, 130–31
    to Rus', 21, 47, 128 and nn. 13 and 16, 153, 155
  Rus', to Byzantines, 198
ambo, 147 and n. 40
ambushes, 41–42
  Bulgarian, against Byzantines, 213–14
  Byzantine
    against Hamdanids, 72, 74–75
    against Rus', 158–60 and n. 110
  Cretan Arab, against Byzantines, 63–64, 66
  Hamdanid, against Byzantines, 81, 106
  Patzinak, against Rus', 200
  Rus', against Byzantines, 185
  Sicilian, against Byzantines, 116
amnesty, 164, 166, 173
anthypatos, 216 n. 87
archers, 5–6, 7, 9, map 5
armor (summary discussion of), 40
army, 4–7
  place in society, 46–47
artillery, 39, 44, 45, 67, 77, 102, 108, 129. *See also* siege engines
assaults. *See* sieges
astrologers, 113, 211 and n. 56
astronomers, 211 and n. 56
asylum, 48, 96 and n. 53, 97–98, 144, 191 and nn. 25–27
augusta, 100, 135, 136, 137, 148, 155, 170
aurora borealis, 217 n. 91

ballasting, 40, 115 and n. 62, 174 and n. 76
banishment, 173 and n. 72, 190, 191, 206
basileopator, 172 n. 65
battering ram, 68 n. 79, 77, 78
battles

mock, 6, 38, 46, 49, 112, 114 n. 55
  pitched, 6, 42, 104, 106–8, 158, 163 and n. 9, 212, 216
  mentioned, 73, 81, 166
beggars, 168
blinding (method of punishment), 164 and n. 18, 165, 167, 170 and n. 53, 172, 189–90, 191
boots, scarlet, 92 and n. 30, 140, 163, 169, 201
booty, 79 n. 45
  Bulgarian, 182
  Cretan Arab, 79–81 *passim*
  Hamdanid, 75, 76, 82, 84, 103, 109
  See also relics
bridges, 101, 176 and n. 12
brotherhood, ritual, 129 and n. 17
burning at stake, 114 and n. 57

caesar, 99 and n. 74, 110, 165 and n. 21
camps, expeditionary, 6, 41, 62 n. 47, 187
  Byzantine, 90, 169, 203, 215–16
    at Antioch, 119, 123
    at Crete, 62, 68
    at Dorystolon, 187, 189, 196, map 5
    at Sardica, 213–14
    at Tarsos, 101, 106
  Hungarian, 72
captives. *See* prisoners of war
cavalry, 5–7, 107 and n. 15, 157 n. 105
  command of, 115
  defensive armor, 40
  deployment, 129, 216
  in battle
    at Antioch, 124
    at Dorystolon, 186, 198, map 5
    at Preslav, 42, 179–80
    at Tarsos, 42, 105, 107 and n. 16
  Rus', 180 n. 32, 188 and n. 4
  size of, 107 n. 16, 125 n. 110
  See also kataphraktoi and "Immortals"
chain (across the Golden Horn), 48 and n. 165, 129–30 and n. 22, map 2
chain mail, 40 n. 141, 43, 158, 188 and n. 9

General Index

General Index

against Bardas Phokas, 216
against Rus', 174, 188, 195, 198
against Bardas Skleros, 213
harbored in dockyards at Constantinople, 48, 97
harbored in Golden Horn, 176
to assist Nikephoros Phokas, 97
to Crete, 59, 60, 80
to Sicily, 115
See also dromones and triremes
flood, 118, 218
fortresses
Arab, 82, 101, 104, 123, 127, 203, 208, 209
Mempetze, 122, 207
Bulgarian, 111, 129, 188
Byzantine, 93, 169–70, 172–73, 213, 216
funeral pyres, 193 and n. 32
funerals, 134–35, 141, 193
furca. See phourka

godparent, 100 and n. 79
gold coins, 112 n. 46, 197 n. 47
as diversion in battle, 75 and n. 27
booty, 81, 204
bribe, 112, 144, 189
donations, 149

harbors, 49, 50, 62, 135, 176, 210
helepolis, 68 n. 79, 76 n. 32. *See also* artillery, siege engines, *and* trebuchets
Hellenic mysteries, 193
Heroon, 141
horoscopes, 211 n. 56
horse races, 100
horses, relays of, 162 and n. 6
hunting, 83

icons, 16, 27
of Christ, 137
of Crucifixion, 209–10 and n. 48
of John the Baptist, 137
of Theotokos, 27, 47, 137, 201 and n. 69
infanticide, 193 and n. 33
infantry, 5–7, 124, 125, 129, 133 n. 42, 179, 193, 216, map 5
iron weights, 150 and n. 59

kataphraktoi (iron-clad horsemen), 6, 7, 40, 107 and n. 15

deployed
against Rus', 42, 129, 185, 195
at Tarsos, 107
See also cavalry *and* "Immortals"
katepano, 5, 216 n. 87
kentenarion, 112 and n. 46
keramion. See Holy Tile of Edessa
key-keepers, imperial, 190 and n. 18
keys, 190
kleisoura, 5, 177
komenton, 194 and n. 40
kouropalates, 99 and n. 75, 112 and n. 48, 144–45, 162, 164, 189–92

laisa (siege shed), 8
lawcourts, 163
leopardskin, 134, 137
lepers, 149, 220 and n. 114
leprosarium, 149 and n. 49
lochagoi, 37
logothetes, 211

magistros, 60 n. 37
Boris II, 201
Symeon, 211
John Kourkouas, 173, 192
Leo Melissenos, 215 and n. 84
Bardas Phokas (father of Nikephoros II), 96
Bardas Phokas (nephew of Nikephoros II), 212
Nikephoros (II) Phokas, 60
Bardas Skleros, 157–58, 159, 166, 173, 183, 198
John Tzimiskes, 94, 99, 135
mandylion, 98 n. 68, 120 n. 88, 121 n. 91
marriage, impediments to, 100 n. 79
marriage, imperial, 99–100, 174 and n. 79
medimnoi, 199 and n. 59
menavlatoi, 6. *See also* infantry
miliaresia, 67 n. 72
military, forces and operations, 4–9, 36–47, *and passim*
moats, 64, 68, 78, 101
modios, 199 n. 59
monks, 99–100, 113, 134, 150, 152, 218
monoxyla, 156 n. 96
musical instruments, military, 42 and n. 154

General Index

navy, 5, 40, 115, 171
night prefect, 145 and n. 21
nose, cutting of, 106 and n. 11, 154 and n. 85
nun, 197

oblong formation (*plaision*), 76 and n. 35

palace life, 49
parakoimomenos (chamberlain), 84 n. 68, 97
   n. 57, 137 n. 64
   Joseph Bringas, 84 and n. 68, 86, 88
   Basil Lekapenos, 97 and n. 57, 143–44
     and nn. 9–10, 147, 218
parrhesia, 85 n. 73
patriarch, deposition of, 205
patriarch, election of, 150 n. 55, 151–52
patrikios, 60 n. 33, 166
   Adralestos, 168
   Kalokyres, 111, 128, 129, 130, 180
   Leo, 191 and n. 24
   Nicholas, 153
   Niketas, 115, 117, 127
   Paschalios, 95 and n. 47
   Peter, 132, 158, 212
   Theophanes, 188 n. 6
   Symeon Ambelas, 163 n. 8
   Marianos Argyros, 88, 95
   Michael Bourtzes, 133 n. 42
   Kalokyres Delphinas, 216
   Constantine Gongyles, 60
   Romanos Lekapenos, 219
   Theodoulos Parsakoutenos, 162 n. 3
   Bardas Phokas, 145, 167
   Manuel Phokas, 115
   Constantine Skleros, 159, 166
   Tornikioi, 95
   John Tzimiskes, 89
phourka, 155 n. 93, 216 n. 89
pipes, drainage, 48, 96 and n. 51
pirates, 79 and n. 46
plunder. *See* booty
poison, 83 and n. 60, 219 and n. 112, 220
praitor, 114 and n. 56, 145
priest (of imperial court), 136
prisoners of war
   Arab, 75–76, 102 n. 89, 102, 134
   Bulgarian, 155
   Byzantine, 74, 75, 117, 126 n. 5, 127,
     154, 216

Cretan Arab, 78–81 *passim*
Rus', 183
   sacrifice of, by Rus', 193 and n. 32
   treatment of, 78–79 and n. 43, 102 n. 89
private life, 50
proedros, 99 n. 76, 143 n. 6
   Basil Lekapenos, 97 n. 56, 99, 143, 179,
     214, 218
prophecies, 113, 124 n. 105, 134, 150, 152,
   169, 211
prostitutes, 76
protovestiarios, 115 n. 64, 137 n. 64, 191 n. 24

rainstorms, 118–19, 197 and n. 47
ramps for landing, 61 and n. 41
regents, 83 n. 63, 84, 170 n. 58
relics
   hair of John the Baptist, 27, 47, 49, 120
     n. 88, 122 n. 95, 207–8 and n. 36
   holy blood from icon of Berytus, 210 and
     n. 50
   keramion. See Holy Tile of Edessa
   mandylion of Edessa, 98 n. 68, 120 n. 88,
     121 and n. 91
   sandals of Christ, 27, 47, 49, 120 n. 88,
     207, 208 n. 36

sacrifices of animals, 193 and nn. 32–33
sappers, 44, 77–78, 102
scholae, tagma of, 5
scouts, 159, 177, 185
scribes, 29
sebastophoros, 219 and n. 109
senate, 83–86 and nn. 62–63 *passim*, 92, 95,
   97, 149, 151
   mentioned, 36
ships. *See dromones*, fireships, transport ships,
   and triremes
siege engines, 7–9, 44–46, 68 n. 79, 69 n. 80
   deployed
     in Bulgaria, 179, 181, 192, 214
     in Crete, 67, 68, 69, 76, 77 and n. 38
     in Syria, 82, 119, 122, 207
   See also artillery *and* ἑλέπολις
siege ladders, 133, 181–82
sieges, 7–9, 44–46
   Abydos, 216
   Antioch, 119–20, 123–25, 132–34
   Arka, 122

258

General Index

INDEX OF NOTABLE GREEK WORDS

An asterisk indicates those words that are found only in the *History* of Leo the Deacon, according to the online version of the TLG.

Index of Notable Greek Words

ῥίψασπις, 106 n. 11
ῥόγαι, 149 n. 52

σάκος, 40 n. 140
σκάφη, 156 n. 96
*σκυτοτρώκτης, 110 n. 36
σύγκλυδες, 80 n. 49
συλλογὴ λόγων, 23, 114 n. 60
συνασπισμός, 61 n. 42

τοπάρχης, 145 and n. 24
τρίδουλος, 110 n. 38
τυραννεῖα, 95 n.44
τύχη, 16–19, 23

ὑπογραφεύς, 202 n. 4

φάσγανον, 39 n. 131
φατρία, 80 n. 49
φιλόψυχος, 195 n. 42
φλογοειδής, 197 n. 51

χαλκοτυπία, 62 n. 51
χάραξ, 41, 62 n. 47

Index Locorum

Only quotations, paraphrases, and allusions in the *History* to earlier sources are indexed, not parallels discussed in the introduction or notes (for which see the index of proper names). The reader is referred to book and chapter references, to facilitate use with other editions and translations of the *History*.

Index Locorum

Index Locorum